P9-DEO-035

LISTENING TO THE GIANTS

LISTENING TO THE GIANTS

A Guide to Good Reading and Great Preaching

WARREN W. WIERSBE

BAKER BOOK HOUSE
Grand Rapids, Michigan

Sketches by Amy Van Martin

ISBN: 0-8010-9618-9

Printed in the United States of America

To
the pastoral staff
of the Moody Church, Chicago,
with whom it was my joy to work
for nearly seven years:
with affection, appreciation
and the remembrance of our happy years together

Paul Craig	*David Lichard*
Richard Dinwiddie	*Fred McCormick*
Don Dix	*James A. Rands*
W. Warren Filkin	*Tom Streeter*

and to the memory of

Donald H. Smith

who has gone before us
into the Glory

Contents

List of Illustrations 9
Preface 11

PART 1 Great Preacher-Authors

1. John Henry Newman (1801–1890) 15
   Unreal Words 21
2. Richard Trench (1807–1886) 35
   Christ Poor That We Might Be Rich 40
3. J. B. Lightfoot (1828–1889) 47
   Girded Loins and Burning Lamps 52
4. George Matheson (1842–1906) 61
   Jonah the Narrow 65
5. C. I. Scofield (1843–1921) 77
   The Test of True Spirituality 81
6. F. B. Meyer (1847–1929) 89
   The All-Sufficiency of Christ 97
7. Henry Drummond (1851–1897) 107
   Dealing with Doubt 113

8. Thomas Spurgeon (1856–1917) *123*
The Soul's Keeping 127
9. W. H. Griffith Thomas (1861–1924) *139*
Knowing and Showing 144
10. John Henry Jowett (1864–1923) *153*
The Ministry of a Transfigured Church 158
11. Joseph W. Kemp (1872–1933) *175*
Revivals and Evangelism 179
12. H. A. Ironside (1876–1951) *197*
Charge That to My Account 201
13. William Culbertson (1905–1971) *211*
Taking the Cross and Following the Lord 216

PART 2 Classic Books for the Preacher

14. Preaching on the Miracles *229*
15. Preaching on the Parables *237*
16. Sermon Series *243*
17. Books of Quotations *249*
18. The Thesaurus *257*
19. Anthologies *263*
20. A Basic Library *269*

PART 3 Miscellania

21. The Theology of Dwight L. Moody *311*
22. The Women in Moody's Ministry *319*
23. Henry Varley (1835–1912) *325*
24. Samuel Johnson (1709–1784) *333*
25. Bunhill Fields *339*
26. Marks of Maturity in the Ministry *345*

Index of Persons *355*

List of Illustrations

John Bunyan *338*
William Culbertson *210*
Henry Drummond *106*
H. A. Ironside *196*
Samuel Johnson *332*
John Henry Jowett *152*
Joseph W. Kemp *174*
J. B. Lightfoot *46*
George Matheson *60*
F. B. Meyer *88*
Betsey Holton Moody *318*
Dwight L. Moody *310*
John Henry Newman *14*
Peter M. Roget *256*
C. I. Scofield *76*
Thomas Spurgeon *122*
W. H. Griffith Thomas *138*
Richard Trench *34*
Henry Varley *324*

Preface

For over six years it was my privilege to edit "Insight for Pastors," a column in *Moody Monthly,* official publication of the Moody Bible Institute, Chicago. As I traveled across the country, and as I read my correspondence, I was amazed at how many people—laymen as well as pastors—read the column and appreciated it. When *Walking with the Giants* was published in 1976, the response was greater than I expected. It seemed that there was a hunger to know more about the great preachers of the past and the books they wrote.

This book is a companion volume to *Walking with the Giants,* with one difference: I have added sermons from each of the preachers so that you can "listen" to as well as "meet" them. The extra chapters that are not biographical contain material that I think is pertinent to the ministry today.

I have added an informal bibliography to help the many people who have asked for guidance in buying books. It is not definitive or complete, but it should be helpful.

Mature readers will realize that my including a preacher in these pages, or my citing of a book, does not mean that I endorse everything the preacher believed or the book contains. I have learned that God blesses people with whom I disagree and that He can make them a blessing to me. The order of biographies in part 1 is strictly chronological and suggests no system of priorities or personal preferences.

I want to thank the Moody Bible Institute for permission to reprint articles that originally appeared in "Insight for Pastors." Also I must thank Moody Press, Baptist Publications, and Marshall, Morgan, and Scott for permission to use copyrighted material.

Special thanks are due to Dr. Raymond Brown, principal of Spurgeon's College, London, for supplying a sermon by Thomas Spurgeon; to Dr. Harald Ellingsen, who knows books as few men do, for locating in his vast library a sermon by Richard Trench; to Mrs. Winifred G. T. Gillespie for invaluable help in gathering information about her father, W. H. Griffith Thomas, for helping to edit the chapter on him, and for supplying the photograph from which the sketch was made; and to the Evangelical Library, London, for photographs of Thomas Spurgeon and Henry Varley.

When I started this book, I was pastor of the Moody Church in Chicago. By the time I had completed it, I had resigned from the church to devote more time to conference ministry and writing. The Lord willing, there will be a third "Giant" book, vastly different from the first two.

If the material in these pages encourages a reader or helps a younger pastor in his ministry, I will be grateful to the Lord. "There were giants in the earth in those days . . .", and perhaps by getting to know them better, we can produce some giants in our own day.

Part 1

Great Preacher-Authors

1

John Henry Newman

(1801–1890)

If people today think at all of John Henry Newman, it is probably as the author of the familiar hymn "Lead, Kindly Light." Those who are somewhat acquainted with church history will identify him as the spiritual genius behind the Oxford Movement, which shook the Church of England and eventually led Newman himself into the Church of Rome. But it is Newman the preacher I want to examine in this chapter, the man whom W. Robertson Nicoll called "the most influential preacher Oxford has ever known,"[1] and whom Alexander Whyte admired so much that he wrote *Newman: An Appreciation.*

Newman was born in London, 21 February 1801. His family would be identified with the moderate evangelicals in the Church of England. At age fifteen Newman experienced conversion. He was educated at Trinity College, Oxford, where he fell under the influence of Richard Whately. "He, emphatically, opened my mind, and taught me to think and to use my reason," Newman later

1. *Princes of the Church,* p. 29.

wrote in his famous autobiography, *Apologia pro vita sua*. This was probably the beginning of Newman's drift from the evangelical emphasis and into the High Church party, and eventually to the Church of Rome.

However it was his dear friend Richard Hurrell Froude who influenced Newman the most. "He taught me to look with admiration towards the Church of Rome," Newman wrote, "and in the same degree to dislike the Reformation." Froude did more than this: he introduced Newman to John Keble—brilliant Oxford scholar, humble Anglican pastor, and a man utterly devoted to the Church of England. Keble is remembered today as the writer of "Sun of My Soul, Thou Savior Dear," taken from his once-popular book of religious poetry, *The Christian Year*.

In 1824 Newman was ordained, and in 1828 he began his ministry as vicar of St. Mary's, Oxford. I can never forget stepping into that historic church one summer day and actually climbing the stairs into Newman's pulpit. As I stood there, I could hear faintly the Oxford traffic outside; but I quickly found myself caught away in imagination to a Sunday afternoon service at which Newman was preaching. The church was filled with worshipers, mostly the younger fellows of the colleges and the undergraduates. Newman came in—"gliding" is the way one observer described it—and made his way to the pulpit, where he adjusted the gas lamp, laid his manuscript before him, and then in a musical voice that haunted you, began to preach in a way that penetrated one's very being. "It was from the pulpit of St. Mary's that he began to conquer and to rule the world," wrote Whyte, one of Newman's most ardent Protestant admirers.

The rest of the story need not delay us. On 14 July 1833 Keble preached the "assize sermon" at St. Mary's, and his theme was "national apostasy." It was this sermon that gave birth to the concern that eventuated in what we know as the Oxford Movement (not to be confused with the Oxford Group Movement begun by Frank Buchman and later renamed Moral Re-armament). The burden of the movement was spiritual renewal in the Church of England. Newman, Keble, Froude, E. B. Pusey, and their associates sought to restore the spiritual authority of the church and to return the church to its ancient moorings. Their motives were commendable; their methods perhaps left something to be desired.

One of their chief ministries was the publication of "tracts for the times." Various men—not all as gifted as Newman—wrote on subjects pertaining to the Church of England. The critics noticed a Rome-ward trend in the tracts, but the writers persisted. It was

Tract Ninety that wrote *finis* to Newman's leadership in the movement and his ministry at St. Mary's. In this famous pamphlet Newman tried to prove that the Thirty-nine Articles of the Church of England could be honestly interpreted from the Roman Catholic point of view. The result was official censure—the "politics" of the controversies from 1833 to 1845 is worthy of study—and Newman could do nothing but step aside or recant. Deeply hurt by the church leaders he thought would encourage him, Newman left Oxford; and on 8 October 1845 he was received into the Roman Catholic church.

I find the history of the Oxford Movement fascinating. In it one finds events and leaders that parallel situations we have today. There is really nothing new under the sun. People today who want to "purify" or "renew" the church would do well to read up on the Oxford Movement and then avoid its mistakes. *The Oxford Movement* by R. W. Church, dean of St. Paul's, is the best introduction. A more modern study is *The Oxford Conspirators* by Marvin R. O'Connell. You will want to read Newman's own account in *Apologia pro vita sua,* and keep in mind that he wrote this some twenty years after these events.

But now to Newman's preaching.

Between 1824, when he was ordained, and 1845, when he left Oxford, Newman preached over one thousand sermons, ten volumes of which are available today. His eight volumes of *Parochial and Plain Sermons* represent the best of his pulpit ministry at St. Mary's. *Sermons Bearing on Subjects of the Day* and *Fifteen Sermons Preached Before the University of Oxford* are two volumes that complete the Protestant years. *Discourses Addressed to Mixed Congregations* and *Sermons Preached on Various Occasions* come from his Roman Catholic years.

I was amazed when I learned that Whyte had been such an admirer of Newman; for if any preacher emphasized the grace of God and the gospel of Jesus Christ, it was Whyte. Yet Whyte told a friend that he valued Newman's sermons more than those of F. W. Robertson! On 14 March 1876 Whyte and some friends visited Newman at the oratory in Edgbaston and were received graciously. Whyte even incorporated in his *Catechism* a revision from Newman that clarified the doctrine of transubstantiation. There is no escaping the fact that Alexander Whyte admired John Henry Cardinal Newman.

Let us begin with the obvious reason: Newman's sermons, not unlike Whyte's, were directed to the conscience. "The effect of Newman's preaching on us young men," wrote William Lockhart, "was to turn our souls inside out!" In this, Whyte is a kindred spirit of Newman, for few evangelical preachers can expose sin and "perform spiritual surgery" like Alexander Whyte! But another factor is Newman's "other-worldliness." He, like Whyte, had an utter disdain of earthly things. Whyte reveled among the mystics and constantly called his congregation to a life of reality in the things of the Spirit. While Whyte would point sinners to the Lamb of God, however, Newman would find this life of the Spirit in a sacramental system.

Newman's ability to examine a text and then develop it into a sermon was something Whyte greatly admired. "For, let any young man of real capacity once master Newman's methods of exposition, discussion, and argumentation; his way of addressing himself to the treatment of a subject; his way of entering upon a subject, worming his way to the very heart of it, working it out, and winding it up," wrote Whyte in his *Appreciation*, and that man will "soon make his presence and his power felt in any of our newspapers or magazines."[2]

Add to this, Newman's pure English style—"the quiet perfection of his English style," wrote Whyte's biographer—and you can understand why the old Covenanter appreciated the preaching of Cardinal Newman.

Whyte was careful to point out his disagreements with Newman, not the least of which was Newman's neglect of preaching the good news of salvation through faith in Jesus Christ. When Newman's sermons are "looked at as pulpit work, as preaching the Gospel," wrote Whyte, "they are full of the most serious, and even fatal, defects. . . . they are not, properly speaking, New Testament preaching at all."[3] "As an analysis of the heart of man, and as a penetrating criticism of human life, their equal is nowhere to be found. But, with all that, they lack the one all-essential element of all true preaching—the message to sinful man concerning the free grace of God."[4] "Newman's preaching—and I say it with more pain than I can express—never once touches the true core, and real and innermost essence, of the Gospel."[5]

Why bother to read the sermons of a man who did not preach the gospel, a man who eventually preached himself right out of an

2. *Newman: An Appreciation*, p. 122.

3. Ibid., p. 90.

4. Ibid., pp. 91–92.

5. Ibid., p. 97.

evangelical tradition and into a sacramental system? Because Newman can help teach us how to preach to a man's conscience, how to get beneath the surface and apply spiritual truth where it is needed. Newman was a better diagnostician than dispenser of healing medicine ("I never take down Newman's sermons for my recovery and my comfort," admitted Whyte); but it is easier to apply the medicine after you have convinced the patient of his need.

It is worth noting that Newman warned against magnifying preaching above the other ministries of the church. In this, I think, he was reacting against the tendency on the part of some evangelicals in that day to make their preachers celebrities. Newman believed strongly in the continuity of the church and the need for sermons to minister to the body collectively. He himself shunned and even fled from becoming "a popular preacher," and he had little confidence in men who used the pulpit to promote themselves.

It is unfortunate that Newman did not know the better evangelical men of that day. He saw only (or perhaps only wanted to see) a ministry that emphasized correct doctrine and dedicated zeal, but that lacked Christian character and true spiritual power. R. W. Church described evangelicals as people with "an exhausted teaching and a spent enthusiasm." The evangelical churches were "respectable" and popular with men of position, but (added Church) "they were on very easy terms with the world."[6] If there was one thing Newman hated with a holy zeal, it was a religion of words without reality, words that described an experience but failed to effect it in the lives of people.

Newman desired to elevate worship in the church. While I do not agree with his sacramentalism, I do applaud his purpose; for it is my conviction that true worship is the greatest need in our churches today. How easy it is to have words without power (Paul was aware of this—read I Thessalonians 1:5) and program without substance, even in a nonliturgical church. Newman would have agreed with William Temple's definition of *worship*: "to quicken the conscience by the holiness of God, to feed the mind with the truth of God, to purge the imagination by the beauty of God, to open up the heart to the love of God, to devote the will to the purpose of God." We do not experience this kind of worship in many churches today, and often the preacher is to blame. Newman spoke about the "rudeness, irreverence, and almost pro-

6. *The Oxford Movement*, p. 15.

faneness . . . involved in pulpit addresses, which speak of the adorable works and sufferings of Christ, with the familiarity and absence of awe with which we speak about our friends."

Next to irreverence and the "unreality of words," Newman abhorred preaching that tries to cover "three or four subjects at once." He insisted that each sermon have a definite purpose expressed in a concrete statement. "Definiteness is the life of preaching," he wrote in *Lectures and Essays on University Subjects*, "a definite hearer, not the whole world; a definite topic, not the whole evangelical tradition; and, in like manner, a definite speaker. Nothing that is anonymous will preach. . . ."[7] Of course the ultimate aim of all preaching is the salvation of the hearer, but this can be accomplished only when the preacher is prepared and knows what his aim is. We preach to persuade, and we must preach to the emotions as well as the intellect, always using simple and concrete language.

The thing that impresses me about Newman's sermons is their freshness of spiritual expression. He did not preach on the "topics of the day." He carefully explained some first principle of the Christian life, some doctrine of the Christian faith, and wedded it to the practical life of the worshiper. He shunned oratory and sought to make the message of the Word the most important thing, the messenger the least important. He did not even debate the great issues involved in the Oxford Movement. Rather he strengthened and extended the movement by avoiding the issues and dealing with the fundamental truths that gave rise to these issues.

There are men called by God to preach on the issues of the hour, and we need their ministry. But for permanent strengthening of the church, we need also the men who will dig again the old wells and lead us intelligently down the old paths; men who, renouncing cheap pulpit rhetoric, will focus the white light of revelation on the human heart and examine us in that light. In short, we need today preaching that appeals to the conscience, penetrating preaching, clinical preaching, preaching that moves men to cry, "Men and brethren, what shall we do?" Newman's preaching did this.

But let us go one step further: let us apply the blessed medicine of the gospel (something Newman did not do) and reply to those under conviction, "Believe on the Lord Jesus Christ, and you shall be saved!" Newman would run to the beaten man at the side of the road and pour in the wine; but he could not pour in the oil.

---

7. P. 218.

If you want to get acquainted with Cardinal Newman, start with *Newman: An Appreciation* by Whyte. Then secure *The Preaching of John Henry Newman* edited by Newman scholar W. D. White. White's scholarly introduction will acquaint you with Newman's world and his philosophy of preaching. I think both Newman and White were too hard on the evangelicals, but this is a minor fault in an otherwise capable essay. White included thirteen sermons that Newman had considered his best. If you are interested in owning more of Newman's sermons, visit your local Catholic bookshop, or watch the used-book stores in your area.

The best modern biography of Newman is Meriol Trevor's two-volume *Newman.* The first volume is subtitled *The Pillar of the Cloud,* the second *Light in Winter.* The author has abridged this work in a one-volume edition titled *Newman's Journey.*

Newman wrote things other than sermons, some excellent and some not so good. *A Newman Reader,* edited by Francis X. Connolly, will give you a rich sampling of his writings. My favorite edition of his autobiography, *Apologia pro vita sua,* is the one edited by David J. DeLaura. It contains all the necessary texts of Newman's controversy with Charles Kingsley, plus helpful notes that clarify material in the text.

One final observation: when I read Newman's sermons, I find myself examining not only my heart, but also my preaching. I find myself asking: Am I a faithful physician of the soul? Am I preaching to the conscience? Am I faithful to declare *truth,* not simply my "clever ideas" about truth? Do I offer Christ as the only Redeemer? Do I get beneath the surface and help my hearers where they need it most? While I disagree with Newman's theology, I appreciate his preaching and have learned from it.

Unreal Words

> Thine eyes shall see the king in his beauty: they shall behold the land that is very far off. **Isa. 33:17**

The prophet tells us, that under the gospel covenant God's servants will have the privilege of seeing those heavenly sights which were but shadowed out in the law. Before Christ came was the time of shadows; but when He came, He brought truth as well as

Author's note: Newman's sermon "Unreal Words" is from *Parochial and Plain Sermons,* 5:29–45. He preached it on Advent.

grace; and as He who is the Truth has come to us, so does He in return require that we should be true and sincere in our dealings with Him. To be true and sincere is really to see with our minds those great wonders which He has wrought in order that we might see them. When God opened the eyes of the ass on which Balaam rode, she saw the angel and acted upon the sight. When He opened the eyes of the young man, Elisha's servant, he too saw the chariots and horses of fire, and took comfort. And in like manner, Christians are now under the protection of a divine Presence, and that more wonderful than any which was vouchsafed of old time. God revealed Himself visibly to Jacob, to Job, to Moses, to Joshua, and to Isaiah; to us He reveals Himself not visibly, but more wonderfully and truly; not without the cooperation of our own will, but upon our faith, and for that very reason more truly; for faith is the special means of gaining spiritual blessings. Hence St. Paul prays for the Ephesians "that Christ may dwell in your hearts by faith," and that the eyes of their understanding may be enlightened. And St. John declares that "the Son of God . . . hath given us an understanding, that we may know him that is true; and we are in him that is true, even in his Son Jesus Christ" (Eph. 3:17; 1:18; I John 5:20).

We are no longer then in the region of shadows: we have the true Savior set before us, the true reward, and the true means of spiritual renewal. We know the true state of the soul by nature and by grace, the evil of sin, the consequences of sinning, the way of pleasing God, and the motives to act upon. God has revealed Himself clearly to us; He has destroyed "the face of the covering cast over all people, and the vail that is spread over all nations." "The darkness is past, and the true light now shineth" (Isa. 25:7; I John 2:8). And therefore, I say, He calls upon us in turn to "walk in the light, as he is in the light." The Pharisees might have this excuse in their hypocrisy, that the plain truth had not been revealed to them; we have not even this poor reason for insincerity. We have no opportunity of mistaking one thing for another: the promise is expressly made to us that our teachers shall not be removed into a corner any more, but our eyes shall see our teachers; that "the eyes of them that see shall not be dim"; that every thing shall be called by its right name; that "the vile person shall be no more called liberal, nor the churl said to be bountiful" (Isa. 30:20; 32:3, 5); in a word, as the text speaks, that our eyes "shall see the king in his beauty"; we shall "behold the land that is very far off" (Isa. 33:17). Our professions, our creeds, our prayers, our dealings, our conversation, our arguments, our teaching must henceforth be sincere, or, to use an expressive word, must be *real*. What St. Paul says of himself and his fellow laborers, that they were true because Christ is true, applies to all Christians: "Our rejoicing is this, the testimony of our conscience, that in simplicity and godly sincerity, not with fleshly wisdom, but by the grace of God, we have had our conversation in the world, and more abundantly to you-ward. . . . the things that I purpose, do I purpose according to the flesh, that with me there should be yea yea, and nay nay? But as God is true, our word toward you was not yea and nay. For the Son of God, Jesus Christ, . . . was not yea and nay, but in him was yea. For all the promises of God in him are yea, and in him Amen, unto the glory of God by us." (II Cor. 1:12–20)

And yet it need scarcely be said, nothing is so rare as honesty and singleness of mind; so much so, that a person who is really honest, is already perfect. Insincerity was an evil which sprang up within the church from the first; Ananias and Simon were not open opposers of the apostles, but false brethren. And, as foreseeing what was to be, our Savior is remarkable in His ministry for nothing more than the earnestness of the dissuasives which He addressed to those who came to Him, against taking up religion lightly, or making promises which they were likely to break.

Thus He, "the true Light, which lighteth every man that cometh into the world," "the Amen, the faithful and true witness, the beginning of the creation of God" (John 1:9; Rev. 3:14), said to the young ruler, who lightly called Him "Good Master," "Why callest thou me good?" as bidding him weigh his words; and then abruptly told him, "One thing thou lackest." When a certain man professed that he would follow Him whithersoever He went, He did not respond to him, but said, "The foxes have holes, and the birds of the air have nests, but the Son of man hath not where to lay His head." When St. Peter said with all his heart in the name of himself and brethren, "To whom shall we go? Thou hast the words of eternal life," He answered pointedly, "Have not I chosen you twelve, and one of you is a devil?" as if He said, "Answer for thyself." When the two apostles professed their desire to cast their lot with Him, He asked whether they could drink of His cup, and be baptized with His baptism. And when "there went great multitudes with him," He turned and said, that unless a man hated relations, friends, and self, he could not be His disciple. And then He proceeded to warn all men to count the cost ere they followed Him. Such is the merciful severity with which He repels us that He may gain us more truly. And what He thinks of those who, after coming to Him, relapse into a hollow and hypocritical profession, we learn from His language towards the Laodiceans: "I know thy works, that thou art neither cold nor hot: I would thou wert cold or hot. So then because thou art lukewarm, and neither cold nor hot, I will spue thee out of my mouth."(Mark 10:17–21; Matt. 8:20; John 6:68–70; Matt. 20:22; Luke 14:25–28; Rev. 3:15–16)

We have a striking instance of the same conduct on the part of that ancient saint who prefigured our Lord in name and office, Joshua, the captain of the chosen people in entering Canaan. When they had at length taken possession of that land which Moses and their fathers had seen "very far off," they said to him, "God forbid that we should forsake the Lord, and serve other gods . . . therefore will we also serve the Lord; for he is our God." He made answer, "Ye cannot serve the Lord; for he is an holy God; he is a jealous God; he will not forgive your transgressions nor your sins." (Josh. 24:16–19) Not as if he would hinder them from obeying, but to sober them in professing. How does his answer remind us of St. Paul's still more awful words, about the impossibility of renewal after utterly falling away!

And what is said of profession of *discipleship* applies undoubtedly in its degree to *all* profession. To make professions is to play with edged tools, unless we attend to what we are saying. Words have a meaning, whether we mean that meaning or not; and they are imputed to us in their real meaning, when our not meaning it is our own fault. He who takes God's name in vain, is not counted guiltless because he means nothing by it—he cannot frame a language for himself—and they who make professions, of whatever kind, are heard in the sense of those professions, and are not excused because they themselves attach no sense to them. "By thy words thou shalt be justified, and by thy words thou shalt be condemned" (Matt. 12:37).

Now this consideration needs especially to be pressed upon Christians at this day; for this is especially a day of professions. You will answer in my own words, that all ages have been ages of profession. So they have been, in one way or other, but this day in its own especial sense—because this is especially a day of individual profession. This is a day in which there is (rightly or wrongly) so much of private judgment, so much of separation and difference, so much of preaching and teaching, so much of authorship, that it involves individual profession, responsibility, and recompense in a way peculiarly its own. It will not then be out of place if, in connection with the text, we consider some of the many ways in which persons, whether in this age or in another, make unreal professions, or seeing see not, and hearing hear not, and speak without mastering, or trying to master, their words. This I will attempt to do at some length, and in matters of detail, which are not the less important because they are minute.

Of course it is very common in all matters, not only in religion, to speak in an unreal way; viz., when we speak on a subject with which our minds are not familiar. If you were to hear a person who knew nothing about military matters, giving directions how soldiers on service should conduct themselves, or how their food and lodging, or their marching, was to be duly arranged, you would be sure that his mistakes would be such as to excite the ridicule and contempt of men experienced in warfare. If a foreigner were to come to one of our cities, and without hesitation offer plans for the supply of our markets, or the management of our police, it is so certain that he would expose himself, that the very attempt would argue a great want of good sense and modesty. We should feel that he did not understand us, and that when he spoke about us, he would be using words without meaning. If a dim-sighted man were to attempt to decide questions of proportion and color, or a man without ear to judge of musical compositions, we should feel that he spoke on and from general principles, on fancy, or by deduction and argument, not from a real apprehension of the matters which he discussed. His remarks would be theoretical and unreal.

This unsubstantial way of speaking is instanced in the case of persons who fall into any new company, among strange faces and amid novel occurrences. They sometimes form amiable judgments of men and things, sometimes the reverse; but whatever their judgments be, they are to those who know the men and the things strangely unreal and distorted. They feel reverence where they should not; they discern slights where none were intended; they discover meaning in events which have none; they fancy motives; they misinterpret manner; they mistake character; and they form generalizations and combinations which exist only in their own minds.

Again, persons who have not attended to the subject of morals, or to politics, or to matters ecclesiastical, or to theology, do not know the relative value of questions which they meet with in these departments of knowledge. They do not understand the difference between one point and another. The one and the other are the same to them. They look at them as infants gaze at the objects which meet their eyes, in a vague unapprehensive way, as if not knowing whether a thing is a hundred miles off or close at hand, whether great or small, hard or soft. They have no means of judging, no standard to measure by, and they give judgment at random, saying yea or nay on very deep questions, according as their fancy is struck at the moment, or as some clever or specious argument happens to come across them. Consequently they are inconsistent; say one thing one day, another the next; and if they must act, act in the dark; or if they can help acting, do not act; or if they act freely, act from some other reason not avowed. All this is to be unreal.

Again, there cannot be a more apposite specimen of unreality than the way in which judgments are commonly formed upon important questions by the mass of the community. Opinions are continually given in the world on matters, about which those who offer them are as little qualified to judge as blind men about colors, and that because they have never exercised their minds upon the points in question. This is a day in which all men are obliged to have an opinion on all questions, political, social, and religious, because they have in some way or other an influence upon the decision; yet the multitude are for the most part absolutely without capacity to take their part in it. In saying this, I am far from meaning that this need be so. I am far from denying that there is such a thing as plain good sense, or (what is better) religious sense, which will see its way through very intricate matters, or that this is in fact sometimes exerted in the community at large on certain great questions; but at the same time this practical sense is so far from existing as regards the vast mass of questions which in this day come before the public, that (as all persons who attempt to gain the influence of the people on their side know well) their opinions must be purchased by interesting their prejudices or fears in their favor—not by presenting a question in its real and true substance, but by adroitly coloring it, or selecting out of it some particular point which may be exaggerated, and dressed up, and be made the means of working on popular feelings. And thus government and the art of government becomes, as much as popular religion, hollow and unsound.

And hence it is that the popular voice is so changeable. One man or measure is the idol of the people today, another tomorrow. They have never got beyond accepting shadows for things.

What is instanced in the mass is instanced also in various ways in individuals, and in points of detail. For instance, some men are set perhaps on being eloquent speakers. They use great words and imitate the sentences of others; and they fancy that those whom they imitate had as little meaning as themselves, or they perhaps contrive to think that they themselves have a meaning adequate to their words.

Another sort of unreality, or voluntary profession of what is above us, is instanced in the conduct of those who suddenly come into power or place. They affect a manner such as they think the office requires, but which is beyond them, and therefore unbecoming. They wish to act with dignity, and they cease to be themselves.

And so again, to take a different case, many men, when they come near persons in distress and wish to show sympathy, often condole in a very unreal way. I am not altogether laying this to their fault; for it is very difficult to know what to do, when on the one hand we cannot realize to ourselves the sorrow, yet withal wish to be kind to those who feel it. A tone of grief seems necessary, yet (if so be) cannot under our circumstances be genuine. Yet even here surely there is a true way, if we could find it, by which pretense may be avoided, and yet respect and consideration shown.

And in like manner as regards religious emotions. Persons are aware from the mere force of the doctrines of which the gospel consists, that they ought to be variously affected, and deeply and intensely too, in consequence of them. The doctrines of original and actual sin, of Christ's divinity and atonement, and of holy baptism, are so vast, that no one can realize them without very complicated and profound feelings. Natural reason tells a man this, and that if he simply and genuinely believes the doctrines, he must have these feelings; and he professes to believe the doctrines absolutely, and therefore he professes the correspondent feelings. But in truth he perhaps does *not* really believe them absolutely, because such absolute belief is the work of long time, and therefore his profession of feeling outruns the real inward existence of feeling, or he becomes unreal. Let us never lose sight of two truths: that we ought to have our hearts penetrated with the love of Christ and full of self-renunciation; but that if they be not, professing that they are does not make them so.

Again, to take a more serious instance of the same fault, some persons pray, not as sinners addressing their God, not as the publican smiting on his breast, and saying, "God be merciful to me a sinner," but in such a way as they conceive to be becoming *under* circumstances of guilt, in a way becoming such a strait. They are self-conscious, and reflect on what they are about, and instead of actually approaching (as it were) the mercy-seat, they are filled with the thought that God is great, and man His creature, God on high and man on earth, and that they are engaged in a high and solemn service, and that they ought to rise up to its sublime and momentous character.

Another still more common form of the same fault, yet without any definite pretense or effort, is the mode in which people speak of the shortness and vanity of life, the certainty of death, and the joys of heaven. They have commonplaces in their mouths, which they bring forth upon occasions for the good of others, or to console them, or as a proper and becoming mark of attention towards them. Thus they speak to clergymen in a professedly serious way, making remarks true and sound, and in themselves deep, yet unmeaning in their mouths; or they give advice to children or young men; or perhaps in low spirits or sickness they are led to speak in a religious strain as if it were spontaneous. Or when they fall into sin, they speak of man being frail, of the deceitfulness of the human heart, of God's mercy, and so on: all these great words, heaven, hell, judgment, mercy, repentance, works, the world that now is, the world to come, being little more than "lifeless sounds, whether of pipe or harp," in their mouths and ears, as the "very lovely song of one that hath a pleasant voice and can play well on an instrument"—as the proprieties of conversation, or the civilities of good breeding.

I am speaking of the conduct of the world at large, called Christian; but what has been said applies, and necessarily, to the case of a number of well-disposed or even religious men. I mean, that before men come to know the realities of human life, it is not wonderful that their view of religion should be unreal. Young people who have never known sorrow or anxiety, or the sacrifices which conscientiousness involves, want commonly that depth and seriousness of character, which sorrow only and anxiety and self-sacrifice can give. I do not notice this as a fault, but as a plain fact, which may often be seen, and which it is well to bear in mind. This is the legitimate use of this world, to make us seek for another. It does its part when it repels us and disgusts us and drives us elsewhere. Experience of it gives experience of that which is its antidote, in the case of religious minds: and we become real in our view of what is spiritual by the contact of things temporal and earthly. And much more are men unreal when they have some secret motive urging them a different way from religion, and when their professions therefore are forced into an unnatural course in order to subserve their secret motive. When men do not like the conclusions to which their principles lead, or the precepts which Scripture contains, they are not wanting in ingenuity to blunt their force. They can frame some theory, or dress up certain objections, to defend themselves withal; a theory, that is, or objections, which it is difficult to refute perhaps, but which any rightly ordered mind, nay, any common bystander, perceives to be unnatural and insincere.

What has been here noticed of individuals, takes place even in the case of whole churches, at times when love has waxed cold and faith failed. The whole system of the church, its discipline and ritual, are all in their origin the spontaneous and exuberant fruit of the real principle of spiritual religion in the hearts of its members. The invisible church has developed itself into the church visible, and its outward rites and forms are nourished and animated by the living power which dwells within it. Thus every part of it is real, down to the minutest details. But when the seductions of the world and the lusts of the flesh have eaten out this divine inward life, what is the outward church but a hollowness and a mockery, like the whited sepulchres of which our Lord speaks, a memorial of what was and is not? And though we trust that the church is nowhere thus utterly deserted by the Spirit of truth, at least according to God's ordinary providence, yet may we not say that in proportion as it approaches to this state of deadness, the grace of its ordinances, though not forfeited, at least flows in but a scanty or uncertain stream?

And lastly, if this unreality may steal over the church itself, which is in its very essence a practical institution, much more is it found in the philosophies and literature of men. Literature is almost in its essence unreal; for it is the exhibition of thought disjoined from practice. Its very home is supposed to be ease and retirement; and when it does more than speak or write, it is accused of transgressing its bounds. This indeed constitutes what is considered its true dignity and honor, viz., its abstraction from the actual affairs of life; its security from the world's currents and vicissitudes; its saying without doing. A man of literature is considered to preserve his dignity by doing nothing; and when he proceeds forward into action, he is thought to lose his position, as if he were degrading his calling by enthusiasm, and becoming a politician or a partisan. Hence mere literary men are able to say strong things against the opinions of their age, whether religious or political, without offense; because no one thinks they mean anything by them. They are not expected to go forward to act upon them, and mere words hurt no one.

Such are some of the more common or more extended specimens of profession without action, or of speaking without really seeing and feeling. In instancing which, let it be observed, I do not mean to say that such profession, as has been described, is always culpable and wrong; indeed I have implied the contrary throughout. It is often a misfortune. It takes a long time really to feel and understand things as they are; we learn to do so only gradually. Profession beyond our feelings is only a fault when we might help it—when either we speak when we need not speak, or do not feel when we might have felt. Hard insensible hearts, ready and thoughtless talkers, these are they whose unreality, as I have termed it, is a sin; it is the sin of every one of us, in proportion as our hearts are cold, or our tongues excessive.

But the mere fact of our saying more than we feel is not necessarily sinful. St. Peter did not rise up to the full meaning of his confession, "Thou art the Christ," yet he was pronounced blessed. St. James and St. John said, "We are able," without clear apprehension, yet without offense. We ever promise things greater than we master, and we wait on God to enable us to perform them. Our promising involves a prayer for light and strength. And so again we all say the creed, but who comprehends it fully? All we can hope is, that we are in the way to understand it; that we partly understand it; that we desire, pray, and strive to understand it more and more. Our creed becomes a sort of prayer. Persons are culpably unreal in their way of speaking, not when they say more than they feel, but when they say things different from what they feel. A miser praising almsgiving, or a coward giving rules for courage, is unreal; but it is not unreal for the less to discourse about the greater, for the liberal to descant upon munificence, or the generous to praise the noble-minded, or the self-denying to use the language of the austere, or the confessor to exhort to martyrdom.

What I have been saying comes to this: be in earnest, and you will speak of religion where, and when, and how you should; aim at things, and your words will be right without aiming. There are ten thousand ways of looking at this world, but only one right way. The man of pleasure has his way, the man of gain his, and the man of intellect his. Poor men and rich men, governors and governed, prosperous and discontented, learned and unlearned, each has his own way of looking at the things which come before him, and each has a wrong way. There is but one right way; it is the way in which God looks at the world. Aim at looking at it in God's way. Aim at seeing things as God sees them. Aim at forming judgments about persons, events, ranks, fortunes, changes, objects, such as God forms. Aim at looking at this life as God looks at it. Aim at looking at the life to come, and the world unseen, as God does. Aim at seeing "the king in his beauty." All things that we see are but shadows to us and delusions, unless we enter into what they really mean.

It is not an easy thing to learn that new language which Christ has brought us. He has interpreted all things for us in a new way; He has brought us a religion which sheds a new light on all that happens. Try to learn this language. Do not get it by rote, or speak it as a thing of course. Try to understand what you say. Time is short, eternity is long; God is great, man is weak; he stands between heaven and hell; Christ is his Savior; Christ has suffered for him. The Holy Ghost sanctifies him; repentance purifies him, faith justifies, works save. These are solemn truths, which need not be actually spoken, except in the way of creed or of teaching; but which must be laid up in the heart. That a thing is true, is no reason that it should be said, but that it should be done; that it should be acted upon; that it should be made our own inwardly.

Let us avoid talking, of whatever kind; whether mere empty talking, or censorious talking, or idle profession, or descanting upon gospel doctrines, or the affectation of philosophy, or the pretense of eloquence. Let us guard against frivolity, love of display, love of being talked about, love of singularity, love of seeming original. Let us aim at meaning what we say, and saying what we mean; let us aim at knowing when we understand a truth, and when we do not. When we do not, let us take it on faith, and let us profess to do so. Let us receive the truth in reverence, and pray God to give us a good will, and divine light, and spiritual strength, that it may bear fruit within us.

Bibliography

Church, R. W. *The Oxford Movement, Twelve Years, 1833–1845*. London: Macmillan, 1891. Reprinted—New York: Archon, 1966.

Newman, John Henry. *Apologia pro vita sua*. London: Longmans, 1864. Reprinted—Edited by David J. DeLaura. New York: Norton, 1968.

———. *Discourses Addressed to Mixed Congregations*. London: Longmans, 1849. Reprinted—Westminster, Md.: Christian Classics, 1966.

———. *Lectures and Essays on University Subjects*. London: Longman, Brown, Green, Longmans, and Roberts, 1859.

———. *A Newman Reader: An Anthology of the Writings of John Henry Cardinal Newman*. Edited by Francis X. Connolly. Garden City, N.Y.: Doubleday, 1964.

———. *Parochial and Plain Sermons*. Edited by W. J. Copeland. 8 vols. London: Rivingtons, 1868. Reprinted—Westminster, Md.: Christian Classics, 1968.

———. *The Preaching of John Henry Newman*. Edited by W. D. White. Philadelphia: Fortress, 1969.

———. *Sermons Bearing on Subjects of the Day.* London: Rivingtons, 1843. Reprinted—Westminster, Md.: Christian Classics, 1968.

———. *Sermons, Chiefly on the Theory of Religious Belief, Preached Before the University of Oxford.* London: Rivingtons, 1843. Reprinted—*Fifteen Sermons Preached Before the University of Oxford, Between A.D. 1826 and 1843.* 1872. Reprinted—Westminster, Md.: Christian Classics, 1970.

———. *Sermons Preached on Various Occasions.* London: Burns and Lambert, 1857. Reprinted—Westminster, Md.: Christian Classics, 1968.

———. *Tract Ninety; or, Remarks on Certain Passages in the Thirty-Nine Articles.* Edited by A. W. Evans. London: Constable, 1933.

Nicoll, W. Robertson. *Princes of the Church.* London: Hodder and Stoughton, 1921.

O'Connell, Marvin R. *The Oxford Conspirators: A History of the Oxford Movement, 1833–45.* New York: Macmillan, 1969.

Trevor, Meriol. *Newman.* 2 vols.: *The Pillar of the Cloud* and *Light in Winter.* New York: Macmillan, 1962–1963.

———. *Newman's Journey.* Cleveland: Collins and World, 1977.

Whyte, Alexander. *Newman: An Appreciation in Two Lectures, with the Choicest Passages of His Writings.* Edinburgh: Oliphant, 1901.

2

Richard Trench

(1807–1886)

The life of Richard Chenevix Trench contained ingredients so diverse that they seem almost contradictory. A scholar by nature, his position in the Anglican church forced him into prominence where he fought and lost unpopular battles. Born into a comfortable and cultured family, he recklessly identified with an abortive "student invasion" to free the oppressed people of Spain, a venture that could have cost him his life. When he returned to Cambridge in 1831 to prepare for the ministry, he admitted to a friend that he had forgotten "well-nigh all" his Greek. Yet he wrote *Synonyms of the New Testament,* a classic in Greek studies that is still valuable. Trench was not recognized as a good preacher. But his two monumental works, *Notes on the Parables of Our Lord* and *Notes on the Miracles of Our Lord,* have helped many preachers prepare better messages.

Trench would have rejoiced to stay out of the public arena and in his study, but circumstances dictated otherwise. He became dean of Westminster Abbey and eventually archbishop of Dublin. Perhaps it was the outworking of the "Peter Principle" (every man rises to his level of incompetence), because Trench was not cut out to fight church battles. He was born to study and write.

His passion was words. Two of his classics, though a bit outdated by modern research, are still helpful and most enjoyable: *On the Study of Words* and *English, Past and Present*. One of the greatest things Trench did was to propose to the Philological Society on 7 January 1858 that "a new and independent dictionary should be prepared." The result was the monumental *Oxford English Dictionary* (OED), originally published in ten huge volumes and now available (micrographically reproduced) in two. One of the assistants who worked with James Murray on the great OED was George H. Morrison. In later years he would be known as Morrison of Wellington and one of Scotland's greatest preachers. Whenever I use my OED, I think of Trench and Morrison and give thanks.

Richard Trench was born on 5 September 1807 in Dublin, Ireland. His father belonged to the Anglo-Irish aristocracy, and his mother, a cultured Christian, had traveled widely. She greatly influenced him in his love for books and poetry and his desire to write. Early in his school career he displayed his love for linguistic studies. When her son was only fifteen, Mrs. Trench wrote to a friend: "My son Richard has a craving for books. . . . he cannot take an airing without arming himself against ennui by one or more volumes. . . . He wishes much we should purchase a certain Polyglot and luxuriates in the idea of finding fifteen readings of the same passage in Scripture."[1]

Trench entered Trinity College, Cambridge, in October 1825. He became a member of an elite group known familiarly as the Apostles. In this group were men who would one day greatly influence England: F. D. Maurice, the Christian socialist; Alfred Tennyson, who would become poet laureate; Arthur Hallam, a friend of Tennyson whose death inspired "In Memoriam"; and others.

He received his B.A. in 1829 and spent the next year traveling. In Spain he saw the desperate need of the people. When he returned to England, he threw himself in with a group of idealistic young men who planned to invade Cadiz and set the masses free. Why would a scholar get involved in such a daring venture? Partly from heredity: his mother's family was of Huguenot origin, and Trench was attracted to anything that smacked of chivalry. While a student at Cambridge, Trench had been fascinated by Spanish history and culture. But perhaps the main reason was his own need for a challenge. He was living rather aimlessly, making him some-

1. John Bromley, *The Man of Ten Talents*, p. 18.

what depressed. The liberation of Spain was just the tonic he needed. The whole enterprise aborted. Some of the men who were involved were arrested and shot. Trench never spoke about the event in later years, nor did he ever visit Spain again. The experience soured him on all revolutionary movements, a fact that played an important role when he became archbishop of Dublin.

Trench returned to Cambridge in October 1831 to study for holy orders. He was married on 31 May 1832; the following October he was ordained a deacon. No churches were available at that time, so once again Trench found himself drifting and waiting. In January 1833 he became curate to Hugh James Rose at Hadleigh in Suffolk, a post he held until September, when Rose left to become professor of divinity at the University of Dublin.

Here we meet one of those quirks of history that makes us want to ask, "What if. . .?" While Trench was serving at Hadleigh, two important events took place that ultimately shook the Anglican church to its foundations. The first was John Keble's "assize sermon" preached at St. Mary's, Oxford, on 14 July. That sermon marked the beginning of the Oxford Movement, although nobody knew it at the time. The second event grew out of the first: Rose, impressed by Keble's sermon on "national apostasy," invited a number of his clerical friends to Hadleigh to discuss ways to stir the church and bring about needed changes. Keble did not attend the conference, nor did his good friend John Henry Newman. How much Trench participated we do not know for certain; probably he was on the fringes of the meetings, being only a lowly curate.

But suppose he had been captivated by the challenge? Suppose he had been enlisted by the influential Richard Hurrell Froude, the man who perhaps more than any other influenced Newman, who eventually left the Anglican for the Roman church? Would Trench's skills have made any difference in the Oxford Movement? He was definitely not a fighter, but he was a scholar. He was not a strong preacher, but he was a capable writer. His sympathies did not lie either with the evangelical party in the church or with Rome. He could never have abandoned the Anglican church because his roots went too deep in her traditions. But could he have influenced others to remain? We will never know.

Once again Trench found himself without a place of ministry. He returned to live with his father until January 1834, when he accepted a curacy at St. Peter's, Colchester. But a health problem ended that ministry almost before it started. He traveled in Europe with his family, arriving back in England in June 1835. On 5 July he was ordained to the Anglican priesthood. In September he became the minister of St. Peter's, Curdridge, where he served for six delightful years. At last he could devote himself to study and service. In 1841 he published his great work on the parables.

Though books on the parables are legion, Trench's volume is outstanding. Be sure to purchase the edition that includes English translations of the quotations from the church fathers. It is unnerving to have the archbishop write, "The greatest insight into this truth is given by St. Augustine," and then follow with three paragraphs of Latin! Even Charles H. Spurgeon recommended Trench on the miracles and parables, although he admitted that Trench's doctrine was not always to his taste.

During his ministry at Curdridge, Trench became a close friend of Samuel Wilberforce, third son of the great William Wilberforce, whose association with the evangelicals in the Church of England helped him in his victory over slavery. Samuel was an energetic leader whose personal charm won him the nickname "Soapy Sam." If opposites attract, then we should not be surprised at Trench's friendship with the future bishop of Oxford and Winchester. Wilberforce enjoyed ecclesiastical politics as much as Trench detested it. Wilberforce asked Trench to become his "examining chaplain" for ordination, a high honor indeed.

At the close of 1844, Trench moved to Itchenstoke, where he served for eleven years. There he prepared his great book on the miracles, another classic. He also got involved in Irish relief ministry. Since Ireland was the land of his birth, he visited and tried to assist the multitudes suffering from the 1846 potato blight. This experience opened Trench's eyes to the real weaknesses and problems of the Irish Church.

Trench was appointed professor of divinity at King's College, London, in February 1846. At last he was in his element. The students not only profited from his lectures, but actually enjoyed them. The substance of his lectures on the vocabulary of the Greek New Testament appears in *Synonyms of the New Testament*. He believed that theology must be grounded on the study of words. "The *words* of the New Testament," he said, "are the *stoikeia* [elements, ABC's] of Christian theology." What a time Trench would have had with a complete set of the *Theological Dictionary of the New Testament* edited by Gerhard Kittel and Gerhard Friedrich!

On 21 June 1856 a statement appeared in the *Times* that Richard Trench had been appointed the new bishop of Gloucester and Bristol. The news hit everybody like a sonic boom, especially Professor Trench. He was even accused of planting the item so he would get the appointment. His friend Wilberforce interceded with Queen Victoria, and Trench was absolved; but the consequences were most unpleasant to the quiet scholar. He received nearly three hundred letters from pastors asking for places in his diocese!

The Lord had something better for the man who would not promote himself. On 15 August 1856 William Buckland died and the deanery of Westminster became vacant. On 23 October Trench was installed as dean of Westminster, the ideal place for the scholar/pastor. It was a difficult move for him and his family, for they were accustomed to the lovely English towns. Now they had to live in the busy, dirty city. At that time the abbey was surrounded by slums, described by one pastor as a "reeking and irreclaimable center of filth and misery."

Nobody expected the new dean to do anything more than enjoy "learned leisure"; but Trench surprised them. He and other London clergy were distressed that great ecclesiastical centers like St. Paul's and Westminster Abbey were not being used to reach the masses. Complicated church rules governed who could and could not preach in these historic pulpits. On 3 December 1857 Trench and his associates decided to open the abbey for Sunday evening services, an unprecedented thing at that time. No doubt the great success of Spurgeon's evening meetings helped them make their decision. On 3 January 1858 the first Sunday evening service was held. The weather was cold and icy, and the dean was certain nobody would attend. But a crowd gathered, Trench preached, and the service was somewhat of a success. The problem was that the service was not "popular" enough, the building was too cold, and the common people in attendance did not follow the liturgy too well. Trench persisted, however, and his experiment encouraged St. Paul's to follow his example.

Trench would have enjoyed remaining at Westminster, but the failing health of Richard Whately, archbishop of Dublin, meant that a successor would be needed. And who would be better than the scholarly Dubliner Richard Trench? When his friend Wilberforce suggested the move, Trench wrote him: "England is my world, the land of all my friends; the English Church seems to feel full of life and hope and vigor, of which I see little in the Irish. Then I know myself deficient in some of the most needful qualifications for the episcopate. I have few or no gifts of government, little or no power of rallying men round me and disciplining them into harmonious action."

Trench himself had told a friend years before that no one could wish to be a bishop who was not a hero or a madman. But on 1 January 1864 he was consecrated archbishop of Dublin and was introduced to one of the most perplexing problems of English church history: the disestablishment of the Irish Church. The Episcopal church in Ireland was a Protestant island in a Roman Catholic sea. It was the church of the well-to-do English landowners, not of the common people. As a missionary church it had failed. The poor citizens accused the Irish Church of bleeding the people. There were less than 700,000 adherents to the Irish Church, while 4,500,000 people claimed loyalty to Rome.

The scholarly Trench lacked the experience and ability to handle so complex an issue. He was not a diplomat; he lacked the political know-how to play one group against another. On 26 July 1869 the Disestablishment Bill was given royal assent and the battle was over. Trench had lost. He was then given the task of reconstructing a new church. This precipitated controversies that the learned archbishop was unable to handle. Bravely he stayed at his post, doing the best he could with a bad situation. On 22 November 1875 he suffered a disabling accident while going to London for a meeting of the New Testament Revision Committee. In the spring of 1883, he was laid low with bronchitis; and by the fall of 1884, it was obvious he would have to resign. This he did on 28 November; on 28 March 1886 he died. He was buried in Westminster Abbey on 2 April.

What choice volumes of Greek word studies and Christian theology might this man have written had he not become involved in ecclesiastical politics? Is becoming an archbishop necessarily a promotion? Would not Trench have made a greater contribution to the church by remaining in "learned leisure" at Westminster? This same fate overtook J. B. Lightfoot when he was translated from the university and made bishop of Durham. Those of us who love the study of words (and we have good company in G. Campbell Morgan and John Henry Jowett) are tempted to wish that Bishop Wilberforce had minded his own business and not moved Richard Trench to Dublin.

Christ Poor That We Might Be Rich

> Ye know the grace of our Lord Jesus Christ, that, though he was rich, yet for your sakes he became poor, that ye through his poverty might be rich. **II Cor. 8:9**

It was but recently that these Corinthians had known this grace of the Lord Jesus Christ, for it was he himself, the writer of these

Author's note: Trench's sermon "Christ Poor That We Might Be Rich" is from *Sermons New and Old*, pp. 249–57.

words, who had first brought to them the knowledge of that grace; who had found them, some the servants of vain idols, and some of a vain philosophy—or some, it might be, the servants of both at the same time—and, delivering them from these sinful and beggarly elements of this world, had imparted to them the knowledge of those unsearchable riches of Christ, whereof he here reminds them. And if you will observe the occasion *on* which, and the motive *with* which he utters these words, you will find them to be as follows: The church at Corinth was comparatively a wealthy one—above all, wealthy if set beside the mother church at Jerusalem. From some cause or another—various causes have been assigned—the poor saints at Jerusalem continually needed the assistance of their richer brethren throughout the world; and St. Paul is here urging the Christians at Corinth to a liberal contribution on their behalf. And now the apostle, who loves ever to appeal to the highest motives, sets before the Corinthians, in these words of my text, why it was their duty to open their hands and their hearts freely, to respond cheerfully and largely to the appeal which he made to them. Ye profess to be followers of the Lord Jesus Christ, to be desirous to walk in His footsteps, to take Him for a pattern and example. And you know what that pattern and example was—what His grace towards us was—rich He became poor for our sakes, that we, through His poverty, might be rich. Shall we refuse to follow, though it be at an infinite distance, in His footsteps? How infinite this distance is, and must always continue, and at the same time how constraining the motive which we may here find for acts of self-sacrifice and self-denial, be they small or be they great, will appear most plainly, when we have a little more closely studied the memorable words: "Ye know the grace of our Lord Jesus Christ, who being rich, he . . ." *Being rich,* or *though He was rich;* to what do these words refer? What were the riches which He had, and which for our sakes He renounced? No doubt the riches of His glory and preeminence in heaven—in His preexistent subsistence—the glory which He had with the Father, before the foundations of the world were laid. All attempts to explain away these words, as though they expressed less than this, as though anything short of this would exhaust and satisfy their meaning, must at once be rejected and set aside as idle and futile. He was *rich*—what words of ours can express, for indeed what thoughts of ours can conceive, the riches which were His? He was in the form of God, the first-born or the born before every creature—in the bosom of the Father—sharing with the Father and the Holy Ghost the incommunicable bliss of Deity, for He thought it not robbery to be equal with God, and taking all, did not account that He was snatching anything which was not rightfully His own. And Him the angels, a living circle of light around the throne, worshiped for evermore; and when the four living creatures gave glory and honor and thanks to Him that sat upon the throne, who liveth for ever and ever, it was to Him, to the Son, the image of the invisible God, that this glory and honor and these thanks were rendered.

But being rich He made himself poor. Here again what comparison drawn from things earthly would make even a remote approximation to this making of Himself poor on the part of the Son of God? Truly it immeasurably transcends them all. It is a real fall when a king, by the turn of fortune's wheel, comes down to a private man's estate; but we have a far greater fall than this to deal with. Let him exchange his royal robes for a beggar's weeds, his scepter for a staff, wander an outcast and an exile over the earth, that too were nothing—that would but feebly help to show forth what we are contemplating here.

For such a change, great as no doubt it would be, would yet find place altogether within fixed and in some respects very narrow limits—that is, within the limits and conditions of our humanity. That king who left his throne—he was but a man at the highest, subject therefore to all the infirmities of our nature, to sorrow, to sickness, to accidents, to death, dwelling in a house of clay which the moth crushes—he continues a man at his lowest. He has but changed his outward garb and trappings, not the essentials of his existence.

A rich man to become a poor man, or a great man a small, or a king a beggar—what is it after all, wherein does it even remotely approach the change which St. Paul speaks of here: God to become man, not to cease from being God, for that it was impossible for Him to do. God could never cease to be God; but to abdicate and renounce for the time all the actings of Deity, to empty Himself of all these, to take upon Him man's nature with all its inherent weaknesses and infirmities, with all the conditions which cling to it, except, indeed, its sin—which is only its miserable accidents and not its essence—to take upon Him the form of a servant, and as lowest and last and least to walk this painful earth of ours, hungering and thirsting, having not where to lay His head, enduring the contradictions of sinners, and at length paying the things which He never took, stripped of all, bare of all, undergoing the extreme penalty of our sin, tasting death and the bitterness of death for every man. Truly He made Himself poor for our sakes—a worm and no man. There was no poverty like His.

But His purpose in all this. *That we through his poverty should be rich.* How strangely these words sound! That the poverty of one should be the riches of many! And yet it is indeed only another putting of the same wonderful paradox which runs through the whole gospel, and through the whole of Christ's dealings with the children of men. Those dealings were throughout a giving and a taking, a wondrous exchange, such as it could only have entered into the heart of God to conceive. He everywhere taking from us whatever was poorest, meanest, saddest, most painful, most ignominious, and giving to us what was highest, noblest, choicest, best, and most glorious; taking earth and giving heaven, taking our poverty and giving to us His riches. But this is not all; taking our shame and giving to us His glory, taking our cross and giving to us His crown, taking our sin and giving to us His righteousness, taking our curse and giving to us His blessing, taking our death and giving to us His life.

Truly He did make Himself poor that we through His poverty might be rich. But of what riches speaks the apostle here? Not of silver and gold, corruptible things, of which if one have more another must have less, which oftentimes corrupt those that have them, which at best perish in the using; which leave us, or which at the best we must leave. Not to make us rich in these; for He knew that man's true life was not in them, that a man abounding in these, rich in all which the world calls riches, might yet still be poor, poor in all the elements of true happiness, poor in time and poor for eternity; poor in time, having no joy in his life here, for the fountains of joy even here are within a man and not without, from above and not from beneath. How poor too may a rich man of this world be, how poor for eternity, how bare, how naked, how miserable, when that world which was his only world shall have passed away from him and the glory of it; this too He knew as none of us *can* know, as it is to be hoped we shall never know, as only that last and terrible day shall declare.

To make us rich, then, in what? Rich in peace, rich in joy, rich in the grace, favor, presence, and benediction of our God. And oh! brethren, how poor is man's life, how mean, how wretched, if it have not these; if it be lived without Christ and without God. Men may array that life outwardly with what gorgeous trappings they can; cover over and conceal the inner squalor and meanness of it as they will; they may hide its loathsome sores under purple and gold; yet the inner meanness and poverty of it cannot effectually be hid, will make themselves felt; its sores refuse to be hidden, will break forth so that all may see them. There is hollowness at the heart of a worldly life, be it outwardly as rich and prosperous as it may; a want of sincerity in its joys; its mirth is madness, and its loudest laughter ever followed by a sigh. What good shall my life do me? is sooner or later the cry of the jaded votary of pleasure. He who thought to enjoy everything in a little while enjoys nothing. The prodigal of yesterday is the bankrupt of today. "I enjoy nothing": those were the very words of one, gifted with all the external helps to happiness—a poet, one of the noble of the earth, gifted with genius, with all that wealth could command, who, having loosed himself from all the painful tasks which duty would impose, sought only to please himself. Having laid himself out to enjoy everything, but without God, against God, this was the sad and forlorn confession which was wrung from his lips ere he had reached half the allotted years of man.

But that Savior with whom we have to do makes the life of His people rich, brings them back to God, the one foundation and spring of all joy, reconciles them to Him in the blood of His cross, and in that same act reconciles them to themselves, healing the deep hurt of their spirits and changing the deep discords of their lives into harmonies. The world in which they live, they behold it now as God's world. The work appointed to them to do is God's work, and this adds dignity and honor to the humblest task which may be allotted to them here.

Toil and labor, sorrow and suffering, all have transformed and transfigured from the moment that the light of heaven, the light of Christ's cross has rested upon them. They are no longer mere heavy crushing burdens, under which our suffering humanity groans as it staggers wearily to its grave; but these very things, seeming to be burdens, are indeed lightsome wings, lifting us heavenward; a divine training and discipline appointed for the children of God; a ladder let down from heaven, by which they may mount, painfully, it may be, and with bleeding feet to the throne of God. Surely the apostle had good right to affirm that Jesus Christ became poor that we through His poverty might be rich.

But whom did St. Paul mean by *we*? Was it only those who were already partakers of these riches that were in Christ; and who should henceforward glorify themselves in the exclusive possession of these riches? Or was it not rather all men—that all whom sin had impoverished might through the grace of our Lord Jesus Christ be made rich? It was not a favored few, but all whose poverty Christ would fain change into riches, their sin into righteousness, their shame into glory, their despair into hope, their death in life into a life even in death; his purposes of love as wide as the world.

Bibliography

Bromley, John. *The Man of Ten Talents: A Portrait of Richard Chenevix Trench, 1807–1886, Philologist, Poet, Theologian, Archbishop.* London: SPCK, 1959.

Trench, Richard. *English, Past and Present: Five Lectures.* London: Parker, 1855.

———. *Notes on the Miracles of Our Lord.* London, 1846. Reprinted—Popular edition. Grand Rapids: Baker, 1949.

———. *Notes on the Parables of Our Lord.* London, 1841. Reprinted—Popular edition. Grand Rapids: Baker, 1948.

———. *On the Study of Words: Five Lectures.* London: Parker, 1851.

———. *Sermons New and Old.* London: Kegan Paul, 1886.

———. *Synonyms of the New Testament.* Cambridge: Macmillan, 1854. Reprinted—Grand Rapids: Eerdmans, 1950.

3

J. B. Lightfoot

(1828–1889)

The English Revised Version of the New Testament was placed in the hands of the British people on 17 May 1881, culminating ten years of work by fifty-four outstanding scholars. Public response was predictable: the new version, with all its announced accuracy, could never replace the Authorized Version with its beauty and, above all, familiarity.

The Anglican clergy were confused: could they legally use the new version when only the old version was officially authorized by the church? The man in the street was critical and skeptical. After all, the translators had promised not to deviate too much from the King James Version, and yet they had made 36,000 changes. Perhaps the new version was more accurate, but the public preferred tradition to scholarship. Prime Minister William Gladstone stated the problem clearly: "You will sacrifice truth if you don't read it, and you will sacrifice the people if you do." But Charles H. Spurgeon put the finger on the real problem: "It is strong in Greek, weak in English."

Indeed the new version *was* "strong in Greek," and one reason was the presence on the New Testament Committee of the "Cambridge triumvirate"—B. F. Westcott, F. J. A. Hort, and J. B. Lightfoot—names that still stand for scholarship in New Testament studies. Of the three, Lightfoot was undoubtedly the best scholar. In fact Owen Chadwick called Lightfoot "the greatest scholar in the Jerusalem Chamber."[1] In his memorial essay on Bishop Lightfoot, W. Robertson Nicoll called him "pre-eminently the scholar of the Church of England."[2]

If you have ever used Lightfoot's commentaries on Galatians, Philippians, and Colossians, or any of his studies in the church fathers, you probably agree with Nicoll's conclusion. But what you may not know is that Bishop Lightfoot was a godly man, a teacher of pastors, and a preacher with a burden for lost souls. "When goodness is joined to knowledge, it counts for much," wrote Nicoll, "and when these are crowned by spiritual power, paramount influence is the result. Lightfoot had all three."

Joseph Barber Lightfoot was born in Liverpool on 13 April 1828. He was taught at King Edward's School, Birmingham, by the noted James Prince Lee, whose pupils seemed to capture every prize and move into places of influence, particularly in the church. Lee taught Lightfoot to love the Greek New Testament; and the teacher saw in the pupil tremendous potential for both Christian character and scholarship. "Give him the run of the town library!" Lee ordered.

At age nineteen Lightfoot entered Trinity College, Cambridge, where he studied under Westcott. ("He was Westcott's best pupil," Hort later admitted.) He captured several honors and prizes and seemed destined for a teaching position. In 1854 he was ordained a deacon in the Church of England, and in 1858 a priest. The next year he became a tutor at Trinity College, and in 1861 he was named Hulsean Professor of Divinity. So popular were his New Testament lectures that they had to be given in the great hall of the college. Ten years later he was made canon of St. Paul's, sharing the ministry with the great Henry Liddon and Dean R. W. Church. He was named Lady Margaret Professor of Divinity in 1875, and it seemed that his ministry as scholar, writer, and teacher was established.

But in 1879 he was appointed bishop of Durham, and the scholar had to make the most critical decision of his life. In the last public

1. *The Victorian Church*, 2 vols. (London: Black, 1966), 2:49.

2. *Princes of the Church*, p. 22.

message Bishop Lightfoot preached, on 29 June 1889, he confessed that he had spent a "long wakeful night" making the decision to leave Cambridge and a life of scholarship for Durham and a life of administration. He wrote to his friend Westcott: "At length I have sent my answer 'Yes.' It seemed to me that to resist any longer would be to fight against God. My consolation and my hope for the future is that it has cost me the greatest moral effort, the greatest venture of faith which I ever made. Now that the answer is sent I intend to have no regrets about the past." Westcott called the decision "a kind of martyrdom," and perhaps it was.

In the months that followed, Lightfoot received letters from all kinds of people urging him to continue his studies and writing in spite of his new ministry. In a memorial sermon to Lightfoot, given on 24 November 1929, George R. Eden said: "Few men can have passed through such an agony of choice as we know he suffered. . . . Yet the choice was made—upon his knees, 'wrestling with the Angel in prayer.'" It is interesting to note that R. W. Dale warned Westcott in 1883: "Forgive me for saying—do not let them make you a bishop. I do not know what Dr. Lightfoot may have done for Durham; for those of us who are outside he has done nothing since his elevation."

What did the great Greek scholar do for Durham and for the Church of England? His years as bishop are still called "the golden age of Durham."

Westcott preached the consecration sermon (25 April 1879) and urged the new bishop to "choose between the important and the routine . . . and do the important." Lightfoot did so gladly, delegating routine matters to his associates and concentrating on the things only a bishop can do. Lightfoot was gifted with the mental, physical, and spiritual equipment a man needs to make a success of such a high office. He had a robust constitution and a love for hard work. An early riser, he put in two or three hours of study before breakfast, and he often remained at his desk when the rest of the staff had gone to bed. He had a remarkable memory and could tell a secretary where a quotation was in a given book, even its location on the page.

During a holiday in Norway, he was seen correcting proofs while riding in a cart on a rather precipitous road. He was a gifted linguist, fluent in French, German, Spanish, Italian, and Latin, as well as Greek; and he was able to use Hebrew, Syriac, Arabic, Coptic, Ethiopic, and Armenian. He enjoyed telling the story about the professor who isolated several newborn babies to discover what language they would speak if not influenced by English.

After a pause, Lightfoot would say, "The poor little children spoke pure Hebrew."

The new bishop was a worker and an innovator, much to the surprise and delight of the clergy under his jurisdiction. One of his first innovations was the "Brotherhood." Never married, Lightfoot each year "adopted" several young men who studied with him for a year before ordination. It was an internship program on the highest level. But the bishop made it clear to applicants that the fellowship was "a brotherhood in Christ, not an exclusive association of clique or caste"; and that their union was based on "participation in a common work and the loving devotion to a common Master." The bishop was their leader, teacher, example, and spiritual father. As one member of the Brotherhood put it, "We read, we worked, because Lightfoot was working and reading."

Men in the Brotherhood—"the sons of the house," as the bishop called them—were kept busy. They breakfasted with Lightfoot at 7:45, at 8:15 were in the chapel for morning prayers, and by 9 were either reading or listening to lectures. They ate lunch at 1:15, then scattered for practical ministry in the diocese. Each man was assigned a district where he worked with resident clergy. The men gathered during the week to share experiences and learn from one another, always under the watchful eye of the bishop. As the program developed, Bishop Lightfoot set aside St. Peter's Day (29 June) for an annual reunion of the "sons of the house." (Spurgeon followed a similar pattern with the men in his Pastors' College.)

The bishop viewed the Christian ministry highly, and he applied high standards to himself before he applied them to others. His essay "The Christian Ministry" in his commentary on Philippians upset more than one Anglican who saw it as a departure from Church of England tradition. His friend Canon Liddon requested him to withdraw the essay, but Lightfoot refused. "The Christian minister, whatever else he is—and I shall not enter upon controversial questions—is, before all things, a pastor, a shepherd," said Lightfoot in his last public appearance in his diocese.

Bishop Lightfoot also blended scholarship and Christian devotion. I once listened to an impassioned sermon by a well-known preacher on the impossibility of being "a soul-winner and a deep Bible student." The apostle Paul would have smiled at that sermon, as would Charles G. Finney, Jonathan Edwards, R. A. Torrey, Spurgeon, and Lightfoot. All Greek students should write on the flyleaf of their Greek New Testament these words of Bishop Lightfoot: "After all is said and done, the only way to know the Greek Testament properly is by prayer."

Lightfoot's own walk with God was the secret power of his life, and his concern to obey God and help others find Christ motivated him. He reorganized his diocese so that pastors might be able to reach more people and build more new churches. A great admirer of John Wesley, Lightfoot organized lay evangelists who helped carry the message from district to district. He mobilized the women of the diocese and encouraged them to serve in "sisterhoods" or as deaconesses. Before long, Durham was vibrating with new power and excitement because a great Greek scholar had placed himself and his ambitions on the altar that he might serve God. What he said to the Brotherhood, he practiced himself: "You go where you are sent, you work till you drop. . . ."

Lightfoot is best remembered as a writer. His commentaries on Galatians, Philippians, Colossians, and Philemon ought to be in every pastor's library. These scholarly works are part of a series that he had projected with his friends Westcott and Hort. The series was not completed, but Westcott did publish excellent commentaries on the Gospel of John, Hebrews, and the Epistles of John. Lightfoot died before he could write his commentary on Ephesians to complete the quartet. Lightfoot also wrote four articles for *Smith's Dictionary of the Bible* (Acts, Romans, I Thessalonians, and II Thessalonians) and published the definitive edition of *The Apostolic Fathers.* The latter work demolished the position of the Tübingen school that centered around F. C. Baur, the German critic. More of a historian than a theologian, Lightfoot was at home with ancient documents and textual problems.

When an anonymous author attacked his friend Westcott in *Supernatural Religion,* Lightfoot took up his pen and wrote a series of articles for the *Contemporary Review* that pushed the best-selling book off the market. His facts were so devastating that the public rejected *Supernatural Religion,* and the book ended up glutting the used-book stores. Lightfoot's book *On a Fresh Revision of the English New Testament* is still available, as are several posthumous collections: *Ordination Addresses, Leaders in the Northern Church, Cambridge Sermons, Sermons Preached on Special Occasions, Sermons Preached in St. Paul's,* and *Historical Essays.*

Lightfoot had requested that no official biography be written; however, a memoir, *Bishop Lightfoot,* was published anonymously in 1894. Hort wrote the excellent article on Lightfoot in *The Dictionary of National Biography;* in fact, it was the last thing Hort wrote before his death. *Lightfoot of Durham: Memories and Appreciations* was edited by George R. Eden and F. C. Macdonald, and published in 1933.

Westcott did not heed Dale's warning. Not only did he become a bishop, but he succeeded Lightfoot at Durham. And his successor was one of Lightfoot's students, Handley C. G. Moule, also a Greek scholar and writer of commentaries. Durham was privileged to have men who combined academic excellence with spiritual fervor, resulting in a balanced ministry.

The day after Bishop Lightfoot died, one of the leading British newspapers, the *Times*, said: "He was at once one of the greatest Theological scholars and an eminent Bishop. It is scarcely possible to estimate adequately as yet the influence of his life and work." In preparing his "sons" for ordination, Bishop Lightfoot used to say: "Forget me, forget the (ordination) service of tomorrow, forget the human questioner. Transport yourselves in thought from the initial to the final inquiry. The great day of inquisition, the supreme moment of revelation, is come. The chief Shepherd, the universal bishop of souls is the questioner.... The 'Wilt thou' of the ordination day is exchanged for the 'Hast thou' of the judgment day...." This is good counsel for all of us, but especially for those who serve as ministers and who want to hear our Master say, "Well done."

Girded Loins and Burning Lamps

> Let your loins be girded about, and your lights burning; and ye yourselves like unto men that wait for their lord, when he will return from the wedding.... **Luke 12:35–36**

A great change in your lives, a tremendous pledge given, a tremendous responsibility incurred, a magnificent blessing claimed, a glorious potentiality of good bestowed—how else shall I describe the crisis which tomorrow's sun will bring, or at least may bring, to all of you, to deacons and priests alike, to those who are entering on the first stage of the ministry most perceptibly, but to those whose ministry is crowned with the duties and the privileges of the higher order most really!

A great and momentous change—momentous beyond all human conception for good or for evil, to yourselves, to your flock, to every one who comes in contact with you. For good or for evil. It must be so. This is the universal law in things spiritual. The same

---

Author's note: Lightfoot's sermon "Girded Loins and Burning Lamps" is from *Ordination Addresses and Counsels to Clergy*, pp. 67–81. He preached this charge to candidates for ordination on Trinity Sunday in both 1882 and 1886.

Christ, who is for the rising of many, is for the falling of many likewise. The same gospel, which is to some the savor of life unto life, is to others the savor of death unto death. A potentiality of glory must likewise be a potentiality of shame. You cannot touch the ark of God with profane hands and live—just because it is the ark of God.

I know not, I never do know, what to say on such occasions as these. Where shall I begin and where shall I end? What shall I say, and what shall I leave unsaid? One short half-hour of exhortation, where the experience of a long lifetime were all too little for the subject! One short half-hour, where the issues involve an eternity of bliss or of woe to many immortal souls of your brothers and sisters for whom Christ died!

At such a moment we cannot do better than steady our thoughts by gathering them about some scriptural text. If all else should be forgotten, if all else should be scattered to the winds, it may be that the text itself will linger on the ears and will burn itself into the heart. I will therefore sum up these parting words of exhortation in the opening sentence of tomorrow's Gospel: "Let your loins be girded about, and your lights burning; and ye yourselves like unto men that wait for their lord, when he will return from the wedding."

I know not how it may be with others; but no words in the ordination service—not even the tremendous and searching question, "Do you trust that you are inwardly moved by the Holy Ghost to take upon you this office and ministration?" not even the solemn words of the higher commission itself, "Receive the Holy Ghost for the office and work of a priest in the Church of God"—no other words sank so deeply into my mind at the time, or affect me so profoundly when I hear them again, as these opening words of the Gospel.

For here is the twofold equipment of the man of God: the loins girded, and the lamps burning. The loins girded: the outward activities, the external accompaniments, the busy ministrations, on the one hand. The lamps burning: the inward illumination, the light of the Spirit fed with the oil of prayer and meditation and study of the Scriptures, on the other.

And both alike are brought to the final searching test of the great, the terrible, the glorious day, when every secret of the heart shall be revealed and every deed of man shall be laid bare.

To such a test I desire you to put yourselves in imagination this night in reference to your ordination vows. All is over. The life's probation is accomplished. The ministrations in the sanctuary have ceased. The voice of the preacher is silenced. The pastoral visits are ended. And now the scrutiny, the review, the trial begins. The great heart-searcher puts His questions: "How didst thou deal with the soul of this sinning brother, or this sorrowing sister, with this, and this, and this? What study, what thought, what pains didst thou bestow on this sermon, and on this, and on this? How hast thou conducted thyself in this church ministration, and in this, and in this—with what reverence, with what concentration of heart and mind, so that the contagion of thy devotion spread through the assembled people, and their sympathetic responsive "Amen" said to thy praise and thanksgiving redounded to the glory of God the giver? Hast thou been faithful to thy church? Hast thou been faithful to thy flock? Hast thou been faithful to thyself?"

"Hast thou been faithful to thyself?" Yes; after all, the many and various questions are gathered up and concentrated in this. If you have only proved true to yourself, you cannot have been found untrue to your office, to your work, to your brothers and sisters, to the church of God. As are the equipments of the minister, so will be his ministrations. Have you kept your loins ever girded, and your lamp ever burning? Then, whensoever and howsoever Christ has come, He has found you ready to meet Him. Has He presented Himself to you in the penitent, burdened with past sin and struggling with present temptation? Has he come to you in the bereavement of the mourner, or in the helplessness of the ignorant? Is His presence manifested in the bitter opposition of some reckless foe, or in the passive resistance of some stolid indifference, in the unreasonableness, or the worldliness, or the overbearingness, or the misunderstanding of those around you? How can you command at a moment's notice the sympathy, the patience, the forbearance, the courage, the resourcefulness, the tact, the wisdom, the power, which the occasion requires? How shall you escape the perplexity, the confusion, the shame, the failure, the desolation, the despair of those foolish five, who at the supreme crisis awoke from their slumber to find the lights quenched and the doors closed—closed forever?

So then I desire today to call your attention more especially to those questions in the ordinal which relate to your intended treatment of yourselves, as distinguished alike from those which test your beliefs and those which enquire after your purposed fulfillment of duties towards others.

These questions are two: the one addressed indeed to priests but hardly less applicable to deacons; the other put in substantially the same words to both orders alike; the one relating to the inner man, to the furniture of the soul; the other to the outward conduct and life.

First, "Will you be diligent in prayers, and in reading of the Holy Scriptures, and in such studies as help to the knowledge of the same, laying aside the study of the world and the flesh?"

Secondly, "Will you apply all your diligence to frame and fashion your own lives . . . according to the doctrine of Christ, and to make yourselves . . .wholesome examples of the flock of Christ?"

These two questions correspond roughly to the two clauses of the text. "Your lamps burning": here is the diligence in prayer and study; "your loins girded": here is the framing and fashioning of your lives.

Well then. Forget me, forget the service of tomorrow, forget the human questioner. Transport yourselves in thought from the initial to the final inquiry. The great day of inquisition, the supreme moment of revelation, is come. The chief Shepherd, the universal bishop of souls, is the questioner. It is no longer a matter of the making of the promises, but of the fulfillment of the promises. The "Wilt thou" of the ordination day is exchanged for the "Hast thou" of the judgment day. "Hast thou been diligent in prayer? Hast thou framed and fashioned thy life?"

First then; as to the inner furniture and equipment of the soul, intellectual as well as spiritual. Has the lamp been kept burning? Has it been constantly trimmed, constantly replenished with oil?

This equipment is set forth in the one question. It is threefold: first, prayer; secondly, the reading of the Holy Scriptures; thirdly, such studies as help to the knowledge of the same.

But it will be pleaded, prayer is good, meditation is good, study is good; but how am I to find the time for all these things? Work presses upon me from all sides—work incomplete and work unbegun. I cannot rest satisfied while the schools are so inefficient; I cannot give myself leisure, so long as whole families, perhaps whole districts, in my parish are untouched, or barely touched, by my ministrations. There are a thousand projects which I have had in my mind, and which, for mere lack of time, I have never been able to carry out. Is it not selfish, is it not unpardonable, to retire into myself, to think of myself, when so many others are uncared for? No, not selfish, for unless in this matter of the inner life you are true to yourself, you cannot be true to others; not selfish, for where there is no fire, there can be no light and no warmth; not selfish, for you cannot draw for others out of an empty fountain. You want recreation, you want relief, you want change, amidst this ceaseless worry, these anxious cares, this turmoil of never-ending business. And what refreshment, what medicine, what recreating of the soul so effective as to take your troubles to God, to tell them one by one to Him, to pour out your heart to your Father, and so to lay down your burden at His footstool? Try to realize the strength of the expression in St. Peter—far stronger in the original Greek than in our translation, *pasan tēn merimnan hymōn epirripsantes ep' auton,* "casting, tossing off, all your anxiety on Him." What completeness, what energy, what promptness, what eagerness and (if I might say so without irreverence) what familiarity in the action! And after all there is time enough for prayer, if only prayer is sought—time enough for the lifting up of the heart to God. All places and all hours are convenient for this. No spare interval is so short but that one unspoken ejaculation of the soul is possible. Do not mistake me. I do not desire to encourage dreaminess, sentimentalism, vagueness, unsubstantiality. Prayer—true prayer—is essentially firm and strong and real. And this firmness, this strength, this reality, it and it only will communicate to your ministerial work.

But side by side with prayer is the reading of the Holy Scriptures. These are the two pillars of the pastoral edifice. This reading of the Holy Scriptures—what does it imply? The devotional study? This certainly; but clearly it involves very much more than this. What place else were there for "such studies as help to the knowledge of the same? Plainly the exegetical, the theological, the historical study of the book is included. Every ray of knowledge, from whatever source it comes, which throws light on this book, will be welcomed by the faithful priest of God. We know the proverbial strength which attaches to the *homo unius libri.* The man of this one book—this book of books—will be strong indeed. But then he must know it; know it within and without, know it in all its bearings, find food for his intellect, his imagination, his reason, as well as for his soul, for his heart, for his affections; find nourishment for his whole man. If Christianity had been a dry code of ethics, then he might have neglected the theology; but now its morality flows from its theological principles. If the gospel had been an abstract system of metaphysics, then he might have ignored the history; but now the gospel dispensation is embodied in a history. The incarnation, the cross, the resurrection are a history.

I wish I could impress upon you, as strongly as I feel myself, the necessity of this faithful, concentrated, diligent study of the Bible. I wish I could make you realize the greatness of the opportunity which lies before you. The greatness of the opportunity. Aye, that is it. There never was a time when men on all sides were more eager after biblical knowledge. Your people are standing open-mouthed, hungering and thirsting for meat and drink. Will you deny it to them—you the appointed stewards and dispensers of God's mysteries, of God's revelations? The appetite, of which I speak, may not always be very spiritual, very exalted. I do not say it is. It may be an undefined craving, it may be a mere vague curiosity, in many cases; though I believe it is more often a deeper feeling. But there it is. And it is your opportunity. But it is knowledge which is required. Mere empty talk, mere repetition of stereotyped phrases, mere purposeless rambling about the pages of the Bible, will not satisfy it. The teaching, which it demands, can only be acquired by earnest, assiduous, concentrated study on the part of the teacher. But then what a speedy and abundant harvest it yields to the teacher and the taught alike! Do not say you have no time. Time can always be made, where there is the earnest desire to make it. The fact is, we want more backbone in our teaching. Instruction is craved; and instruction, as a rule, is just what our people do not get in our sermons. We want more systematic teaching on the great doctrines of the faith; we want more continuous elucidation of particular books of Holy Scripture; we want more detailed exposition of the duties and responsibilities of churchmen as members of a body—of the meaning of the church as the spouse of Christ, of its ordinances and its seasons. The incarnation, the incarnation itself, is the type, the pattern, of the best form of teaching. God is immanent in man. God speaks through man. So too the Bible is the most human of all books, as it is also the most divine. Use its humanity, if I may so speak, that you may enforce its divinity.

And so it is that you are encouraged in the question of the ordinal to range outside the sacred volume itself. You pledge yourself to be diligent in such studies as help to the knowledge of the same. This is a large subject, and I cannot venture to go into it. Only I would apply to this intellectual food the words which St. Paul uses of the material food. "Nothing is to be refused"; but, observe, on this condition that "it is sanctified by the word of God and prayer." It must be studied in the light of God's Word; it must be employed for the elucidation of God's Word; it must be hallowed by the uplifting of the soul to Him. Biography furnishes illustrations; poetry supplies images; science and history are the expression of God's laws and God's dealings with man. Have you eyes to see? Then for you heaven and earth are full of His glory.

But the great Judge, the searcher of hearts, passes on to that second and not less momentous question: "Hast thou framed and fashioned thy life—thy life and the lives of those about thee—according to the doctrine of Christ? Hast thou, and have they, been wholesome examples and patterns to the flock? Answer this, thou teacher in Israel; answer this, thou priest of the most high God. Hast thou never brought scandal on the church of Christ? Hast thou never by the evil deed of a moment, neutralized, discredited, held up to scorn and blasphemy, the teaching of months and years?" What! Do I wrong you, if only for a moment I entertain in my mind the possibility of such an issue to your ministry? Indeed I hope so; I believe so. Otherwise it were better for me—better far—that my right hand were cut off, than that I should lay it on the head of such a one. It were better for him—a thousand times better—that he should skulk home this night under cover of darkness, unordained, disgraced, cast helpless and hopeless on the sea of life, to shape his course afresh, than that he should thus betray the Son of man with a kiss. And yet such things have happened. Already in the few short years of my episcopate, I have seen the fall of one and another and another. This incumbent or that curate has brought blasphemy on the name of God, has scandalized the church of Christ by intemperance or even worse than intemperance. Therefore I say, "Let him that thinketh he standeth take heed lest he fall." Check the first risings of the evil passion in you. You, the ministers of Christ, are beset with many and great perils by virtue of your very office. You enjoy confidences, you excite sympathies, you stir sensibilities, which may be most pure, most holy, most heavenly. But beware, beware. The opportunity of boundless good is the opportunity of incalculable evil. There is no fall so shocking, so terrible, as the fall of a minister of Christ.

But I desire rather to warn you against lesser faults of character—trifling unimportant faults they might be regarded in laymen, but with you nothing is unimportant, nothing is trifling. There is the fault of temper, the impatience of opposition, the stiffness of self-assertion, a magnifying of self which veils itself from itself under the guise of magnifying of your office. It is not in vain that at the outset of your ministry the prayer is offered for you that you may be modest and humble, as well as constant, in your ministrations. There is again the recklessness of an unbridled tongue; there is the indulgence in idle gossip; there is the absence of self-restraint in the character and the limits of your recreations. All these things, and far more than these, are involved in the pledge of tomorrow to frame and fashion your lives, that you may be a wholesome example and pattern to the flock of Christ.

The pledge of tomorrow! The hour is fast approaching, the hour which binds you to a lifelong devotion, to a lifelong labor. Answer to the "Wilt thou," as remembering the great day when you must answer to the "Hast thou"; answer to it, as purposing henceforward by God's grace to ask and to answer to yourselves continually "Am I?" "Am I diligent in prayers and in reading of the Holy Scriptures? Am I framing and fashioning my life according to the doctrine of Christ?"

The hour is fast approaching. What satisfaction, what joy, what thanksgiving should be yours! On you the highest of all honors is conferred. To you the noblest of all endowments is pledged—the earnest of God's Spirit, the gift of God's grace, the germ and the potentiality of untold blessings to many, many souls of men. What joy and thanksgiving; and yet what awe and trembling! This priceless treasure, and these earthen vessels! This high commission, and my utter feebleness! This Holy Spirit—the all-pure and all-righteous—and my sullied heart, my sinful life! O God, my God, what a contrast, what a contradiction, what an impossibility is here! Help me, strengthen me, cleanse me with the blood of Thy dear Son; purge me with the fire of Thy blessed Spirit. Take me to Thyself this day, and make me wholly Thine.

Bibliography

Bishop Lightfoot. London: Macmillan, 1894.

Eden, George R., and Macdonald, F. C., ed. *Lightfoot of Durham: Memories and Appreciations.* Cambridge: Cambridge University, 1932.

Lightfoot, J. B. *The Apostolic Fathers.* Edited by J. R. Harmer. London: Macmillan, 1891. Reprinted—Grand Rapids: Baker, 1956.

______. *Cambridge Sermons.* London: Macmillan, 1890.

______. *The Epistles of St. Paul.* 3 vols. London: Macmillan, 1865–1875. Reprinted—Grand Rapids: Zondervan, 1957.

______. *Historical Essays.* London: Macmillan, 1895.

______. *Leaders in the Northern Church.* Edited by J. R. Harmer. London: Macmillan, 1890.

______. *On a Fresh Revision of the English New Testament.* London: Cambridge, 1871.

______. *Ordination Addresses and Counsels to Clergy.* London: Macmillan, 1890.

______. *Sermons Preached in St. Paul's Cathedral.* London: Macmillan, 1891.

______. *Sermons Preached on Special Occasions.* London: Macmillan, 1891.

Nicoll, W. Robertson. *Princes of the Church.* London: Hodder and Stoughton, 1921.

4

George Matheson

(1842–1906)

Most people know two things about George Matheson: he was blind, and he wrote "O Love That Will Not Let Me Go." Some people still believe the myth that he wrote the hymn after his sweetheart broke their engagement because he was going blind. Matheson began to go blind at eighteen months, and he was never engaged. "I have never been in love," he once told his friend M'Kenzie Bell.

Matheson told about composing the hymn: "It came to me spontaneously, without conscious effort; and I have never been able to gain once more the same fervor in verse." He admitted a crisis had been involved, but he did not say what it was. "My hymn was composed in the manse of Innellan on the evening of 6th June 1882. I was at that time alone. It was the day of my sister's marriage, and the rest of the family were staying overnight in Glasgow. Something had happened to me, which was known only to myself, and which caused me the most severe mental suffering. The hymn was the fruit of that suffering. It was the quickest bit of work I ever did in my life. I had the impression rather of having it dictated to me by some inward voice than of working it out myself. I am quite sure that the whole work was completed in five minutes. . . ."[1]

I believe Matheson made far greater contributions to the cause of Christ than his hymn, as beautiful as that is. His courage and accomplishment are a tremendous inspiration to anyone in the ministry who has to fight a handicap.

George Matheson was born in Glasgow on 27 March 1842. His eyesight began to fail, but he managed to complete his basic schooling wearing very strong glasses. By the time he was eighteen, however, he had to have assistance. His two sisters were his greatest helpers, even learning foreign languages to tutor him. At the University of Glasgow he devoted five years to earning his M.A. and another four years to the M.Div. He won honors, particularly in debate and public speaking, and he was popular. At one point he wanted to train for a legal career, but the call of Christ prevailed. On 13 June 1866 he was licensed by the presbytery; six months later he was named assistant to John Ross MacDuff at Sandyford Church. MacDuff was a devotional preacher whose books sold in the millions. Influenced by MacDuff, Matheson also became a very successful devotional writer.

Early in 1868, Matheson was recommended to the church of Innellan in one of Glasgow's resort areas. When Glasgow citizens relaxed in Innellan during summer months, they wanted to hear good sermons. Matheson's blindness gave rise to some strong opposition in the church, and they called him by a very narrow majority. Before long, however, the new pastor won the hearts of the people. They ordained him on 8 April 1868, and he remained with them for eighteen years. Not only was he faithful in his preaching, but he also spent time with his people. Like most Scottish pastors, he invested his mornings in the study and his afternoons in visitation and counseling. Imagine what it would be like for a blind man to pastor a church. Matheson did have the capable assistance of his sister and the officers of the church. But only he could gather the material for his messages, plan the Sunday services, and lead the church in worship. He memorized not only his message, but also the hymns and the Scripture readings. And he never missed a word!

Early in his Innellan ministry Matheson experienced an eclipse of faith that would have defeated a person without handicaps. "With a great thrill of horror," he told a friend, "I found myself an absolute atheist! After being ordained at Innellan, I believed noth-

1. Donald Macmillan, *The Life of George Matheson*, p. 181.

ing; neither God nor immortality." He shared his problem with his officers and even offered to resign. They wisely counseled him to wait; he was young, and all young ministers (they said) had times of doubt. He waited and won the battle. Without abandoning his traditional faith, he saw deeper meaning in it and felt he could still preach it without losing his integrity.

In 1879 he was granted a D.D. by Edinburgh University. He also became one of Innellan's greatest attractions. When he resigned the church in 1886 to go to St. Bernard's, Edinburgh, he temporarily threatened the economic stability of the resort!

His call to St. Bernard's Church is an interesting story in itself. One stormy winter's Sunday, Matheson preached to only a handful of worshipers. He went home rather discouraged because he felt his message had been especially good. A stranger in the congregation, however, never forgot either the sermon or the preacher. More than seven years later, when St. Bernard's needed a pastor, this man recommended Matheson. Each occasion of ministry deserves our best. The results may be slow in coming, but they will come.

Matheson was installed as pastor of St. Bernard's Church on 12 May 1886. He remained with the church for thirteen years. In 1896 he offered his resignation, but it was rejected. He preached his farewell sermon on 17 November 1899, and then retired to write and occasionally to preach. He preached his last sermon on 14 February 1904, at Morningside Church, Edinburgh, a pulpit made famous in recent years by James S. Stewart. While on his annual holiday, George Matheson took sick; he died on 28 November 1906.

His friends claimed that Matheson's blindness was actually his making. It compelled him to "walk by faith" and live in the highest levels of spiritual meditation. He was not deceived or distracted by the surface things of life. He had the ability to penetrate deeper even though he could not see. A presbyterian council heard him preach once and responded: "The Council all feel that God has closed your eyes only to open other eyes, which have made you one of the guides of men."

Beside being a courageous man and an outstanding preacher, Matheson was an exacting scholar and capable writer. His first book was *Aids to the Study of German Theology* (1874). Preachers with normal vision would hesitate to tackle a subject like that. Three years later he published a two-volume work, *Growth of the Spirit of Christianity*, attempting to apply Hegelian philosophy to church history. In 1881 he published *Natural Elements of Revealed*

Theology, the Baird Lectures for that year. But we most remember Matheson as a devotional writer of amazing perception and poetic ability. *My Aspirations* (1883) was his first devotional book. He also wrote *Moments on the Mount, Words by the Wayside, Leaves for Quiet Hours, Rests by the River, Sidelights from Patmos,* and many others. Any preacher who has ever delivered a series of biographical sermons would appreciate *The Representative Men of the Bible* (two volumes), *The Representative Men of the New Testament,* and *The Representative Women of the Bible.* His *Studies of the Portrait of Christ* (two volumes) and *Spiritual Development of St. Paul* are valuable contributions to these areas of Bible study.

So much "devotional writing" today is shallow and sentimental and not at all spiritual. A Bible verse, a paragraph of approved platitudes, an exhortation, and a prayer make up the average "meditation." The people who manufacture these things need to listen to Matheson's convictions about devotional writing: "Devotion must be the child of reflection; it may rise on wings, but they must be the wings of thought. . . . it should aim at the marriage of qualities which are commonly supposed to be antagonistic—the insight of the thinker and the fervor of the worshiper. . . . Religious sentiment, if it is worth anything, must be preceded by religious perception."[2] Matheson blended the intellectual power of the theologian and the spiritual perception and devotion of the mystic. In the preface to *Times of Retirement,* he wrote: "It is often said that devotion is a thing of the heart. I do not think it is either mainly or merely so. I hold that all devotion is based upon intellectual conviction." No wonder his writing is like that "sea of glass, mingled with fire." His devotional writings are characterized by depth and variety. He laid hold of a great spiritual truth, saw new and exciting possibilities in it, and then applied it in a way that is practical without being preachy. He combined fact and feeling. Each selection generally has two parts: the spiritual thought for the mind and a prayer directed to the heart. George H. Morrison once defined "sentiment" as "feeling without responsibility." Matheson would have agreed, because he avoided the mawkish or maudlin. He never used religious words to manufacture artificial feeling.

Perhaps the secret of his balanced devotional experience was sincere prayer. One of his faithful parishioners wrote: "Dr. Matheson's first prayer [in the worship service] was often the finest part of the service. And what a prayer it was!. . . How many of our preachers draw tears from the eyes of the worshipers as they

---

2. Ibid., pp. 172–73.

pray?" Another worshiper said: "In that prayer we have been to the mount of worship, and we could go away content even if we heard no more. It was wonderful the way in which that blind preacher talked with God and uttered the aspirations of the people." Matheson himself admitted: "Prayer never causes me an effort. When I pray, I know I am addressing the Deity, but when I preach, the Devil may be among the congregation."

In his early days of ministry, Matheson attempted to reconcile evangelical doctrine with the new German theology and the views of evolution. For some he succeeded; but he failed to minister to the needs of the masses. In his later years he wrote for the common people, and God gave him a wide and useful ministry. That ministry continues in his many books.

Matheson did not try to generate false fire. He warmed one's heart as had the Savior those of the Emmaus disciples: Matheson opened up the Scriptures and revealed Jesus Christ. He fed himself on the truths of the Word in long hours of meditation and then shared those truths with others. He made truth luminous. He made it exciting. We would do well to rediscover Matheson in this day of much superficial devotional preaching and writing. Some publisher could do us a great service by reprinting his best books, or perhaps an anthology of his best selections. The preacher would be wise to read Matheson and seek to attain that beautiful blending of doctrinal precision and devotional passion. George Matheson was blind. Yet through his books he helps us see better.

Jonah the Narrow

There is no book of the Bible which to my mind has suffered such undue disparagement as the Book of Jonah. It is popularly treated as the butt of literature. It is regarded as the product of a very superficial intellect—a writing which has crept into the canon unaccountably, and whose presence there should be held to be a mistake. I hold, on the other hand, that the Book of Jonah is second to no part of the Old Testament in originality of thought and breadth of conception. I hold that, so far from being the production of a superficial intellect, it is the work of a mind greatly in advance of its own time, and abreast of the highest religious culture in ours. I look upon the Book of Jonah as the counterpart of the Book of Job.

Author's note: Matheson's sermon "Jonah the Narrow" is from *The Representative Men of the Bible*, 2:217–41.

Job is the study of a moral problem; Jonah is the delineation of an intellectual difficulty. Both are designed to indicate an enlarged sense of the presence of God. Job battles against the doctrine that *pain* is a banishment from God; Jonah refutes the belief that space is a banishment from God. Job selects a suffering individual and shows that he had the divine spirit; Jonah selects a foreign heathen city and shows that it had the divine care. Job says, "If I make my bed in hell, Thou art there"; Jonah cries, "If I flee unto the uttermost parts of the sea, even there shall Thy hand find me."

Let me pass from the Book of Jonah to the figure it delineates. I have often imagined an exercise proposed to the pupils of a Sunday school to this effect: "Write the life of Jonah in modern terms." I think the responses to that demand would run very much in the same groove. Something like the following, it seems to me, would typify the view of the scholars: "There once was a very loose-living youth, who cared little about religion and spent his time in idle pleasures. This was a great grief to his parents, who had all along wanted to bring him up for the church. In the hope that years might lend him wisdom, they tried to force him to study for the ministry. But this youth had a passion for another kind of life; he wanted to go to sea. He dreamed with rapture of the blue waves of the Mediterranean, and longed to be tossed upon its bosom. At last the importunity of his parents became so irksome and the attraction of the sea became so great, that he fled from home. He went down to the harbor and attached himself to a ship about to sail for the coast of Spain. He thought he would there be free from all moral lessons, all grave lectures, all individual restraints. But he found that in the attempt to get away he had run into the lion's den. He had come to a life which sobered him more effectually than all the lectures of his father and mother. His proud spirit was subdued; his recklessness was cured. He had been sick of home; he now became homesick. He longed for even the dull Sabbaths and the tedious sermons. He repented of his bad life; he resolved to make amends. He said, 'As a punishment for my wicked conduct I will do what my parents desire; I see that their will was God's call; I will obey the call; I will become a minister.'"

Such, I think, would be the typical essay of the Sunday school child; and I doubt not that many of its elders would say, "Well done!" Now, we all know that there is such a youth as the one here described; the boy who runs off to sea is a very familiar object in modern life, and the result of his nautical experience is almost invariably the same as is here portrayed. But Jonah is not that boy. He is not a boy at all; already, at the opening of the scene, he is a mature man—a man of position, a man of reputation. Far from being averse to the ministry, he is already a great preacher. He is chaplain to Jeroboam II—the greatest sovereign who, since the days of Solomon, had filled a Jewish throne. In that monarch's brilliant court Jonah ben-Amittai lives and labors ere ever has opened the story of the book that bears his name. We gather from II Kings 14:25 that he was the foreteller of the royal triumphs and the inspirer of the royal counsels. This is not the picture of a youth who became nautical to continue the privilege of being naughty. The truth is, if you accept the view of my hypothetical scholar, you are on a track leading in the opposite direction to the right one. Jonah is in want of discipline; but it is precisely for the contrary reason to that supposed. He needs it, not to narrow him, but to widen him—not to sober him down, but to give him wings. He is not the wild spirit of youth requiring to be contracted; he is the contracted nature requiring the spirit of youth. He must be made more intellectually daring, more sympathetically venturesome, more emotionally expanded. The danger from which he has to fly is not the danger of a fast life, but of a slow life; he awaits the opening of the prison door.

Jonah was brought up in the most narrow period of Jewish orthodoxy—the time when Israel believed in the limitation of divine sympathy to her own work and her own borders. She looked upon herself as the only child of the human family on whom the eye of the Father could complacently gaze. It was for her the earth was allowed to bloom. It was for her the natural mercies of God were still continued. It was for her the thunders of divine judgment were prevented from falling. She believed herself to be the salt of the earth—that which kept the earth alive. All heathen lands were outside the sympathy of the Eternal. They moved in a circle of their own—a circle which had no point of contact with the plan of the world. The kingdom of God was a Jewish kingdom. The providence of God was a Jewish providence. The triumph of God was a Jewish triumph. Into this faith Jonah was born; in this faith he grew. He was reared in the belief of the *tribal* sympathy of God. He reached manhood in the persuasion that the salvation of the world meant the salvation of Israel, and that the climax of divine grace would be attained in the glory of the Jewish nation.

But all at once something happened to Jonah. It is described at the opening of the book as a coming to him of the word of the Lord. You must not imagine it was an outside catastrophe. You must not think it came in handwriting on the wall or sounded with audible accents from the sky. When we think of it thus we miss the real feature of the portrait of Jonah; we rob him of his credit. The divine voice that came to Jonah was a voice within him, an aspiration. He may have connected his first hearing of it with something physical—I cannot tell. But the voice itself was within; it was a part of the man, a thought in the man. And it was a thought unlike all his previous thoughts—new, startling, disturbing. It set him at variance with *himself*. It came to him in a form something like this: "Are there no cities of the world which are great in the sight of God except Jerusalem and Samaria? Is it conceivable that the metropolis of the mighty Assyrian Empire is disregarded by the eye of heaven? Is not that metropolis—that city of Nineveh—the home of human hearts which are beating with all the impulses common to the life of man? Are not the chords of these hearts swept by the same winds that sweep the strings of the hearts of Israel? Are the chords of Nineveh to have no minstrel on earth and no listening ear in heaven? Can no human hand be found that shall weave these notes into harmony—a harmony that God Himself will hear? Why should not *yours* be that hand? You are a prophet to the court of Jeroboam; why should you not be a prophet to the court of Nineveh? Are you only to preach to those who need no conversion? Are there to be no *foreign* missions—no messages of God to those who specially require them? Do you not hear a voice calling you to quit your native land, to claim fresh lands for God?"

That was the call that sounded in the ear of Jonah, and it came to the inner ear of Jonah. It came as a movement of his heart—as a missionary impulse. It was the dim dawning of that message which was hereafter to be written in golden light: "Other sheep I have which are not of this fold." But though it spoke to Jonah's inner ear, it did not yet speak to the whole man. It was a voice to but one side of his nature—the higher side. There was a lower side of his nature to which there spoke another voice—the voice of expediency. For remember, this new thought of Jonah was, to the age in which he lived, a social heresy. It was something which, if revealed, would ostracize him. It would shake his prophetic glory; it would destroy his ministerial influence. Was he prepared to speak aloud the word which had been spoken within? Two forces strove in his heart—the old world and the new. On one side was the favor of God; on the other was the respect of man. On the one was enlarged sympathy; on the other was ancient custom. On the one was the breath of poetry; on the other was the warning touch of prudence. On the one was a vision of the future; on the other was a memory of the past. It was a choice which, on either side, involved a sacrifice.

Was there any way of avoiding both alternatives? Yes. A mode of escape was suggested to him, not by the spirit of atheism, but by the very orthodoxy of his original creed. Might not he cease to hear the divine voice by a simple act of flight? He had been trained in the belief that the God of Israel never let His voice be heard amid objects entirely foreign—and that even the pious Jew, when he sojourned in distant lands, had to carry with him some relic of his own country which would serve as a talisman of divine communion. Had not Naaman the Syrian when he embraced the faith of Israel been obliged, ere departing from Damascus, to carry with him a heap of Jewish earth whereon to build the altar to his future God (II Kings 5:17)? Jonah remembers the incident, and it suggests to him an open door. Might not he fly from his country *without* transporting the heap of earth? Might he not avoid both the voice of conscience and the voice of contumely by a flight from his native land which would be also a flight from the divine presence? If he could leave every relic of Israel behind him, if he could get away into some region where the Jew had left no track, if he could sojourn in a land where he would find no fellow countryman, meet no transplanted product and hear no borrowed song, would not the troublesome voice then be still? Would he not thenceforth interpose a wall between himself and that haunting presence whose accents were at once so convincing and so dreadful?

But where, asks Jonah, is this region to be found? Where can he find a land in which there dwells not a reminder of *his* land—a world absolutely divorced from every Jewish association? He looks round on all the nations of the earth to find a spot which the influence of Israel has not touched. He looks in vain. In every land to which his eye turns he sees some footprint of the steps of Judaism; he feels that the presence of God will *find* him there. Suddenly a thought strikes him. There is a spot he has not yet considered. He has reconnoitered all the *land*; but is there not an element besides the land—the sea? Is not the sea a track where Judaism has seldom journeyed? Has it not been an element hateful to the son of Israel—a path which, since the days of Moses, his countrymen have traversed with trembling? Surely *here* there will be no sacramental symbol to wake communion with God! If he can only get out upon the deep, he feels that he will be free from this haunting divine presence—this perpetual missionary call which, like the moaning of the wind, will not let him sleep. He will throw himself upon the bosom of this dreaded sea. The very thing which makes it dreaded by his countrymen will make it desired by him—the sense which it gives of the absence of God.

So Jonah goes down to Joppa and embarks in a ship bound for

the land which is now called Spain. I do not think he had any wish to go to Spain. He wanted a sea voyage, and he chose the ship bound for the extreme west as likely to afford him the longest journey—the journey, also, towards the point most remote from Nineveh. He is seeking to drown a voice by the inpouring of new associations— associations which have always suggested something foreign and unfamiliar. He has launched himself into another world. Everything about it is un-Jewish. The sea is un-Jewish; the ship is un-Jewish; the crew is un-Jewish; the objects worshiped by the crew are un-Jewish. Surely here he will escape the haunting conscience—the disconcerting message from the God of Israel!

And now something happens—something which is commonly called Jonah's punishment, but which I would rather call Jonah's revelation. Jonah's revelation comes through the sea—through the very element which he expected to obstruct revelation. It is the sea, and not the whale, that is the real savior of Jonah. A storm darkens the face of the deep. All the winds of heaven break forth upon this ship bound for Spain; all the waves of the Mediterranean aspire to sweep over her. That storm is Jonah's deliverance—his deliverance from delusion. It brings him a message—the very message he needs. Its voice is to him the voice of God. It says: "Jonah, you have been trying to escape from Me. You have been thinking that Mine is a *limited* presence. You have thrown yourself on the bosom of the deep to avoid lying on *My* bosom. And on the bosom of the deep you have found Me. I have been here before you—waiting for you, expecting you. I have interrupted your journey, your flight from duty, your effort to evade My call. I have a way even through the sea, a path even through the deep; whither shall you flee from My presence?"

I have said that this voice of the storm is the real rescue of Jonah; it rescued his soul, his manhood. Long before his salvation from the outward shipwreck, he is saved from the shipwreck of his inner life. The storm made a man of him, a missionary of him. His missionary spirit took fire on the spot. Are these heathen sailors to die on *his* account? Is not he the aggressor, the delinquent? Is it not for him that the storm has been sent? Is it not he that has brought discredit on this foreign ship? Is it not he that should atone? He calls upon the sailors to throw him into the sea—to purchase their peace by his sacrifice. That call is the finest thing in the picture. It is the real miracle. It marks the enlargement of the man. It implies a transformation akin to that of Saul of Tarsus. The greatest prodigy is not Jonah's escape from the waves, but Jonah's immersion in the waves—his immersion at his own desire. He could only ask to be thrown into that element of death by reason of the fact that he had already entered into an element of larger life—an environment in which his Jewish nature had recognized the common need of man.

Here, so far as the moralist is concerned, closes the first scene in the life of Jonah. When the second scene opens we are in a new atmosphere. Jonah has been physically rescued from the storm and he has been spiritually rescued *by* the storm. He has reached a definite conviction that the Spirit of God is brooding over the face of the heathen waters. He has arrived at the conclusion that his pity for Nineveh is God's pity for Nineveh—God's imperative mandate to his soul to give that city the words of eternal life. He has obeyed that mandate. He has gone down to Nineveh. He has stood in her streets and proclaimed her danger. He has called on her to repent and flee from the wrath to come. But a question remains. What does Jonah *understand* by Nineveh's repentance? Does he mean that if the city experiences the natural remorse of conscience and resolves to lead for the future a better life, she will receive the mercy of God? No, Jonah is not broad enough for *that*. He has only learned half of the truth. He has learned that God desires the salvation of the heathen city from an impending doom. But will God avert the doom of that city while it *remains* heathen? Jonah says no. To him the escape of Nineveh must be made via Jerusalem, via Samaria, via some part of Israel. If the heathen city would be saved, it must become a Jewish city. It must kneel as a suppliant at the altar of Jonah's people. It must keep the Sabbath. It must be circumcised, or, at the least, must become "a proselyte of the gate." Will God accept mere natural religion? Will He be content to receive as an offering the fruits of a heathen soil? Will He consent to pardon Nineveh, not for the sake of Moses, but for her own sake—not because she has accepted the laws of Sinai, but because she has heard the voice of the secular conscience?

Let me put Jonah's difficulty clearly. His message has been, "Yet forty days, and Nineveh shall be overthrown!" It has been entirely effective. The city has been stirred to its depths. Panic has seized all classes, from the king to the beggar. A fast has been proclaimed in the hope of obviating the wrath of heaven, and by a royal decree all ranks of society are commanded to conform to it. Now, remember what this fast was. It was a purely Assyrian ceremony. It did not take the form which a fast would have taken in Israel. It took a heathen form, a Gentile form, a thoroughly grotesque form. The rules given were such as betokened a benighted condition. Will God *accept* this foreign sacrament? asks Jonah. Will He extend pardon to men who seek it through a heathen ceremony? "Surely not!" he answers; the very thought makes him angry. He wants the city to be saved, but saved by legitimate means—means consistent with Jewish patriotism. If the Ninevites want to fast, let them come up to his wilderness and fast; if they want to pray, let them come up to his temple and pray; thus and not otherwise may they hope for the mercy of God.

But the forty days pass, and the destruction comes not. A wave of Jewish reaction sweeps over Jonah. He has been liberal up to a certain point—liberal beyond his age. But he finds here an arrest to his opening liberality. It offends him as a patriot that a Ninevite, as a Ninevite, should win the heart of God. There is required for Jonah a second rescue from his own narrowness. The first stage of his deliverance had been secured by the storm. From that storm he had come forth enlarged, but not perfected. There is still a dividing wall between him and freedom. Who shall break it down? Who shall usher him into the open? Who shall bring him into the presence of a God without fences, without barriers, without limits? Who shall reveal to him the truth that divine love can travel by its own wings and reach a heathen city without the aid of Jewish chariots?

That revelation comes to Jonah in a most extraordinary way—extraordinary in its simplicity. The first revelation had been remarkable in its pageantry. It had come in the rolling of the waves, in the shrieking of the winds, in the darkening of the skies. But this second revelation is to enter by a silent door—a door whose opening none will hear. It is to reach the heart of Jonah by a commonplace avenue—an avenue which has been for years but an ordinary carriage-drive. With no moaning of the sea, no shaking of the trees, no flying of the birds, is it to come. It is to manifest its presence in an incident too trifling to be historical, in an experience too minute to be recorded by human annals. We make a transition from the roaring ocean to the restful arbor. We pass from the Mediterranean into the meadow. We exchange the sublime for the simple. We follow the prophet of God from the scene where man feels his insignificance to the scene where man realizes his superiority—from the heaving of the great deep to the waving of the autumn field.

Jonah has gone to sit in that field. He is in discontented mood—inclined to murmur against the order of things. The day is sultry; the sunbeams smite the grass like shafts of fire. The prophet is oppressed with the heat; he feels weary and jaded. Suddenly he remembers a delightful little arbor which had sheltered him yesterday—a resting-place in the field, overshadowed by a gourd or shrub of wide-spreading leaves. He will go to that cooling shade, he will recline under that protective foliage; it will be to him as the shadow of a great rock in a weary land. He repairs to the spot where used to spread the healing plant. The spot is there, the seat is there; but the plant is gone; it has faded in the past night. Jonah's rage bursts forth; this is the last straw, and it breaks his last thread of patience. He pours out the vials of his wrath over this vacant spot of the universe—this little bit of ground despoiled of a plant which had been its tenant for a day.

All at once another voice spoke within Jonah—a voice very like that which he had heard in the court of Jeroboam. It said: "Jonah, are you not at this moment refuting the grounds for your own discontent? Is not your very anger an argument against yourself? You have taken an interest in a most insignificant thing—a thing which you admit to be unfit for your companionship; why should not the Almighty have the same interest in *Nineveh?* Nineveh cannot reach up to *Him* any more than the gourd can reach up to *you;* but you can come down to the gourd; you can give your presence and your interest to the insignificant plant. Are you to have a power that the Almighty has not—the power of going down? You accepted the service of a plant which was a plant of Nineveh. You did not insist on first bearing it to Jerusalem, to Samaria, to some part of Israel. You sat down yesterday beneath its foliage in this very spot; its shade was as precious to you as if it had been a Jewish shade. And shall not *God* accept the service of Nineveh? Though its fast be a heathen fast, though its cry be a cry of nature, though its repentance be the repentance of the natural conscience, though its voice be the voice, not of the man in the temple, but of the man in the street, shall not God accept its service? By the very anger of your soul you have justified the ways of heaven."

From that hour in the fields of Nineveh Jonah returned, a changed man. The voice that spoke *to* him was the voice that spoke *in* him. He never could have heard it if the door of his heart had not been already open. For the second time God had revealed to him that he could not flee from His presence. For the second time he had found that presence in an unlikely spot. He had already found it in the solitudes of the great deep, where one would have thought it unnecessary; and he had now discovered it in the midst of a heathen city, in the observance of a heathen ritual, in the conscience of a heathen community. In the silent thoughts of one human soul there had struck another hour in the progress of life's day; and in the heart of an individual man humanity had taken its first step into a field of wider development.

Reveal to me, O Father, the breadth of Thy divine presence! I *too* am prone to narrow Thee. I have refused to see Thy presence in Nineveh. I have been quite willing that Nineveh should come to my Jerusalem, to my temple, to my altar; I have always offered her an open door into the house where I worship. But I have never dreamed that Nineveh can get a blessing within her own temple. I have never dreamed that a fast in a heathen city may be a fast of real communion. I have never dreamed that an altar built to other names than Thine can have a step leading to the sky. Teach me that truth, O Lord! Teach me that Thou claimest all prayers as prayers to *Thee*! I see the men of Nineveh adoring inferior things, and I cry, "These are idolators!" But *Thou* sayest, "Inasmuch as they did it unto the least, they have done it unto Me." Often have I thought of these words of Thine, "Shall I not spare Nineveh, in which are more than six score thousand infants and much cattle?" I think I understand their meaning. It is that even the unspoken cry of the infant, even the inarticulate cry of the cattle, has to Thee the import of a prayer. O Love, divine love, imputing to me, to Nineveh, to all things, more than the voice can ask or the thought express, let us magnify Thy name together! Thou answerest, not our words but our needs; unite us by our needs! Unite us under the withered gourd, the common want, the kindred pain! Whether our fast be at Jerusalem or at Nineveh, it is the same want and the same cry; let us feel it to be the same worship too! Send us the day of Pentecost once more! We have many tongues in the flesh; let us speak one language in the spirit. We have many creeds in the mind; let us recognize a common craving in the heart! We fix our trembling gaze each on a different star; tell us that through them all we see one golden light!

Bibliography

Macmillan, Donald. *The Life of George Matheson*. London: Hodder and Stoughton, 1907.

Matheson, George. *Aids to the Study of German Theology*. Edinburgh: Clark, 1874.

———. *Growth of the Spirit of Christianity, from the First Century to the Dawn of the Lutheran Era*. 2 vols. Edinburgh: Clark, 1877.

———. *Leaves for Quiet Hours*. London: Clarke, 1904.

———. *Moments on the Mount: A Series of Devotional Meditations*. London: Nisbet, 1884.

———. *My Aspirations*. Heart Chords. London: Cassell, 1883.

———. *Natural Elements of Revealed Theology*. London: Nisbet, 1881.

———. *The Representative Men of the Bible.* 2 vols. London: Hodder and Stoughton, 1902–1903.
———. *The Representative Men of the New Testament.* London: Hodder and Stoughton, 1905.
———. *The Representative Women of the Bible.* Edited by William Smith. London: Hodder and Stoughton, 1907.
———. *Rests by the River: Devotional Meditations.* London: Hodder and Stoughton, 1906.
———. *Sidelights from Patmos: Thoughts Suggested by the Book of Revelation.* London: Hodder and Stoughton, 1897.
———. *Spiritual Development of St. Paul.* London: Blackwood, 1890.
———. *Studies of the Portrait of Christ.* 2 vols. London: Hodder and Stoughton, 1899–1900.
———. *Times of Retirement: Devotional Meditations.* London: Nisbet, 1901.
———. *Words by the Wayside.* Small Books on Great Subjects, vol. 1. London: Clarke, 1896.

5

C. I. Scofield

(1843–1921)

Strictly speaking, the Authorized (or King James) version of the Bible was never "authorized." King James favored the project for both personal and political reasons. But as the spiritual head of the Church of England, he did not *order* the use of the new translation. For years the new translation received severe criticism similar to the criticism leveled today at modern translations. Even Lancelot Andrewes, one of the most learned of the King James Version translators, preferred to use the Geneva Bible.

Perhaps the Geneva Bible most irritated King James and convinced him that a new version was needed. The marginal notes in the Geneva Bible were critical of monarchies and national churches. The fact that the Calvinists in Geneva had helped produce the Geneva Bible was an added incentive for a new version in the language of the people. At any rate, one of the rules given to the King James translators was: "No marginal notes to be affixed," except notes relating to Hebrew or Greek.

Today the situation is reversed: we honor the King James Version and resist its critics, and we prefer it with as many notes as possible. Annotated editions of the King James Bible continue to be published, and the public buys them. Like makes of cars or brands of toothpaste, each edition has its promotors and detractors, almost to the point of making one's choice of study Bibles a test of orthodoxy or spiritual fellowship. The young Bible student looking for a study Bible has so many choices that he may not know how to make a sane selection. Perhaps the best known is the *Scofield Reference Bible,* edited by C. I. Scofield and published in 1909 by the Oxford University Press. A corrected edition appeared in 1917, and in 1967 *The New Scofield Reference Bible* was published. More than a million and a half copies of this new edition have been sold. (I understand that there is a group dedicated to preserving the *original* edition! Apparently they feel the editors of the 1967 edition deviated too much from Scofield's interpretations.)

Cyrus Ingerson Scofield was born on 19 August 1843 in frontier Lenawee County, Michigan. While he was still a lad, his family moved to Wilson County, Tennessee, where he lived until he was seventeen. When he should have been enrolled in college, he enlisted in the Confederate Army and served with distinction for four years. He received the Cross of Honor for bravery at Antietam. After the war he located in St. Louis with his oldest sister, who had married into a wealthy family. Unwilling to permit his brother-in-law to pay for his education, Scofield went to work as a land clerk, examining titles. In two years his promotion to chief clerk provided sufficient money to study law. He passed his bar examinations at age twenty-six and was elected to the Kansas legislature. An efficient lawyer and politician, he was appointed by President Grant as U.S. Attorney for Kansas. He served for two years and then returned to St. Louis to practice law.

Another attorney, Thomas S. McPheeters, a dedicated Christian, was one of Scofield's close friends. Scofield was battling alcohol. McPheeters came to Scofield's office in September 1879 and said: "For a long time I have been wanting to ask you a question that I have been afraid to ask, but that I am going to ask now. Why are you not a Christian?" He then took out his pocket New Testament and reasoned with the lawyer. Scofield wanted more time to consider the matter, but McPheeters would not give in. The Holy Spirit won the case: the two men prayed together, and C. I. Scofield gave his heart to Jesus Christ. Instantly the chains were broken, never to be forged again. Scofield wrote in later years: "The passion for drink was taken away! Divine power did it, wholly of grace. To Christ be all the glory!"

Like Dwight L. Moody, with whom he would be associated,

Scofield became active in the YMCA. He also grew under the ministry of James H. Brookes, whom he called "the greatest Bible student I have ever known." Scofield developed a hunger to know the Word of God. One day he visited C. E. Paxson, a Christian friend, and found him drawing lines in a new Bible. "Man, you're spoiling that fine new Bible!" Scofield protested. But Paxson showed him he was connecting Acts 8:5 and 8:8 to demonstrate that Philip's preaching of Christ brought great joy to the city. Scofield's logical mind instantly caught the importance of the lines that were "ruining" Paxson's Bible, and from that hour he marked cross references in his Bible. Scofield's experience in Paxson's office was his first step toward editing the most famous study Bible in English.

Scofield abandoned law in 1882 to pastor a new congregational church in Dallas. There were twelve members, eleven of them women. Within two years a new building had to be constructed to accommodate two hundred members. Scofield's Bible-teaching ministry was blessed by God both at home and in the various conferences where he spoke, including the famous ones at Niagara and Northfield.

In 1895 Scofield became Moody's pastor at the East Northfield Congregational Church, where he ministered for seven years. He also served as president of the Northfield Bible Training School. He returned in 1902 to the First Congregational Church in Dallas; but the most important event of that year took place in New York City. While there to minister, Scofield visited Alwyn Ball, a Christian businessman who had encouraged his ministry. Ball asked what projects he was working on now that he had finished writing a correspondence course. Scofield replied that he had been thinking for years of preparing a reference Bible to help serious students study the Word more systematically. Ball immediately approved the project, and the two of them took it as confirmation of the Lord.

Scofield tried pastoring the church while preparing the reference Bible, but after a year of frustration, he resigned. Much of his work from 1902 to 1909 was done in Montreaux, Switzerland. On several occasions Scofield was too ill to work, but his wife continued the project until he could join her. We who read the *Scofield Reference Bible* today can appreciate the enormous amount of editorial work and proofreading. Of course Scofield consulted other Bible teachers (whose names appear on the title page), but the final writing and editing were his own.

On two occasions the work was almost destroyed. After he shipped the material from Europe to America, the boxes were lost. He and his wife prayed fervently until they located the priceless shipment among the baggage of immigrants who had come over on the same ship. While completing the final manuscript, the Scofields lived in a tent in New Hampshire, and the tent caught fire. Had the wind shifted, the manuscript in a nearby shed would have been destroyed.

Scofield did his work well. Even those who do not follow the dispensational approach to Scripture can benefit from the chain-reference system, the definitions, and the doctrinal summaries. The men who gave us the revised edition helped strengthen some points and solve some problem areas of interpretation.

The success of the Scofield Bible had encouraged other editors and publishers to enter the field. One of the latest—and best—is the *Ryrie Study Bible*, published in various editions by Moody Press, and edited by Charles C. Ryrie, professor of systematic theology at Dallas Theological Seminary. Ryrie's credentials as a Bible scholar and teacher certainly need no defense; even those who do not follow the Scofield-dispensational approach to the Bible admit that Ryrie is well-equipped for such an ambitious task.

This is not a "reference Bible" as such, although it does have a good system of cross-references. Rather it is an annotated Bible, with hundreds of marginal notes that explain and apply the text. While much of this information is available in standard Bible helps, it is good to have it alongside the text. These annotations cover more ground than those of Scofield, including historical data, archaeological information, cultural background, and doctrinal definitions and explanations. There is such a great wealth of information in these annotations that even the seasoned student will find them useful.

Ryrie introduces and outlines each book of the Bible. Some of the outlines are analytical (e.g., Matt., John, Acts, and I Thess.), while others are interpretive (e.g., II Tim. and I Peter). I prefer interpretive outlines that "open up" the book. But all the outlines are good, though some are a bit long. I am glad Ryrie did not caption the outlines, "*The* Outline of. . ." As G. Campbell Morgan said, "There is no such thing as *the* outline of a Bible book. I prefer to say *an* outline." No outline is inspired or final.

The editor is to be congratulated for breaking away from some time-honored dispensational "doctrines," such as a pre-Adamic race and a "gap" between the first and second verses of Genesis. He also makes it clear that Cain's sin was his unbelief, not his bloodless sacrifice. I have not yet read every note, but the ones I have read are helpful and practical. The experienced student who finds some of the annotations rather obvious (Luke 7:24–25, for example) must remember that this Bible will be used by believers who are at much earlier stages in their spiritual growth and Bible knowledge.

The *Ryrie Study Bible* is available in two texts: the Authorized Version and the New American Standard Bible. I commend Ryrie for preparing notes for both texts; it must have been a monumental task. He has also provided at the back of the Bible a number of extra helps: a harmony of the Gospels, a summary of Bible doctrine, various articles about the Bible and its origin, a topical index, an index to the annotations, maps, and others. There is also a concordance.

Ryrie's is probably the best study Bible for the serious Christian today. I have used other study Bibles and been helped by them in one way or another, but the *Ryrie Study Bible* must take first place on my shelf. It will not replace the Scofield, nor was it meant to; but it is the perfect complement to the Scofield. The student who owns and uses both will benefit tremendously.

We have come a long way since King James ordered the omission of interpretive notes, and I am glad we have. As long as we keep in mind that the text, not the notes, is inspired, and that even the wisest men make mistakes, we will profit from the dedicated scholarship that produces such tools. There is no excuse except laziness for the Christian who lacks a working knowledge of the Bible. Which study Bible is the best? The one that helps you the most. Let every man be fully persuaded in his own mind. The important thing is to study God's Word consistently, using whatever helps are available, and then put it into practice.

The Test of True Spirituality

Two epistles are notable for the severity of their tests of Christian profession—James and I John. James is concerned with the reality of the professor's faith, John with the reality of the believer's experience, that is, of any pretensions which he may set up to spirituality of life. The key phrase of James is: "Yea, a man may say . . ." The key phrase of this aspect of I John is: "If we say . . ." or "He that saith . . ." Profession is easy, but false profession is supremely dangerous. The man who is living in sin and unbelief, and knows it, is fairly open to the gospel appeal; but the man who in self-

---

Author's note: Scofield's sermon "The Test of True Spirituality" is from *In Many Pulpits with Dr. C. I. Scofield*, pp. 201–12.

deception answers the gospel appeal by saying, "But I am a Christian," is in the most dangerous place conceivable.

If one be a Christian, there is always the grave danger of living in mere positional truth on the one hand, or of assuming a false spirituality on the other. In the first case one would resemble a noble who should exalt his mere patent of nobility while living most ignobly. In the second case, one falls into the snare of spiritual pride based on some supposed experience or attainment.

James exposes a false or mistaken profession of faith; John a spurious spirituality. This exposure John effects by six tests applied to profession. Let us look at these.

The first applies to the profession of fellowship with God: "If we say that we have fellowship with him . . ." (I John 1:6). The test is severe but simple. To such a profession he says in effect, "Where do you walk?" The "walk" is the daily life. Now, says John, there are two places and but two where a believer may walk—darkness and light. Light is where God is and what God is: "In him is no darkness at all" (I John 1:5). Observe it is not *how* we walk, but *where* we walk. David, in Psalm 51, all broken and crushed with the sense of his sin, is in the very whitest of the light, for he is saying: "Have mercy upon me, O God" (Ps. 51:1). He is saying: "Wash me throughly from mine iniquity, and cleanse me from my sin" (Ps. 51:2). He is saying: "Against thee, thee only, have I sinned, and done this evil in thy sight: that thou mightest be justified when thou speakest, and be clear when thou judgest" (Ps. 51:4). In the light, though his whole talk is of his sins.

Now see a man in darkness—a good, moral man too, and a believer in God: "The Pharisee stood and prayed thus with himself, God, I thank thee, that I am not as other men are" (Luke 18:11). That man in the very act of prayer is in thick darkness.

To walk in the light is not to walk sinlessly, but it is to bring the sin instantly to God. It is not to serve perfectly, but it is to bring the imperfection to Him. It is to live the daily life in His presence. Now, if we say that we have fellowship with Him, and have two lives, a religious life for Him and a secular life for ourselves, we walk in darkness, and our profession of fellowship is a lie, John says.

John's second test strikes down at one blow the most subtle of the errors into which men have fallen concerning this most vital subject of holiness—the notion that by regeneration, or by "the baptism with the Spirit" or by the "baptism with fire," or some other experience, the old Adamic nature has been eradicated, so that such a one no longer has sin as an indwelling fact. As to this John's word is clear: "If we say that we have no sin, we deceive ourselves, and the truth is not in us" (I John 1:8). Note carefully, John does not say that those who make that profession are not saved. What he says is they are deceived, because they are not judging the matter by revealed truth, but by some supposed experience of feeling. The underlying rule here is one which if duly heeded will save the child of God from every excess of fanaticism. It is: Judge experience by the Word, not the Word by experience. "For the word of God is quick, and powerful, and sharper than any twoedged sword, piercing even to the divid ing asunder of soul and spirit, and of the joints and marrow, and is a discerner of the thoughts and intents of the heart" (Heb. 4:12). Beloved, the old nature unchanged and unchangeable is within; all victory lies in the recognition of that fact, and then in self-distrustful resort to the provision of grace for that fact—the indwelling Spirit. So long as we walk in the Spirit we do not "fulfil the lust of the flesh" (Gal. 5:16). "For the flesh lusteth against the Spirit, and the Spirit against the flesh: and these are contrary the one to the other: so that ye cannot do the things that ye would" (Gal. 5:17). How subversive of this constant watchfulness, how sure to end—as all experience shows—in humiliating defeat, is the notion that the flesh has been eradicated.

And, as closely connected with that error, is the one to which John opposes his third test, the error of sinless perfection in the flesh: "If we say that we have not sinned . . ." (I John 1:10). Mark well, this message is to the little children of the Father. We have not here a word to the self-righteous sinner but to the presumptuous child of God. And it is not, "If we say that we have not sinned in the past . . ."; it is a present word, a word for every moment of our lives. If we say right in the midst of our best prayer, of our purest aspiration, that "we have not sinned"—what? "We make him a liar" (I John 1:10). Are we ready for that? Do we want to do that? But how can a little child of the Father possibly find himself in such a case? For the old reason: inattention to the Word. "His word is not in us" (I John 1:10) when we say such things. And His Word is uncompromising about sins. His grace has made a way of forgiveness and cleansing for confessing children who sin, but that Word will never permit us to lower the standard as to what sin is. Have we forgotten that an offering was provided for sin? Have we forgotten that in His eyes, the very heavens are not clean? No, we need this humbling Word, this searching test.

The fourth test applies to profession of a different kind, to the claim to intimate acquaintanceship with God: "He that saith, I know him . . ." (I John 2:4). Bear with a cautionary word. Knowing about God is one thing: knowing God is quite another. Job's confession illustrates this: "I have heard of thee by the hearing of the ear" (Job 42:5). And upon the hearing there had come to Job a true faith, a faith which had withstood tremendous shocks. Well, we all begin there. Our saving faith is based on testimony. But Job goes on: "But now mine eye seeth thee" (Job 42:5). A very different matter. Are we then content to remain with a hearsay knowledge of God? By no means. In John 17 our Lord tells us that the ultimate end of the gift of eternal life is that we may know Him. He is our Father, and can our hearts rest with anything short of that personal knowledge of Him of which John speaks? At this point, John's test of spirituality is not to discourage a true knowledge of God, but to expose a false assumption of such knowledge. What is that test? "He that saith, I know him, and keepeth not his commandments, is a liar" (I John 2:4). Does John mean to put us back under law? Not at all. He speaks in his characteristic way, meaning that he who is living outside the known will of God and who says "I know God," is a liar. It is not sinless obedience, but it is a heart set to live in the known will of God. Such a one will have many a failure, but, though often stumbling, he will keep on. The needle in the compass is often deflected by influences about it—it trembles and is unquiet, but it resumes its steady alignment with the object of its devotion. Now a life aligned to the will of God, is in the way to know God. It is not an arbitrary requirement. In no other way, to no other man, can God reveal Himself. Paul's prayer for the Colossians runs along that road: "That ye might be filled with the knowledge of his will in all wisdom and spiritual understanding... increasing in the knowledge of God" (Col. 1:9–10).

John's fifth test of the profession of spirituality of life, also applies to the walk: "He that saith he abideth in him ought himself also so to walk, even as he walked" (I John 2:6). Upon a superficial view, this seems most discouraging. What is it "to abide" in Him? Many earnest souls have known much distress just here. They have been told that "to abide" in Him means to be always occupied with Him. Now I make bold to say, this is an unattainable counsel of perfection.

We are in the world, and however sedulous we may be to keep the world out of us, we are charged with engrossing duties calling for the utmost concentration of mind, heart, and hand. We cannot be in conscious constant occupation with Him. I do not so understand that great word.

For a moment think of that other phrase, "in Him." What does that mean? Ephesians explains it: "in Christ Jesus" is the sphere of the Christian's life. That is where grace has put him. We have not to concern ourselves about getting that place: we are there. Now, what is "abiding in Him?" Why, simply having nothing apart from Him, living in the sphere of the things which interest Christ; bringing Him into the sphere of all our necessary occupations, joys, and innocent pleasures down here; having no business in which He is not senior partner; no wedding feast or other feast at which He is not chief guest; no failures which are not brought to Christ for forgiveness and cleansing.

What is John's test of such a life? In degree, though not as perfectly, it will be a walk even as He walked. It will lead along the same road; it will encounter the same trials, enlist the same sympathies. Apply the test; it is easy, if humbling. "He that saith he is in the light, and hateth his brother, is in darkness even until now" (I John 2:9). God is love as surely as God is light. The light and the love are one. Then, how impossible to walk with God—for that is to walk in the light—and have hatred for one of the other of God's children. Remember, John speaks in an absolute way of these things. It is not what we may *call* our feeling for our brother, "dislike" or "instinctive aversion" or "annoyance"; John has one name for the insincere evasions—*hate*. That is John's word.

Think of this. Is there some brother against whom we have taken up a breath of accusation which we have whispered about to his detriment? Is there one whose ways annoy us so that we avoid him? Is there one whose habits, though within his liberty in Jesus Christ, do not happen to be the habits in which we have been more narrowly reared and against which we whisper? My friends, till we are cleansed in the laver, till our feet have been in His blessed hand, let us not talk of walking in the light. So we come to John's final test: "If a man say, I love God, and hateth his brother, he is a liar" (I John 4:20). With John, love is more than sentiment, more than a feeling. It is a principle which moves the hand and opens the purse. If I am not my brother's keeper; if I am not, in the measure of my power, my brother's providence—wisdom for his folly, a hiding place for his shame, openhanded for his need, wet-eyed for his sorrow, glad in his joy—oh, then let me at least spare him the insincerity of my profession, "I love God."

Bibliography

Gaebelein, A. C. *The History of the Scofield Reference Bible*. New York: Our Hope, 1943.

Scofield, C. I. *Addresses on Prophecy*. New York: Gaebelein, 1910.
———. *In Many Pulpits with Dr. C. I. Scofield*. New York: Oxford University, 1922. Reprinted—Grand Rapids, Baker, 1966.
———. *Plain Papers on the Doctrine of the Holy Spirit*. New York: Revell, 1899. Reprinted—*A Mighty Wind: Plain Papers on the Doctrine of the Holy Spirit*. Grand Rapids: Baker, 1973.
———, ed. *The Scofield Reference Bible*. New York: Oxford University, 1909.
Trumbull, Charles G. *The Life Story of C. I. Scofield*. New York: Oxford University, 1920.

6

F. B. Meyer

(1847–1929)

When Jack Johnson defeated James Jeffries for the 1911 world heavyweight championship, negotiations were begun to pit Johnson against the British champion, Bombardier Wells. But a well-known British Baptist preacher stepped into the ring and opposed the contest. So effectively did he protest from pulpit and platform, as well as in the press, that the fight was called off. The sporting public was enraged. F. B. Meyer hardly seemed the type to get involved in controversy. A harmless mystic with a saintly face, he was popular throughout the English-speaking world as a devotional preacher. Even today his devotional books and biblical biographies are on almost every pastor's shelves.

But Frederick Brotherton Meyer was a *militant* mystic. He was, as Carl Sandburg described Abraham Lincoln, "velvet steel." His gentleness was not weakness, but power under control. Once he determined that something was wrong, he fought it even if he had to fight alone. Attacked in one church because of his strong evangelistic ministry, he resigned and built a church of his own. Hindered in his program of rehabilitating exconvicts, he organized his own business and put the men on his payroll. There was no stopping F. B. Meyer.

Nothing in Meyer's birth hinted that a spiritual soldier had come on the scene. In fact he was born with the coveted silver spoon in his mouth. As they said in that Victorian Era, the family had "good connections." He was born on 8 April 1847 at Lavender Terrace, Wandsworth Road, London (even the address seems to glitter). Home life in Brighton was happy and comfortable, but also spiritual. His mother taught the children the Bible, and his father set the example as a dedicated Christian businessman. On Sunday mornings they attended the Bloomsbury Chapel, and in the evenings they held family services at home.

When Meyer was fifteen, business reverses forced the family to leave their lovely home in Brighton and return to London. His father tried to settle all the accounts honestly, which left little for the family. Meyer's silver spoon was gone, but not his sterling Christian character. In later years Meyer gave thanks for the experience because it helped him discover the things that matter most. In his itinerant ministry he was always sensitive about large offerings and honoraria. More than once he returned love offerings he thought were too large.

From his earliest years Meyer felt called to the ministry. He had even preached during family devotions. When sixteen he told his father his decision to enter the ministry, and both went to see William Brock, pastor of Bloomsbury Chapel. The great preacher asked young Meyer to preach a trial sermon for him—hardly easy for a teenager. But he passed the test.

At this critical point Brock counseled Meyer to spend at least two years working in a London business office before entering college. So Meyer joined the tea firm of Allan Murray, working there for two years. He saw city life firsthand. He learned to keep accurate records, make sensible decisions, plan his day well, and use his time efficiently. Later he counseled theological students to get business experience. "By all means let them graduate in the college of city life," he would say, "and study attentively the great books of human nature. It is impossible to preach to young men unless you *know* young men, and possess some knowledge of their peril and temptation." Not surprisingly, Meyer's Saturday afternoon meetings for young men were successful. In all his churches he attracted men from every level of life. The seed sown during those two years in the tea business bore fruit.

Meyer graduated from Regent's Park College in 1869. While a

student, he ministered for about a year at Duke Street Baptist Chapel, Richmond, Surrey, a church made famous in recent years by the ministries of Alan Redpath and Stephen Olford. Upon graduation he was appointed assistant to Charles M. Birrell at the Pembroke Baptist Chapel, Liverpool. A godly scholar, Birrell unconsciously overpowered his young assistant, who imitated him almost to the point of idolatry. "In preparing my sermons and addresses," wrote Meyer, "I naturally followed the lines of the senior minister. This was a mistake, for Birrell's habit was to write out and memorize. Such a method was totally unsuitable for me. . . ."

Meyer was married in 1871. The next year he and his wife moved to York, where he pastored Priory Street Baptist Chapel. This move proved to be the turning point in his life and ministry, for two years later Dwight L. Moody and Ira Sankey ministered at Meyer's chapel. Moody had a gift for "finding" men—and Meyer was one of his greatest discoveries.

The other side of the coin is this: humanly speaking, the Moody-Sankey ministry in Britain received a boost from Meyer. The meetings at the York Independent Chapel had not begun too successfully, and the noon prayer meeting at the Cooney Street "Y" were limping along. At one of the prayer meetings Meyer heard Moody preach on the Holy Spirit. So convicted was the young pastor that he spent the next two days wrestling with God. He returned to the prayer meeting on Saturday and testified that God had met him and given victory. For two years he had preached without any special blessing. "I was just beating the air," he confessed. But now he had experienced a new touch from God. In spite of ministerial opposition. Meyer courageously opened his chapel to Moody and Sankey. For the first time in Meyer's ministry there, he saw the place filled. People were converted; the inquiry rooms were busy. Meyer learned some of his greatest spiritual lessons from Moody.

Moody taught this "proper" Baptist minister to be himself and not imitate others. "What an inspiration when this great and noble soul first broke into my life!" wrote Meyer. "I was a young pastor then . . . and bound rather rigidly by the chains of conventionalism. Such had been my training, and such might have been my career. But here was a new ideal! Mr. Moody was absolutely unconventional and natural."

Moody also taught Meyer the value of winning souls by every legitimate means. Those few days in York with Moody lit a fire in

Meyer's soul. He once told Moody, "I have not preached one sermon, since God gave me that anointing, that there have not been conversions."

But Moody taught Meyer a third lesson: ministry is much larger than one church or denomination. In one of his autobiographical books, *The Bells of Is*, Meyer wrote: "I caught a glimpse of a wider, larger life, in which mere denominationalism could have no place, and in which there was but one standard by which to measure men, namely their devotion to, and knowledge of, the Son of God."[1] Meyer's church became the base of his ministry, not its sphere.

Meyer accepted a call from the Victoria Road Baptist Church, Leicester, in 1874. This was a typical "wealthy and influential church," and the young pastor gave himself sacrificially to his ministry. Had he still been a "proper pastor," the church would have been happy. But his concern for the lost and his willingness to pioneer new trails irked the comfortable officers. The tension climaxed when a wealthy deacon burst in one Sunday evening and told the pastor: "We cannot have this sort of thing here. This is not a gospel shop!" A few years before, Meyer would have apologized and resumed business as usual. But he had been with Moody and had experienced the blessing of serving God in the Spirit, letting the wind blow where it would. Meyer promptly resigned the church and planned to leave Leicester. No doubt fault lay on both sides: Meyer's enthusiasm had not yet caught fire in the congregation, and the comfortable officers felt threatened by his zeal.

When word got out that Meyer had resigned from Victoria Road, several other churches immediately issued him calls. Meyer wrote a letter of acceptance to the Glossop Road Church, Sheffield. On his way to mail the letter, he providentially met Arthur Rust (brother-in-law of W. Y. Fullerton, the evangelist who would later assist Charles H. Spurgeon). Meyer told Rust about the letter he was mailing, and Rust told Meyer about a group of earnest Christians in Leicester who wanted him to form a new church; fifteen young merchants would guarantee his salary. Meyer agreed, and the eventual result was the church at Melbourne Hall. At first the group met in one of the museum halls. (One lady arrived early each Lord's Day to cover the statues and pictures!) In five months they were strong enough to organize into a church. On 2 July 1881 they held their first service in their own building, Melbourne Hall. The building was a combination local church, rescue mission, social center, Sunday school, and Bible institute.

---

1. *The Bells of Is*, p. 17.

At Melbourne Hall Meyer practiced another lesson learned from Moody: organize your work and enlist the help of new converts. Before long, Meyer was ministering to a congregation of two thousand. They in turn were ministering to thousands outside the church. The congregation did not pay their pastor to do the work; they worked *with him* and relieved him of routine matters. They were willing for him to "leave the ninety-and-nine" and search for that one lost sheep.

The ministry at Melbourne Hall can be described by one word: *miracles*. Meyer carried on a great work among prisoners, a work that resulted from a young girl's request of him: "My father is going to be released from jail tomorrow morning, and I'm afraid he will get into bad company. Could you meet him at the gate and try to keep him from his bad companions?" The successful pastor of a new church certainly did not need one more task. But how could he say no? He promised to be at the gate the next morning. When he arrived, he discovered that the prisoner had been transferred to another jail. Instead of hurrying home, Meyer waited across the street and watched the newly released prisoners. Almost to a man they headed for a nearby public house. "Is this what goes on here most mornings?" he asked some men lounging in the street.

"Yes, sir, mostly," they replied.

"But if a man comes out at yonder jail door and goes into the door of the public house," Meyer protested, "he appears to me to come out of the jail by the *front* door and go into it again by the *back* one! For I reckon that the public house is the back door to the jail."

"Well, what's a chap to do?" the men argued. "There's nowhere else for him to go."

Without replying, Meyer walked across the street to the jail and asked to see the governor, Miles Walker. Walker received him courteously, listened to his plea, and agreed to cooperate in every way. "All I want to do," Meyer explained, "is meet these men and take them to a nearby coffee-house for some decent food and a word of encouragement."

Little did Meyer know that this ministry would result in some of his greatest burdens, as well as his greatest blessings. In his delightful *The Bells of Is,* Meyer admitted that his second thoughts about the new ministry made him miserable. "I fear that I more than once repented of the promise I had given the Governor, and wished that I have never undertaken the cause of the discharged jail-birds. . . . Altogether, between my fear of what the discharged prisoners would do to me, and what my own people and towns-folk would think of me, I had an uncomfortable time of it. . . . I had not then learned what it is to be the slave of Jesus Christ—a condition of mind in which one becomes blessedly oblivious to what men may say or do, so long as the light of His approval shines warm and fresh upon the heart."[2]

That first morning the entire group of men agreed to go to breakfast with him. During his years at Melbourne Hall, Meyer gave breakfast to nearly five thousand men. Many were converted; some, in spite of the hard work of both pastor and people, fell back into their old ways. The ministry continued even after Meyer left. Since many of the men could not find work, Meyer organized a window-washing brigade. Then he got into the wood-cutting business. He established a savings bank for the men, and even founded Provident House to give them a place to live while getting back on their feet. The citizens of Leicester were never sure what the creative pastor of Melbourne Hall would think of next. They saw signs announcing "F. B. Meyer—Firewood Merchant" and "F. B. Meyer—Window-Washing."

Meyer even bought a man a glass of ale to get him to stop drinking. "My friend, what do you say to signing the pledge this morning?" Meyer asked the former prisoner. "You know as well as I do that you have been falling under the power of drink." The man hesitated, then explained he had vowed to drink a pint of ale when he got out of jail. He wanted to keep his vow. Meyer explained that the vow was a bad one, but the man insisted on a pint of ale. "If you have that pint of ale," Meyer asked, "will you give me your solemn word and honor that you will sign the pledge immediately?" The man agreed, so Meyer went to the nearest public house to purchase the ale. The man greedily took a large swallow, then two more. "This is the miserablest pint of ale that I ever drank!" he exclaimed, putting down the mug. "Where is the card, sir? I may as well sign it as drink any more." He gave up alcohol and later was converted.

Meyer became pastor of Regent's Park Chapel in London early in 1888. The church was at low ebb when he arrived, but before long it was flooded with activity. Though this was one of London's select congregations, Meyer was not happy serving a denominational church and limiting his sphere of ministry. He longed to reach the lost.

After four years Meyer resigned and started fifteen years of

---

2. Ibid., pp. 32–33.

ministry at Christ Church, Westminster Bridge Road, London, which had been founded in 1873 by Rowland Hill. Nominally Anglican in its association, congregational in government, and operated on nondenominational lines, it was ideal for a man like Meyer. "I never was an ardent denominationalist," Meyer confessed. But he did ask the trustees of Christ Church, which required no one form of baptism for membership, to install a baptistry.

Attendance averaged about one hundred when Meyer began, but within two years the 2,300-seat auditorium was filled. He organized fellowships for women, children, youth, and men. The Men's Brotherhood became a great power in Christ Church. "No leader of men should ever ask another to do what he is not prepared to do himself," Meyer affirmed. "On the other hand, never do work yourself that you can get another to do. To set one soul at work is to open stores of blessedness."

Meyer expressed his view of the local church: "It is urgently needful that the Christian people of our charge should come to understand that they are not a company of invalids, to be wheeled about, or fed by hand, cossetted, nursed, and comforted, the minister being head-physician and nurse—but a garrison in an enemy's country, every soul of which should have some post of duty, at which he should be prepared to make any sacrifice rather than quit it."[3] Anyone pastoring a city church ought to read Meyer's book *Reveries and Realities,* in which he gave some practical principles for a successful city ministry.

Meyer resigned Christ Church in 1907 for a two-year world tour, then returned to Regent's Park Chapel. He resigned that work in 1915 and went back to Christ Church for five years. His remaining years were spent in an itinerant ministry. During his lifetime he made twelve trips to the United States and visited many other countries as well.

Meyer always claimed that he was "an ordinary man" and that God could do as much through anyone who is yielded to Him. Perhaps so, but Meyer was unique. His close friend Fullerton listed seven factors that contributed to Meyer's success: (1) Puritan heredity and training; (2) the spiritual influence of Birrell, Meyer's senior minister in Liverpool; (3) an enthusiasm for the whole church without "artificial and narrow boundaries"; (4) a willingness to be himself and not copy others; (5) a practical mysticism, "that sense of the Unseen"; (6) a democratic sympathy that enabled him

3. *Reveries and Realities,* p. 41.

to touch people in every level of life; and (7) a fervent spiritual idealism, "devotion to great aims."[4]

He may have been a mystic, but Meyer worked hard and never wasted time. His ability to concentrate on one task at a time enabled him to work his way through a long agenda without being distracted. Constantly on the go, he learned to use his hours of railway travel productively. "If he had a long journey before him," one friend wrote, "he would settle himself in his corner of the railway carriage with a sigh of relief, open his dispatch case (which was fitted up as a sort of stationery cabinet), and set to work in supreme contentment on some abstruse article, quite oblivious of his surroundings." He could also go to sleep almost at will and awaken himself at just the right time. "The Lord always wakes me up just when I ask Him," Meyer once told a friend. To prove his point, he said he would take a nap for twenty minutes. He awoke on time, fresh and ready for the evening's meeting.

In some respects Meyer had so much to do he had to keep going. Once he was browsing through W. Robertson Nicoll's huge library, complaining because he did not have enough leisure to examine the books as he should. "Now you know, Meyer," Nicoll replied, "you would not be here an hour before you would be asking for *Bradshaw's Railway Guide!*"

Meyer said he had spent "many a holy hour . . . while rushing through the country at express speed" and had "felt the railway carriage to be the house of God and the gate of heaven."

F. B. Meyer is known primarily as a devotional preacher and writer. Besides his two autobiographical volumes, he wrote ten books on great men of the Old Testament and three on those of the New Testament.[5] He wrote expositions on such books as Exodus, Isaiah, John, Hebrews, and I Peter, and on such passages as the Sermon on the Mount. His more than twenty books of devotional messages still challenge believers hungering for a deeper life. *Light on Life's Duties* and *Back to Bethel* have always been favorites of mine, perhaps because they were put into my hands shortly after my conversion. *Our Daily Homily* is a priceless collection of expositions drawn from every chapter in the Bible, useful as both a daily devotional guide and a "pump primer" for the preacher.

---

4. *At the Sixtieth Milestone: Incidents of the Journey* (London: Marshall, 1917), pp. 80–81.

5. Abraham, Jacob, Joseph, Moses, Joshua, Samuel, David, Elijah, Jeremiah, Jonah, John the Baptist, Peter, and Paul.

Meyer majored in Bible exposition. He explained his approach in *Expository Preaching*. His early mentor, Birrell, pointed him in that direction. "That was quite a good sermon you gave this evening," Birrell told Meyer as they walked home after the service, "but it was a topical sermon, and if you are going to make topical sermons your model, you will presently come to the end of your topics, and where will you be then? I advise you to do as I have done for the last thirty years—become an expositor of Scripture. You will always retain your freshness and will build up a strong and healthy church." Meyer's method was not unlike that of G. Campbell Morgan: he read a Bible book repeatedly until he grasped its central message, then divided the book into sections and related them to that central truth. In each section he located what he called a "pivot text."

"Meyer preaches," said Spurgeon, "as a man who has seen God face to face." A printed sermon by Meyer transformed the ministry of J. Wilbur Chapman, who confessed, "I owe more to this man [Meyer] than to anyone in the world."

Meyer preached his last sermon on 10 February 1929 in Wesley Chapel, City Road, London. Three days later he entered a nursing home where, in spite of loving care, his health failed rapidly. "Read me something from the Bible," he whispered the day before he died, "something brave and triumphant!" He died on 28 March.

The next time you read one of Meyer's more than fifty books, remember him as much more than a devotional writer. He was an evangelist with a burden for the city; a pastor who loved the whole church; a crusader who hated social evils; a spiritual man who guided many believers into a closer fellowship with Christ; an ambassador whose calling carried him far beyond his own local church and denomination. Joseph Parker put it perfectly: "He never leaves me without the impression that I have been face to face with a man of God."

The All-Sufficiency of Christ

I am Alpha and Omega **Rev. 1:8, 17; 2:8; 22:13**

It is hardly necessary to explain that these are the first and the last letters in the Greek alphabet. Obviously they represent all the

---

Author's note: Meyer's sermon "The All-Sufficiency of Christ" is from *The Call and Challenge of the Unseen*, pp. 148–60.

intervening letters, which they enclose as in a golden clasp. On those letters was built the entire literature of that wonderful people. Plato, Socrates, Sophocles, Thucydides, and Aristotle built up their reasoning, teachings, systems, and histories on the letters contained between alpha and omega. This metaphor, as the references indicate, is in frequent use throughout the Apocalypse.

The majestic announcement at the opening of the book (1:8) refers to the eternal God. His nature underlies the whole created universe, all races of being, the entire work of redemption, the destiny of His children, the ultimate victory of righteousness, order, and peace; all that has been, is, or shall be is conditioned by His existence. It would be difficult, if not impossible, to discover a more comprehensive formulary for Him who was, and is, and is to come, than this, "Of him, and through him, and to him are all things, to whom be glory for ever and ever." We can almost hear the unceasing chant of the four living creatures, which are before the throne, who rest not day and night, saying, both when God's purposes are evident and when they are veiled, "Holy, holy, holy, Lord God Almighty, which was, and is, and is to come." Let us worship before the immutable and eternal Lord God Almighty, joining in that ceaseless chant. He is the first and the last, and beside Him there is no other!

In our thinking we must distinguish between that side of His ineffable nature, which has revealed itself in the universe, in the creation of man, and in Jesus Christ, and that side of His nature which transcends our thought, infinite, eternal, self-existent. In the one He has revealed Himself so far as the naked spirit of man can endure the almost insufferable light. In the other is that which no man hath seen or can see, that which we can only describe by negatives, that before which angels veil their faces with their wings. "No man hath seen God at any time; the only begotten Son, which is in the bosom of the Father, he hath revealed him."

What audacity it is to rush into His presence, without the due preparation and reverence of the heart. Even Moses was bidden to unloose his sandals when the bush burned with fire. But does it not stand to reason that, as we cannot know this great Being by the intellect, so we must give time to our fellowship with Him? We must wait before Him till the glare and noise of this clamorous world cease to monopolize our sense, and we are acclimatized to the conditions of His manifested presence. Dr. Lyman Abbott has said truly that the profoundest truths of spiritual experience are those which are not intellectually ascertained, but spiritually discerned. They are not taught to us, but revealed. They defy definition; they transcend expression. So it must be in our fellowship with God. He is our Father. He loves us infinitely, but He is the blessed and only potentate, the King of kings and Lord of lords, who only hath immortality, dwelling in the light which no man can approach unto, whom no man hath seen or can see; to whom be honor and power everlasting. Such is the abyss of the Godhead for which we have no fathoming-line! We have, as Job puts it, only a whisper of Him in His works, and in Jesus a manifestation of only so much as can be translated into human speech.

In the other quotations named above, the Lord Jesus appropriates to Himself these august words, though He was meek and lowly, and emptied Himself. When the fainting disciple whom He loved fell at His feet as one dead; when the church at Smyrna needed encouragement to remain faithful unto death; when spirits athirst for God, in this life or the next, cry out for the living water; when the way has to be opened through the gates of the city to the Tree of Life, He quotes, in part or as a whole, these majestic words, "I am Alpha and Omega, the beginning and the end, the first and the last" (Rev. 22:13).

The very pressing question of this hour is to ascertain whether each of us is making enough of personal contact with Christ. We hear about Him, read of Him, talk about Him, but how far do we really know Him? Might He not say rather sadly to some of us, as to Philip: "Have I been so long a time with you, and yet hast thou not known me?" On the other hand, Paul said: "I count all things but loss for the excellency of the knowledge of Christ Jesus, my Lord . . . that I may know him!"

We may sometimes question whether we should ever have known Jesus Christ had it not been for the urgent needs forced on us by this human life. We have seen that we are tempted in order that we may know things by knowing their contrasts and opposites. To know light, we must needs know darkness; to know good, we must know evil, not by yielding to it but by resistance. Let us carry that thought further, and question whether the blessed beings in other worlds will ever appreciate the Savior as we can, who have wintered and summered with Him, during our earthly life. May not this have been in Paul's mind when he said: "I know Him whom I trusted"? He trusted Christ almost before he knew Him; but having traveled with Him for thirty years, he had come to know Him. In an Alpine village, you engage your guide to take you to the summit of Mont Blanc. He has been recommended as eminently reliable, and you trust him with your life. But during every subsequent hour you are testing him; you see how carefully he picks the path, how strong his arm and keen his eye, how quick he is to notice and prepare against the gathering avalanche. At the end of your sojourn in that mountain village you know him for yourself. You trusted in the word of another, but you now believe in him because of your personal experience. So with our Lord, we trust Him at the beginning of life on what we are told, but as the years pass we come to know Him with a certainty which asks no confirmation elsewhere.

A mathematical figure may help us here. Draw on paper or slate a small curve. That is obviously far away from being a circle; but you can easily *complete the circle*, of which the curve becomes a part. So in human life, Jesus Christ is the complement, or "completement," of our need. He comes to us in the smallness of our patience, faith, hope, or love, and He adds Himself to our great need, and makes the perfect circle.

We may go further, and say that very often God allows our helplessness and failure to become extraordinarily acute in order that His grace may have a larger opportunity. It is only when we have reached our greatest extremity that we begin to realize what Jesus is prepared to be and do.

It was only when Sennacherib came against Jerusalem with scaling-ladders and the full equipment for capturing a fortified city that Isaiah and Hezekiah discovered that God was prepared to be "a place of broad rivers and streams," and that there was a river—the river of His protecting care—which could make glad the city of God. Of course there was no literal river; but God made good that lack, and Himself became all that a river could have been. He was thus the complement of their need!

It was only when Ezra, on the return of the Jews to their own land, halted at the river Euphrates, that he awoke to the peril of crossing the great wilderness, inhabited by robber tribes. But in answer to united prayer, God promised to go before the procession, and become its rear guard. Jehovah Himself became the complement of their need! They would not have realized what He could do for them in this direction had they been fully defended by bands of soldiers.

The sisters of Bethany would never have known the Master's imperial glory as the Resurrection and the Life, had mortal sickness not overtaken Lazarus and carried him to his grave. In their dire sorrow and distress Jesus became their complement as the Resurrection and the Life. In after years they were glad to have had such a sorrow, which left them enriched forever with that unexpected revelation.

Paul himself would never have known what Jesus could be unless he had been beset by that thorn in his flesh. There was a phase in the Savior's grace which he had never known unless that infirmity had befallen him. Then he realized that his sufferings had provided a new angle of vision, a better platform for God's saving help. Therefore he was willing rather to suffer, that the power of Christ might compensate for his deficiency; for when he was weak the strength of the Son of God was more than enough.

Let us look at some of the disabilities named in this book; and when we have set them down, let us take the letters out of the alphabet of our Lord's nature, and spell out the word most suited to bring out salient characteristics of the saving help of His right hand.

Rev. 1:17—*Loneliness is an opportunity for Jesus to make Himself known.* The beloved apostle was alone on the Isle of Patmos, but at the same moment he was "in the Spirit," and the Spirit revealed the Lord. There ensued that fellowship, which began in what seemed at first a revelation almost too great to be borne by human flesh and blood. "I fell at his feet as one dead." Then Christ laid His hand upon him and lifted him up, and revealed to him the mystery of His own eternal life. The ancient mystics went to the deserts in order to obtain that vision; but in quiet lonely hours, as we walk beside the ocean, or climb the mountain, or sit in our own room, He will come and manifest Himself as He does not to the world. But you must let the silt fall to the bottom; you must allow time for the glare of the world to die out from your eyes. There must also be the spirit's steadfast attention turned towards the unseen; the unwearied and loving meditation and prayer, and the atmosphere of Christian love. The failure of any of these will make it impossible to see or feel Jesus nigh.

Thomas a Kempis says: "Shut thy door upon thee and call unto Jesus, thy love. When Jesus is nigh all goodness is nigh and nothing seemeth hard; but when He is not nigh all things are hard. If Jesus speaks one word, there is great comfort. To be without Jesus is a grievous hell, and to be with Jesus is a sweet paradise. If Jesus be with thee, there may be no enemy hurt thee. It is a great craft for a man to be conversant with Jesus; and to know how to hold Jesus is a great prudence."

But it must be remembered that fellowship like this is full of inspiration. The revelation given to John was instantly followed by *the command to write.* The soul, therefore, that is illumined by fellowship with Christ becomes, to use an ancient illustration, like the cherubim who went and came as the Lord directed. Thus holy souls, invigorated and renewed by communion with Jesus, whilst they wait upon Him, receive direction and instruction as to the errands they are to undertake, and they go forth to minister as He may direct. The heavenly character, seated within them, wills their movements through His loving guidance given to their hearts. He nourishes them with food celestial and enables them with grace sufficient for their day.

When, therefore, you are lonely; when, like John on the Lord's day in Patmos, you seem to hear the hymns and prayers which you can join only in spirit, turn to the Lord Himself and ask Him to bear you company. That loneliness constitutes a claim on Him. If you had not experienced it, you would not have learnt what He can be and do when He draws near saying, "Fear not." He will not leave you orphaned, He will come to you. Though lover and friend forsake, and you are passing through a dark valley unattended, the Good Shepherd will accompany you, armed with a crook to help you out of pitfalls, and a club for your foes. Therefore out of the letters of the alphabet of His being let us choose those that spell "unfailing Friend."

Rev. 3:8–11—*Hours of suffering give opportunities for Jesus to become known.* Like the church at Smyrna, on which the first sparks of fiery trial were falling, the child of God is often called to take the way of the cross. With its suffering, its injustice, its humiliation, its bitterness, it has been trodden by millions, and has been called "the King's highway." One holy soul says: "There is none other way to life and inward peace but the way of the cross." But nothing has brought out so much of the love and help of Jesus!

This is specially marked in the life of the apostle Paul. Few men have come anywhere near him in the ordeal of anguish and pain. "We are made as the filth of the world, the off-scouring of all things." He was always bearing about the dying of Jesus. Poverty, persecution, ill health, the hatred of the Jewish party: these were the deep waters he was called to cross and recross. But in it all he was more than conqueror through Him that loved him. Jesus was nearer him than the chill waters. True, he suffered for Christ, but Christ suffered with him. His Lord stood by him, then who could stand against him? His spirit seems to have become full of a divine optimism, as he challenges life and death, height and depth, to separate him from the love of God. Do not let us fear suffering or pain. Do not allow yourself to shrink back when Jesus leads you into the dark chamber. He walks the furnace kindled to seven times its ordinary heat. Martyrs have asked that they might not be taken from the rack, so ecstatic were the peace and joy poured into their hearts. Sufferers for long years on beds of pain have affirmed that they would not have chosen otherwise, since the Savior has made that chamber of pain as the vestibule of heaven. There are also experiences of suffering which are worse than most of those endured in the physical sphere, but Jesus is always standing there with the crown of life to place on the head of the overcomer. Let us not complain of our sufferings, or the lack of human sympathy, or allow people to criticize the divine Lover; let us rather rejoice that He has trusted us with pain and disability that His power may more richly rest on us. "Be thou faithful unto death, sentry, at thy post." The first and the last is with thee. He passed through death to a fuller life; so shalt thou!

The thousands of sick folk who were brought from every part of Galilee revealed healing qualities in Jesus that would have remained unknown had they not thronged around Him. The leper revealed His purity; the paralyzed His nervous energy; the dying His power of life. Each was a prism to break up rays of color hidden in His pure manhood. So each trial and sorrow which He comes into our lives to share reveals to us, and to the principalities and powers in the heavenlies, some new phase of that wonderful Being who is the complement of our infirmities.

Therefore, out of the alphabet of His being, let us choose the letters that spell "wonderful Healer."

Rev. 21:6–7—*Hours of thirst give opportunities for a more intimate knowledge of Jesus.* If the woman of Sychar had not been driven by thirst, she would not have visited the well at the noon of that memorable day; and if it were not for the thirst of their souls for satisfaction, men would never say with David: "As the hart panteth for the water brooks, so panteth my soul after thee, O God." If we were perfectly supplied from ourselves, we should never know what Christ can be. We are suffered to hunger and thirst that we should not trust in ourselves, but in the living God, who gives us all things richly to enjoy. There are those amongst us who have an immense capacity for love, but have never been married because a suitable partner has never been forthcoming. They love children, but have none of their own. They thirst, but perhaps, like Hagar, they have never realized that a fountain is within reach; it is the personal love of Jesus.

But the special reference in this passage is not to the present, but to the future. The first heaven and the first earth have passed away! The judgment is over, and death and Hades have ceased forever! The seas of division and storm are no more! The conquerors and overcomers have come into their blessed heritage, of which they have been made heirs! Yet even in that beatific state there will be thirst! Jesus says: "All is over, I am Alpha and Omega, I will give to him that is athirst."

Yes, even in that life there will be need for supplies from outside ourselves. Even there we shall not be independent of Him. As the circle of light grows, the circumference of darkness will grow. As we know more, we, like Newton, shall feel we are but gathering shells on the shores of a boundless ocean. The flock will lie down in green pastures, and be led in paths of righteousness, but we shall never reach the last fountain nor be able to dispense with the presence or lead of our Savior. When we have drunk of one set of wells, He will lead us further and more deeply into the recesses of eternity. He will still guide us to further fountains of living water. Oh, blessed absence of self-sufficiency! We shall never be self-contained! Never able to dispense with Christ! But, as our nature expands, as new yearnings arise, as fresh deeps call to deeps, we shall only learn more and more of His all-sufficiency, as the way, the truth, and the life.

Therefore, out of the letters of His alphabet of being, let us choose those that spell "immortal Lover."

Rev. 22:14—*When we are most deeply conscious of sin, it will reveal the purity and redeeming love of Jesus.* In these closing verses of the Apocalypse we are back again in the earth-life, though the Master assures us that He is coming very soon. This verse contains the last beatitude that is uttered from the throne of His ascension. The reading of the Revised Version is full of beauty, and is to be preferred to that of our Authorized Bibles. Thus for "Blessed are they that keep his commandments," we now read, as in an earlier passage (7:14) of those who *have* washed their robes. It is evidently a glance back from the eternal world at an experience long past, although its blessed influence still abides. But here it is: "They are washing their robes." It is the present tense, and therefore a present experience, in a present world.

Alas! that we ever had to come to wash our robes in His most precious blood. Alas! that we need to come so often to wash them. It is a terrible thing to be a sinner! It does not seem so terrible, because this is a world of sinners, and we have never seen a sinless one. The child born in a leper colony cannot realize what leprosy is, nor what the child of noble and pure birth is like. But we know enough to repent in dust and ashes and cry "Unclean," as did Isaiah when he beheld the glory of the Lord. And yet! And yet!—we should never otherwise have known the love of Christ, the wonder of His forgiving grace, His patience, His tender forbearance, His fathomless humility in stooping to wash our feet. Yes, Augustine, we understand what you mean when you say, "*O beata culpa,*" "O blessed fault!" Yet we dare not sin that grace may abound, lest we open again His wounds. But, in our hours of contrition, we have glimpses into the heart of God in Christ, which unfallen natures cannot share. Therefore, out of the alphabet of His being, let us choose letters to spell "the Friend of sinners."

Move through the flames with transcendent form
  As of the Son of God, in splendor move!
Divide the anguish, breast with us the storm,
  Companion perfect grief with perfect Love!

Bibliography

Fullerton, W. Y. *F. B. Meyer: A Biography.* London: Marshall, 1929.

Meyer, F. B. *Back to Bethel: Separation from Sin and Fellowship with God.* Chicago: Bible Institute Colportage Association, 1901.

______. *The Bells of Is; or, Voices of Human Need and Sorrow.* London: Morgan and Scott, 1894.

______. *The Call and Challenge of the Unseen.* London: Morgan and Scott, 1928.

______. *Christ in Isaiah.* London: Morgan and Scott, 1895. Reprinted—Fort Washington, Pa.: Christian Literature Crusade, 1970.

______. *The Directory of the Devout Life: Meditations on the Sermon on the Mount.* London: Morgan and Scott, 1904. Reprinted—Grand Rapids: Baker, 1954.

______. *Exodus.* 2 vols. A Devotional Commentary, edited by A. R. Buckland. London: R.T.S., 1911-1913.

______. *Expository Preaching: Plans and Methods.* London: Hodder and Stoughton, 1912.

______. *The Life and Light of Men: Expositions of John 1-12.* London: Morgan and Scott, 1891.

______. *Light on Life's Duties.* Chicago: Bible Institute Colportage Association, 1895.

______. *Love to the Uttermost: Expositions of John 13-21.* London: Morgan and Scott, 1898.

______. *Our Daily Homily.* 5 vols. London: Morgan and Scott, 1898-1899.

______. *Reveries and Realities; or, Life and Work in London.* London: Morgan and Scott, 1896.

______. *Tried by Fire: Expositions of the First Epistle of Peter.* London: Morgan and Scott, 1895. Reprinted—Fort Washington, Pa.: Christian Literature Crusade, 1970.

______. *The Way into the Holiest: Expositions of the Epistle to the Hebrews.* London: Morgan and Scott, 1893.

7

Henry Drummond

(1851–1897)

"Never have I known a man who, in my opinion, lived nearer the Master, or sought to do His will more fully." So wrote Dwight L. Moody in the May 1897 issue of the *Record of Christian Work*. He was writing about Henry Drummond, who died on 11 March 1897 at age forty-five. Drummond was one of Moody's friends, and Moody called Drummond "one of the most lovable men I have ever known." Moody wrote to James Stalker: "No man has ever been with me for any length of time that I did not see something that was unlike Christ, and I often see it in myself, but not in Henry Drummond. All the time we were together he was a Christ-like man and often a rebuke to me."

And yet Drummond was an evolutionist and an advocate of higher criticism. His approach to evangelism was different from that of Moody in that he rarely preached about the cross or referred to the atonement. "As to his theology," wrote W. Robertson Nicoll, "no theologian would admit that it was satisfactory or coherent. Of the atonement, for example, he made nothing; not that he rejected it, but that he had no place for it, and received it as a mystery."[1]

Drummond's ministry was more than once a source of trouble to Moody, and yet the great evangelist remained true to his friend. In July 1893, when Drummond came to Northfield to speak, a deputation of concerned ministers asked Moody to remove Drummond from the conference program. Some questioned the soundness of Drummond's theology: he did not defend verbal inspiration and even questioned some of the miracles. Others opposed his evolutionary teachings and his cigar smoking. Moody asked for a day to think the matter over. He met the deputation after breakfast the next morning and informed them that he had "laid the matter before the Lord, and the Lord had shown him that Drummond was a better man than himself; so he was to go on." Apparently this frank reply did not solve the problem, for Drummond reported: "At Northfield I felt a good deal out of it, and many fell upon me and rent me. . . . it was not a happy time."

That same year Drummond refused to help Moody in the Chicago World's Fair campaign, a decision that cut Moody deeply. "Well, Mr. Moody, you know why he refused," George Adam Smith told Moody while visiting Northfield in the summer of 1899. "It was because he was afraid to compromise you further with the men with whom you were working."

"I know it," Moody replied. "He did it out of pure love, but that he should have had to do it cut me."

Perhaps this explains why, in spite of their differences, Moody and Drummond were dear friends: both of them preached "God is love" and practiced that love.

Henry Drummond was born into a devout evangelical family in Stirling, Scotland, on 17 August 1851. At age fifteen he entered the University of Edinburgh, graduating in 1870. He then entered New College, Edinburgh, but he did not get his degree until 1876; the reason for this delay is the most important part of the story. On 23 November 1873 Moody and Ira Sankey opened the "Great Mission" in the Edinburgh Music Hall, an event that was to change Drummond's life. Nobody is quite sure how Drummond became involved in the campaign. More than one student had gone to hear Moody "on a lark," only to be arrested by God and put to work by the evangelist. Drummond was keenly interested in personal work, and personal work was what Moody emphasized. In fact just a few weeks before the meetings opened, Drummond had read a

---

1. *Princes of the Church*, p. 100.

perceptive paper on "Spiritual Diagnosis" before the Theological Society, advocating the very thing Moody was practicing in his inquiry room. So Drummond began as a counselor in the inquiry room, and Moody was quick to detect his gifts.

When the mission moved to Glasgow and was so singularly blessed of God, Moody sent to Edinburgh for reinforcements and Drummond rallied to the cause. Before long he was not only dealing with inquirers, but also speaking to large meetings of new converts; and God was using his messages. He was Moody's "Timothy," and the bond between the two men grew stronger as the months passed.

"I got a treat last night," Drummond wrote to his mother from Liverpool on 15 February 1875. "Moody sat up alone with me till near one o'clock telling me the story of his life. He told me the whole thing. A reporter might have made a fortune out of it." In 1894 Drummond wrote a personal tribute to his friend, titled simply *D. L. Moody,* and it is a valuable contribution to Moody lore. After Moody's death Smith added "A Personal Tribute" to Drummond's tribute, and the two were published together in 1900.

After the mission ended, Drummond returned to New College and graduated in 1876. Moody wanted Drummond to go with him to America, but Drummond remained in Scotland. How he made this decision is the first of four providential events that could be considered coincidences were it not for the impact they made on his life and ministry.

In the early days of the Moody mission, Drummond became fast friends with Robert W. Barbour, son of the wealthy cotton merchant, George F. Barbour. Often Drummond would visit his friend at the family home, Bonskeid House. During one of these visits Drummond stumbled over a stone and wrenched his knee, resulting in confinement for nearly two weeks. During that time he discussed Moody's invitation with Mrs. Barbour, who wisely counseled him to finish school and let God give him a ministry of his own. This counsel he followed; but during that final school year he continued his evangelistic ministry by holding meetings on Sunday evenings in the Gaiety Theater not far from school. Some of the students who assisted him in these services were Stalker, John Watson (later known as Ian Maclaren), Charles William Gordon (later known as Ralph Connor the Sky Pilot), and Smith.

After graduation Drummond became an assistant at the Barclay Free Church. In 1877 he began lecturing in natural science at the Free Church College in Glasgow. During the second year he became pastor of a mission in Possilpark, a suburb of Glasgow. The mission was under the jurisdiction of the Renfield Free Church, whose pastor, Marcus Dods, was to have tremendous influence over Drummond for the rest of his life.

At this point we must pause to examine the spiritual and academic situation that prevailed in the Free Church in the last quarter of the nineteenth century. There were two forces beating away at the citadel: biblical criticism and evolution. In 1878 W. Robertson Smith, professor of Old Testament at the Free Church College in Aberdeen, was charged with heresy because of an article he had written for the *Encyclopaedia Britannica.* The church was divided over the issue, and even the godly Alexander Whyte defended Smith's orthodoxy and his right to academic freedom. In 1881 Smith was finally suspended; Drummond wrote that Smith had been "lynched." Charles Darwin had published his *Origin of Species* in 1859, and evolution was the "going thing" by the time Drummond began studying science in Edinburgh. Higher criticism was basically an application of evolutionary theory to the documents of the Bible. First and foremost, Drummond was a scientist. Though ordained, he preferred to be called *Professor* Drummond rather than *Reverend* Drummond. One hundred years later we have a clearer view of both evolution and higher criticism, so we must be somewhat sympathetic with men like Drummond who faced the impact of these issues in ways that we do not today.

Now for the second "coincidence" in Drummond's life. During his regular ministry as a pastor, Drummond had delivered a number of sermons that sought to express spiritual truth in terms of the scientific beliefs of that day. He felt there was no conflict between science and Christianity if each was properly understood. He saw the Christian life in terms of evolution, something his friend Moody certainly did not do. Nicoll explained Drummond's ministry in this way: "He saw that the age was essentially scientific. He saw that there appeared to be between science and religion a spanless and fathomless abyss. He saw that the materialists were swiftly poisoning the nation. . . . he threw himself with all his strength into the work of effecting a reconciliation, and though we do not propose in this place to discuss the value of his work, it may certainly be said at the very least that it helped to change the situation, and to bring into many minds, scientific and religious, more than a ray of hope."[2]

One day Drummond "happened" to meet H. M. Hodder on Paternoster Row, London; and the publisher asked about some of

2. Ibid., p. 101.

Drummond's papers that had been rejected by two or three other houses. Drummond promised to send the manuscript to the firm of Hodder and Stoughton, and the result was the publication of *Natural Law in the Spiritual World,* a book that took both the scientific and religious worlds by storm. But when the book came off the press in June 1883, Drummond was steaming toward East Central Africa to investigate for a trading firm in Scotland the area's natural resources. Not until he received his mail somewhere near Tanganyika did Drummond discover his book was a best seller and he was famous. By the time he died in 1897, well over 100,000 copies had been sold, and the book had been reviewed in practically every major journal.

In 1884 Drummond was promoted to professor of natural sciences. In his inaugural address, titled "The Contribution of Science to Christianity," he reaffirmed his belief in evolution as God's method of both creation and revelation. Drummond's new position, plus the success of *Natural Law in the Spiritual World,* made him somewhat of a folk hero among the students, and he used this popularity as a means of reaching them for Christ.

On Sunday evening, 25 January 1885, Drummond gave the first of his "addresses" in the Oddfellows Hall, Edinburgh; and for nine years these meetings continued, reaching students by the hundreds. The meetings were supervised by a "secret committee" composed of Whyte, A. R. Simpson, A. H. Barbour (brother to Robert) and Dods. (Whyte's interest in Drummond stemmed from the fact that Mrs. Whyte was Jane Elizabeth Barbour, sister to Henry's dear friend, Robert. G. F. Barbour, Whyte's nephew, wrote Whyte's biography.)

It is worth noting that Moody as well as Drummond had tremendous appeal to students, but for different reasons. Both were utterly transparent and sincere; but Moody appealed to the authority of Scripture while Drummond spoke to the intellect and reasoned with students. Drummond felt that the Christian faith had to be presented in the language and categories of a scientific age—the "new evangelism" he called it. Moody presented the Christ of the cross; Drummond emphasized Christ's perfect life.

That Drummond believed in the efficacy of the atonement is beyond question; his scientific attitude, however, prevented him from trying to explain it. Even Sankey, Moody's song leader, had his doubts about the professor; in 1892 Sankey wrote Drummond and asked why he did not emphasize the cross. Drummond's explanation was that he was called to preach "the forgotten truths," not those that are being repeated by others again and again.

In 1887 Drummond came to Northfield. While in this country, he visited many Eastern colleges and universities. Everywhere he went the students turned out in droves, and from every indication tremendous spiritual results followed. William Lyon Phelps said of Drummond's visit to Yale, "I have never seen so deep an impression made on students, by any speaker on any subject."

But 1887 is important for another reason: Drummond delivered his famous address on I Corinthians 13, and Moody insisted that he publish it. *The Greatest Thing in the World* is still in print today.

The third "coincidence" in Drummond's life occurred in 1890, when he was ministering in Australia. It was decided that Drummond should visit mission stations in the New Hebrides, and for the first time Drummond came face to face with the gospel's confrontation with raw heathenism. He was so impressed that he delivered a powerful paper at the college that November on "The Problem of Foreign Missions." This paper influenced a number of mission leaders and was indirectly responsible for the great Edinburgh missionary conference in 1910.

Drummond was always interested in children and young people, though he never married. A Glasgow businessman and Drummond, while walking down the street one day, saw a merchant throw a stack of round strawberry boxes into the gutter. Instantly a group of boys swooped down upon the boxes and put them on their heads for caps. Then they lined up in military formation and "marched" away. "There's an idea for you," Drummond told his friend; and out of that "coincidence" grew the Boys' Brigade program that God still uses to win boys to Christ.

After two years of suffering, Drummond died on 11 March 1897. He was laid to rest next to his father in Stirling.

If you want to become better acquainted with Drummond, begin with *Henry Drummond: An Anthology*, edited by James W. Kennedy. The brief biographical chapter will give you the basic facts about Drummond's life and ministry, and the selections from his writings will give you insight into his thinking. I know of no single volume that better explains Drummond to space-age Christians. The official biography was written by Smith: *The Life of Henry Drummond* (1899). Smith included several extracts from Drummond's addresses to students, but Kennedy's selections are, I think, better. Not long after his death, Drummond's *"The Ideal Life" and Other Unpublished Addresses* was published. Two memorial sketches are prefixed to the fifteen popular addresses, one by Nicoll and the other by Watson, Drummond's lifelong friend. Drummond's address "Ill Temper" is one of the best sermons on the elder brother of Luke 15 that I have read.

After Moody's death in 1899, some cited his friendship with Drummond as proof that Moody was liberal theologically. Even his son Paul Moody wrote an article for *Christian Century* suggesting that the evangelist had been liberal; but this was immediately refuted by no less an expert on the subject than R. A. Torrey. He wrote from Los Angeles on 20 August 1923: "It is true that Mr. Moody loved Henry Drummond as he loved very few other people. . . . But Mr. Moody did not sympathize at all with some of the views into which Prof. Henry Drummond was led. . . . though Mr. Moody loved him still, and loved him to the end, he would not use him, and greatly regretted the position which Prof. Henry Drummond had taken up."

At one of the memorial services for Moody, J. M. Buckley said: "Mr. Moody had his prejudices, for I once heard him declare that he would own fellowship with everybody that believed himself to be a sinner and trusted in Christ; but, said he, 'God being my helper, I will never own fellowship with a man who denies the deity of my God and Savior Jesus Christ, or sneers at His atonement.'" Moody and Drummond had their differences, but each was used to bring Jesus Christ to lost sinners. Had Drummond ever cast one slur on the person or work of Jesus Christ, Moody would have defended his Lord and denounced his friend. Moody loved his friend, but he loved his Savior more.

Dealing with Doubt

There is a subject which has not yet been touched upon at this conference, and which I think we as workers amongst young men cannot afford to keep out of sight—I mean the subject of doubt. We are forced to face that subject. We have no choice. I would rather let it alone; but every day of my life I meet men who doubt, and I am quite sure that most of you have innumerable interviews every year with men who raise skeptical difficulties about religion. Now, it becomes a matter of great practical importance that we should

Author's note: Drummond's sermon "Dealing with Doubt" is from T. J. Shanks, ed., *A College of Colleges*, pp. 35–44. He preached it during the "Summer School for College Students" held at Northfield, Massachusetts, June 30–July 12, 1887.

know how to deal wisely with these men. Upon the whole, I think these are the best men in the country. I speak of my own country. I speak of the universities with which I am familiar, and I say that the men who are perplexed—the men who come to you with serious and honest difficulties—are the best men. They are men of intellectual honesty, and cannot allow themselves to be put to rest by words, or phrases, or traditions, or theologies, but who must get to the bottom of things for themselves. And if I am not mistaken, Christ was very fond of these men. The outsiders always interested Him, and touched Him. The orthodox people—the Pharisees—He was much less interested in. He went with publicans and sinners—with people who were in revolt against the respectability, intellectual and religious, of the day. And following Him, we are entitled to give sympathetic consideration to those whom He loved and took trouble with.

First, let me speak for a moment or two about the origin of doubt. In the first place, we are born questioners. Look at the wonderment of a little child in its eyes before it can speak. The child's great word when it begins to speak is *why*. Every child is full of every kind of question, about every kind of thing that moves, and shines, and changes, in the little world in which it lives. That is the incipient doubt in the nature of man. Respect doubt for its origin. It is an inevitable thing. It is not a thing to be crushed. It is a part of man as God made him. Heresy is truth in the making, and doubt is the prelude of knowledge.

Secondly, the world is a sphinx. It is a vast riddle—an unfathomable mystery; and on every side there is temptation to questioning. In every leaf, in every cell of every leaf, there are a hundred problems. There are ten good years of a man's life in investigating what is in a leaf, and there are five good years more in investigating the things that are in the things that are in the leaf. God has planned the world to incite men to intellectual activity.

Thirdly, the instrument with which we attempt to investigate truth is impaired. Some say it fell, and the glass is broken. Some say prejudice, heredity, or sin have spoiled its sight, and have blinded our eyes and deadened our ears. In any case the instruments with which we work upon truth, even in the strongest men, are feeble and inadequate to their tremendous task.

And in the fourth place, all religious truths are doubtable. There is no absolute proof for any one of them. Even that fundamental truth—the existence of a god—no man can prove by reason. The ordinary proof for the existence of God involves either an assumption, argument in a circle, or a contradiction. The impression of

God is kept up by experience, not by logic. And hence, when the experimental religion of a man, of a community, or of a nation wanes, religion wanes—their idea of God grows indistinct, and that man, community, or nation becomes infidel. Bear in mind, then, that all religious truths are doubtable—even those which we hold most strongly.

What does this brief account of the origin of doubt teach us? It teaches us great intellectual humility. It teaches us sympathy and toleration with all men who venture upon the ocean of truth to find out a path through it for themselves. Do you sometimes feel yourself thinking unkind things about your fellow students who have intellectual difficulty? I know how hard it is always to feel sympathy and toleration for them; but we must address ourselves to that most carefully and most religiously. If my brother is shortsighted I must not abuse him or speak against him; I must pity him, and if possible try to improve his sight or to make things that he is to look at so bright that he cannot help seeing. But never let us think evil of men who do not see as we do. From the bottom of our hearts let us pity them, and let us take them by the hand and spend time and thought over them, and try to lead them to the true light.

What has been the church's treatment of doubt in the past? It has been very simple. "There is a heretic. Burn him!" That is all. "There is a man who has gone off the road. Bring him back and torture him!" We have got past that physically; have we got past it morally? What does the modern church say to a man who is skeptical? Not "Burn him!" but "Brand him!" "Brand him!—call him a bad name." And in many countries at the present time, a man who is branded as a heretic is despised, tabooed, and put out of religious society, much more than if he had gone wrong in morals. I think I am speaking within the facts when I say that a man who is unsound is looked upon in many communities with more suspicion and with more pious horror than a man who now and then gets drunk. "Burn him!" "Brand him!" "Excommunicate him!" That has been the church's treatment of doubt, and that is perhaps to some extent the treatment which we ourselves are inclined to give to the men who cannot see the truths of Christianity as we see them. Contrast Christ's treatment of doubt. I have spoken already of His strange partiality for the outsiders—for the scattered heretics up and down the country; of the care with which He loved to deal with them, and of the respect in which He held their intellectual difficulties. Christ never failed to distinguish between doubt and unbelief. Doubt is *can't believe;* unbelief is *won't believe.* Doubt is honesty; unbelief is obstinacy. Doubt is looking for light; unbelief is content with darkness. Loving darkness rather than light—that is what Christ attacked, and attacked unsparingly. But for the intellectual questioning of Thomas, and Philip, and Nicodemus, and the many others who came to Him to have their great problems solved, He was respectful and generous and tolerant.

And how did He meet their doubts? The church, as I have said, says "Brand him!" Christ said, "Teach him." He destroyed by fulfilling. When Thomas came to Him and denied His very resurrection, and stood before Him waiting for the scathing words and lashing for his unbelief, they never came. They never came. Christ gave him facts—facts. No man can go around facts. Christ said, "Behold my hands and my feet." The great god of science at the present time is a fact. It works with facts. Its cry is, "Give me facts." Found anything you like upon facts and we will believe it. The spirit of Christ was the scientific spirit. He founded His religion upon facts; and He asked all men to found their religion upon facts. Now, gentlemen, get up the facts of Christianity, and take men to the facts. Theologies—and I am not speaking disrespectfully of theology; theology is as scientific a thing as any other science of facts—but theologies are human versions of divine truths, and hence the varieties of the versions, and the inconsistencies of them. I would allow a man to select whichever version of this truth he liked *afterwards;* but I would ask him to begin with no version, but go back to the facts and base his Christian life upon that. That is the great lesson of the New Testament way of looking at doubt—of Christ's treatment of doubt. It is not "Brand him!" but lovingly, wisely, and tenderly to teach him. Faith is never opposed to reason in the New Testament; it is opposed to sight. You will find that a principle worth thinking over. *Faith is never opposed to reason in the New Testament, but to sight.*

Well, now; with these principles in mind as to the origin of doubt, and as to Christ's treatment of it, how are we ourselves to deal with our fellow students who are in intellectual difficulty? In the first place, I think we must make all the concessions to them that we conscientiously can. When a doubter first encounters you he pours out a deluge of abuse of churches, and ministers, and creeds, and Christians. Nine-tenths of what he says is probably true. Make concessions. Agree with him. It does him good to unburden himself of these things. He has been cherishing them for years—laying them up against Christians, against the church, and against Christianity; and now he is startled to find the first Christian with whom he has talked over the thing almost entirely agrees with him. We are, of course, not responsible for everything that is said in the name of Christianity; but a man does not give up medicine because there are quack doctors, and no man has a right to give up his Christianity because there are spurious or inconsistent Christians. Then, as I already said, creeds are human versions of divine truths; and we do not ask a man to accept all the creeds, any more than we ask him to accept all the Christians. We ask him to accept Christ, and the facts about Christ, and the words of Christ. But you will find the battle is half won when you have endorsed the man's objections, and possibly added a great many more to the charges which he has against ourselves. These men, gentlemen, are in revolt against the kind of religion which we exhibit to the world—against the cant that is taught in the name of Christianity. And if the men that have never seen the real thing—if you could show them that, they would receive it as eagerly as you do. They are merely in revolt against the imperfections and inconsistencies of those who represent Christ in the world.

Second, beg them to set aside, by an act of will, all unsolved problems: such as the problem of the origin of evil, the problem of the Trinity, the problem of the relation of human will and predestination, and so on—problems which have been investigated for thousands of years without result—ask them to set those problems aside as insoluble in the meantime, just as a man who is studying mathematics may be asked to set aside the problem of squaring the circle. Let him go on with what can be done, and what has been done, and leave out of sight the impossible. You will find that will relieve the skeptic's mind of a great deal of unnecessary cargo that has been in his way.

Thirdly, talking about difficulties, as a rule, only aggravates them. Entire satisfaction to the intellect is unattainable about any of the greater problems, and if you try to get to the bottom of them by argument, there is no bottom there; and therefore you make the matter worse. But I would say what is known, and what can be honestly and philosophically and scientifically said about one or two of the difficulties that the doubter raises, just to show him that you can do it—to show him that you are not a fool—that you are not merely groping in the dark yourself, but you have found whatever basis is possible. But I would not go around all the doctrines. I would simply do that with one or two; because the moment you cut off one, a hundred other heads will grow in its place. It would be a pity if all these problems could be solved. The joy of the intellectual life would be largely gone. I would not rob a man of his problems, nor would I have another man rob me of my problems. They are the delight of life, and the whole intellectual world would be stale and unprofitable if we knew everything.

Fourthly, and this is the great point, turn away from the reason, and go into the man's moral life. I don't mean, go into his moral life and see if the man is living in conscious sin, which is the great blinder of the eyes—I am speaking now of honest doubt—but open a new door into the practical side of the man's nature. Entreat him not to postpone life and his life's usefulness until he has settled the problems of the universe. Tell him those problems will never all be settled; that his life will be done before he has begun to settle them; and ask him what he is doing with his life meantime. Charge him with wasting his life and his usefulness; and invite him to deal with the moral and practical difficulties of the world, and leave the intellectual difficulties as he goes along. To spend time upon these is proving the less important before the more important; and, as the French say, "The good is the enemy of the best." It is a good thing to think; it is a better thing to work; it is a better thing to do good. And you have him there, you see. He can't get beyond that. You have to tell him, in fact, that there are two organs of knowledge: the one reason, the other obedience. Now tell him, as he has tried the first and found the little in it, just for a moment or two to join you in trying the second. And when he asks whom he is to obey, you tell him there is but One, and lead him to the great historical figure who calls all men to Him: the one perfect life—the one Savior of mankind—the one Light of the world. Ask him to begin to obey Christ; and, doing His will, he shall know of the doctrine whether it be of God.

That, I think, is about the only thing you can do with a man: to get him into practical contact with the needs of the world, and to let him lose his intellectual difficulties meantime. Don't ask him to give them up altogether. Tell him to solve them afterward one by one if he can, but meantime to give his life to Christ and his time to the kingdom of God. And, you see, you fetch him completely around when you do that. You have taken him away from the false side of his nature, and to the practical and moral side of his nature; and for the first time in his life, perhaps, he puts things in their true place. He puts his nature in the relations in which it ought to be, and he then only begins to live. And by obedience—by obedience—he will soon become a learner and pupil for himself, and Christ will teach him things, and he will find whatever problems are solvable gradually solved as he goes along the path of practical duty.

Now, gentlemen, let me just, in closing, give you a couple of instances of how to deal with specific points. The commonest thing that we hear said nowadays by young men is, "What about evolution? How am I to reconcile my religion, or any religion, with the doctrine of evolution?" That upsets more men than perhaps anything else at the present hour. How would you deal with it? I would say to a man that Christianity is the further evolution. I don't know any better definition than that. It is the further evolution—the higher evolution. I don't start with him to attack evolution. I don't start with him to defend it. I destroy by fulfilling it. I take him at his own terms. He says evolution is that which pushes the man on from the simple to the complex, from the lower to the higher. Very well; that is what Christianity does. It pushes the man farther on. It takes him where nature has left him, and carries him on to heights which on the plane of nature he could never reach. That is evolution. "Lead me to the Rock that is higher than I." That is evolution. It is the development of the whole man in the highest directions—the drawing out of his spiritual being. Show an evolutionist that, and you have taken the wind out of his sails. "I came not to destroy." Don't destroy his doctrine—perhaps you can't—but fulfil it. Put a larger meaning into it.

The other instance—the next commonest question perhaps—is the question of miracles. It is impossible, of course, to discuss that now. But that question is thrown at my head every second day: "What do you say to a man when he says to you, 'Why do you believe in miracles?'"

I say, "Because I have seen them."

He says, "When?"

I say, "Yesterday."

He says, "Where?"

"Down such-and-such a street I saw a man who was a drunkard redeemed by the power of an unseen Christ and saved from sin. That is a miracle."

The best apologetic for Christianity is a Christian. That is a fact which the man cannot get over. There are fifty other arguments for miracles, but none so good as that you have seen them. Perhaps you are one yourself. But take you a man and show him a miracle with his own eyes. Then he will believe.

Bibliography

Drummond, Henry. *Dwight L. Moody: Impressions and Facts.* New York: McClure and Phillips, 1900.

———. *The Greatest Thing in the World: An Address.* London: Hodder and Stoughton, 1890. Reprinted—Old Tappan, N.J.: Revell, 1968.

———. *Henry Drummond: An Anthology.* Edited by James W. Kennedy. New York: Harper, 1953.

———. *"The Ideal Life" and Other Unpublished Addresses.* London: Hodder and Stoughton, 1897.

———. *Natural Law in the Spiritual World.* London: Hodder and Stoughton, 1883.

Nicoll, W. Robertson. *Princes of the Church.* London: Hodder and Stoughton, 1921.

Shanks, T. J., ed. *A College of Colleges: Led by D. L. Moody and Taught by Henry Drummond, Joseph Cook, John A. Broadus, L. T. Townsend, A. T. Pierson, and Jacob Chamberlain, with Others.* New York: Revell, 1887.

Smith, George Adam. *The Life of Henry Drummond.* London: Hodder and Stoughton, 1899.

8

Thomas Spurgeon

(1856–1917)

"The first time I saw my future husband, he occupied the pulpit of New Park Street Chapel on the memorable Sunday when he preached his first sermons there." So wrote Mrs. Charles H. Spurgeon of that "memorable Sunday," 18 December 1853.

It was not easy to be the fiancée of London's most popular preacher. So engrossed was Charles Spurgeon in his ministry that he often shook hands with Susannah at church meetings without recognizing her! When they were alone, he would correct proofs of his sermons while his beloved sat by quietly. "It was good discipline for the pastor's intended wife," she wrote in later years. Spurgeon baptized Susannah on 1 February 1855, and she became a member of New Park Street. A year later, on 8 January, they were married. After a ten-day honeymoon in Paris, they returned to London and to what would be one of the greatest ministries in the history of the church.

Susannah presented her husband with twin sons on 20 September 1856. The first-born was named Charles, the other Thomas. The boys attended local schools and also had a private tutor. It was discovered early that Thomas had a gift for drawing. Both boys became Christians early and often distributed copies of their father's sermons. On 20 September 1874 their father preached from the text "I and the children" (Gen. 33:5); the following evening he baptized his sons.

Their famous father sometimes hinted that he would rejoice if one of his sons succeeded him at the Metropolitan Tabernacle. In a sermon titled "Now: A Sermon for Young Men and Women," Spurgeon said: "It may not be my honor to be succeeded in this pulpit by one of my sons, greatly as I would rejoice if it might be so; but at least I hope they will be here in this church to serve their father's God, and to be regarded with affection by you for the sake of him who spent his life in your midst." At first it did not appear that either son would enter the ministry. The boys preached when opportunities came, and they helped found the Northcote Road Baptist Church. But Charles entered a mercantile career, and Thomas was apprenticed to a wood-engraver named William Holledge. Both young men served the Lord zealously, but neither devoted full time to the Christian ministry.

Tom's health was poor, so he went on a sea voyage to Australia. Tom Holledge, son of William, went along. Their three-masted schooner left on 15 June 1877 and arrived in Melbourne on 28 August. During the voyage Spurgeon preached often to the passengers and crew. His father had given Thomas a letter of introduction in which he said, "He can preach a bit." Thomas had intended to set up an engraving business in Melbourne, but the name *Spurgeon* opened doors of ministry that he could not ignore. "Young Spurgeon does not possess the fire and dash of his father," one newspaper reported, "but he has much originality, humor, and force." Wherever he preached, he drew great crowds. Some came to criticize and compare, but many went away convicted. Young Thomas was not C.H.S., but he was still God's servant and a capable preacher.

About this time Thomas was falsely accused of conduct unbecoming to a minister. "Whether it was the tongue of slander in the old land, or some misinformation or mistake, I do not know," he once said. "But there came to my dear father's ears a story which did not reflect credit upon his absent son. It came in such a form that he was almost bound to believe it." (We wonder if C.H.S. remembered the slander that had been spread about him in early years.) "I left the matter with God," said Thomas, "and He espoused my cause." In a few days his father cabled: "Disregard my letter; was misinformed."

In September 1878 Thomas received word that his mother was

ill. Immediately he sailed for home. When he arrived, he found her much improved, but his father was suffering. On Sunday, 10 November, Thomas Spurgeon had to preach for C.H.S. at the great tabernacle. His brother Charles also came to his aid during his father's illness.

Thomas enrolled in the Pastors' College, but his poor health forced him to miss so many classes that he decided to return to Australia. This decision deeply hurt his father, who had long hoped his son would share his ministry and eventually take his place. Spurgeon's dear friend and associate, W. Y. Fullerton, wrote: "Only twice in his life C. H. Spurgeon spent a whole night in prayer. . . . One of these nights of intense supplication was for a personal need. . . . The other was when the hopes he had built on his son Tom being by his side were shattered." Tom settled in New Zealand, and for the first year he supplied the pulpit of the Hanover Street Church in Dunedin. Family history repeated itself, for in that church he met Lila Rutherford, who on 10 February 1888 became Mrs. Thomas Spurgeon. In January 1882 Thomas became pastor of the Baptist church in Aukland. The work prospered, they built a new auditorium (a tabernacle, of course!), and many found Christ. The pastor returned to Great Britain for five months in 1884 to raise funds for his work. On 14 December 1884 he sailed for New Zealand, bidding goodbye to his father, who told him he could not bear the pain of another parting.

There were to be no further partings. On 7 June 1891 C.H.S. preached his last sermon at the tabernacle; and on 31 January 1892 he was "called home." The death of "the governor" (as his officers called him) ushered in the "tabernacle tempest" that was watched with great interest by Christians all over the English-speaking world. The question was: Who will keep the tabernacle going? Spurgeon's brother James, who had assisted in the tabernacle ministry, was asked to serve as acting pastor. A. T. Pierson had been preaching at the tabernacle during Spurgeon's last illness; but since he was a Presbyterian, he could not be a candidate for the pulpit. Pierson stayed with the work for a year, but then he had to return to the States. The officers asked Thomas Spurgeon to come to preach for three months; and on 10 June 1892 he arrived in London with his wife and son. He closed his ministry on 9 October and then Dwight L. Moody arrived for a series of meetings at the tabernacle.

Pierson returned following Moody's ministry and discovered a deep division in the congregation. The "tabernacle tempest" was dividing families and breaking lifelong friendships. On 28 March 1893 some two thousand members met and asked the officers to call Thomas Spurgeon home for a year's ministry, after which the church would decide what to do next. Thomas accepted the call. He also remembered something Moody had said to him during his previous ministry at the tabernacle: "You are yet to come back to this place, and I am going to pray God here and now that it may be so!" He began his ministry in London on 30 July 1893. Before the year was over, the church knew that Thomas Spurgeon was the man for the pulpit. On 21 March 1894 the church called him as pastor, and he remained until 1908.

One of the most tragic events in the ministry of Thomas's father had occurred when young Charles was preaching to a huge crowd at the Surrey Gardens Music Hall. Trouble-makers in the audience began to cry "Fire! Fire!" and the result was catastrophe. Seven people were killed, twenty-eight hospitalized. It seemed that Spurgeon's ministry was doomed. God overruled, however, and vindicated His servant. A trying time in Thomas's ministry also involved fire.

On 20 April 1899 the great Metropolitan Tabernacle burned to the ground, leaving Spurgeon with a congregation and no place to house it. The fire was caused by an overheated flue in the adjacent Pastors' College. At the Pastors' Conference the day before, the Scripture reading, Hebrews 12, had ended with "Our God is a consuming fire." Thomas Spurgeon preached on the theme "No Strange Fire." The slogan for the annual conference was "Does the fire burn brightly on the altar?" And oddly enough, *Old Moore's Almanack* had predicted, "About the middle of the month [April] the destruction of a famous building by fire may be expected." Spurgeon had built a tabernacle in New Zealand; now he would rebuild one in London. When he was standing by the ruins shortly after the fire, a stranger approached him and slipped some money into his hand. "This is to build it up again, sir!" he said. God multiplied those five shillings into thousands of dollars; and on 19 September 1900 the new tabernacle was opened. Ira Sankey sang at the dedication services, and F. B. Meyer and John Henry Jowett assisted Spurgeon in the preaching.

Thomas Spurgeon resigned as pastor of the tabernacle on 8 February 1908, and the church reluctantly accepted his resignation. They held a great farewell service for him on 22 June. For the next nine years he preached often, assisted in raising funds for the orphan homes his father had founded, and worked hard to maintain his health. He celebrated his diamond jubilee on 20 September 1916 and received well-deserved honors from an appreciative Christian public. He died on 20 October 1917 and was buried near his father's tomb in Norwood Cemetery. A. C. Dixon, the new pastor of the tabernacle, read the Scripture; Dinsdale Young prayed; the children from the orphanage sang; and F. J. Feltham preached. At C.H.S.'s burial service, a dove had flown from the direction of the tabernacle towards the tomb, glided over the sorrowing crowd, seemed almost to hover, and then flown away. For Thomas Spurgeon there was no dove, but there certainly was peace.

Early in his ministry Thomas wrote to his father: "If I can have but a portion of my father's mantle, I might be well content." Did his illustrious heritage cripple him? I think not. He knew himself and accepted himself. He did not try to be his father, although he certainly learned from his father. No doubt many people came to hear him because he was a Spurgeon; but after they heard, they came back. They detected an authentic note. Thomas Spurgeon was a voice for God, not an echo of his father. The gifts God had given him would have made him a successful minister of the gospel even without the name *Spurgeon*.

Certainly Thomas Spurgeon is to be honored for daring to be himself. He never permitted his father to determine God's will for his ministry. When Thomas returned to London for a year's ministry at the tabernacle, he wisely left his wife and son in New Zealand, lest their presence be interpreted as overconfidence on his part. He had great gifts as an evangelist. His itinerant ministry in Australia and New Zealand was greatly blessed by God. Like his father, he had a keen sense of humor and often had to struggle to control it. To say that Thomas Spurgeon was not as gifted or as marvelously used by God as his father is to say nothing. How many preachers even begin to measure up to the stature of Charles Haddon Spurgeon? In uniting a great congregation, maintaining a wide and varied ministry, and rebuilding a great and historic structure, Thomas Spurgeon performed, under God, one of the greatest ministries of modern times. He will always be overshadowed by his father, but nevertheless will receive his own "Well done!" when all Christians stand before the Lord.

The Soul's Keeping

Wherefore let them that suffer according to the will of God commit the keeping of their souls to him in well doing, as unto a faithful Creator.
I Peter 4:19

Author's note: Spurgeon's sermon "The Soul's Keeping" is from *Sermons Preached in the Metropolitan Tabernacle*. He preached it on 14 July 1901.

This word is addressed preeminently to the persecuted. A time of fiery trial was about to come upon the church of God; and Peter, himself a man who had been tested and proved, determines that he will, now that he is returned again, strengthen the brethren. The closing verses of this chapter—indeed, almost the larger part of it—is devoted to such encouragement. He addresses the tried ones affectionately, and gives them heart and hope in God their Lord. It may be that—though days of persecution may, in a sense, be said to be past and gone—it may be that some are here who know what suffering for the cause and cross of Christ is. The reproach of the cross is not ended; I am not sure that the fires of persecution are out. They may be smoldering still, and in some particulars and circumstances they are doing more than smoldering. Slow fires they may be, but slow fires are not less hard to bear than the quicker and the fiercer flames.

Well, let us run through these items of strong encouragement. May the Spirit abide in the hearts of those who are distressed, persecuted, buffeted, tempted! In verse 12 I notice that Peter speaks to such in his most affectionate style. "Beloved"—he greets them thus. He would have them know that he, for one, thinks of them, and thinks graciously and tenderly concerning them. But if Peter—who, with all respect to him, was not particularly strong in this department: he was rather a stern, rough, rugged man—if Peter felt his heartstrings stirred as he thought of the suffering saints, what of Jesus whose heart is full of tenderness—so full that it overflows with love? The whole church is with you, dear suffering friends; the Spirit looks lovingly upon you; the Bride would greet you, too; and Jesus Himself exclaims, "Ye are my beloved ones."

Peter further encourages them, by reminding them that no strange thing has happened unto them. The judgment has begun at the house of God, but this is nothing novel. All through its history the house of God has been thus proved and tested. Your case is not unique, my brother; you are not alone in this sorrow, my suffering sister. So far from being unique, you are but one of many. This is universal; you are sailing in the same boat with ten thousand of God's people, who, in proportion as they are true to their trust and loyal to their Christ, suffer persecution for His name.

Notice further, that you are "partakers of Christ's sufferings." This is a wonderful word. It reminds one of the still more striking passage in Colossians, in which Paul tells the persecuted and suffering that they are filling up, as he himself was doing, that which was lacking, that which was behind, in the sufferings of Christ. Not that there was any incompleteness in the suffering—that could not be. The atonement was fully wrought, and all He had to bear He bore right bravely. But it is a case of being, shall I say, "continued in our next." We are one with Christ—one with Him in His sufferings, as we shall be in His glory. You are just running on the same lines, carrying on the same experience. You are one with Jesus, partakers of His sufferings. Rejoice therein: for "when His glory shall be revealed, ye shall be glad also with exceeding joy." Ah, there is comfort here. The banner that has trailed in the dust, the standard that is shot-riven and stained with smoke and blood, shall yet wave in God's cathedral, and hang forever in the place of honor. Meanwhile, the Spirit of God rests upon you: the blessed Dove overshadows you. You may rest in Him who rests on you.

A somewhat strange source of comfort it may seem to be; but it looks to me as if, even from verses 17 and 18, the apostle would have the persecuted and the tried find some comfort. "The time is come that judgment must begin at the house of God: and if it first begin at us, what shall the end be of them that obey not the gospel of God?" You are suffering, but you are not suffering as they do or as they will. You are in the furnace, but it is with different purpose from that which they must know who disobey the gospel of God. "And if the righteous scarcely be saved"—if there is so much stress and strain and distress and difficulty in bringing many sons to Glory—"where shall the ungodly and the sinner appear?" Thank God you are not with them! You are stooping, but you are *stooping to conquer*. Grace has made you to differ.

> And though 'tis painful at present,
> 'Twill cease before long;
> And then, oh how pleasant!
> The conqueror's song.

Wherefore, envy not those to whom the lines seem for the present to have fallen in pleasant places; consider their end, and thank God with all the gratitude your heart can put forth, that your sufferings are working for you, "a far more exceeding and eternal weight of glory"; that they are, indeed, refining you to see His face.

There is further comfort in the verse which we have taken as our text. There, reference is made to those who suffer "according to the will of God." I know not what it is that has come upon you, my beloved Christian friends—the nature of the distress may be a secret in your own breast; but if you can only realize that it is "according to the will of God," if you know assuredly that you are not to blame in this matter, or that if there were blame originally the sin has been forgiven, what comfort you should suck out of this flower! It is full of nectar; it is "according to the will of God," by His appointment: or, at least, by His permission you suffer thus. And even the stings and arrows of tortuous fortune, even the bolts and buffets of the enemy, are welcome: since God has sent them for your good, and that He, when you have done all and still stood, shall be glorified by your brave endeavor and endurance. "According to the will of God." Ah, that is *the gleam that lightens every gloom;* that is the sunshine which makes it daylight, even in the darkest night. It is Thy will, my Father, and I can only say, "Amen: Thy will, not mine, be done."

The apostle Peter, however, is very practical; and whereas he is more than willing to give this sympathetic word, he follows it by instruction which would serve his hearers in the evil day. I believe that this instruction is equally applicable to those who are in any sort of sorrow, to those who are enduring any sort of trial: so I pass it on to the great congregation, hoping that God Himself will apply it to the neediest hearts. All who suffer "according to the will of God" in mind or body or estate, in things temporal or in things spiritual, are included here. And this is the advice: "Let them commit the keeping of their souls to him in well doing, as unto a faithful Creator."

I. Now, in the first place, after a rather lengthy preface, let me say that it is evident that *the chief danger to be apprehended* in such cases as I have referred to is of a spiritual sort. Those who suffer thus are charged to commit the keeping of their souls to Him. Remember to whom the apostle spoke, to those who were suffering, persecuted, for the name and cause of Jesus Christ. They were in constant peril. They died daily. They knew what it was to suffer shame and nakedness and famine and sickness. They were in constant poverty. They were in frequent pain. And Peter comes to them and says, "What you have to do is to commit your souls to Him." I think I can imagine some of them saying to Peter, "Oh, but Peter, it is our bodies we are most concerned about. See these gaping, aching wounds; see these emaciated frames; see how almost naked we have been stripped by our relentless enemies." Well, whether they said that or no, Peter's advice remains the same, "Commit your souls to Him": because souls are more than bodies, and because the danger to the soul is more to be dreaded than the danger to the outward frame.

My dear hearer, I know not, as I have said, what suffering presses on you now; how it may affect your mind or your body or your estate; what loss you have already suffered of prestige, of business, of health, of friends, for Christ's sake and the gospel's. I know that sometimes it looks as if all these evil things came upon one as soon as he became devoted to the cause and kingdom of Christ; but I say that, whatever has come, and whatever threatens to come, *what concerns you chiefly is the result of these trials upon your soul.* They work upon your body; they affect your mind by the way. But it is your soul the enemy is aiming at. And even God's providences and strange dispensations may work you spiritual harm, unless they are taken from His hand, wisely used, thankfully received. The soul suffers most of all: the enemy is after that. It is not the casket he wants, but the jewel that lies within. It is not the shell that he is after, but the kernel. Hence, be not so taken up with the sorrows that affect your person, that you forget to be on your guard lest these sorrows sink through your person into your inmost mind, and make you fretful or perhaps rebellious; that is where the danger comes in. Commit the keeping of your souls to Him, "as unto a faithful Creator." In sorrow, as in sunshine, seek first the kingdom of God and His righteousness, "and all other things"—so runs the promise—"shall be added unto you."

Another reason why the apostle says commit your souls, rather than your bodies, to Him, in these distressful circumstances, lies here—*that the soul involves and includes the body.* Of course, there is a sense in which the body includes the soul; but in this case the greater includes the less, the most important involves also that which is of lesser moment. Your Father knows that you have need of means to keep the business going, to keep the family intact, to continue the home in existence, to maintain your health which seems to be failing: your Father knows how you suffer when men reproach you for your religion, and He is not unmindful of the mental and bodily distress these things cause; but oh, if your soul is rendered and surrendered to Him, if you have yielded your inmost self to Him, definitely and distinctly, concerning this particular matter, well then, does not that include the body? You mean to tell me that the Lord will overlook that, in His anxiety to save and succor your soul? No, no. He who hath trod the thorny road, will He lead our feet along the briary way? And He who has borne the greatest load of all, the tremendous burden of our sins, will not refuse to care for us in these minor matters, these trivial details: for such they really are, in comparison with the main matter of the keeping of the soul, the maintaining of our integrity, the holding up of the head in the midst of the 'whelming waters, and the carrying out of God's purposes concerning His chosen and redeemed. The soul is *the main matter* then: and I believe you will find your relief, if not your release, from your present trial, by thinking less about its influence upon your person and your business and your prospects and your children, and more about how, if it be rightly used and truly sanctified, it may bless you as nothing else can do and glorify your life by making you patient and bringing out of you what is most manly and Christlike in you.

II. *The remedy*—this is the second point—the remedy is as plainly prescribed, as is the difficulty pointed out. The remedy is this—the soul, or the keeping of it, is to be committed to God. Every heart is to be garrisoned by the Holy Spirit. The inmost man, the spiritual life, the source and center of the new creation, has to be handed over to God that He may preserve and protect. Beloved, you should not need to be persuaded to this. The task is too great for you.

> Myself I cannot save,
> Myself I cannot keep:
> But strength in Thee I surely have,
> Whose eyelids never sleep.

No one can accept the responsibility for you—none but the faithful Creator. No forms and ceremonies will suffice, neither are feelings sufficient or efficient; there must be a handing over of the soul in all its perplexity and its persecution, and the trouble that these bring—there must be a handing over of the soul to God. This means definite surrender. This means *an absolute disposal of the soul to God.* This means a committal of the manhood in its triple nature—body, soul, and spirit—to the three-one God, even as we had it in our prayer just now. My beloved hearer, are you prepared for this? Have you done this? Or, having done it, are you prepared to do it yet again?

> My body, soul, and spirit,
> Jesus, I give to Thee:
> A consecrated offering,
> Thine evermore to be.

There are a great many things we do not know—there are some things we cannot know; but "I know in whom I have believed, and am persuaded that he is able to keep that which I have committed unto him against that day." Persecution, tribulation, of every sort—let them do their best or their worst; my soul is beyond the reach of harm—I have committed it to God. My spiritual life is not in my own keeping: else, indeed, it would be an easy prey to its multitude of enemies. But it is in the keeping of the pierced hands; it is in the keeping of Jehovah's palms; and none can pluck away the sheep for whom Christ Jesus died.

Now this committal of the soul to God, though it has been definitely and distinctly done, should, I think, be *constantly repeated.* It may be that the committal can never be again quite what it was at first. There is not quite the same meaning as there was originally. But I am not one of those who holds that the thing, having been done, there should be entirely left. The vow is registered above, and there is, in one sense, no need for another vow; but will it not be well for a repetition of the same vow?

> High heaven that heard that solemn vow,
> That vow renewed shall daily hear.

It will be for our good, and perhaps for God's own gratification, to hear us pledge ourselves again and again and yet again as to our absolute dependence upon Him, as to our complete surrender to His love and will. Ah, that is what is wrong with some of you. The vow has been forgotten—I will not say that it has been broken. But you have not repeated it; you have not renewed it; you have not brought it up to date; you have not uttered it in the presence of God's people; you have not paid your vows now in the presence of His people. I pray you here and now, just where you sit and as I speak to you, let your hearts go out and up to Him, and say, "Lord, I am Thine—save me. I am Thy servant; I am Thy servant; and the son of Thine handmaid. Thou hast loosed my bonds: my soul is in Thy keeping. I need not fear; I will not be afraid—what can man do unto me?"

But when this committal has been truly made, and as often as it is repeated, it must be, *it must be relied on.* That is not exactly what I mean; I do not know whether I can find the exact word to describe my meaning. But oh, how necessary it is that, having in so many words committed the keeping of the soul to God, we should act as if we believed that we had thus committed it, and that He had accepted the committal. That is the point. We are to act and live according to this vow, and as if we were assured, as indeed we may be, that the vow has been registered on high, and has met with God's approval and acceptance. Do not you know what I mean? I think you do by sad experience. You have joined in the committal of your soul to God, and then you forget you have done it. Then you forget—and it involves this—you forget that God is pledged to see you through. It is useless making vows after that fashion. It is mere mockery to hand oneself over, and then take oneself back again. It is ridiculous, to say the least, to say, "Lord, I entrust myself to Thee," and then find oneself as fretful and as careful and anxious as ever. We are eating our own words, we are contradicting ourselves, in so doing. I pray you, *do as you have said:* having done it, believe that it is done. Believe that the Lord takes you at your word; believe that you have taken Him at His; believe that the contract is settled, sealed, and signed; believe that He will keep the feet of His saints, and that, even when persecution of the fiercest rages and flames, His grace will be sufficient for you.

When you come to think of it, is it not quite childish to act as we so often act? The little one is laughed at, not blamed, because, having planted a bush, it goes occasionally to see how it is getting on, and pulls it up by the roots. That is just what we do, and we are much more to blame than the little ones. Oh, if you have yielded yourself to God, God has accepted you; the sacred trust will never be forgotten. And this tree which you have planted is to be judged, not by its roots, but by its fruits; and it will have no fruits, unless you let it grow. Be restful, be trustful, be confident: so will you be fruitful and victorious.

At the same time, beloved, this does not absolve us from *the duty of watchfulness and holiness*. It is "in well doing" that we are to commit the keeping of our souls to Him. His angels have charge concerning us, so long as we are found in His ways. You must not wonder if there is an explosion, if you, who carry so many sparks in your bosom, go where the gunpowder is stored. I pray you, be watchful, be careful, for all depends upon yourself. This is God's way of keeping your soul. The work is His, but *the watchfulness is yours*. "Let none of you suffer as a murderer, or as a thief, or as an evildoer"—do you think these sins can never be chargeable to you? Ah, but you may be a murderer, or a thief, or an evildoer, without slaying your fellow man, or purloining his treasure, or laying yourself open to the law of the land. There are sins of word, as well as sins of hand: and it is very striking that the apostle Paul includes in this list such a matter as being a busybody in other men's affairs. Ah, you may well expect persecution, if you do that. If you will put your finger in the pie, you expect to get it burned. Do not interfere with other people's affairs, or you cannot expect God to keep your soul in His hand. Moreover, it is only as you walk before Him in all holiness that He will keep your soul as in the hollow of His hand.

III. And this the third and closing point. I refer you to the name, *the name and nature of Him to whom this solemn committal is to be made.* "... as unto a faithful Creator." Did it ever strike you as not a little remarkable, that God should be called by that name in this connection? It is the only time, if I remember rightly, that it appears in the New Testament: and why just here? Why not commit our souls unto the great Jehovah who rides upon the heavens? Or why not commit our souls unto the Father, by whose Spirit we have been taught to call Him "Abba"? Does He not care for our souls, for He is the Father of spirits? Or why should you not commit your soul unto your Savior? He who bled for you, lives for you; He who died for you, pleads for you. Why is not the sweet name of Friend introduced here, or the still sweeter name, if sweeter can be, of Comforter? Commit your souls unto the Holy Ghost, who will quicken and keep and illuminate and comfort them. All of these, or any of these, might have been used, and we think they would have been suitable. But the Holy Spirit Himself taught Peter to say, "Commit your souls unto him, as unto a faithful Creator." Ah, here again, the greater term includes the less. Who is the Creator? Father, Son, and Holy Ghost. They were all engaged in the work of creation, were they not? If you commit your souls to the Creator then, it is, as Mr. Olney had it in his prayer, for which we thank God, *the committal of the three-one nature to the three-one God:* body, soul, and spirit are given over to the keeping of Father, Son, and Holy Ghost.

Then, as I am trying to show you, there is a great deal here about the suffering of the frame. The fire has come upon it to burn it, the sword has been drawn from its sheath and has cut it: and there have been other things that have marred and maimed the frame. Well, says the apostle, "Commit your soul to the keeping of this faithful Creator." He that made it, knows how to keep it; He that made your heart, knows how to comfort it. Whatever is your distress, and whatever particular portion of your frame and being it affects, He is acquainted with it. Here I am: foot, heart, mind, soul, body, all; He knows all about it, for was He not the Creator and Maker of it? He who made it, can mend it. Commit the keeping of your soul to the Creator.

Then, I think it was in view of *the soul's needs*—for, as I told you, these are paramount and preeminent—that the apostle said, "Commit your souls to the Creator." For I fancy he had in mind the fact, that the God who created the universe and the world created us in Christ Jesus. There is such a thing as the new creation, which transcends the miracle of the creation of the world from nothing. Well, says the apostle, your soul is likely to suffer under this persecution. It may become hardened; its best aspirations may become damped. There are a thousand perils for the soul, arising from these perplexities and persecutions and tribulations. Well, just yield your soul to the Creator. He made you what you are. By the grace of God, you are what you are. He begat in you those holy aspirations that you are now so fearful about—He will not let them be quenched if you will entrust Him with the keeping of them. All your spiritual life has sprung from Him—well then, commend it to Him; He will keep it.

> The love that lit the torch of life
> Will keep it burning still.

And the graces that are from God will be revived and strengthened, as Father, Son, and Holy Ghost step forward. As in the days of the creation of the world, and as in the day when you were born again, they will step forward and work in you anew—the love, the grace, the hope, the patience, the joy, the faith, and all the other virtues persecution and tribulation are cutting at the root of: but which, thank God, must live, because the trees of the Lord are full of sap. That is it. Commit the keeping of your soul unto Him, "as unto a faithful Creator."

And there is just this other word; it is the greatest and grandest argument of all. *He is "faithful."* Ah yes, you would not like to give your soul up to one whose faithfulness you had a doubt about. You are very chary about giving your treasures up to others to take care of them, whose honesty you question. When you go away for your holiday, you will see to it that those who are put in charge are trustworthy. Well, He is the "faithful Creator." There is no promise-keeper like the Lord; there is no bank like the bank of faith, for God Himself is the manager of it. Put your souls into His keeping. Oh that I could induce you to do it! Come, ere we close; and ere you give of your substance to the Lord, will you take that which is more precious than your gold and silver: take this life, this spiritual life of yours, and hand it to Him. See, He seems to me to hold His hand out for it. Here, Lord, I come—it is all that I can do; and Thou wilt care for me, and keep me, till the day of Thine appearing. The Lord bless His truth! For Christ's sake. Amen.

Bibliography

Fullerton, W. Y. *Thomas Spurgeon: A Biography*. London: Hodder and Stoughton, 1919.

Hayden, Eric W. *A History of Spurgeon's Tabernacle*. Pasadena, Tex.: Pilgrim, 1971.

Spurgeon, Thomas. *Down to the Sea: Sixteen Sea Sermons*. London: Passmore and Alabaster, 1895.

______. *"God Save the King!" Addresses Concerning King Jesus*. London: Passmore and Alabaster, 1902.

______. *The Gospel of the Grace of God*. London: Passmore and Alabaster, 1884.

______. *Light and Love: A Series of Sermons*. London: Stockwell, 1897.

______. *"My Gospel": Twelve Addresses*. The Baptist Pulpit, vol. 23. London: Stockwell, 1902.

______. *Sermons Preached in the Metropolitan Tabernacle*. London: Stockwell, 1897–1902.

9

W. H. Griffith Thomas

(1861–1924)

When William Henry Griffith Thomas died in Duluth, Minnesota, on 2 June 1924, the religious press in both America and England paid tribute. In the *Sunday School Times* for 21 June 1924 W. Graham Scroggie wrote: "By the passing of Dr. Thomas the Christian Church has lost a scholar and teacher. . . . I can with utmost confidence say that the reading of Dr. Thomas's books creates in one a deeper love of and desire for God as is revealed in His Word, and that is more than can be said of much which the Christian press of today is turning out." (Scroggie should have seen some of the books being published now!)

R. A. Torrey wrote in the 5 July issue of the same publication: "The first thing that impressed me about Dr. Thomas was his sound, wide, thorough, sane, well-balanced scholarship. His interpretations of Scripture were always scholarly and dependable. . . . Along with his scholarship and his clearness of vision there went a very unusual ability to state profound truth with a clearness and a simplicity to which very few attain."

James M. Gray, president of Moody Bible Institute at the time, wrote in the 28 June issue: "Many will speak of Dr. Thomas as an author, editor, preacher, and expositor; but I should like to say a word about him as a contender for 'the faith which was once for all delivered unto the saints.' He had a great advantage there in his broad knowledge and his early experience as an evangelical leader in the Anglican church before he came to this country."

Griffith Thomas had no advantages in childhood or early manhood. From the beginning, circumstances seemed to be against him. Yet in the furnace of affliction and on the battlefield of life, God made him a great man. His mother had been widowed before he was born on 2 January 1861 in Oswestry, Shropshire. He spent his early years with his grandfather William Griffith. His mother married again, but family financial pressure forced young Will to leave school when only fourteen. In later years he was recognized throughout the English-speaking world as a brilliant educator, teacher, and writer; yet his own education was obtained with the greatest difficulty and sacrifice.

When he was sixteen, he was asked to teach a Sunday school class at Holy Trinity Church in Oswestry. Not yet a professed believer, he thought he was volunteering for the choir! For four months he did his best, but he found it impossible to teach something he had never experienced. God used the witness of two young men in the church to bring him to salvation on 23 March 1878. "When I awoke the next morning," he related, "my soul was simply overflowing with joy, and since then I have never doubted that it was on that Saturday night I was born again, converted to God."

He moved to London in 1879 and worked in his uncle's office. From 10:30 p.m. to 2:30 a.m. he devoted himself to serious study, a discipline that made him a scholar. He always admonished his students to devote themselves to reading and thinking no matter what price had to be paid. His vicar, the Rev. B. Oswald Sharp, offered him a lay curacy in 1882. This enabled him to attend morning lectures at King's College in London while fulfilling his pastoral responsibilities during the afternoons and evenings. He earned his A.K.C. (Associate of King's College) degree and was ordained in 1885. At that service the bishop of London, Frederick Temple, admonished him never to neglect his Greek New Testament for a single day. (We wonder how seriously a young minister today would take that admonition.) "G. T." kept his promise to Bishop Temple by reading a chapter each day the rest of his life.

After three and a half years as curate of the church in London, Griffith Thomas accepted a curacy at St. Aldate's Church, Oxford.

While there he earned his B.D. in 1895 at the university, again as the result of disciplined study and the wise investment of early and late hours. When I visited the Bodleian Library in Oxford, I thought of Griffith Thomas studying there, hiding in a special corner known only to the rector, the beloved Canon Christopher. The canon, a kind, spiritual man and a great soul-winner, was failing in health and becoming deaf. Consequently much of the parish work fell to Griffith Thomas, who entered into it with as much zest as he did his Greek studies. He preached often, led the Sunday school, managed the various parish organizations, and did a thorough job of visitation. He was a scholar, but never in the slightest degree a recluse. Both young and old loved him, and he had a particular love for them.

About this time the larger fellowship of the Anglican church began to notice him. I have in my file a copy of the *Record* for Friday, 17 January 1896, which includes a full report of the Islington Clerical Meeting held the preceding Tuesday. The vicar of Islington, Dr. Barlow, had invited the young curate to read a paper on the doctrine of the church, the first young assistant thus to be honored. "Mr. Thomas treated his subject popularly," the *Record* reported, "and he received the cordial recognition and praise of the entire Meeting." The great scholar Handley C. G. Moule, later the bishop of Durham, was also on the program; so young Griffith Thomas was in good company.

Later that year Griffith Thomas accepted a call to St. Paul's, Portman Square, now devoted almost entirely to small hotels and business offices. St. Paul's Church today is located a few blocks from its original site.

Scholar that he was, Griffith Thomas did not make the mistake of trying to build his ministry on bookish sermons. He depended on prayer as well as careful preparation. The church conducted six prayer meetings each week! To be sure, there were a multitude of organizations within the church. They even had an orchestra society and a cycling club. (Griffith Thomas, a cycling enthusiast, was such a big man that his bicycle had to be specially made.) The main meetings of the church emphasized the study of the Word. Most of Griffith Thomas's later expository books grew out of these early Bible classes. To learn his philosophy of Bible study, read *Methods of Bible Study*, published originally in 1902 and recently reprinted. For his views on preaching and pastoral work, read *The Work of the Ministry* (reprinted as *Ministerial Life and Work*).

In October 1905 Griffith Thomas was named principal of Wycliffe Hall, Oxford, the center of ministerial training for evangelical

Anglicans. During his five years there he was the pastor, teacher, and friend of more than eighty students. He also conducted a weekly Greek New Testament reading at the university on Sunday afternoons. Attending one of these meetings were undergraduates T. E. Lawrence (Lawrence of Arabia) and his two brothers. During the years at Oxford Griffith Thomas earned his doctor's degree (D.D.Oxon). His dissertation was titled "A Sacrament of Our Redemption." Also during those years he began to minister at the British Keswick Convention. He was also busy writing, editing, and taking a leading part in church affairs that affected evangelicals.

He and his family moved in 1910 to Toronto, where he joined the faculty of Wycliffe College, having been persuaded that a wider ministry would be his in Canada. Originally he had been invited to serve as professor of systematic theology, but when he arrived, he discovered that one of the local graduates had been given the position instead! A lesser man would have resigned and returned to England. But Griffith Thomas believed so strongly that God had called him to Canada that he remained and taught Old Testament literature and exegesis for nine years. The students were the losers in that nobody in the Anglican church at that time surpassed Griffith Thomas in teaching biblical theology. It was largely by this means, however, that he became known in both North America and many other parts of the world. When approached to return to an English parish, he replied, "But now a continent is my parish!"

In 1919 the family moved to Philadelphia, and Griffith Thomas carried on an extensive conference and writing ministry. He joined with Lewis Sperry Chafer and Alex B. Winchester in founding Dallas Theological Seminary. He was to have served as a visiting lecturer and later as a faculty member, but his untimely death in 1924 intervened. Today his library continues its ministry to the hundreds of students at the school, however, and his memory is also kept green through the annual W. H. Griffith Thomas Memorial Lectures.

Today we know W. H. Griffith Thomas primarily from the printed page. Add every one of his books to your library. Begin with his great commentaries on Genesis and Romans. Unfortunately some of his best books have gone out of print, including *The Apostle John, The Apostle Peter,* and *Christianity Is Christ.* Still available are his masterly Stone Lectures, presented at Princeton Theological Seminary in 1913, on *The Holy Spirit of God* and his commentary on the Epistle to the Hebrews, *"Let Us Go On."* You do not have to be Anglican to appreciate *The Principles of Theology* and *The Catholic Faith,* both published in London by Vine Books (formerly Church Book Room Press), which plans to issue new editions of as many of his books as possible. *The Prayers of St. Paul* is a devotional gem, as is *Grace and Power.* He published twenty-six booklets and twenty-four larger works, a tremendous accomplishment for a man who began his career with severe educational limitations.

Griffith Thomas's daughter, Winifred G. T. Gillespie, has also edited and issued posthumously several volumes of her father's unpublished material: *Outline Studies in the Gospel of Matthew, Outline Studies in the Gospel of Luke, Outline Studies in the Acts of the Apostles, Through the Pentateuch Chapter by Chapter*, and *Studies in Colossians and Philemon.* She is now working on notes he used at Toronto in his course on Old Testament introduction.

Griffith Thomas's advice to young preachers was: "Think yourself empty, read yourself full, write yourself clear, pray yourself keen—then enter the pulpit and let yourself go!" He practiced this counsel himself, becoming a first-rank evangelical scholar and preacher, always keenly alert to encroachments of both modernism and ritualism. Academic achievement did not come without sacrifice, but then it rarely does. He dedicated and applied himself, and the Lord did the rest. His books are exposition at its best—sound exegesis, pastoral concern, clear outlining, practical application, relevance to the needs of the day. He did not attempt to be sensational; he wanted only to be biblical. Griffith Thomas was a rare blend of spirituality and scholarship, a true "pastor-teacher."

"We cannot make up for failure in our devotional life by redoubling energy in service," he wrote. "As water never rises above its level, so what we do never rises above what we are. . . . We shall never take people one hair's breadth beyond our own spiritual attainment. We may point to higher things, we may 'allure to brighter worlds,' but . . . we shall only take them as far as we ourselves have gone." In other words, the pastor must be both a man of God and a student. If he is careless in either his praying or his studying, he cannot enjoy God's blessing. One of his students at Wycliffe Hall, G. R. Harding Wood, wrote in the 29 December 1960 issue of *Life of Faith:* "One was conscious that all his work, especially his teaching, was steeped in prayer; and it was the same in the more intimate talks about personal problems. . . . He truly walked with God, and made that spiritual exercise something to be coveted and practiced." Can a man be both saint and scholar, a man of books and a man of *the* Book? W. H. Griffith Thomas is convincing proof that one can—if one is willing to pay the price.

Knowing and Showing

> And he said, The God of our fathers hath chosen thee, that thou shouldest know his will, and see the Just One, and shouldest hear the voice of his mouth. For thou shalt be his witness unto all men of what thou hast seen and heard. **Acts 22:14**

When Saul of Tarsus was met on the way to Damascus by the Lord Jesus Christ, he asked two questions: "Who art thou, Lord?" and "What wilt thou, Lord?" The first question referred to a desire for a personal knowledge of the One who had appeared to him; the second expressed readiness to do His will.

These two questions which were thus closely connected at the time of the conversion of St. Paul, were inseparably associated with the rest of his life on earth. So must it be with the life of every Christian. The first step in the Christian life is to be followed by a lifelong relationship to the One who has revealed Himself to us. The second of these two questions, "What shall I do, Lord?" according to the version in this chapter, practically sums up everything from the moment of conversion onwards. It was in the lifelong willingness to know and to do what Jesus should reveal to him that the apostle Paul found the secret of peace and power, of satisfaction and of service. Surely this message has a special bearing upon the gatherings of this week. What does Keswick mean? It means the Christian life in its fullness of power, of privilege, of responsibility. It means that we have come up here to learn more deeply what it means to be a Christian, whether from the standpoint of character or of conduct, of privilege or of responsibility, of life or of service. I desire to take this text as giving to us some at least of the reasons why we are gathering at Keswick, and as revealing some of the aspects of that Christian life which we desire to study afresh.

First of all, we have here the *divine purpose*. The God of our fathers has appointed us to know His will. This is the divine purpose for every one of us—to know His will. The will of God is the first and last thing in His revelation to us. To know and to do the will of God is everything. In the Psalms we hear the coming Messiah using these words: "Lo, I come to do Thy will, O my God."

Author's note: Thomas's sermon "Knowing and Showing" is from Herbert F. Stevenson, ed., *Keswick's Authentic Voice*, pp. 325–31 and is used by permission. He preached it in St. John's Church, Keswick, on the opening Sunday of the Keswick Convention in 1907.

When God would describe the ideal man, it is in these words: "A man after mine own heart, who shall fulfil all my will." When we think of that model prayer for all disciples in all generations, the culminating point of the first part, which has to do with the divine glory and purpose, is, "Thy will be done." If we are concerned with the salvation of mankind, we read, "It is not the will of your heavenly Father that one of these little ones should perish." "God willeth all men to be saved, and to come to the full knowledge of the truth." If we are concerned about the sanctification of the believer, "This is the will of God, your sanctification." And if, looking forward to the future, we think of the home above, we at once recall the words of the Master, "Father, I will that they may be with me where I am." So that in everything, and from all points of view, to know God's will is everything. The will of God—it gives joy, it gives dignity, it gives power, it gives glory to life. When we realize that everything in our daily affairs is included, in some way or other, in the will of God, what inspiration it gives us for what we are accustomed to call the most trivial and common of our duties.

Teach me, my God and King,
In all things Thee to see,
And what I do in anything,
To do it as to Thee;
A servant, with this clause,
Makes drudgery divine,
Who sweeps a room as for Thy laws,
Makes that and th' action fine.

We have been singing "Thy will be done"; but there is one note running through that exquisite and beautiful hymn which is untrue, in the sense of being inadequate in its teaching concerning the will of God. We remember the sufferings of the authoress, and we know that for her the will of God was expressed in suffering. But the will of God is for action, as well as for suffering. There is no need for us to wait for that "happier shore" before we *sing* "Thy will be done." We may sing it here and now, as we pray here and now, not merely "Thy will be suffered," but "Thy will be done."

God's purpose, then, is that we should know His will. What a startling lesson and revelation this must have been to Saul of Tarsus. To know His will? Surely he knew it. The Jew, the scholar, the leader, the member of the Sanhedrin—did he not know God's will? And yet this humble disciple Ananias comes to him and speaks of "the God of our fathers." Saul had been on the wrong tack. He thought he knew God's will; but he did not. And there are many today who are just in his position. They have been professing Christians, it may be, for years; they have prided themselves on their knowledge, their orthodoxy, their churchmanship, on their standing among their fellows. And yet all the while they have not known His will! It may be—yea, it shall be—that this week there will be a revelation of God's will to such, which will come with all the startling features of a perfect surprise. "Except ye become like little children," that is the condition for knowing His will. Like Naaman we say, "Behold, I thought"; and that is where we make our mistake. "I thought Christianity was so-and-so; I thought that the evangelical doctrine of Christian holiness was such and such a thing; I thought that church membership was such and such a thing; I thought that Christian life, and work, and preaching, and practice, in the pulpit and parish, were such and such things." "Behold, I thought!" And this week will come with its revelation. "The God of our fathers has appointed" many of us this week to know His will. Before next Friday night is passed there will be scores and hundreds who will know God's will as they have never known it before. The divine purpose will have come into our life.

Second, the *divine plan:* to see the righteous One, and hear the voice of His mouth. For the realization of the divine purpose, this was the divine plan. First, personal contact with Jesus Christ—to see the righteous One. The sight of Jesus Christ was to be everything to Saul of Tarsus all through his life. But will you notice in what respect Saul was to see Him? To see Him as the righteous One. What is this sight of Jesus as the righteous One? You will remember that on the eve of His crucifixion our blessed Lord told the disciples that the Spirit was coming to convict the world of righteousness, "because I go to the Father." The world's impression of Jesus Christ at that time was that He was an "unrighteous" One, and they put Him to death. They were determined to believe that He was unrighteous, a blasphemer, and so they rejected Him. But God raised Him from the dead, and He would not have been allowed to go to the Father had He been other than righteous. So He said that the world should be convicted of sin because "I go to the Father."

And Saul of Tarsus was convicted of that very thing. "I am Jesus of Nazareth, whom thou persecutest." If the voice had said, "I am the Son of God whom thou persecutest," Saul would have been able to say, "I never persecuted Him!" So the word came, "I am Jesus of Nazareth"—that hated word—"whom thou persecutest." Jesus of Nazareth was thus revealed to be with the Father, and therefore, righteous.

That righteous One—this is only another way of saying "the Lord our Righteousness." Personal contact with Christ as "the Lord our Righteousness" is still God's plan for the life of every one of us. The sight of that Lord, our righteousness—it purifies; the sight of the Lord, our righteousness—it sanctifies; the sight of the Lord, our righteousness—it qualifies; the sight of the Lord, our righteousness—it glorifies. I wonder whether this is true of everyone here? Have we all had a vision of the Lord as our righteousness—our righteousness for a guilty past, our righteousness for a sin-stained present, our righteousness in view of a perfect future?

> Jesus, Thy blood and righteousness
> My beauty are, my glorious dress;
> 'Midst flaming worlds, in these arrayed,
> With joy shall I lift up my head.

To see the righteous One: I have no doubt whatever that during this week there will be many who will see the righteous One. They will see Him, perhaps, first of all for their justification, and they will see Him also for their sanctification.

See Him for their justification. And yet someone says, "Surely that is not why people come to Keswick!" No, but I am perfectly certain that there are those who come to Keswick for the second step of sanctification who have never taken the first step, that of justification. You and I will never learn a single lesson about sanctification unless, first of all, we know the Lord our righteousness for justification. Romans 3 and 4 must come before 6–8. That is the gateway—justification, not sanctification; not justification through sanctification, but the opposite; sanctification through justification, through the vision of the Lord our righteousness.

But a part of the plan was also a personal communication from Jesus Christ—not only to see that righteous One, but to "hear the voice of his mouth." What a blow to the pride of Saul of Tarsus this must have been—to hear the voice of His mouth, the voice of the One of Nazareth, the One whom he had been persecuting: to hear the voice of God's will, the word from His mouth. There were more things in heaven and earth than were dreamed of in Saul's philosophy that morning on his way to Damascus. God had a new way of revealing His will; Saul was to "hear the word from his mouth." And so it must be today. Doubtless we shall hear, this week, many a word of Christ through His servants. But this will not suffice. We must hear the voice of *His* mouth; we must have contact with Christ through His Word; we must come face to face with Christ direct, and hear the voice of God speaking by the Holy Spirit. We shall probably hear it in the tent; we shall hear it as we come to the services and celebrations in this church this week. We shall hear it in our own rooms. We shall hear it, it may be, at the lakeside, or on the hillside. But wherever we are, Keswick will fail for us if we do not hear the voice of His mouth. The vision and the voice of the Lord this week—this is the divine plan for the realization of the divine purpose.

Third, the *divine project:* "For thou shalt be his witness unto all men of what thou hast seen and heard." This is the culminating point. The purpose and the plan lead up to this project. What does it mean? "Thou shalt be his witness." Not a judge. Saul had been attempting the work of a judge, and the issue was disaster. Not an echo, vague, empty, and practically useless; not a philosopher, not even a theologian; but a witness. This is the meaning of Keswick this week. Everything that God says to us, everything that God gives to us, is for the purpose of witnessing to Christ, rendering our testimony to Him. There is scarcely any other word in the New Testament more frequently used than this word *witness* to express what the Christian has to be and to do.

A witness—one who has direct knowledge; a witness—one who has personal experience; a witness—one who speaks and lives with the knowledge of experience, truthfully, frankly, fearlessly always. Are we parents? We must be witnesses. Our authority as parents will fail in proportion as we are without the authority of the witness. Are we teachers? We shall teach with authority when we teach as the result of our personal experience. Are we writers? Our pens must be dipped in our personal experience. The reason why so many books today upon the Bible and theological subjects are dry, dull, unprofitable and unconvincing, is that they have no note of personal testimony behind the aspects of truth they bring forward. Are we philosophers—has God given to us powers for thinking, and writing, and speaking? Our philosophy will be as nothing unless it is based upon personal experience. Are we leaders in church or state? Has God given us great gifts of organization? Everything will count for nothing except so far as all our life is permeated with the glow of a personal experience.

"Thou shalt be his witness." Where? "Unto all men." Our first witness will be in our home. Those who are nearest and dearest to us will be watching us, and scanning us more closely than ever when we go down from Keswick. They will want to know what Keswick has been to us, and what the Lord Jesus has been to us; whether we have had the vision, whether we have heard the voice.

Then we shall have to witness in our church. I should not be at all surprised if many a sermon next Sunday in parish churches and elsewhere will be transformed as the result of the vision this week. We shall have to declare that which God has done for our soul; and whether in preaching, or in parish organization, or in our methods of church life and work, this great personal testimony to Christ must run through everything.

It may be we shall have to witness in the town in which we live, on behalf of morality, social righteousness, municipal purity. And I am perfectly certain that to some the "all men" of my text will be realized in foreign missionary work, and this will be primarily the work of witnessing. Not only the work of teaching and training, but of witnessing to all men of those things of which we have heard and seen. And the power of this is incalculable. The power of personal testimony—it is a power to *ourselves*. St. Paul was telling this story in Jerusalem a good many years after his vision, but the facts were coming back to him as fresh and fragrant as ever. So it will be with us as we look back. And although five, ten, twenty, thirty years after our conversion, we shall not be living merely on that, we shall be glad to go back to the foundation and to the facts of personal experience, and find in them the promise of everything in our Christian life. We shall be able to say, "I know whom I have believed." As we tell the story of what God has been all through those years, our own faith will be strengthened, our confidence rooted and grounded in Christ: and, in spite of all temptations to doubt and despair, we shall look up to Him and say:

> Whoso hath felt the Spirit of the Highest,
> Cannot confound, nor doubt Him, nor deny;
> Yea, with one voice, O world, though thou deniest,
> Stand thou on that side, for on this am I.

And the power of it to *others*. It is an unanswerable argument for Christianity, the testimony of personal experience. Paul was in Jerusalem among his old friends. He had a great crowd around him. "Now is the opportunity for ability, thought, eloquence?" No, nothing of the kind; but for a personal witness of what Jesus Christ had been to him. There is no greater foe to Christianity today than mere profession. There is no greater discredit to Christianity today than to stand up for it, and yet not to live it in our lives. There is no greater danger in the Christian world today than to stand up for the Bible, and yet to deny that Bible by the very way we defend it. There is no greater hindrance to Christianity today than to contend for orthodoxy, whatever the orthodoxy may be, and to deny it by the censoriousness, the hardness, the unattractiveness with which we champion our cause.

Oh, this power of personal testimony—with the heart filled with the love of Christ, the mind saturated with the teaching of Christ, the conscience sensitive to the law of Christ, the whole nature aglow with the grace and love of our Lord Jesus Christ! This is God's purpose; this is God's plan for us.

Not happiness but holiness, not happiness but helpfulness, is the keynote of Keswick this week. And when holiness and helpfulness are realized, then happiness must of necessity come. So it is for us to know, to see, to hear, and then to show. Are we doing this? There are people in the world around us who never open, who never read this Book. But they are reading us. Are they able to see God in our lives? Are they able to say of us to others, "That man"—or that woman—"reminds me of Christ"? Do we let our light so shine that men may see, not us, but our Father, our Savior in us; and glorify, not us, but our Father in heaven? This is the real test of a gathering like this. So let us live in the presence of God; let us surrender ourselves to the Christ of God; let us keep very close to the Word of God; let us welcome into our hearts the grace of God; let us seek the fullness of the Spirit of God: and then live evermore to the glory of God.

Bibliography

Clark, M. Guthrie. *William Henry Griffith Thomas.* London: Church Book Room, 1949.

Stevenson, Herbert F., ed. *Keswick's Authentic Voice: 65 Dynamic Addresses Delivered at the Keswick Convention, 1875–1957.* Grand Rapids: Zondervan, 1959.

Thomas, W. H. Griffith. *The Apostle John: Studies in His Life and Writings.* Philadelphia: Sunday School Times, 1923. Reprinted—Grand Rapids: Eerdmans, 1953.

———. *The Apostle Peter: Outline Studies in His Life, Character, and Writings.* New York: Revell, 1904. Reprinted—Grand Rapids: Eerdmans, 1946.

———. *The Catholic Faith: A Manual of Instruction for Members of the Church of England.* London: Hodder and Stoughton, 1905. Reprinted—London: Church Book Room, 1952.

———. *Christianity Is Christ.* The Anglican Church Handbooks, edited by W. H. Griffith Thomas. London: Longmans, 1909. Reprinted—Grand Rapids: Eerdmans, 1955.

———. *Genesis.* 3 vols. A Devotional Commentary, edited by A. R.

Buckland. London: R.T.S., 1907–1908. Reprinted—Grand Rapids: Eerdmans, 1946.

———. *Grace and Power: Some Aspects of the Spiritual Life.* New York: Revell, 1916. Reprinted—Grand Rapids: Eerdmans, 1949.

———. *The Holy Spirit of God.* London: Longmans, 1913. Reprinted—Grand Rapids: Eerdmans, 1955.

———. *"Let Us Go On": The Secret of Christian Progress in the Epistle to the Hebrews.* London: Morgan and Scott, 1923. Reprinted—*Hebrews: A Devotional Commentary.* Grand Rapids: Eerdmans, n.d.

———. *Methods of Bible Study.* London: Marshall, 1902. Reprinted—Rev. ed. Chicago: Moody, 1975.

———. *Outline Studies in the Acts of the Apostles.* Edited by Winifred G. T. Gillespie. Grand Rapids: Eerdmans, 1956.

———. *Outline Studies in the Gospel of Luke.* Edited by Winifred G. T. Gillespie. Grand Rapids: Eerdmans, 1950.

———. *Outline Studies in the Gospel of Matthew.* Edited by Winifred G. T. Gillespie. Grand Rapids: Eerdmans, 1961.

———. *The Prayers of St. Paul.* The Short Course Series, edited by John Adams. Edinburgh: Clark, 1914.

———. *The Principles of Theology: An Introduction to the Thirty-Nine Articles.* London: Longmans, 1930. Reprinted—Grand Rapids: Baker, 1979.

———. *St. Paul's Epistle to the Romans: A Devotional Commentary.* Grand Rapids: Eerdmans, 1946.

———. *Studies in Colossians and Philemon.* Edited by Winifred G. T. Gillespie. Grand Rapids: Baker, 1973.

———. *Through the Pentateuch Chapter by Chapter.* Edited by Winifred G. T. Gillespie. Grand Rapids: Eerdmans, 1957.

———. *The Work of the Ministry.* London: Hodder and Stoughton, 1911. Reprinted—*Ministerial Life and Work.* Grand Rapids: Baker, 1976.

10

John Henry Jowett

(1864–1923)

If someone should erect a Sunday school teachers' hall of fame, he must enshrine J. W. T. Dewhirst of Halifax, Yorkshire. Dewhirst said to one of his pupils, "I had always hoped that you would go into the ministry." The pupil did, and he became "the greatest preacher in the English-speaking world." His name was John Henry Jowett.

Born on 25 August 1864 into a middle-class Christian home, Jowett planned to be a lawyer and perhaps enter politics. But two people strongly influenced him to enter the ministry: his mother and his pastor, Enoch Mellor. "At my mother's knee," he often said, "I gained my sweetest inspirations."

Mellor had come to the Square Road Congregational Church, Halifax, in 1847. The membership grew so large that they had to erect a new building. From 1861 to 1867 Mellor ministered in Glasgow. But in 1867 he returned to Halifax and served another fourteen years. During that second term young Jowett came under his godly influence. The lad never met the pastor personally, but he nevertheless idolized him and listened attentively to his preaching. In later years Jowett modeled his own preaching after that of his boyhood pastor. "He was the finest platform orator it was ever my fortune to hear," he admitted. "Square Church was to me a very fountain of life, and I owe to its spiritual training more than I can ever express."

Jowett concentrated on his education from 1882 to 1889. He attended Airedale College, of which A. M. Fairbairn was principal, and also Edinburgh University. At that time the city of Edinburgh was enjoying the ministries of some of the great preachers—Alexander Whyte, George Matheson, and Henry Drummond, to name but a few. What a place for study and for preaching!

Jowett's first church was St. James's Congregational at Newcastle-on-Tyne. He began his ministry in October 1889 and was ordained on 19 November. The building seated more than a thousand. The young preacher responded to this challenge with faith and courage. During his six-year ministry there, he always preached to large crowds. In fact Jowett drew crowds throughout his lifetime. The great R. W. Dale died on 13 March 1895, leaving vacant the influential pulpit of Carr's Lane Church, Birmingham. The church officers turned immediately to John Henry Jowett, and on 6 October 1895 he began his ministry there. Many had predicted that Carr's Lane would die with Dale, but their predictions proved false. Not only did Jowett help save the church, but the church helped save Jowett.

The young pastor, overwhelmed by his new responsibilities, read everything Dale had written. Dale, a massive intellect, preached Bible doctrine with clarity and passion. His books are still worth reading: *The Atonement, The Living Christ and the Four Gospels, Christian Doctrine, The Jewish Temple and the Church,* to name several. As Jowett assimilated these books, he confronted the great themes and texts of the Bible. In his first sermon as pastor of Carr's Lane Church, Jowett said: "This pulpit has never been belittled by the petty treatment of small and vulgar themes." He determined to preach the great truths of the Word (what he liked to call "the fat texts"). This determination motivated his ministry for the rest of his life. "The grace of God" became his central theme.

His church officers made it easy for their new pastor to preach well. They relieved him of the many details of church administration that can rob a pastor of precious hours needed for study and meditation. They were rewarded, for the church prospered in every way. A. T. Pierson once called Carr's Lane Church "the greatest church in the world." During his ministry at Carr's Lane,

Jowett was elected chairman of the Congregational Union and president of the National Council of Evangelical Free Churches. He was quite young, but he wore the honors with distinction. He received as many as thirty invitations a day to preach. But Jowett kept his life in balance and majored on building the church.

It was inevitable that calls would come from other churches. Late in 1909 Jowett received a call from the prestigious Fifth Avenue Presbyterian Church, New York City. He graciously refused, but they issued a second call in June 1910. Again he said no; but when the call was repeated at the end of the year, he felt led to accept, saying, "The scale of decision . . . turned by a hair."

On 2 April 1911 Jowett opened his ministry in New York City. The American press made a great deal out of his arrival, headlining him as "the greatest preacher in the world!" Retiring by nature, Jowett despised anything that smacked of promotion; he never quite adjusted to the "American system of ballyhoo." His preaching attracted great crowds, not only "up-and-outers" (for which Fifth Avenue was famous), but also common people who heard the gospel gladly. New York City was desperately in need of solid biblical preaching. "What a time this is for the preacher," he wrote in a letter to a friend. "Congregations tense, strained, burdened, wanting some glimpse of spiritual things amid this riot of material things, and yearning for a glimpse of the things which abide in all the fierce rush of things which are transient."

The advent of the war created new problems for the Jowetts, who longed to be in England but knew they had been called to New York. One good by-product of Jowett's sojourn was the opportunity to give the Yale Lectures on preaching in April 1912. If you had to name the six best volumes in this valuable series, surely you would include Jowett's *The Preacher: His Life and Work*.

The lecturer himself did not enjoy the experience. "I am here for ten days delivering the Yale lectures on preaching," he wrote to a friend. "The lectures have been a nightmare to me, and I am glad I am getting rid of them this week!" The theme of his seven lectures is summarized in one of Jowett's favorite sayings: "Preaching that costs nothing accomplishes nothing." "If they will only learn one thing," he wrote in a letter, "that preaching is not easy and that it costs blood, and if they will only learn another thing—that no one can attend to the deep wants of a church if he is running all over the country, I shall have discharged a very real service." I try to reread Jowett's lectures annually, if only to catch his passion for preaching. Some books on preaching and pastoral work almost make you want to turn in your ordination certificate; this is not one of them.

"I love my calling," he said on the first page. "I have a glowing delight in its service. . . . I have had but one passion, and I have lived for it—the absorbingly arduous yet glorious work of proclaiming the grace and love of our Lord and Savior Jesus Christ."

This book gives good counsel not only on sermon preparation, but also on the making of the minister himself and the conducting of public worship. Jowett was known as much for his public prayers as for his sermons. That friend and student of great preaching W. Robertson Nicoll, after visiting Carr's Lane when Jowett was minister there, wrote: "The great simplicity, reality, sympathy, and tenderness of the prayers moved one strangely." Jowett's public worship, including the prayers, grew out of his private devotional life. "We cannot be strong leaders of intercession unless we have a deep and growing acquaintance with the secret ways of the soul," Jowett told the Yale students. He never considered the exercises before the sermon as "mere preliminaries." The hymns, the prayers, and even the offering are all part of worship and need to be prepared with spiritual discernment. "If men are unmoved by our prayers," he said, "they are not likely to be profoundly stirred by our preaching."

He gave equal emphasis to the public reading of the Word of God. "It is a mighty experience when a lesson is so read that it becomes the sermon," he stated, "and the living word grips without an exposition!" It was said of G. Campbell Morgan that you learned more from his *reading* of the Word than from anyone else's *preaching* of the Word. Jowett was almost as skilled as Morgan in this area.

If Jowett worshiped in some of our churches today, he would behold careless "preliminaries" hastily thrown together; he would hear prayers that sound tragically the same week after week; he would listen to the inspired Word of God read without much feeling or understanding. He would miss that vital element he called "the strong gracious presence of reverence and order." He would be appalled by seeing preachers threatened by "the peril of ostentatious display." He warned his Yale listeners: "We never reach the innermost room in any man's soul by the expediences of the showman or the buffoon. The way of irreverence will never lead to the Holy Place."

While ministering in New York, Jowett received calls to return to England. He was invited to succeed Whyte in Edinburgh and J. D. Jones in Bournemouth. Both calls he rejected. But on 26 February 1917 he received a call to succeed Morgan at Westminster Chapel, London; this call he accepted. He asked the church to wait one year while he fulfilled his commitments in America. On 14 April 1918 he said farewell to his church. On 19 May he preached his first sermon as pastor of Westminster Chapel. The next years should have been the most fruitful in his ministry, but Jowett was dying and did not realize it. Preaching in Westminster Chapel was taxing. More than one previous minister, including Morgan, had lost his health while preaching in the building. (D. Martyn Lloyd-Jones always claimed that the building had "killed" Samuel Martin, the pastor who had built it.) Jowett had anemia, and his strength slowly ebbed. On 17 December 1922 he preached his last sermon in the chapel; a year later, on 19 December, he was "called home."

I urge you to secure every Jowett book you can find, not only his Yale lectures, but also his sermons. Begin with the volume in the "Great Pulpit Masters" series. This collection of twenty-seven sermons, which will introduce you to Jowett's ministry, has been reprinted in recent years, as have *The Eagle Life* (Old Testament devotional studies), *Life in the Heights* (devotional studies in the Epistles), and *Springs in the Desert* (devotional messages from the Psalms). Other books by Jowett are: *The Passion for Souls* (Christian discipleship), *The Silver Lining*, *Things That Matter Most*, *Apostolic Optimism*, and *God—Our Contemporary*. I enjoy his devotional book *My Daily Meditation*. While you are at it, get a copy of Arthur Porritt's biography *J. H. Jowett*. The foreword was written by Randall Davidson, archbishop of Canterbury. (Jowett once preached at an ecumenical service in Durham Cathedral and incurred the wrath of several Anglican divines: the archbishop was not one of them.)

The thing I appreciate most about Jowett is the dedication to preaching that he demonstrated. He constantly battled the subtle thieves that would steal his time. He arose early in the morning and devoted himself to study and prayer. He toiled over his messages. His hobby was words (he read the dictionary for a pastime), and he used them as an artist uses colors. He was a master of the perfect expression. He never used "almost the right word"; it was always exactly the right word. Perhaps his craftsmanship occasionally overshadowed his passion, so that the sermon was a sea of glass *not* "mingled with fire." But before we criticize him, let us be sure that we use words as accurately as he did.

Jowett was a devotional preacher. His major theme was the grace of God. His purpose was to win the lost and encourage the saved. He followed Joseph Parker's rule: "Preach to broken hearts." But his ministry was not sentimental. It was solidly doctrinal, and it centered in the cross. Jones, who knew Jowett well, called him "the greatest preacher of his generation." Jowett would blush to hear such a statement. But he was a great preacher, a homiletical craftsman with a compassionate heart.

The Ministry of a Transfigured Church

> And when the day of Pentecost was now come, they were all together in one place. And suddenly there came from heaven a sound as of the rushing of a mighty wind, and it filled all the house where they were sitting. And there appeared unto them tongues parting asunder, like as of fire; and it sat upon each one of them. And they were all filled with the Holy Spirit, and began to speak with other tongues, as the Spirit gave them utterance. . . . And when this sound was heard, the multitude came together. . . . **Acts 2:1–4, 6**

The wonder inside the church aroused inquisitive interest without. There came to the church an exceptional and plentiful endowment, and, as by the constraint of a mystic gravitation, the outside crowd began to move, like the waters swayed by the moon. The crowd may have moved toward the church in the temper of a flippant curiosity, or in the spirit of unfriendly revolt, or in the solemn mood of appropriating awe. Whatever may have been the constraint, the waters were no longer stagnant, the masses were no longer heedless and apathetic; the heedlessness was broken up, interest was begotten, and "the multitude came together."

Is the modern church the center of similar interest and wonder? Is there any awed and mesmeric rumor breathing through the streets, stirring the indifferent heart into eager questions? The modern church claims immediate kinship and direct and vital lineage with that primitive fellowship in the upper room. Does she manifest the power of the early church? Does she reveal the same magnetic influence and constraint?

I know that "the kingdom of God cometh not with observation." And so it is with the spring. The spring "cometh not with observation," but you speedily have tokens that she is here. She can hide her coming behind March squalls, and she can step upon our shores in the rough attire of a blustering and tempestuous day; but even though her coming may be without observation, her presence cannot be hid. And even so it is with the kingdom: she may make no noisy and ostentatious display of her coming, but the sleeping

---

Author's note: Jowett's sermon "The Ministry of a Transfigured Church" is from *J. H. Jowett*, ed. Elmer G. Homrighausen, pp. 53–69.

seeds feel her approach, and the valley of bones experiences an awakening thrill, and "there is nothing hid from the heat thereof." I think, therefore, that we are justified in seriously inquiring as to the "resurrection power" of our churches, the measure of their quickening influence, their net result in reaching and stirring and consecrating the energies of a community. How do they stand in the judgment? Is the Pentecostal morning repeated, and is the gracious miracle the talk of the town? Does the multitude come together, "greatly wondering"?

Carry the inquisition to the regular and frequent fellowship of the church. So many times a week her members gather together in the upper room. What happens in the hallowed shrine? Are we held in solemn and enriching amazement at the awful doings? And when we come forth again, is there about us a mysterious impressiveness which arrests the multitude, and which sends abroad a spirit of questioning like a healthy contagion? Can we honestly say that by our ordinary services the feet of the heedless crowd are stayed, and that the people come together "greatly wondering"? In answer to all these searching questions I think that even the most optimistic of us will feel obliged to confess that the general tendency is undisturbed, that we do not generate force enough to stop the drift, and that the surrounding multitude remains uninfluenced.

Now, when we consider these unattracted or alienated peoples, we can roughly divide them into three primary classes. First, there are those who never think about us at all. So very remote are the highways of their thought and life that the impulse of the church is spent before it reaches their mental and moral abode. We can scarcely describe their attitude as one of indifference, because the mood of indifference would imply a negligent sense of our existence, and I can discern no signs of such perception. We contribute no thread to the warp and woof of their daily life. We bring no nutriment to the common meal; we do not even provide a condiment for the feast. Our presence in the city brings neither pleasure nor pain, neither sweet nor bitter, neither irritation nor ease; their souls are not disquieted within them, neither are they lulled into a deeper and more perilous sleep. We are neither irritants nor sedatives; to this particular class we simply do not exist.

And then, secondly, there are those who have thought about us, and as a result of their thinking have determined to ignore us. For all simple, positive, and progressive purposes we are no longer any good. We are exhausted batteries; we have no longer the power to ring a loud alarm, or to light a new road, or to energize some heavy and burdensome crusade. Our once stern and sacrificial warfare has now become a bloodless and self-indulgent quest. It is not only that the once potent shell cases have been emptied of their explosive content, they have been converted into dinner gongs! The once brilliant and unconditional ethical ideal has been dimmed and shadowed by worldly compromise. The pure and oxygenated flame of righteous passion has been changed into the fierce but smoky bonfire of sectarian zeal. We are looked upon as engaged in petty and childish controversy, losing ourselves in vague and nebulous phraseology, decking ourselves in vestures and postures as harmless and indifferent as the dresses worn at a fancy ball. That is the estimate formed of us by a vast section of the thinking crowd. You will find it reflected week by week in the labor papers, where we are regarded as straws in some side bay of a mighty river, riding serenely round and round and round, and we do not even show the drift of the stream, the dominant movement of our age. Our speech and our doings are of interest to the antiquary, but for all serious, practical, forceful, and aspiring life our churches do not count.

And, thirdly, there are those who think about us and who are constrained by their thinking into the fiercest and most determined opposition. To these men the church is not like Bunyan's "Giant Pope," alive but impotent, and "by reason of age, and also of the many shrewd brushes that he met with in his younger days, grown so crazy and stiff in his joints that he can do little more than sit in his cave's mouth, grinning at pilgrims as they go by, and biting his nails because he cannot come at them." No, to this class the church can do more than grin; it can reach and tear, and its ministry is still destructive. Its influence is perverse and perverting. Its very faith is a minister of mental and moral paralysis. Its dominant conceptions befog the common atmosphere, and chill and freeze "the genial currents of the soul." Its common postures and practices, its defenses and aggressions, perpetuate and confirm human alienations and divisions. The church cannot be ignored; it is not a harmless and picturesque ruin; it is a foul fungus souring the common soil, and for the sake of all sweet and beautiful things its nefarious influence must be destroyed.

This is by no means an exhaustive analysis of the alienated multitude, but it is sufficiently descriptive for my present purpose. In each of these three great primary classes the people stand aloof, indifferent, and resentful, and the church is not endowed with that subduing and triumphant impressiveness which would turn their reverent feet toward herself. Now, how stands it with the church? Does she seem fitted to strike, and arrest, and silence, and allure the careless or suspicious multitudes? What is there unique and amazing about her? Her Lord has promised her a marvelous distinctiveness. She is to be "a glorious church, not having spot or wrinkle, or any such thing." "A glorious church," shining amid all the surrounding twilights with the radiance of a splendid noon! "Not having spot": no defect, no blemish, no impaired function, no diseased limb! "Or wrinkle": there shall be no sign of age about her, or any waste; she shall never become an anachronism; she shall always be as young as the present age, ever distinguished by her youthful brow, and by her fresh and almost boisterous optimism! "Or wrinkle, or any such thing." Mark the final, holy swagger of it, as though by a contemptuous wave of the hand the apostle indicates the entire rout of the unclean pests that invade and attack an apostate church. "Or any such thing"! Are these great words of promise in any high degree descriptive of our own church? Is this our distinctiveness? "Not having spot": have we no withered hands, no halt, no blind, no lame, no lepers? "Or wrinkle": are we really distinguished by the invincible and contagious energies of perpetual youth? Does not the holding up of this great ideal throw our basal defects into dark and ugly relief? The pity of it all is just this, that the church, with all its loud and exuberant professions, is exceedingly like "the world." There is no clean, clear line of separation. In place of the promised glories we have a tolerable and unexciting dimness; in place of superlative whiteness we have an uninteresting gray; and in place of the spirit of an aggressive youthfulness we have a loitering and time-serving expediency. There would be no difficulty if only we had seized upon the fullness of our resources, and had become clothed with the riches of our promised inheritance, in men being able to distinguish, in any general company, the representatives of the church of the living God. There would be about them the pervasive joy of spiritual emancipation, resting upon all their speech and doings like sunlight on the hills. There would be about them a spiritual spring and buoyance which would enable them to move amid besetting obstacles with the nimbleness of a hart. "Thou hast made my feet like hinds' feet!" "By my God have I leaped over a wall!" There would be about them the fine serenity which is born of a mighty alliance. And there would be the strong, healthy pulse of a holy and hallowing purpose, beating in constant and forceful persistence. Such characteristics would distinguish any man, and any company, and any church, and the startled multitude would gather around in questioning curiosity. But the alluring wonder is largely absent from our church. Men pass from the world into our precincts as insensible of any difference as though they had passed from one side of the street to the other, and not feeling as though they had been transported from the hard, sterile glare of the city thoroughfare into the fascinating beauties of the Devonshire lane.

What, then, do we need? We need the return of the wonder, the arresting marvel of a transformed church, the phenomenon of a miraculous life. I speak not now of the wonders of spasmodic revivals; and, indeed, if I must be perfectly frank, my confidence in the efficient ministry of these elaborately engineered revivals has greatly waned. I will content myself with the expression of this most sober judgment, that the alienated and careless multitude is not impressed by the machinery and products of our modern revivals. The ordinary mission does not, and cannot, reach the stage at which this particular type of impressiveness becomes operative. The impressiveness does not attach to "decisions," but to resultant life. The wonder of the world is not excited by the phenomena of the penitent bench, but by what happens at the ordinary working-bench in the subsequent days. The world is not impressed by the calendar statement that at a precise particular moment winter relinquished her sovereignty to spring; the real interest is awakened by the irresistible tokens of the transition in garden, hedgerow, and field. It is not the new birth which initially arrests the world, but the new and glorified life. It is not, therefore, by spasmodic revivals, however grace-blessed they may be, that we shall excite the wonder of the multitude, but by the abiding miracle of a God-filled and glorious church. What we need, above all things, is the continuous marvel of an elevated church, "set on high" by the King, having her home "in the heavenly places in Christ," approaching all things "from above," and triumphantly resisting the subtle gravitation of "the world, the flesh, and the devil." It is not only multitudes of decisions that we want, but preeminently the heightening of the life of the saved, the glorification of the saints. The great Evangelical Revival began, not with the reclamation of the depraved, but with the enrichment of the redeemed. It was the members of the Holy Club, moving amid the solemnities of grace and sacred fellowship, who were lifted up into the superlative stages of the spiritual life, and who in that transition took a step as great and vital as the earlier step from sin to righteousness. Their life became a high and permanent miracle, and their subsequent ministry was miraculous. That is the most urgent necessity of our day, a church of the superlative order, immeasurably heightened and enriched—a church with wings as well as feet, her dimness changed into radiance, her stammering changed into boldness, and presenting to the world the spectacle of a permanent marvel, which will fascinate and allure the inquiring multitude, drawn together "not that they might see Jesus only, but Lazarus also whom he has raised from the dead."

Now, what is the explanation of the comparative poverty and impotence of our corporate life? Why is the church not ladened with the impressive dignities of her destined inheritage? Look at the manner of our fellowship. Is it such as to give promise of power and wealth? When we meet together, in worshiping communities, do we look like men and women who are preparing to move amid the amazing and enriching sanctities of the Almighty? Take our very mode of entry. It is possible to lose a thing by the way we approach it. I have seen a body of flippant tourists on the Rigi at the dawn, and by their noisy irreverence they missed the very glory they had come to see. "When ye come to appear before me, who hath required this at your hands, to trample my courts?" That loud and irreverent tramp is far too obtrusive in our communion. We are not sufficiently possessed by that spirit of reverence which is the "open sesame" into the realms of light and grace. We are not subdued into the receptiveness of awe. Nay, it is frequently asserted that in our day awe is an undesirable temper, a relic of an obsolete stage, a remnant of pagan darkness, a fearful bird of a past night, altogether a belated anachronism in the full, sweet light of the evangel of grace. I remember receiving a firm, but very courteous remonstrance from one of the children of light, because on the very threshold of a lovely summer's morning I had announced the hymn:

> Lo! God is here: let us adore
> And own how dreadful is this place.

And my friend said it was like going back to the cold, gray dawn, when disturbed spirits were speeding to their rest! It was like moving amid the shadows and specters of Genesis, and he wanted to lie and bask in the calm, sunny noon of the Gospel by John! I think his letter was representative of a common and familiar mood of our time. I have no desire to return to the chill, uncertain hours of the early morning, but I am concerned that we should learn and acquire the only receptive attitude in the presence of our glorious noon. It is certain that many of the popular hymns of our day are very far removed from the hymn to which I have just referred. It is not that these hymns are essentially false, but that they are so one-sided as to throw the truth into disproportion, and so they impair and impoverish our spiritual life.

Here is one of the more popular hymns of our time:

> Oh that will be glory for me,
> When by His grace I shall look on His face,
> That will be glory for me!

Well, we all want to share in the inspiration of the great expectancy! It is a light and lilting song, with very nimble feet: but lest our thought should fashion itself after the style of these tripping strains, we need to hear behind the lilt "the voice of the great Eternal," sobering our very exuberance into deep and awful joy. "When by His grace I shall look on His face!" That is one aspect of the great outlook, and only one, and therefore incomplete. I find the complementary aspect in these familiar words, "With twain he covered his face!" That is quite another outlook, and it introduces the deepening ministry of awe, which I am afraid is so foreign to the modern mind. "I feel like singing all the day!" So runs another of our popular hymns. That would have been a congenial song for my friend on that radiant summer morning when his thoughtless minister led him up to the awful splendors of the great white throne! "I feel like singing all the day," and the words suggest that this ought to be the normal mood for all pilgrims on the heavenly way. I am not so sure about that, and I certainly have grave doubts as to whether the man who feels "like singing all the day" will make the best soldier when it comes to "marching as to war." "The Lord is in his holy temple: let all the earth keep silence before him." That is a contemplation which seeks expression in something deeper than song. "There was silence in heaven about the space of half an hour." What had they seen, what had they heard, what further visions of glory had been unveiled, that speech and song were hushed, and the soul sought fitting refuge in an awe-inspired silence?

When I listen to our loud and irreverent tramp, when I listen to so many of our awe-less hymns and prayers, I cannot but ask whether we have lost those elements from our contemplation which are fitted to subdue the soul into silence, and to deprive it of the clumsy expedient of speech. We leave our places of worship, and no deep and inexpressible wonder sits upon our faces. We can sing these lilting melodies, and when we go out into the streets our faces are one with the faces of those who have left the theaters and the music halls. There is nothing about us to suggest that we have been looking at anything stupendous and overwhelming. Far back in my boyhood I remember an old saint telling me that after some services he liked to make his way home alone, by quiet byways, so that the hush of the Almighty might remain on his awed and prostrate soul. That is the element we are losing, and its loss is one of the measures of our poverty, and the primary secret of our inefficient life and service. And what is the explanation of the loss? Preeminently our impoverished conception of God. The popular God is not great, and will not create a great race. The church must not expect to strike humanity with startling and persistent impact if she carries in her own mind and heart the enfeebling image of a mean divinity. Men who are possessed by a powerful God can never themselves be impotent. But have we not robbed the Almighty of much of His awful glory, and to that extent are we not ourselves despoiled? We have contemplated the beauties of the rainbow, but we have overlooked the dim severities of the throne. We have toyed with the light, but we have forgotten the lightning. We have rejoiced in the fatherhood of our God, but too frequently the fatherhood we have proclaimed has been throneless and effeminate. We have picked and chosen according to the weakness of our own tastes, and not according to the full-orbed revelation of the truth, and we have selected the picturesque and rejected the appalling. "And he had in his right hand seven stars"—yes, we can accept that delicate suggestion of encircling love and care! "And his countenance was as the sun shineth in his strength"—yes, we can bask in the distributed splendor of the sunny morn! "And out of his mouth went a sharp two-edged sword!"—and is that too in our selection, or has our cherished image been deprived of the sword? Why leave out that sword? Does its absence make us more thoughtful and braver men, or does it tend to lull us into an easefulness which removes us far away from the man who when he saw Him, "fell at his feet as dead"?

This mild, enervating air of our modern Lutheranism needs to be impregnated with something of the bracing salts of Calvinism. Our very evangelicalism would be all the sturdier by the addition of a little "baptized Stoicism." Our water has become too soft, and it will no longer make bone for a race of giants. Our Lutheranism has been diluted and weakened by the expulsion of some of the sterner motive-elements which it possessed as its source. If we banish the conceptions which inspire awe, we of necessity devitalize the very doctrines of grace, and if grace is emasculated then faith becomes anemic, and we take away the very tang and pang from the sense of sin. All the great epistles of the apostle Paul being in the awe-inspiring heights of towering mountain country, and all through the changing applications of the thought these cloud-capped eminences are ever in sight. Paul's eyes were always lifted up "unto the hills," and therefore his soul was always on its knees. If he rejoiced, it was "with trembling"; if he served the Lord, it was "with fear"; if he was "perfecting holiness," it was gain "in the fear of the Lord!" Always, I say, this man's eyes were upon the awful, humbling, and yet inspiring heights of revealed truth. Our modern theological country is too flat; there are not enough cool, unlifted snow-white heights—heights like Lebanon, to which the peasant can turn his feverish eyes even when he is engaged in the labors of the sweltering vale. "Wilt thou forsake the snows of Lebanon?" "His righteousness is like the great mountains!" "Go! stand on the mount before the Lord!" "In the year King Uzziah died I saw the Lord, high and lifted up!" "Holy, holy, holy is the Lord." That was a mountain view. "And I said, Woe is me!" And that was the consequent awe. If the ministers of the church were to swell in those vast uplifted solitudes strange things would happen to us. Our speech would be deepened in content and tone, and we should speak as they say John Fletcher of Madeley used to speak, "like one who had just left the immediate converse of God and angels." But not only so, there would be added to our speech the awful energy of a still more powerful silence. "Every year makes me tremble," said Bishop Westcott toward the end of his years—"every year makes me tremble at the daring with which people speak of spiritual things." Is not the good bishop's trembling justified?

Some time ago I preached a sermon on the bitter cup which was drunk by our Lord and Savior Jesus Christ. I noticed that one of the papers, in a reference to the sermon, said that I had spoken on the sufferings of Christ "with charming effect." The words sent me to my knees in humiliation and fear. Soul of mine, what had I said, or what had I left unsaid, or through what perverting medium had I been interpreted? For the flippancy can be in the reporter as well as in the preacher; it can be in the religious press as well as in the consecrated minister. But let the application stand to me alone and let me once again remind myself of Westcott's trembling "at the daring with which people speak of spiritual things." Ay, we are reckless and therefore forceless in our speech: we are not mighty in our silences. There are some things which our people must infer from our reverent silences, things which can never be told in speech, and these mountain experiences are among them. That awe of the heights will deepen and enlarge both the ministry and the church; it will enrich both her speech and her silences; and it will make her character unspeakably masculine, forceful, and impressive. "If in any part of Europe a man was required to be burned, or broken on the wheel, that man was at Geneva, ready to depart, giving thanks to God, and singing psalms to Him." A mighty God makes irresistible men. History has proved, and experience confirms it today, that this mountain-thinking, with all its subduing austerities and shadows, would create a powerful and athletic church, a church of most masculine temper, courageous both in its aggressions and in its restraints, both in its confessions and its reserves, a church that would rouse and impress the world by the decisive vigor of its daily life—never dull, never feeble, but always and everywhere "fair as the moon, clear as the sun, and terrible as an army with banners." "O Zion, get thee up into the high mountains!"

But our impoverished conception of God is not the only cause of our comparative poverty and enfeeblement. The life of the church is expressed in two relationships, the human and the divine. The divine fellowship has been impoverished by lack of height; the human fellowship has been impoverished by lack of breadth. We have not drunk the iron water from the heart of the mountains, and we have therefore lacked a healthy robustness; we have not accumulated the manifold treasures of the far-stretching plain, and we have therefore lacked a wealthy variety. Our fellowship with God has been mean: our fellowship with man has been scanty. Nay, would it not be just the truth to say that the human aspects of our church fellowship suggest a treasure-house which has never been unlocked? The church is poor because much of her treasure is imprisoned; but she herself carries the liberating key to the iron gate! Our riches are buried in the isolated lives of individual members instead of all being pooled for the endowment of the whole fraternity. A very large part of the ample ministry of the *koinōnia* has been atrophied, if indeed it has ever been well sustained. I gratefully recognize the mystic, silent fellowship among the consecrated members of the church of Christ. I know that out of the very heart of "him that believeth" there inevitably flow "rivers of living water," and I delight to allow my imagination to rest upon the well-irrigated country of this sanctified society. There is a mystic commerce altogether independent of human expedient or arrangement. We cannot bow together without some exchange of heavenly merchandise, without angel ministries carrying from island to island the unique and peculiar products of their climes. The rich and enriching history of the Society of Friends is altogether corroborative of this great truth of spiritual experience. "When I came into the silent assemblies of God's people," says Robert Barclay, "I felt a sweet power among them which touched my heart, and as I gave way unto it, I found the evil weakening in me and the good raised up."

But the human side of the apostolic *koinōnia* includes riches other than these. It is not only a mystic interchange in the awful depths of the spirit: it is a fellowship of intelligence; it is a community of experience; it is the socializing of the individual testimony and witness. It is not only the subtle carriage of spiritual energy: it is the transference of visions, the sharing of discoveries, the assemblage of many judgments, whether in the hour of triumph or of defeat. "When ye come together, every one of you hath a psalm, hath a doctrine, hath a tongue, hath a revelation, hath an interpretation." That is the broader fellowship we lack, and we are all the poorer for it. The psalm that is born in one heart remains unsung, and the sadness it was fitted to remove from the heart of another abides like a clammy mist. The revelation that dawned upon one wondering soul is never shared, and so another remains in the cold imprisonment of the darkness. The private interpretation is never given, and for want of the key, many obstructing doors are never unlocked.

This is the neglected side of the apostolic fellowship, and for the want of it the church goes out to confront the world in the poverty of a starved individualism rather than in the rich and full-blooded vigor of her communistic strength. We are not realizing the social basis of the church's life; Christian fellowship comprehends not only a meeting at a common altar, but a meeting at a family hearth, for the reverent and familiar interchange of our experiences with God, and of what has happened to us in our warfare with the world, the flesh, and the devil. In lieu of the broader and richer fellowship we have exalted the ministry of one man, and out of the limited pool of his experience—and sometimes they are not even experiences, but only fond and desirable assumptions—the whole community has to drink, while the rest of the many pools remain untapped. And, oh, the treasures that are hidden in these unshared and unrevealed experiences! What have our matured saints to tell us of the things we wish to know? How did they escape the snare, or by what subtlety were they fatally beguiled? How did they take the hill, and where did they discover the springs of refreshing? What did they find to be the best footgear when the gradient was steep, and how did they comfort their hearts when they dug the grave by the way? And what is it like to grow old, and what delicacies does the Lord of the road provide for aged pilgrims, and have they seen any particular and wonderful stars in their evening sky? Are not all of us unspeakably poorer because these counsels and inspirations are untold? And our younger communicants—how are they faring on the new and arduous road? What unsuspected difficulties are they meeting? And what unsuspected provisions have they received? And what privilege of service has been given them, and what inspiring vision have they found in the task? And what have our stalwart warriors to tell us? How goes the fight in the business fields, on market and exchange? And what hidden secret has the Lord of light been unveiling to the ordained layman? What wealth of truth and glory? I say, these are breadths of the *koinōnia* we do not traverse; these are mines we do not work. And the output of our moral and spiritual energy is consequently small.

I know the perils which abound in these particular regions of exercised communion. Those who have the least to say may be readiest to speak. The spiritually insolvent may rise and talk like spiritual millionaires. The bloom of a delicate reserve may be destroyed, and flippant witnessing may become a substitute for deep experience. Easy familiarity may be made the standard of spiritual attainment, and sensational statements may be engendered by the hotbed of vanity and pride. In a fellowship-meeting some members may speak from a subtle love of applause, while others may speak from an equally illicit sense of shame. I know all this, but I know also that there is nothing in the entire round of Christian worship and communion which is not exposed to abomination and abuse. There is not a single plant in your garden which is not the gathering ground of some particular pest; ay, and the more delicate and tender the plant, the more multitudinous are the foes. But you do not banish the plant because of the pests; you accept the plant and guard against the pests; and I for one think it not impossible to cultivate this larger, richer, more social and familiar fellowship, and at the same time to create an atmosphere in which these invasive perils shall be unable to breathe. Under God, everything depends upon your leader; and under God, cannot wise leaders be grown leaders who shall be able, with a rare delicacy of tact, born of deep and unceasing communion with God, to draw out the individual gift of witness and experience, and by the accumulated treasure to enrich the entire church? Our church is comparatively poor and unimpressive; here is a storehouse of untouched resources which I am convinced would immeasurably enrich and strengthen our equipment in our combined attack against the powers of darkness. We need to get higher up the mountains. And we need, too, to get farther out upon the plains. "O, for a closer walk with God!" And, "O, for a closer walk with man!" Closer to the great and holy God, that we may be possessed by a deepening and fertilizing awe; and closer to our brother, that we may move in the manifold inspiration and comfort of "mutual faith" and experience.

I have not been concerned with the suggestion of new expedients. It has not been my purpose to advocate or defend aggressive and unfamiliar enterprises. My eyes have not been upon the church's conduct, but upon her character; not upon her prospectus, but upon her capital; not upon her plan of campaign, but upon her fighting strength. "Like a mighty army moves the church of God!" Yes, but does she? Are not her regiments sometimes almost Falstaffian in their bedraggled impotence? How shall she increase her fighting power? How shall she enrich her spirit of discipline? And I have answered: By taking thought of the untrodden heights and the untrodden breadths within her own circle, by claiming her purposed and buried resources in humanity and in God. I am convinced that in these ways we should make undreamed-of additions to the energy and impact of the church's strength. No church can walk along these unfrequented paths without acquiring the moments of sacrificial grace; and when the power of the church becomes awful and sacrificial, when she bears in her body the red "marks of the Lord Jesus," when there is "blood upon the lintel and the two side posts" of her door, you may be assured that the arrested multitude will come together, drawn by the mesmeric gravitation of her own irresistible strength. And not only strong shall the church become, strong in unselfish daring and persistence, but because of the very robustness of her strength she shall be tender with an exquisitely delicate compassion. I have yielded to none in the advocacy of "the wooing note" in the ministry of the word, and with a growing and richer confidence I advocate it still. But there is the wooing not of a silly, simpering sentimentalism, and there is the wooing note of strong and masculine men who have been cradled and molded and homed in the austere nursery and school of the mountains. And where can you make your fine wooers if not among the deepening ministries of the mountains? "How beautiful upon the mountains are the feet of them that bring glad tidings!" I shall have no fear about the strength and sweetness of the wooing note when we are all the children of the heights.

Given these conditions, and I believe the church will move among the alienated multitudes with an illumined and fascinating constraint. The alienation of the people is not fundamental and ultimate. Deep down, beneath all the visible severances, there are living chords of kinship, ready to thrill and to respond to the royal note. Those living chords—buried, if you will, beneath the dead and deadening crust of formality and sin, buried, but buried alive—are to be found in Belgravia, where Henry Drummond, that man of the high mountains and the broad plains, awoke them to response by the strong, tender impact of a great evangel and a great experience. And those living chords are also to be found at the pit's mouth, among the crooked and pathetic miners, and they become vibrant with responsive devotion, as Keir Hardie has told us that his became vibrant, in answer to the awakening sweep of the strong, tender hands of the Nazarene. The multitude is not sick of Jesus; it is only sick of His feeble and bloodless representatives. When once again a great church appears, a church with the Lord's name in her forehead, a church with fine muscular limbs and face seamed with the marks of sacrifice, the multitude will turn their feet to the way of God's commandments. I sat a little while ago in one of the chambers of the National Gallery, and my attention was caught by the vast miscellaneous crowd as it sauntered and galloped through the rooms. All sorts and conditions of people passed by—rich and poor, the well-dressed and the beggarly, students and artisans, soldiers and sailors, maidens just out of school and women bowed and wrinkled in age: but, whoever they were, and however unarresting may have been all the other pictures in the chamber, every single soul in that mortal crowd stopped dead and silent before a picture of our Savior bearing His cross to the hill. And when the church is seen to be His body—His very body: His lips, His eyes, His ears, His hands, His feet, His brain, His heart, His very body—and when the church repeats, in this her corporate life, the brave and manifold doings of Judea and Galilee, she too shall awe the multitude, and by God's grace she shall convert the pregnant wonder into deep and grateful devotion.

Our times are disturbed, and hopefully and fruitfully disturbed, by vast and stupendous problems. On every side the latch is lifting, and the door of opportunity stands ajar. But we shall fail in our day, as other men have failed in their day, unless by faith and experience we enter into "the fellowship of his sufferings," and become clothed with "the power of his resurrection." Sound social economics are not enough; sound political principles are not enough; sound creeds and politics are not enough. The most robust and muscular principle will faint and grow weary unless it is allied with character which is rendered unique and irresistible by unbroken communion with the mind and will of God. It is "Christ in us" which is "the hope of glory," both for the individual and the state.

Let us abide in Him in total and glorious self-abandonment. Let nothing move us from our rootage. Let us "pray without ceasing," and let our consecration be so complete and confident that there may be presented unto the world a church "alive unto God"; a church as abounding in signs of vitality as hedgerows in the spring; a church quickened in moral vision, in intellectual perception, in emotional discernment; a church acute, compassionate and daring, moving amid the changing circumstances of men in the very spirit of her Lord, and presenting everywhere the arresting ministry of "a hiding-place from the wind, a covert from the tempest, rivers of water in a dry place, and the shadow of a great rock in a weary land!"

Bibliography

Jowett, John Henry. *"Apostolic Optimism" and Other Sermons.* London: Hodder and Stoughton, 1901.

———. *"The Eagle Life" and Other Studies in the Old Testament.* London: Hodder and Stoughton, 1921. Reprinted—Grand Rapids: Baker, 1976.

———. *God—Our Contemporary: Sermons for the Times.* London: Clarke, 1922.

———. *J. H. Jowett.* Edited by Elmer G. Homrighausen. Great Pulpit Masters. New York: Revell, 1950. Reprinted—Grand Rapids: Baker, 1972.

———. *Life in the Heights: Studies in the Epistles.* London: Hodder and Stoughton, 1924. Reprinted—Grand Rapids: Baker, 1973.

———. *My Daily Meditation for the Circling Year.* London: Clarke, 1914.

———. *The Passion for Souls.* London: Clarke, 1905.

———. *The Preacher: His Life and Work.* New York: Hodder and Stoughton, 1912. Reprinted—Grand Rapids: Baker, 1968.

———. *The Silver Lining.* London: Melrose, 1907.

———. *Springs in the Desert: Studies in the Psalms.* London: Hodder and Stoughton, 1924. Reprinted—Grand Rapids: Baker, 1976.

———. *Things That Matter Most: Short Devotional Readings.* London: Clarke, 1913.

Porritt, Arthur. *John Henry Jowett.* London: Hodder and Stoughton, 1924.

11

Joseph W. Kemp

(1872–1933)

"God pity the man who comes here!" said Joseph W. Kemp at a committee meeting in famous Charlotte Baptist Chapel, Edinburgh. The Baptist church in Hawick, of which Kemp was pastor, was enjoying remarkable blessing; Charlotte Chapel was in sad shape. Then Charlotte Chapel called Kemp. "Don't go!" his friends warned. Why exchange a successful work for a derelict one? Kemp prayed, and then he accepted the call. His ministry in Edinburgh not only restored a great church, but also brought salvation and revival to thousands.

Joseph W. Kemp was born in 1872 in Hull, Yorkshire. He was only seven when his father died; two years later his mother died. The six little children were scattered. Joseph, with only eighteen months of schooling, had to go to work. When he was twelve, he went to Bridlington to work as a pageboy; but he soon returned to Hull, where he lived with a devoted Christian named J. H. Russell. Russell helped train the lad and witnessed to him lovingly about Jesus Christ.

Kemp was converted in September 1886. He was chatting with

an old sailor who suddenly asked, "Lad, when are you going to accept Christ?" Kemp arose from his chair, walked across the room, took the sailor by the hand, and said: "I'll do it now!" His own salvation experience no doubt contributed to his later boldness and decisiveness in evangelism. Two years later he was asked to lead a Bible-study class. About the same time he began attending meetings conducted by J. M. Scroggie, uncle of W. Graham Scroggie. These meetings revealed to him some of the wealth in the Word of God. He determined to study his Bible and appropriate its wealth for himself—and then share it. A generous friend sent Kemp to Glasgow Bible Training Institute, from which he graduated in 1894. While studying his Bible, he concluded that immersion was the scriptural form of baptism, a painful decision since he was at the Prospect Street Presbyterian Church. (The pastor was W. P. Mackay, author of the classic *Grace and Truth.*)

During his student days and for a year after graduation, Kemp conducted evangelistic meetings for the Ayrshire Christian Union. He could have become an itinerant soul-winner, but on 4 April 1897 he accepted a call from the Baptist church in Kelso. Horatius Bonar had ministered in that town for many years. Like Bonar, Kemp preached the doctrine of Christ's second coming; and he practiced evangelism.

The Baptist church in Hawick called him in July 1898; he ministered there until he moved to Edinburgh in February 1902. Before leaving Kelso, he married a daughter of a key church family. Kemp found a divided church at Hawick and left it united and growing. The young pastor spent his mornings in study and prayer. (As a student, he read every book he could find on prayer. After hearing an address by Andrew Murray, he determined to be a man of prayer.) He used afternoons for visitation and evenings for Bible classes and training sessions for church workers. Evangelism, Bible teaching, and prayer were the main elements in his ministry at Hawick, and they remained so throughout his life.

On Kemp's first Sunday at Charlotte Chapel, only thirty-five members came. But he was not discouraged: God had called him, and God would honor His Word. Kemp began by cleaning and remodeling the chapel. "Worldly places are bright and attractive," he said, alluding to the nineteen pubs in the neighborhood. "Why should God's house be dingy and musty?" Church members removed from their building thirteen cartloads of rubbish. But the spiritual changes at Charlotte Chapel were the most important. The new pastor started two Sunday prayer meetings, one beginning at 7 A.M., the other at 10 A.M. At every public meeting he gave solid Bible teaching with an evangelistic fervor that eventually caught fire in the church. Kemp and his congregation often "took to the streets" and conducted open-air meetings. Before long the crowds were going to Charlotte Chapel and not the pubs!

Early in 1905 an evangelist held meetings in the church, but nothing exceptional happened. The officers wisely agreed to have the church continue in prayer until God sent the needed blessing. About this time the great Welsh revival broke out; Kemp went to seek some of the blessing for himself and his people. He urged the people to continue praying for revival. Night after night throughout 1905 multitudes met in different prayer meetings. The blessing came on 22 January 1906 at a special church conference. All that year attendance increased, souls were saved in unusual numbers, and the church felt the power of God. People confessed sin, and broken fellowship was restored. The blessing continued into 1907, when the pastor celebrated his fifth anniversary.

A new church building, designed to accommodate the congregation's increased size, formally opened on 6 October 1912. During its construction the church met in the two-thousand-seat Synod Hall, with the blessing of God continuing unabated. During the dedication services Andrew Urquhart, secretary of Charlotte Chapel, explained the reasons for God's blessing during Kemp's ministry: first was "a firm and unchangeable belief in the power of prayer"; second, the preaching of the gospel; third, "hearty cooperation among as loyal and devoted a band of workers as ever any church possessed"; fourth, "an unfaltering faith in the promises of God."

Kemp's ministry in Edinburgh ended on 5 September 1915, when he left to pastor Calvary Baptist Church, New York City. During the farewell service John Henry Jowett, then pastoring in New York, unexpectedly showed up. And when the Kemp family was sailing out of Liverpool, they heard a voice calling from another ship: "Good-bye, Kemp! Good-bye, Kemp!" They discovered it was A. C. Dixon, then pastor of the Metropolitan Tabernacle in London. Calvary in New York in many respects resembled Charlotte Chapel when Joseph Kemp arrived. One of the first things he did was remove a thousand names from the church roll. He called it "ecclesiastical hypocrisy" to advertise inflated statistics. Unfortunately Kemp's health began to break, and he resigned from Calvary in February 1917. He ministered a short time at the new Metropolitan Tabernacle in New York City, but a complete breakdown forced him to leave the work in 1919.

In the spring of 1920, he accepted a call to the Baptist Tabernacle founded by Thomas Spurgeon in Auckland, New Zealand. God miraculously restored Kemp's health, and he entered the new ministry with great expectations. So popular were his Bible classes that many of the bookstores ran out of Bibles. One by-product of his ministry was the founding of the New Zealand Bible Training Institute. Again Kemp organized daily prayer meetings for revival; but he did not see the results he had seen in Edinburgh. He wrote a friend: "We often wonder why revival tarries. For over eighteen months a daily prayer meeting has been held in the Tabernacle, in addition to two or three prayer meetings of the regular order—the burden of all of which has been, 'Wilt Thou not revive us again?' Still the revival tarries. People do not respond so readily now to the appeals as they did twenty-five years ago."

Kemp paid his last visit to Great Britain in 1926. He preached at Keswick and ministered in the United States and Canada on the return trip. Back in Auckland he took up his work with characteristic zeal; but in 1932 his health again began to fail. He died on 4 September 1933 after seven months of serious illness. He was buried the next day in the Hillsborough Cemetery, with six thousand people lining the streets to pay tribute to a great preacher-evangelist who is almost forgotten today.

Joseph Kemp was a Spirit-taught man, spending hours searching the Bible. He did not borrow other men's sermons; he got his messages from God and always preached the Word. He was a man of prayer. *Bounds on Prayer* (now *Power Through Prayer*), written by E. M. Bounds, was one of his favorite books. Like the apostles of old, he gave himself to prayer and the ministry of the Word (Acts 6:4).

Kemp was not content to minister in a comfortable church; he went after lost souls and preached the gospel to them. He refused to be controlled by what he called "the tyranny of statistics." He taught the Word of God. He saw that new Christians studied the Bible and served the Lord in the church. To Kemp the church is not a field to work in; it is a force to work with. He expected and received the cooperation of his church officers, and God blessed their work together.

His ministry at Charlotte Chapel was no passing thing. His successor, W. Graham Scroggie, ministered for seventeen years with great blessing. The work then prospered under Scroggie's successor, J. Sidlow Baxter. When I visited Charlotte Chapel a few years ago, I gave thanks to God for the ministry of Joseph Kemp.

Kemp was influenced greatly by the life of George Whitefield and the sermons of Charles H. Spurgeon. Charles G. Finney's

Lectures on Revivals also made an impact on his life. "I have frequently been asked, 'What is the secret of Mr. Kemp's success?'" said one of his church officers. "It is this: he believes in the gospel which he preaches, because he knows what it has done for himself, and what he has seen it do for others. . . . He believes in prayer. In other words, he preaches the gospel in faith, and expects and waits for the results. God honors his faith, and he gets the answer he expects." Prayer, Bible teaching, and evangelism: there is no reason why the formula should not work today.

Revivals and Evangelism

I am now in the tenth year of my ministry in Auckland, and in the thirty-third year of my ministry in the denomination. I have been in Christ for forty-one years. Who can surmise what mental mood or spiritual condition I might have been in today, had I not been introduced then to the "strong Son of God" by a humble working man, who was wondrously versed in the things of the kingdom and who knew by what avenue to approach the soul of a boy in order to take it captive for his Lord. I bring my wreath of gratitude to his memory on this notable occasion. I have set myself to address you on a theme in which my soul has bathed ever since the Lord put me into the ministry.

Revivalism and *evangelism:* the terms must not be confused. *Revivalism,* strictly speaking, means the reanimating of that which is already living, but in a state of declension. It has to do principally with the church as a whole and Christians as individuals.

Evangelism, in our usage of the word, as well as in its derivative sense, refers primarily to the proclamation of the gospel to the unsaved. To make *evangelism* a synonym of *revivalism* is untrue to the teaching of the New Testament. The church is responsible for evangelism and not for revival. We are summoned to evangelism; for revival we are cast upon the sovereign grace of God.

To evangelize is to proclaim the glad tidings. It is to declare the salvation of God wrought out by Jesus Christ His Son, once crucified, the now living and exalted Redeemer; to tell men who believingly commit themselves to the Savior, that they will be saved from their sins. We must give to the word *evangelize* all its

---

Author's note: Kemp's sermon "Revivals and Evangelism" is from Winnie Kemp, *Joseph W. Kemp*, pp. 142–59. This was a presidential address to the Baptist Union of New Zealand.

New Testament meaning and value without making the possibly natural but somewhat stupid mistake of confusing it with something that is not intended in the New Testament at all. As Kilpatrick points out, "God never says, 'Revive yourselves, and convert the world.' God's word to His servants is 'Preach the gospel to every creature.' Their word to Him is 'Revive Thy work, O Lord.'"

In the laws of the spiritual universe faithful evangelism is normally followed by genuine revival. Let the church realize as its first responsibility and the first charge upon its strength the duty of preaching the gospel of Jesus Christ, and there will be added to it revival: that is, a constant renewal of its vital energy and increase of moral force which will be manifest in the spiritual growth of its own members and in the attraction to it of them that are without. But let it be well understood that the church is not directly responsible for revival. It *is* directly and immediately responsible for its duty of evangelism. There is a type of revival which condemns the evangelism which produced it. A superficial scratching of the surface which does not reach down to the roots of moral being is a mockery of the gospel. A revival which emphasizes spirituality at the expense of morality, or the making a speciality of a certain type of "holiness" while neglecting the plain virtues of truthfulness and sobriety, is a scandalous misrepresentation of the gospel. I am profoundly convinced of the truth of a recent critic: "A revival satisfied with frothy results, which leaves behind it a trail of moral defeat and spiritual disaster, forms a hindrance to the progress of the gospel in the territory cursed by its appearance, worse than the most violent hostility of wicked men."

Evangelism is for the nonce suffering an eclipse. It has passed under a cloud. I do not suppose that evangelism will ever become popular. The "offense of the cross" will ever be with us. The "carnal mind" is not sympathetic towards evangelism, and even in quarters once sympathetic, a prejudice against evangelism has been, and is being fostered. How are we to account for this? For several decades evangelism has been identified with special missions and mass movements, the after-gain of which has been almost negligible. There has been a parading of statistics and often with a reckless mode of reckoning, forgetting that numerical estimates are very deceptive and misleading. The spectacular and the sensational are amongst the means resorted to. Fabulous expenditure in advertising, hotels, and transportation, together with the smallness of the number of genuine converts to be found afterwards has contributed to the serious reaction from which the church is now suffering.

Moreover, the crudity of thought, poverty of expression, and a sentimentalism of method combine to make another ground of prejudice. To such, right-thinking people cannot subscribe. Is it any wonder that the very name *evangelism* sickens a congregation when we think of "the insipid style, the vapid thinking, the meager arguments, the impossible illustrations, the spurious emotion, and the parrot-like repetitions which characterize much so-called evangelistic preaching." The average congregation of intelligent people demands, not something to satisfy its intelligence merely, but a word which carries with it the sense of reality and forms a link between infinite grace and urgent need.

Then we are faced with the passing of the evangelical stalwarts and few, if any, rising to take their places. When I commenced the Christian life, among the Baptists, C. H. Spurgeon was at the Metropolitan Tabernacle, London. He regarded no sermon as a success that did not prove effective to save and to sanctify. Archibald G. Brown was evangelizing in East London Tabernacle. William Cuff, the converted butcher, was at Shoreditch. Alexander Maclaren, that prince of expositors, was in Manchester. F. B. Meyer was in Melbourne Hall, Leicester. Among the Presbyterians, Dr. Alexander Whyte was in Edinburgh. For two generations he retained his hold upon one of Scotland's most fashionable and cultured congregations largely by the emphasis he laid on sin. Dr. Elder Cumming was at Sandiford Church in Glasgow, and Dr. James Stalker in St. Matthew's of the same city. George H. C. Macgregor—the saintly Macgregor, as Bishop Moule styled him—was impressing the young life of Scotland with his fervid evangelism. He literally burned himself out with a consuming zeal for God. Professor Henry Drummond, who is said to have kept Edinburgh University morally clean for ten years, was exercising an incomparable ministry amongst young men. As was also Professor Orr, a man of profound erudition and evangelical fervor.

Among the Anglicans were to be numbered—Canon Hay Aitken, Bishop Handley Moule, William Haslam, whom I delight to call my spiritual grandfather, and Prebendary Webb-Peploe.

Among the Methodists—how they blazed and burned!—Charles Garrett, Richard Roberts, Thomas Champness, Hugh Price Hughes, Peter Mackenzie, W. L. Watkinson, and Gregory Mantle.

Among the Congregationalists—London had Joseph Parker at the City Temple, Newcastle had Jowett, Birmingham had R. W. Dale, Westminster Bridge Road, London, had Newman Hall.

Others of worldwide ministry and servants of all the churches were: Dr. Grattan Guinness and his son Harry, George Muller, Sir Robert Anderson, Frank White, A. T. Pierson, A. J. Gordon, George F. Pentecost, D. L. Moody, Ira D. Sankey, General Booth, A. C. Dixon, Major Whittle, Henry Varley, Richard Weaver, Andrew Murray, R. A. Torrey, J. Wilbur Chapman, Charles M. Alexander, and others of lesser fame. Not one in this imposing list is with us today. All have gone to their reward. You will agree they are a noble host, and the age that was blest with such men was rich indeed. When shall we see their like again? Our regret is, not that they have passed, but that others are not rising to take their places.

Let me say it emphatically: It is for the churches to redeem evangelism from ordinariness to a place of dignity worthy of the church of God.

This is the first and in a sense the supreme mission of the church. Apart from evangelism the church would not have come into being and certainly would not have continued its vitality. When this work is not sedulously done, the life of the church suffers a heavy loss. When the passion to evangelize grows faint, there is something gravely wrong at the heart of the church. This work touches her nerve center. Listen to these weighty words from an influential quarter: "The church of Jesus Christ may cultivate a reverent and brilliant scholarship, maintain an inspiring and progressive ministry of teaching, and achieve a dignity and beauty of worship appealing to the most aesthetic taste. She may acquire a social conscience keenly sensitive to the needs and problems of the hour, an outlook at once broadly catholic and deeply sympathetic, and a charity sufficient to excite the imagination of the most fastidious. But if she fails to display a living and vigorous evangelism, she has failed in her essential and ultimate mission and the days of her influence are numbered."

"A living and vigorous evangelism"—that is the word which indicates what is the supreme business of the church. How few have faced the question, "What is the work of the church?" Rev. Dr. Harry Miller of Edinburgh rightly says "that this is vaguely conceived and little understood and consequently the church is expected to do some things that are certainly not her work and is blamed for leaving other things undone. Her critics are strangely ignorant of what is the real work of the church." What that work is our Lord declared when He went forth "to seek and to save that which was lost," and when upon the disciples He put the onus of "preaching the gospel to every creature." The apostles by their work and writings show what that work is. Here there is no dubiety or mist. The evangel was known and preached with certainty, courage, and candor. The example of the New Testament warrants us in concluding that the place of evangelism in the churches' activities is that of "absolute primacy." Nothing can take precedence of this. Manifold are the duties of the modern church. Their range and scope are wide as human nature, but if evangelism be treated as separate from them, they lose their distinctively Christian significance and cease to form part of the function of the Christian church.

This leads me to voice the conviction that there is no organization so capable of doing this work as the church. We are trusting too much to organizations outside the church. It is the church's work, and it is in the church the work must be done. Our greatest evangelists realize this, and they are less inclined now to the monster gathering and readier to cooperate with the work of the individual church. This opens a very wide question; for it is beyond doubt that the church, as an institution, is regarded by multitudes of people with feelings ranging from utter indifference, through suspicion, to absolute dislike, and even bitter animosity. "The masses will not come to our churches." We have been told it so often that we have actually come to believe it true, and have not only ceased to expect them, but to gape with open-eyed wonderment if they should.

The church that wants the masses can get them if she goes the right way about it. Some churches are frankly class churches, where the poor are not wanted and are warned off. "Some," as W. J. Dawson described them, are "social clubs, united by moral ideals, rather than spiritual communities quick with divine fire." So far as my own experience goes, this class of church is rare. Is it really true that the masses of people have an aversion to the church, so strong and obstinate that some other building must be provided for them when you wish to evangelize them? I do not believe it. My own experience, during a ministry exercised on three continents, disproves the assumption. I know it is much easier to get the masses of people to a hall than a church. There is a sense of freedom in a hall, an absence of restraint not found in a church, and for many reasons such a neutral center might be preferable where city-wide evangelism is contemplated; but my plea just now is for the constituting of the existing church an evangelistic center, and that implies the use of the church building itself for the work.

Our very methods of conducting modern evangelism have lent color to the belief that the average church is antagonistic to evangelism. There is much to be said for familiarizing the people with our church buildings. In conducting evangelistic work in "public halls," whatever immediate advantage may accrue, do we not give the impression that there is something about the church which is out of sympathy with evangelism? All things being equal, evangelism in the church is likely to have more durable results than that carried on outside. Moreover, for the sake of her own life the church must evangelize. Says Campbell Morgan: "No church ought to be allowed to exist that has not added to its membership by confession of faith. If a church is existing only by letters of transfer, it is time its doors were closed, and 'Ichabod, the glory is departed' inscribed across them." This evangelism must begin within the church.

"It is not spurt evangelism, but the spirit of evangelism" we need in all our churches. Dr. Duff declared that "the church that ceases to be evangelistic soon ceases to be evangelical." It is not enough to be evangelical, we must be evangelistic. "The evangelical church," says A. C. Dixon, "is a reservoir of pure water without a pipe running anywhere. The evangelistic church is a reservoir of pure water with a pipe to every heart in the community." Evangelical is a bomb-proof for defense—evangelistic is an army on the march with every face to the foe. An evangelical creed, merely held and defended, becomes a fossil; but to fossilize is not to evangelize. No church is truly evangelical that is not evangelistic also. Can we hold the doctrines of our most holy and historic faith and not propagate them? Evangelical faith affirms that Christ died for the race. Can we hold that faith without making it known to all for whom He died? The evangelical church is necessarily evangelistic. If the cross has meant to us deliverance, cleansing, freedom, and uplift, then common gratitude should drive us to evangelistic work and effort. To be evangelical and not evangelistic is an absurd contradiction.

We are now led to a consideration of some of the elements which go to make up a sane evangelism. In order to evangelize, the church must know the evangel. Nothing could satisfy William Jay in his preaching—said one who knew him well—but bringing forth the whole story of Matthew Henry's three R's: ruin, redemption, and regeneration. This, the church must know herself if she is to impress the world. A living sense of the wonder of redeeming grace and of gratitude to God is the spring of effective preaching. The church has worn an anxious and troubled face in recent years because of the inroads of Modernism, and well she may, for if the church loses faith in her message, masses will pass her door and leave the church to her naked destitution. Our fear is that if modern thought proceed much further, the fashion of our religion will be as much Mohammedan as Christian; in fact, it will be more like infidelity than either. A church which is not sure of Christ cannot preach Him. The church and her preachers must know whom they have believed and know what they owe to Him. At times she seems to have lost faith in Christ's power; and the cross, which ought to be a dynamic, is only a doctrine.

Our evangelism must be supported by a sane theology. The contention is that evangelism is thin, anemic, and without much body. To redeem it from its shallowness and superficiality it must have a theological basis. Dr. Denney, no small theologian himself, said emphatically, "Our evangelists must be theologians and our theologians evangelists." The keenest controversies of the centuries have raged around some great evangelical word. All the great evangelists of the past have been great theologians. We must not dream of scrapping the old theological terms, we must explain them. Nothing is gained by saying that the word *incarnation* is not in the New Testament and that the word *atonement* is mentioned only once, and that even there it ought not to be. Henry Drummond reminds us that an egg is as much an egg mixed in a pudding as in a shell. The ideas of the incarnation and the atonement are diffused through the whole of the New Testament and constitute its principal message.

In sending out men from our theological halls we must be sure that they have their proper directions. Theological professors who are cutting their students adrift from the old evangel have an awful scene to face at last in the ministries they have wrecked. In 1869 a passenger train was running into New York as another train was emerging. There was a head on collision. Fifty lives were snuffed out. An engineer was pinned under his engine. The blood was pouring from his nostrils, and tears were running down his cheeks. In his dying agonies he held a yellow paper crushed in his hand, and he said, "Take this. This will show you that some one gave me the wrong orders." When Moses became leader of the children of Israel he was anxious about his credentials, and asked God, "What shall I say unto them?" And God said unto Moses, "Say 'I am' hath sent you." "One might well hesitate," says Hubert Simpson, "to handle this verse because of its sheer sublimity. Two words, three letters, and we need 'Thirty-nine Articles,' thirty-three chapters of a 'Confession,' and 'Fourteen Points,' and I know not what all. And a precious lot of good they have done us. Let the evangelist pronounce 'I am.'"

Our evangelism must be biblical. An evangelism that is not biblical is imperfect and false. I despair of any great revival movement coming to our churches until there is a return to great biblical words—words which wound and heal human hearts. The anecdotal, the spicy, the feathery, and the flippant may please the crowd and bring fading laurels to the preacher, but they are poor substitutes for the Word of God. The sacred writers deal with living issues, and touch the great practical things of human experience. Their message never becomes effete. Sin, repentance, faith, justification, righteousness, peace, wrath, death, heaven, hell: these all need to be emphasized if "by all means we might save some."

Our evangelism must emphasize the deity of our Lord. "Let all the house of Israel know assuredly that God hath made that same Jesus whom ye crucified, both Lord and Christ." Thus on the day of Pentecost did Peter proclaim the Lordship of Christ. Confronting blind belief and flippant skepticism, and idle curiosity and surging sorrow and blinding sin and masterful passion, he said, "Jesus is Lord." He is our message—One from whose verdict there can be no appeal, and who is at this moment the Lord Jesus Christ.

We, moreover, seek to demonstrate that He is Lord because of His inherent royalty. "We challenge the world today," says Morgan, "and we say that the Jesus of the New Testament, the Jesus of the virgin birth, the virtuous life, the vicarious dying, and the victorious resurrection, stands amid this age with all its fierce light, its boasted civilization and its new psychology, '*facile princeps,*' the crowned Lord because of the supernal glory of His own character." "Half a century ago," it is told by Dr. W. Y. Fullerton, "there was a clergyman of wide friendships and ample means, whose delight it was to bring together people of dissimilar tastes and ideas. On one occasion he entertained about thirty guests at Westminster Palace Hotel, with Dean Stanley in the chair. All sorts of ideas were represented, and the dean suggested as a topic of discussion, 'What man will dominate the future?' A High Churchman, a Broad Churchman, and a Low Churchman each sought to show that their own view of things would prevail. Then Professor Huxley was called upon, and he declared that the future would belong to the men who stuck most closely to facts. The rest were much impressed; and when Edward Miall rose to speak, everybody felt he had a very difficult task. But he took it quite calmly, and expressed his agreement with Huxley. 'I also believe,' he said, 'that the future will belong to the men who stick most closely to the facts, and all the facts—the facts of nature and the facts of history.

And the greatest fact of history lies with Him.'" On this, it is absolutely essential that evangelism should be clear.

No evangelism can be termed New Testament evangelism that does not take sin into account. The age is peculiarly characterized by a loose sense of sin amongst men. Few are really willing to admit that they are sinners. But sin is a tremendous reality. It is in man's nature. The blood of the race is poisoned at its source. It may be that more people are troubled about their sin than Sir Oliver Lodge gives credit for. Sin is man's tormentor. It plagues him, and its ramifications are endless. "The recognition of sin," says Luther, "is the beginning of salvation." The church's task is to create a consciousness of sin, of its guilt, and power and punishment. Punishment! yes—it used to be that there was in religious minds an awful sense of the claims of God on human beings, and the violation of these was felt to involve awful guilt. The Shorter Catechism says, "Every sin deserveth God's wrath and curse, both in this life and in that which is to come." The consciousness of sin, when it was awakened, was, therefore, the sense of an angry God and of infinite ill-desert, for which no punishment could be too severe. But now sin is rather what impedes a good development; it is what degrades; it is an infection which makes the man, who allows it to spread in his soul, a vitiating element in society. In a writer like George Eliot you find most powerful delineations of the tendency of sin to grow from less to more, and of the certainty with which its consequences ensue, not only for the sinner, but for the innocent connected with him. And this is the kind of appeal which goes home in our time. The conscience of the time feels the power of sin, but is indifferent to its guilt.

With that conception of sin has come a changed attitude to the biblical doctrine of eternity.

Not long ago references to heaven and hell entered into nearly every sermon. Now we tell men that, even if there were no life to come, godliness would be the best mode of spending the present life. We tell them the purpose of God in salvation is, not to rescue a man from everlasting punishment and to make him a sharer of everlasting bliss, but to make him worthy of himself, and to use him as an instrument for making the world better. The true heaven is in the soul, and to be a bad man is to be in hell already.

This may be wholesome doctrine, and it may go home to the mind of the modern man with startling power; but whether it is fitted to be a substitute for what it has displaced or only a supplement to it, is another question. No teacher in the Bible unfolds the scenery of the other world so much as our Lord Himself; and the doctrine of reward has a place in His teaching which Protestantism has always found it difficult to embody in its own scheme. Death, judgment, and eternity are the primordial terrors of the human conscience, and the truth about them is not ours to give or withhold as we list; but to preach it earnestly and contantly belongs to the faithfulness of the Christian ministry.

No one will charge Dr. Dale with a narrow, hidebound theology. What does he say? Listen, for his words are weighty: "Are we as anxious—minister and people—about men as our fathers were? On any theory of eschatology, there is a dark and menacing future for those who have been brought face to face with Christ in this life and have refused to receive His salvation and submit to His authority. I do not ask whether the element of fear has a great place in our preaching, but whether it has a great place in our hearts—whether we ourselves are afraid—of what will come to men who do not believe in Christ; whether we, whether our people, are filled with an agonizing earnestness for their salvation."

Again: "The words of Christ, however indefinite they may be with regard to the kind of penalty which is to come upon those who live and die in revolt against God, and however indefinite they may be with regard to the duration of the penalty, are words which shake the heart with fear." It is that which makes the pulpit an awful place and preaching the most awful business in which man can engage. I agree with Dr. Charles Brown when he says, "I think that the modern preacher says far too little about heaven and hell. It seems to me that the modern sermon is too soft. That is the defect in modern preaching."

The evangelism we think of will necessarily make much of the cross. The modern church has many tasks laid upon it, none of which she would wish to refuse. But whatever else she undertakes, evangelism—the direct appeal of the cross to the heart of man—she dare not neglect, else the doom of fruitlessness will fall on her labors. From the very beginning the death of Christ was preached as the heart of the gospel; and Christ is never preached in the New Testament sense unless it be declared that sin, its guilt and power, has been vanquished through our Lord's cross and passion. When the church talks, no matter how eloquently, of Christ as "Teacher," "Example," "Reformer," and the like, and terminates there, its mission in the world will have ceased.

Every element of power in the life and organization of the church ought to be possessed of this passion of evangelism. Anything in the activities of the church that hinders the spirit of evangelism is a high-handed enemy of the life and mission of that church. Every department ought to be mastered with this passion. Dr. L. R. Scarborough told at a meeting of the Southern Baptist Convention in Hot Springs, Arkansas, of an experience which he had when visiting two great churches in the same city. They were alike in wealth, in magnificence, and in the intellectual and social qualifications of their pastors. The one church was visited in the morning and the other in the evening. The weather was ideal in both cases. In the one there was a congregation of fifty and no fellowship abounded. The service was dry and lifeless. The visitor did not feel that he had been to worship. The other church had a congregation of three thousand; glorious fellowship abounded. Intense and spiritual and full of buoyant life were the services. The sermon was stirring and awakening. The choir of three hundred strong sang the songs of Zion, and the visitor felt as the service closed he wanted to go out and win souls. Dr. Scarborough asked—Why this crowd? Why this swelling tide of spiritual life? Why this crowd of young people? The pastor modestly answered, "We go after souls here." The more the church does that, the larger the congregation, better the fellowship, greater the liberality, and mightier the missionary spirit. Surely God's approval today is shown in the spiritual progress of the evangelistic churches.

This is a task for every member of the church. How many a godly minister has his hands and tongue tied because of the false presentation of Christ by many church members? It is pitiful to see an evangelist begging men to call upon the Lord in the arctic atmosphere of a worldly church. A large church membership may be as weak as it is large. Let our church members stop aping the world and get down to the business for which they pledge themselves by the fact of their subscribing to the teaching of the New Testament, and we shall soon see a great change in the world. To declare oneself a member of an evangelical church and contradict the church's teachings by an unevangelical life is to proclaim a living lie. A membership of regenerated and sanctified souls would be invincible. The church needs a revival of personal holiness. The adjustment of the saint precedes the salvation of the sinner. The churches of all denominations are bewailing their losses. Memberships have decreased and conversions have declined. Yet if the evangelistic spirit were truly alive in our churches, and each member won only a single soul for Christ during the whole year, the membership of each individual church would be practically doubled.

This is exactly what is not being done. The average church member feels little or no responsibility in the matter. It never occurs to the average Christian that the very business of life is to win men for God. There is, in consequence, a curious philosophical calm resting upon the churches. There is no sense of urgency; no atmosphere of earnest longing. The unconverted walk in and out, and no one seems to inquire whether they find pasture. It never seems to strike the quiet, peaceful Christian members that they ought to take no rest until someone is converted. If we go to the average church and speak about conversions, we shall discover that such epoch-making events are quite exceptional. We shall hear glowing tales of political sympathies, of social clubs, and literary guilds; almost every church has these things; the one society each church needs is a League of St. Andrew. I wish I could persuade all my friends to read and master Dr. Conant's book, *Every-Member Evangelism.* Let the church get back to apostolic methods of carrying out the divine commission. The saints then were witnessing and they were all witnessing. It was the private witnessing of all the disciples, reaching its climax and culmination in the public witnessing of one disciple, that brought the results of Pentecost. Let each Christian go with the gospel into his own sphere, and a spiritual revolution will soon take place. The church stands in need of such. Imagine a church full of soul-winners. My Lord! What a millennium!

There must be evangelism among the young. I do not limit this to the Sunday school. It covers all departments. Go after the young. We are much more likely to get a boy at seven than at seventeen, and certainly much more likely to get the youth of seventeen than the old man of seventy. And, hear me, your evangelism must commence in the home. A wise evangelism will not neglect the home, but will make that the starting point in the great campaign to evangelize the world. The child must not be treated as though he were an adult. Many have erred by making the same appeal to the children as to men grown old in sin. Others again fall into the error of supposing a child is without the intellectual capacity to understand the doctrines of grace and make a profession of faith. Thus parents, as it were, defend their children from religion; meanwhile moral habits are forming and character is growing towards fixity. So that at the very time when parents are anxious for their child's conversion it has become impervious to the appeal. The truth is, there is scarce a stage so early when Jesus may not be presented to the child mind, and the child soul may not go out to the Lover of little children. If parents are not helping their children's spiritual progress, they are hindering it. What chance has a child's soul, growing up in a professedly Christian, yet worldly home, where neither father nor mother cares enough for Christ to direct their children to Him? There is need of a revival of family religion. Parents cannot be held responsible for the conversion of their children, but they are responsible for the evangelism of the home.

The Sunday school is a fruitful field for labor. Other things there may be which the teacher must do, but he or she must be the unwearying in their quest until the child is won to Christ. Be encouraged to seek their conversion. Many of the great leaders of the church were won in childhood: Polycarp, one of the apostolic fathers, at nine; Matthew Henry, prince of commentators, at eleven; Jonathan Edwards, noted theologian, evangelist, and college president, at seven; Isaac Watts, the greatest of hymnwriters, at nine; Henry Drummond, the scientist-evangelist, at nine. Such shining examples leave no room for doubt as to the possibility of child conversion. It was the faithful efforts of a Sunday-school teacher that led Robert Morrison, the first Protestant missionary to China, to accept Christ. That teacher multiplied her power a thousandfold in the salvation of that boy. John Wanamaker, the Philadelphia merchant, said truly: "When you save a man or woman you save a unit; but when you save a boy or a girl you save a whole multiplication table." It will repay the church over and over again to take care of the young. "Sirs," Mr. Spurgeon was once heard to say, "I tell you that in God's sight he is no preacher who does not care for the children." Some even depreciate the conversion of children, so that when a child comes to Christ very little is thought of it. I am old enough now to look back on a fairly long ministerial life. In it there are some things of which I cannot be proud, and the memory of them makes me uneasy; but the labor I spent amongst children is giving me to this day unalloyed joy. I have just finished reading a book of sermons by one of my Edinburgh boys who was hardly more than an infant when I went to that city. I saw him develop, I remember his beginning to open his mouth in the prayer meeting. He is now a graduate of a Scottish university and an honored minister of the Word. I received a letter from Damascus a while ago, addressed to "My dear pastor," signed by a familiar Christian name of a medical doctor in the hospital there. The doctor was a child in the Sunday school of my Edinburgh ministry.

In concluding our discussion, the question may well be asked, "Who is sufficient for these things?" Where shall power be found for our tasks? I do not underestimate the value of academic training. For this task we need the best training we can bring to bear upon it. In view of the present-day conditions, any revived interest in evangelism must take into account the need of a thorough intellectual as well as spiritual preparation of its preachers. We may differ as to the nature of the training. To some of us it would appear that certain subjects could well be dropped from the curriculum, and others with advantage included. In any event the modern divinity school in its zeal for scholarship must not forget that its only right to exist, and its only claim upon the sympathy and support of Christian people, lie in its affording an effective training for that work of which evangelism is its crowning glory. The man who has the evangelistic passion must exercise it, or else the gifts within him will burn down to white ashes. But while exercising his gift he should let himself be trained in every way possible. Other vocations of life, like that of lawyer, doctor, businessman, demand preparatory hard work and training; then why should we put untrained men into the work of God? If God takes hold of a man called to the work, and such suggested training is not possible, and he becomes a veritable flame, that is no reason why others should shirk the training and slip into the work carelessly. Ignorance is not a qualification for evangelism. The men that the world and the church wait for are men described by Morgan: men "with the vigor of physical strength, with the acumen of mental equipment, with the dynamic of spiritual force."

The deepest and most important thing is that we translate into our lives the teachings which we enunciate from day to day. The man who preaches the cross must be a "crucified" man. Dr. Parker said that what Thomas said of Christ the world is saying of every preacher: "Except I shall see in His hand the print of the nails, . . . I will not believe." We shall take our stand at the cross whereon was purchased our redemption, and thence will survey the world for which Christ died. We shall go to the people with the message we have proved in our own experience. We shall so live the inner Christian life as well as the outer life of conduct, that our evangelism shall not be affronted by our character, nor our teaching be contradicted by our behavior.

The church further needs self-examination. She needs to give heed to her own inward condition. Is the church strong, vigorous, triumphant? Are Christian liberality and Christian service commensurate with the Christian indebtedness to her Lord? Are members of the church living in practical righteousness and holiness? What impression are they producing on the mind of those who make no confession? Is the conscience of the church alert, keen, and active? Are we not conscious of a "sag" rather than of a strong and steady upward movement in the church's condition? A revival of divine life in her is needed before she can be used in the great task of evangelism.

"Our own times," Dr. Jowett remarks, "are in some respects very similar to those of the early nineteenth century. There is widespread discontent with the churches, and many remedies are suggested for their imagined shortcomings. Some would permit smoking in the back pews; shorten the sermon; abolish the sermon; keep the whole service within an hour, or, better, half an hour; employ the cinematograph; get chairs instead of pews; use more ritual; use less ritual—these are the voices of a crowd of counselors. They are concerned with the fire-grate, when what we need is fire; with cake-plates, when what we want is bread; with electrical fittings, when we need the power. The cardinal necessity of the church today is to recover the fullness of her holy gospel and to exult in the incomprehensible glory of her spiritual status." Such power is available, and if we will but turn to the source of it we shall know it. We are to go where we went for forgiveness, to Christ Himself; and as we renew our act of faith with deepening consecration, there will be given to us the Holy Spirit of power, and in that gift we shall have the Father and the Son. God Himself, Father, Son, and Spirit, is the power of evangelism.

The operation of His power is conditioned by prayer. The workmen whom Jesus employs in erecting His church are those who labor much of their time upon their knees. A prayerless evangelism is useless for the accomplishment of the divine purposes. Called to evangelism, the church is also called to a ministry of intercessory prayer. All spiritual victories are gained in answer to prayer. Moses prayed and Israel prevailed. Daniel was more powerful than the king, because he prayed. Elijah carried with him the keys which locked and unlocked heaven. Paul and Silas prayed, and the earth shook and jail doors were opened. At the back of the Reformation of the sixteenth century were the calloused knees of Melanchthon. It was not the thunderbolt of Luther's anathema, but the power of persistent prayer, that broke the arm of the papacy. At the back of the great revival under Wesley and Whitefield there was prayer. So with Finney, Edwards, Moody, and Roberts. There never was a genuine revival of Christianity which did not have its roots in prayer. This is apt to be forgotten even in a church which has been aroused to a sense of its evangelistic function. Let it be well understood that to attempt the work of evangelism without prayer is to insure humiliating defeat, however much time and money have been spent on preparation of a different kind.

Is the program too severe? Is the cost too high? These questions we answer in the light of His cross. We declare no labor is too great to spend on this ministry. Such work has its burden of reward here in changed lives and, I venture to add, changed churches. "The work," says Goodell, "challenged the Son of God and consumed Him with passion, and there is nothing so godlike among men." This is our task; let us take it up.

In church and congregation there remain
The undecided still, beneath your eyes;
Rest not till all new life in Christ obtain:
    Evangelize!

O church of the Redeemer! Look around;
Within your reach a population lies
In ignorance of Christ and unbelief:
    Evangelize!

The greatest joy the church of Christ can have—
The highest service and the noblest prize—
Is to see multitudes brought to the cross:
    Evangelize!

Indifference is foolishness indeed:
Would ye most truly in God's sight be wise?
Spend strength and time to save the souls of men:
    Evangelize!

Train men for home and missionary work:
Be urgent in the task! Time flies! Time flies!
Trust in the Spirit's power; uplift the cross!
    Evangelize!

Bibliography

De Plata, William R. *Tell It from Calvary: The Record of a Sustained Gospel Witness from Calvary Baptist Church of New York City Since 1847*. New York: Calvary Baptist Church, 1972.

Kemp, Joseph W. *Outline Studies in the Book of Revelation*. New York: The Book Stall, 1917.

———. *Outline Studies on the Tabernacle in the Wilderness*. London: Marshall, 1913.

———. *The Soul-Winner and Soul-Winning*. New York: Doran, 1916.

Kemp, Winnie. *Joseph W. Kemp: The Record of a Spirit-Filled Life*. London: Marshall, Morgan, and Scott, 1936.

12

H. A. Ironside

(1876–1951)

The last time I heard H. A. Ironside preach was in the late 1940s at Winona Lake, Indiana. His text was from chapter 32 of his beloved Isaiah (which he pronounced "I-SIGH-ah"). In his own quiet way Ironside exalted Jesus Christ as man's only refuge from the coming wrath of God. I still remember a story he told that day, based on his experiences with the American Indians, of their hurrying into the shelter of a huge rock to escape a sudden storm. I remember too that when he read from his big Bible, he held it close to his eyes, for by that time he was almost blind. One more memory remains: that of Ironside sitting on a bench in the Billy Sunday Tabernacle, watching young Billy Graham preach a dramatic message on the temptation of Christ. Ironside's facial expression was one of appreciation as his younger brother preached the gospel of Jesus Christ. 14 October 1976 marked the centenary of the birth of Henry Allan Ironside. The official biography, *H. A. Ironside* by E. Schuyler English, has been revised and updated by the author. The new edition is published by Loizeaux, publisher of most of Ironside's books.

When Ironside was born, the attending physician thought the baby was dead. Since the mother desperately needed attention, the doctor concentrated on her. Nearly an hour later, a nurse detected the child's pulse. Immediately they plunged the baby into a hot bath, and he began to cry. It seemed evident to the godly parents that the Lord had marked their son for something special.

When Henry, nicknamed Harry, was about two and his brother only three weeks old, his father died. Harry's mother taught him to trust God for everyday needs. Some of the family's experiences read like miracles from the life of Elijah or Paul. Sophia Ironside asked God to make her children preachers of the Word and winners of souls. Under his mother's guidance Harry began to memorize Scripture when he was three. By age fourteen, he had read through the Bible fourteen times, "once for each year." During the rest of his life he read the Bible through at least once a year. A pastor friend told me of a Bible conference at which he and Ironside were two of the speakers. During the conference the speakers discussed their approaches to personal devotions. Each man shared what he had read from the Word that morning. When it was Ironside's turn, he hesitated, then said, "I read the book of Isaiah." He was saturated with the Word of God.

Sophia decided in 1886 to move her family to California. Even though he was not yet converted, young Harry started a Sunday school, which about sixty neighborhood children attended. When he was twelve, Harry went to Hazzard's Pavilion to hear Dwight L. Moody and was deeply stirred by the message. He prayed that evening, "Lord, help me some day to preach to crowds like these, and to lead souls to Christ." Four decades later he became the pastor of Moody Church in Chicago. In several respects Ironside's sermons would be similar to Moody's. They were always directed to the common man and free of theological jargon. They were not long and were filled with the Word of God. Like Moody, Ironside was a master of illustrating truths with personal experiences. From the illustrations in his published expositions one could almost produce an autobiography.

Ironside finally gave his heart to Christ in February 1890, and almost immediately he identified with the Salvation Army. The Army represented just what he wanted in Christian fellowship and service: separation from sin, courage to witness, a burden for souls, and willingness to live by faith. Two years later he was a respected officer. But disillusionment with the Army's position on sanctification resulted in his resigning his commission in 1895. The full story is given in his book *Holiness: The False and the True*, one of the best books available on practical holiness in the Christian life. The next year Ironside identified himself with the Brethren in San Francisco, and the Brethren remained his "ecclesiastical fellowship" until his death.

Several things about Ironside will amaze you as you read English's excellent biography. First is Ironside's faith. God often provided his needs in miraculous ways, especially in the early days of his ministry. Reading about such instances will encourage you greatly to trust God daily. One is tempted to add to Hebrews 11: "By faith Harry Ironside, needing a new suit of clothes . . ." Second is Ironside's willingness to go where God sent him and do what God wished. He never promoted himself or played politics to "get meetings." Whether preaching to small crowds on street corners or to large congregations, he always did his best. Third is his constant study of the Word of God. To compensate for his academic limitations, Ironside literally studied himself blind. (As a hobby, he taught himself Chinese!) His ministry was one of Bible exposition, simply opening the Word of God and allowing the Spirit to speak for Himself. And finally, Ironside always went for souls. To him, Bible exposition was a means to glorify Christ and to call sinners to trust Him.

Ironside first visited the Moody Church in Chicago in 1925, just two months after P. W. Philpott had moved his congregation into their new 4,000-seat auditorium. Ironside was to conduct a two-week conference, but when Philpott was called out of town, Ironside stayed over another week. Philpott invited him back each year, and his ministry was always appreciated. After Pastor Philpott resigned, the congregation inevitably turned to Ironside. The Brethren, with whom Ironside was associated, believed that local assemblies should have several pastor-teachers and that none should be paid. Ironside had agreed with this conviction. Some of the Chicago Brethren talked of breaking fellowship with him if he accepted the call from the Moody Church. But when Ironside was called to the church unanimously on 24 February 1930 and when he accepted, even his Brethren friends promised to pray for and support him.

Today it is still impossible to think of the Moody Church without thinking of Ironside. Those of us who lived in the Chicago area during his long pastorate (1930–1948) thank God for his ministry of the Word. He would select a book of the Bible and preach through it on successive Sundays; most of these series have found their way into print.

Ironside's preaching was the despair of every homiletics professor. I can still hear students arguing with our seminary professor: "But Dr. Ironside doesn't preach with an outline like you're asking us to make." And I can hear the professor's reply: "If you are as good as Dr. Ironside, you don't belong in this class!" While Ironside's messages did not usually follow an obvious outline, they were always organized. He knew where he was going, and he got there. To the casual listener it seemed like the preacher was merely going from verse to verse, making a few comments and explanations and perhaps adding a story. But the careful listener always found a thread of doctrine woven throughout the message. Ironside knew how to compare spiritual things with spiritual. He used the Bible to illustrate and interpret itself. The thing that impressed me most about his preaching was what I call its "personal practicality." He had a message for you, and he wanted you to get it. Usually you did.

Ironside did not "run" the Moody Church. He was often away at conferences during the week and left the day-to-day organizational matters with the staff and church officers. Ironside was the preacher. Everybody knew it, and nobody wanted it any other way. I recall seeing a letter from the elders to Ironside, however, requesting that he limit his summer conference ministry so that he would be at the church when many visitors came. It would be interesting to calculate exactly how many days he was gone during those eighteen years of fruitful ministry. One thing is certain: hardly a Lord's Day went by without one or more persons responding to the invitation at the close of the service and trusting Christ.

Some have criticized Ironside for preaching through Bible books instead of preaching "more contemporary messages" in such a strategic pulpit. But time, I think, has vindicated his ministry. His expositions are as fresh and meaningful today as when they were preached. I have many books of "contemporary sermons" in my library, and they read like old newspapers in comparison. Not every preacher is called to be an expositor, but I encourage every preacher to strive to be one. People everywhere are hungry for the Word of God, and the best way to give them a balanced diet is to preach Bible books, week by week.

On Sunday, 14 January 1951, the Moody Church was joyfully installing their new pastor, S. Franklin Logsdon, when the cablegram arrived from Mrs. Ironside in New Zealand: "Dr. Ironside died in his sleep this morning after short illness." He had been sick less than a week when, on 15 January (the date in New Zealand), he died. At his request he was buried in New Zealand. A great memorial service was held at the Moody Church on Sunday afternoon, 4 February, with Pastors Logsdon and Howard A. Hermansen officiating, assisted by Ironside's good friend Alex H. Stewart, his biographer English, Carl Armerding, William Culbertson, and Homer Hammontree. The blessed influence of Ironside still hovers over the Moody Church. His ministry has strengthened me and encouraged me to do my best.

A Christian bookseller said to me, "There has arisen a generation that knows not Ironside." If that be true—and I am not sure it is then it says nothing about Ironside. But it does say a great deal about the new generation! Ironside was not a dazzling preacher; he did not aim to be sensational. He stepped into the pulpit with exclamation points, not question marks. A generation of preachers that has tried every gimmick available to get people's attention would do well to become acquainted with Harry Ironside and to learn afresh the meaning of living by faith and preaching the Word of God in simplicity and love.

Charge That to My Account

> If thou count me therefore a partner, receive him as myself. If he hath wronged thee, or oweth thee ought, put that on mine account; I Paul have written it with mine own hand, I will repay it; albeit I do not say to thee how thou owest unto me even thine own self besides.
>
> **Philem. 17–19**

Someone has said that this Epistle to Philemon is the finest specimen of early private Christian correspondence extant. We should expect this, since it was given by divine inspiration. And yet it all has to do with a thieving runaway slave named Onesimus, who was about to return to his former master.

The history behind the letter, which is deduced from a careful study of the epistle itself, seems to be this: In the city of Colossae dwelt a wealthy Christian man by the name of Philemon, possibly the head of a large household, and like many in that day, he had a number of slaves or bondsmen. Christianity did not immediately overturn the evil custom of slavery, although eventually it was the means of practically driving it out of the whole civilized world. It began by regulating the relation of master and slave, thus bringing untold blessing to those in bondage.

Author's note: Ironside's sermon "Charge That to My Account" is from *Charge That to My Account*, pp. 5–15, and is used by permission.

This man Philemon evidently was converted through the ministry of the apostle Paul. Where they met, we are not told; certainly not in the city of Colossae, because in writing the letter to the Colossians, Paul makes it clear that he has never seen the faces of those who formed the Colossian church. You will recall that he labored at Ephesus for a long period. The fame of his preaching and teaching was spread abroad, and we read that "all in Asia heard the word." Among those who thus heard the gospel message may have been this man Philemon of Colossae, and so he was brought to know Christ.

Some years had gone by, and this slave, Onesimus, had run away. Evidently before going, he had robbed his master. With his ill-gotten gains he had fled to Rome. How he reached there we do not know, but I have no doubt that upon his arrival he had his fling, and enjoyed to the full that which had belonged to his master. He did not take God into account, but nevertheless God's eye was upon him when he left his home, and it followed him along the journey from Colossae to Rome. When he reached that great metropolis, he was evidently brought into contact with the very man through whom his master, Philemon, had been converted. Possibly Onesimus was arrested because of some further rascality, and in that way came in contact with Paul in prison, or he may have visited him voluntarily. At any rate God, who knows just how to bring the needy sinner and the messenger of the cross together, saw to it that Onesimus and Paul met face to face.

Some years ago there happened a wonderful illustration of this very thing: the divine ability to bring the needy sinner and the messenger of Christ together.

When Sam Hadley was in California, just shortly before he died, Dr. J. Wilbur Chapman, that princely man of God, arranged a midnight meeting, using the largest theater in the city of Oakland, in order to get the message of Hadley before the very people who needed it most. On that night a great procession, maybe one thousand people, from all the different churches, led by the Salvation Army band, wended their way through the main streets of the city. Beginning at 10:30, they marched for one-half hour, and then came to the Metropolitan Theater. In a moment or two it was packed from floor to gallery.

I happened to be sitting in the first balcony, looking right down upon the stage. I noticed that every seat on the stage was filled with Christian workers, but when Sam Hadley stepped forward to deliver the stirring message of the evening, his seat was left vacant. Just as he began to speak, I saw a man who had come in at the rear of the stage, slip around from behind the back curtain, and stand at one of the wings with his hand up to his ear, listening to the address. Evidently he did not hear very well. In a moment or two he moved to another wing, and then on to another one. Finally he came forward to one side of the front part of the stage and stood there listening, but still he could not hear very well. Upon noticing him, Dr. Chapman immediately got up, greeted the poor fellow, brought him to the front, and put him in the very chair which Sam Hadley had occupied. There he listened entranced to the story of Hadley's redemption.

When the speaker had finished, Dr. Chapman arose to close the meeting, and Hadley took Chapman's chair next to this man. Turning to the man he shook hands with him, and they chatted together. When Dr. Chapman was about ready to ask the people to rise and receive the benediction, Hadley suddenly sprang to his feet, and said, "Just a moment, my friends. Before we close, Dr. Chapman, may I say something? When I was on my way from New York to Oakland a couple of weeks ago, I stopped at Detroit. I was traveling in a private car, put at my disposal by a generous Christian manufacturer. While my car was in the yards, I went downtown and addressed a group at a mission. As I finished, an old couple came up, and said, 'Mr. Hadley, won't you go home and take supper with us?'

"I replied, 'You must excuse me; I am not at all well, and it is a great strain for me to go out and visit between meetings. I had better go back to the car and rest.'

"They were so disappointed. The mother faltered. 'Oh, Mr. Hadley, we did want to see you so badly about something.'

"'Very well, give me a few moments to lie down and I will go with you.'"

He then told how they sat together in the old-fashioned parlor, on the horsehair furniture, and talked. They told him their story: "Mr. Hadley, you know we have a son, Jim. Our son was brought up to go to Sunday school and church, and oh, we had such hopes of him. But he had to work out rather early in life and he got into association with worldly men, and went down and down and down. By and by he came under the power of strong drink. We shall never forget the first time he came home drunk. Sometimes he would never get home at all until the early hours of the morning. Our hearts were breaking over him. One time he did not come all night, but early in the morning, after we had waited through a sleepless night for him, he came in hurriedly, with a pale face, and said, 'Folks, I cannot stay; I must get out. I did something when I was drunk last night, and if it is found out, it will go hard with me. I am not going to stay here and blot your name.' He kissed us both and left, and until recently we have never seen nor heard of him.

"Mr. Hadley, here is a letter that just came from a friend who lives in California, and he tells us: 'I am quite certain that I saw your son, Jim, in San Francisco. I was coming down on a streetcar, and saw him waiting for a car. I was carried by a block. I hurried back, but he had boarded another car and was gone. I know it was Jim.'

"He is still living, Mr. Hadley, and we are praying that God will save him yet. You are going to California to have meetings out there. Daily we will be kneeling here praying that God will send our boy, Jim, to hear you, and perhaps when he learns how God saved one poor drunkard, he will know there is hope also for him. Will you join us in daily prayer?"

"I said I would, and we prayed together," said Hadley. "They made me promise that every day at a given hour, Detroit time, I would lift my heart to God in fellowship with them, knowing that they were kneeling in that room, praying God that He would reach Jim, and give me the opportunity of bringing him to Christ. That was two weeks ago. I have kept my promise every day. My friends, this is my first meeting in California, and here is Jim. Tonight he was drinking in a saloon on Broadway as the great procession passed. He heard the singing, followed us to the theater, and said, 'I believe I will go in.' He hurried up here, but it was too late. Every place was filled, and the police officer said, 'We cannot allow another person to go inside.' Jim thought, 'This is just my luck. Even if I want to go and hear the gospel, I cannot. I will go back to the saloon.' He started back; then he returned determined to see if there was not some way to get in. He came in the back door, and finally sat in my own chair. Friends, Jim wants Christ, and I ask you all to pray for him."

There that night we saw that poor fellow drop on his knees, and confess his sin and guilt, and accept Christ as his Savior. The last sight we had of Jim was when J. Wilbur Chapman and he were on their way to the Western Union Telegraph office to send the joyful message: "God heard your prayers. My soul is saved." Oh, what a God, lover of sinners that He is! How He delights to reach the lost and needy!

This same God was watching over Onesimus. He saw him when he stole that money, and as he fled from his master's house. He watched him on his way to Rome, and in due time brought him face to face with Paul. Through that same precious gospel that had been blest to the salvation of Philemon, Onesimus, the thieving runaway slave, was also saved, and another star was added to the Redeemer's crown.

Then I can imagine Onesimus coming to Paul, and saying, "Now, Paul, I want your advice. There is a matter which is troubling me. You know my master, Philemon. I must confess that I robbed him and ran away. I feel now that I must go back, and try to make things right."

One evidence that people are really born of God is their effort to make restitution for wrong done in the past. They want a good conscience both before God and man.

"Paul, ought I to go back in accordance with the Roman law? I have nothing to pay, and I don't know just what to do. I do not belong to myself, and it is quite impossible to ever earn anything to make up for the loss. Will you advise me what to do?"

Paul might have said, "I know Philemon well. He has a tender, kind, loving heart and a forgiving spirit. I will write him a note and ask him to forgive you, and that will make everything all right."

But he did not do that. Why? I think that he wanted to give us a wonderful picture of the great gospel of vicarious substitution. One of the primary aspects of the work of the cross is substitution. The Lord Jesus Christ Himself paid the debt that we owe to the infinite God, in order that when forgiveness came to us it would be on a perfectly righteous basis. Paul, who had himself been justified through the cross, now says, "I will write a letter to Philemon, and undertake to become your surety. You go back to Philemon, and present my letter. You do not need to plead your own case; just give him my letter."

We see Onesimus with that message from Paul safely hidden in his wallet, hurrying back to Colossae. Imagine Philemon standing on the portico of his beautiful residence, looking down the road, and suddenly exclaiming, "Why, who is that? It certainly looks like that scoundrel, Onesimus! But surely he would not have the face to come back. Still, it looks very much like him. I will just watch and wait."

A little later, he says, "I declare, it *is* Onesimus! He seems to be coming to the house. I suppose he has had a hard time in the world. The stolen money is all gone, and now perhaps he is coming to beg for pardon."

As he comes up the pathway, Onesimus calls, "Master, Master!"

"Well, Onesimus, are you home again?"

"Yes, Master, read this, please."

No other word would Onesimus speak for himself; Paul's letter would explain all.

Philemon takes the letter, opens it, and begins to read: *Paul, a prisoner of Jesus Christ.*

"Why, Onesimus, where did you meet Paul? Did you see him personally?"

"Yes, Master, in the prison in Rome; he led me to Christ."

Unto Philemon our dearly beloved, and fellowlabourer.

"Little enough I have ever done, but that is just like Paul."

And to our beloved Apphia. (That was Mrs. Philemon.)

"Come here, Apphia. Here is a letter from Paul." When Mrs. Philemon sees Onesimus, she exclaims, "Are you back?"

One can imagine her mingled disgust and indignation as she sees him standing there. But Philemon says: "Yes, my dear, not a word. Here is a letter for us to read—a letter from Paul."

Running on down the letter he comes to this: *Yet for love's sake I rather beseech thee, being such an one as Paul the aged, and now also a prisoner of Jesus Christ. I beseech thee for my son Onesimus.*

"Think of that! He must have been putting it over on Paul in some way or another."

Whom I have begotten in my bonds.

"I wonder if he told him anything about the money he stole from us. I suppose he has been playing the religious game with Paul."

Which in time past was to thee unprofitable.

"I should say he was."

But now profitable to thee and to me.

"I am not so sure of that."

Whom I have sent again.

"Paul must have thought a lot of him. If he didn't serve him any better than he did me, he would not get much out of him." He goes on reading through the letter.

"Well, well, that rascally, thieving liar! Maybe Paul believes that he is saved, but I will never believe it unless I find out that he owned up to the wrong he did me."

What is this? *If he hath wronged thee, or oweth thee ought, put that on mine account; I Paul have written it with mine own hand, I will repay it: albeit I do not say to thee how thou owest unto me even thine own self besides.*

Oh, I think in a moment Philemon was conquered. "Why," he says, "it is all out then. He has confessed his sin. He has acknowledged his thieving, owned his guilt, and, just think, Paul, that dear servant of God, suffering in prison for Christ's sake, says: 'Put that on my account. I will settle everything for him.' Paul becomes his surety." It was just as though Paul should write today: "Charge that to my account!"

Is not this a picture of the gospel? A picture of what the Savior has done for every repentant soul? I think I see Him as he brings the needy, penitent sinner into the presence of God, and says, "My Father, he has wronged Thee; he owes Thee much. But all has been charged to My account. Let him go free." How could the Father turn aside the prayer of His Son after that death of shame and sorrow on Calvary's cross, when He took our blame upon Himself and suffered in our stead?

But now observe it is not only that Paul offered to become Onesimus's surety, it was not merely that he offered to settle everything for Onesimus in regard to the past, but he provided for his future too. He says to Philemon: "If thou count me therefore a partner, receive him as myself."

Is not that another aspect of our salvation? We are "accepted in the beloved." The blessed Savior brings the redeemed one into the presence of the Father, and says, "My Father, if thou countest Me the partner of Thy throne, receive him as Myself." Paul says, "Not now as a servant, but above a servant, a brother beloved, specially to me, but how much more unto thee, both in the flesh, and in the Lord." He is to take the place, not of a bondsman, but of an honored member of the family and a brother in Christ. Think of it—once a poor, thieving, runaway slave, and now a recognized servant of Christ, made welcome for Paul's sake. Thus our Father saves the lawless, guilty sinner, and makes him welcome for Jesus' sake, treating him as He treats His own beloved Son.

Jesus paid it all,
All to Him I owe;
Sin had left a crimson stain:
He washed it white as snow.

And now every redeemed one is "in Christ before God—yes, made the righteousness of God in him." Oh, wondrous love! Justice is satisfied. What a picture we have here then of substitution and acceptance. The apostle Paul epitomized it all for us: "Who was delivered for our offences, and was raised again for our justification" (Rom. 4:25).

We are accepted in the Beloved. The Lord Jesus became our Surety, settled for all our past, and has provided for all our future. In the Book of Proverbs there is a very striking statement: "He that is surety for a stranger shall smart for it; and he that hateth suretiship is sure" (11:15). These words were written centuries before the cross, to warn men of what is still a very common ground for failure and ruin in business life. To go surety for a stranger is a very dangerous thing, as thousands have learned to their sorrow. It is poor policy to take such a risk unless you are prepared to lose.

But there was One who knew to the full what all the consequences of His act would be, and yet, in grace, deigned to become "surety for a stranger." Meditate upon these wonderful words: "For ye know the grace of our Lord Jesus Christ, that, though he was rich, yet for your sakes he became poor, that ye through his poverty might be rich" (II Cor. 8:9). He was the stranger's surety.

A surety is one who stands good for another. Many a man will do this for a friend, long known and trusted; but no wise man will so act for a stranger, unless he is prepared to lose. But it was when we were strangers and foreigners and enemies, and alienated in our minds by wicked works, that Jesus in grace became our surety. "Christ also hath once suffered for sins, the just for the unjust, that he might bring us to God."

All we owed was exacted from Him when He suffered upon the tree for sins, not His own. He could then say, "I restored that which I took not away" (Ps. 69:4). Bishop Lowth's beautiful rendering of Isaiah 53:7 reads: "It was exacted and He became answerable." This is the very essence of the gospel message. He died in my place; He paid my debt.

How fully He proved the truth of the words quoted from Proverbs, when He suffered on that cross of shame! How He had to "smart for it" when God's awful judgment against sin fell upon Him. But He wavered not! In love to God and to the strangers whose surety He had become, He "endured the cross, despising the shame."

His sorrows are now forever past. He has paid the debt, met every claim in perfect righteousness. The believing sinner is cleared of every charge, and God is fully glorified.

> He bore on the tree
> The sentence for me,
> And now both the surety
> And sinner are free.

None other could have met the claims of God's holiness against the sinner and have come out triumphant at last. He alone could atone for sin. Because He has settled every claim, God has raised

Him from the dead, and seated Him at His own right hand in highest glory.

Have you trusted "the stranger's surety?" If not, turn to Him now while grace is free.

Bibliography

English, E. Schuyler. *H. A. Ironside: Ordained of the Lord.* Grand Rapids: Zondervan, 1946. Reprinted—*Ordained of the Lord, H. A. Ironside: A Biography.* Rev. ed. Neptune, N.J.: Loizeaux, 1976.

Ironside, H. A. *Addresses on the Gospel of John.* New York: Loizeaux, 1942.

______. *"Charge That to My Account" and Other Gospel Messages.* Chicago: Bible Colportage Association, 1931.

______. *Expository Messages on the Epistle to the Galatians.* New York: Loizeaux, 1940.

______. *Expository Notes on the Prophet Isaiah.* New York: Loizeaux, 1952.

______. *Holiness: The False and the True.* New York: Loizeaux, 1939.

______. *In the Heavenlies: Practical Expository Addresses on the Epistle to the Ephesians.* New York: Loizeaux, 1949.

______. *Lectures on Daniel the Prophet.* New York: Loizeaux, 1920.

______. *Lectures on the Book of Revelation.* New York: Loizeaux, 1919.

______. *Lectures on the Epistle to the Romans.* New York: Loizeaux, 1951.

______. *Random Reminiscences from Fifty Years of Ministry.* New York: Loizeaux, 1939.

______. *Studies in the Epistle to the Hebrews . . . Lectures on the Epistle to Titus.* New York: Loizeaux, 1942.

13

William Culbertson

(1905–1971)

"In whatever man does without God, he must fail miserably—or succeed more miserably." So wrote saintly George Macdonald, and his counsel is desperately needed by Christian leaders and organizations today. An evil idea is abroad in the land that spiritual life is not important to spiritual leadership. So long as the leader projects a "successful image" and manifests "dynamic," he will be successful. Holiness of life, spiritual growth, and obedience to the Word of God have been replaced by promotion, public relations, and obedience to the latest conclusions of the Madison Avenue geniuses.

I do not want to be misunderstood. Christian organizations ought to learn all they can about business methods and leadership principles. Our Lord reminds us that "the children of this world are in their generation wiser than the children of light" (Luke 16:8), and we ought to borrow their wisdom (shortsighted as it is) and put it to work for God. But we dare not undermine the spiritual foundations on which God's work is built. Alas, there are Christian organizations today that have a "form of godliness" (so as not to upset the donors), but in which godliness *as a force* is sadly lacking. Not that there are chinks in the armor; sad to say, the armor was taken off long ago and the organization left naked and ashamed before her enemies. To change the picture, the veneer on the building will peel off little by little, and the foundation of sand will crumble. One day the whole edifice will fall, and a great fall it will be.

In my brief ministry I have met several Christian leaders who knew how to exercise spiritual leadership without sacrificing good business principles. To borrow the old Youth for Christ slogan, they were "geared to the times but anchored to the Rock." One such man was William Culbertson, bishop of the Reformed Episcopal Church, dean of education at the Moody Bible Institute (1942–1948), and president of that school for twenty-three fruitful years. Wilbur M. Smith stated it perfectly: "My first impression and the lasting one is that he is a man of God."

William Culbertson was born on 18 November 1905 into a very godly home in Philadelphia. He was an only child but not of the "spoiled" variety. He trusted Christ as Savior at age nine, and the experience was so real to him that shortly afterward he led his uncle to the Lord. He graduated from West Philadelphia High School in 1924 (where he had taken four years of Greek!), and that same year entered the Reformed Episcopal Seminary in Philadelphia. The Reformed Episcopal Church had been founded by G. D. Cummins in 1873, mainly because of doctrinal "deterioration" in the American Episcopal church. The group was opposed to the "ritualism and sacerdotalism" of the parent body. James M. Gray, another president of Moody Bible Institute, also belonged to this denomination.

After Culbertson graduated from seminary in 1924, he became pastor of Grace Reformed Episcopal Church, Collingdale, Pennsylvania. He studied at Temple University in Philadelphia and taught at Philadelphia School of the Bible (now Philadelphia Bible College) and at his alma mater. In 1939 he graduated from Temple and was granted an honorary D.D. from Reformed Episcopal Seminary. He pastored St. John's-by-the-Sea, Ventnor, New Jersey, and the Church of the Atonement, Germantown, Philadelphia, before moving to Chicago in 1942 to become dean of education at Moody Bible Institute.

Will H. Houghton was president of the school at that time, and he was excited about the new dean God had provided, a man who blended deep spirituality with solid education and common sense. Culbertson's years as a bishop in his denomination (he had been elected in 1937) gave him wide experience in "managing spiritual business," and his academic credentials gave him acceptance in the field of education. Preaching and teaching were his first love, and he especially enjoyed teaching the Pauline epistles and Bible geography. It was an open secret on campus that when Culbertson was bored with a speaker or a meeting, he would study the maps at the back of his Bible! Houghton died on 14 June 1947, and five days later Culbertson was appointed acting president. He never moved into Houghton's office, nor did he exercise any "evangelical politics" to succeed Houghton. Members of the administrative staff urged him to seek the position of president, but he quietly refused. Then on 4 February 1948 the trustees named him president of the school, and he accepted.

According to S. Maxwell Coder, who succeeded Culbertson as dean of education, "William Culbertson moved the Moody Bible Institute out of the nineteenth century and into the twentieth century." Some of the new president's associates did not think he moved things fast enough. One of his favorite expressions was, "Well, let's sleep on it." But when you examine the progress report for his years of administration, you cannot help but conclude that God used him and things were accomplished. The physical campus was greatly improved, the curriculum updated, and the spiritual life of the campus family strengthened. Old ministries were expanded (or quietly buried), and new ministries inaugurated. All of this was accomplished during a turbulent era in American church history when more than one Christian organization either compromised the faith or went out of business. God "called home" Culbertson on 16 November 1971. His last words summarized the deep spiritual passion of his entire life: "God—God—yes!"

It was my privilege to know Dr. Culbertson, and it was my further privilege to be chosen to write his biography, *William Culbertson: A Man of God* (1974). During months of research, I found a few people who disagreed with his program, and some who were impatient with his deliberate style of management; but I found no one who questioned his character or attacked his reputation. Even his enemies (and he had a few) had to admit he was a man of God.

So much for his life and ministry. Now let us go deeper and explore the spiritual principles that operated in his life. Above all else, Culbertson walked with God. He spent time in the Word and in prayer. He looked at the practical decisions of life with the eyes of a man who first looked to God. He did not call committee meetings, make decisions, and then ask God to bless them. He prayed about matters, pondered them long and hard, and brought to bear upon his decisions every experience with God, every truth God had taught him from the Word. You could not be with him very long before saying to yourself, "This is a man of God." This does not mean Culbertson was solemn and ultraspiritual, a fragile saint only to be admired from a distance. He had a great sense of humor, and he lived in contact with people. He did not waste his time "building a public image." He was what he was whether preaching in a church or playing handball with men on the staff. He practiced a healthy kind of holiness that convinced you it is a joyful, robust thing to be a Christian.

I am impressed by the way God prepared him for his strategic ministry. His years of study (and they were difficult years), his experience as a teacher, his work as a bishop: all contributed to his ministry at Moody Bible Institute. He did not seek any office, and to "politic" for position would have been utterly foreign to him. He was content to do the work God had given him until the Master called him to another ministry. I suppose every organization has its "pyramid climbers" who jockey for promotion and position. Culbertson would not be in their company. A Christian leader lamented to me recently about the small number of younger men and women who are prepared to move into positions of greater leadership. "Where are the replacements?" he asked me. "Isn't God preparing people today as He did in Bible days?" My answer may not be the correct or only one, but it is worth considering: Many Christians today will not permit God to prepare them. They go too fast too soon. When they get "to the top," they discover the shoes are too big for their pygmy feet. The applause of the crowd is not always the approval of the Lord.

Culbertson was a lifelong student of the Word and of related subjects. Stephen Olford's evaluation of Culbertson's preaching is apt: "You sense reality in his preaching." He did not depend on other people for either his sermons or the articles he wrote. What he produced came from God and was (as Robert Murray McCheyne used to say) "oil, beaten oil for the sanctuary." His Monday morning chapel addresses at the institute were filled with solid spiritual food, some of which the students did not completely digest until years later. I have read scores of letters from former students at the institute who had become pastors and missionaries and who wrote something like this: "We did not always fully understand what you taught us in chapel, but now that we are in the heat of the battle, your messages come back to us with new power and blessing."

I have always felt that Culbertson lived under the shadow of Houghton, his predecessor. Houghton was a dynamic leader and eloquent pulpiteer; Culbertson was a quiet leader who preferred to work through organizational channels, and a preacher who depended more on depth of character and thought than on heights of oratory. Each man had to be true to his own gifts and calling, and we must not say that one was better than the other. Each made his contribution to the work and then was "called home." Certainly Culbertson had no reason to doubt his abilities or question his competence because his style of leadership was different from Houghton's.

I get the impression that some Christian leaders are too busy to meditate on the Word, pray, and wait for God to speak to them personally. I have heard many sermons and read many books that merely recycle old material; they are the shallow products of a busy life. Whenever you heard Culbertson speak (or pray), you knew he had just come from the throne with a live coal ready to burst into flame. Christian leaders must realize that if they suffer from shallowness, the malady will spread throughout the entire organization.

I have touched on three factors that contributed to Culbertson's ministry: a deep devotion to Christ, a period of God-directed preparation, and a disciplined effort to "take time to be holy." Let me add a fourth: a loving conviction about biblical separation. Culbertson believed in separation, but not in the pharisaical sort that separates true believers. "There is a schismatic separation," he said in an early sermon, "when *our notions* separate us from true believers, when we separate ourselves unto men or mere opinions. There is no cause for separation when men differ in minor details but not in the great doctrines of Scripture." It was not easy to maintain the school on a steady course during those stormy days of the 1950s and 1960s when evangelical groups were debating and dividing over the matter of separation. Because Culbertson feared God, he feared no man; but he was always gracious and kind when he disagreed. He held to his position courageously, but he did not require you to stand with him. He respected your right to disagree, but he expected you to do the same.

Not only are some Christian leaders neglecting spiritual and intellectual growth, but they tend to cater to the constituency, especially if they depend on the constituency for support. I have seen Christian organizations completely reverse a policy or abandon a principle because of a few letters of criticism. While it is true we must listen to the counsel and even the criticism of others, it is also true that we dare not be "reeds shaken in the wind." Culbertson listened, pondered, and prayed; but he did not impulsively make radical changes just to please people. "For if I yet pleased men, I should not be the servant of Christ" (Gal. 1:10). I suppose the word that best describes his leadership is *integrity*. In a letter to Culbertson in 1939, Houghton said: "With modernism as dead as ever . . ., with the worldly churches dying of dry rot, and with so much of Fundamentalism impotent through various causes, there is surely a place of tremendous need for an institution of integrity, loyalty, faith, and power." Integrity is the opposite of duplicity; it speaks of wholeness of character. Like David, William Culbertson "fed them according to the integrity of his heart, and guided them by the skilfulness of his hands" (Ps. 78:72). And like David he was a "man after God's own heart"—a man of God.

Unfortunately not many of Culbertson's messages have been published. Only three volumes have appeared: *God's Provision for Holy Living*, his Bible readings at British Keswick in 1957; *The Faith Once Delivered*, his keynote addresses for the institute's annual Founder's Week; and *For Times like These*, his editorials in *Moody Monthly*. A book of his "man to man" addresses to pastors would be valuable, as would a book of his chapel talks.

In time there arises "a generation that knows not Joseph," and we must not complain if yesterday's spiritual heroes become but memories. But there are many of us who give thanks for the privilege of living in the same century as William Culbertson, and we trust we will not forget the lessons he taught us.

Taking the Cross and Following the Lord

I am sure that any soul spiritually sensitive, looking upon conditions in the church today, is disturbed. There is a great deal of easygoing "Christianity." We seem to know little of discipleship. It was this burden that led a writer in the United States to say: "Millions of Christians live in a sentimental haze of vague piety, soft organ music, trembling in the lovely light from stained glass windows. Their religion is a thing of pleasant emotional quivers, divorced from the real, divorced from the intellect, and demanding

---

Author's note: Culbertson's sermon "Taking the Cross and Following the Lord" is from Herbert F. Stevenson, ed., *Keswick's Triumphant Voice*, pp. 301–9, and is used by permission. He preached this sermon at the Keswick Convention in 1957.

little except lip service to a few harmless platitudes. I suspect that Satan has called off the attempt to convert people to agnosticism. If a man travels far enough away from Christianity he is always in danger of seeing it in perspective, and deciding that it is true. It is much safer, from Satan's point of view, to vaccinate a man with a mild dose of Christianity, so as to protect him from the real thing."

The keenness of that analysis is tragic, is it not? I can say from the depths of my heart that I abhor that kind of Christianity; and God being my helper, in so far as I can influence what goes on at Moody Bible Institute, we are not there to train easygoing Christians; we are there to graduate disciples. To that end pray for us, for in many senses of the term we are going against the current.

Now in Matthew 16:24–27 we have in succinct form the demands of the Lord of those who are His children. He speaks forthrightly and clearly, that if we are to go after Him—to use His language: "If any man would come after me, let him deny himself, and take up his cross, and follow me" (ASV).[1] Now this passage is tremendously moving. There are two little words, one of which occurs three times, which lead us into the movement of the passage, and prepares us to understand what our Lord says. The first of these words is *then*. "*Then* said Jesus unto his disciples . . ." That points to a precise occurrence; that sets the stage in a particular circumstance. *Then* He said it. There was something in the environment of that particular time that elicited from our Lord this particular teaching. *Then* He said, "If any man would come after me, let him deny himself."

Having articulated the principle, having laid down the call to discipleship, He followed that call by three reasons why we should obey that call: and each of the reasons is introduced by the little word *for*. You will see it at the beginning of verse 25, at the beginning of verse 26, and at the beginning of verse 27. "Then said Jesus . . . If any man would come after me, let him deny himself, and take up his cross, and follow me. *For* . . ." and He gives the reason. "*For* . . ." He says the second time, and gives the second reason. "*For* . . ." He says the third time, and gives the third reason. And if only God the Holy Spirit will use these lips of mine to strike home to your hearts these reasons which the Lord Jesus gave, then entirely apart from anything else, my coming to Keswick will have been wonderfully worthwhile.

"Then said Jesus . . ." When? The context gives the answer. It is that context which begins with the word concerning the confession

1. The American Standard Version is quoted throughout this sermon.

of Peter, "Thou art the Christ, the Son of the living God." Oh, how that must have thrilled the heart of the Lord Jesus, as the apostle Peter, undoubtedly the spokesman for the rest, enunciated so perfectly the identity of our Lord. "Who do men say that I am?"

"Some say that you are John the Baptist; some say that you are Elijah; some say that you are Jeremiah; some say that you are one of the prophets."

"Who say *ye* that I am?"

"Thou art the Christ, the Son of the living God."

Peter's understanding of the identity of his Lord was not the result of some special acumen on his part. The Lord Jesus said, "Blessed art thou, son of Jonah; for flesh and blood hath not revealed it unto thee, but my Father who is in heaven. . . . You have believed what God the Father has said about me."

Oh, how thrilled our Lord must have been! Here He was, working with these men, teaching them, leading them, living with them, all to the point that they should understand who He was, and why He had come; and now here is one who has grasped clearly His identity. "Thou art the Christ."

Now they were ready for the next lesson—and that is the way God always works. When we learn one lesson, He will teach us the next. The trouble with a lot of us is that we have attended conventions and conferences, and gotten a lot of information that is merely theoretical. When God teaches us, it is experimental; and He does not teach us the second lesson until we have learned the first one.

Their having understood the first lesson—who He was—He proceeded to tell them why He had come. And so I read in verse 21, "From that time began Jesus to show unto his disciples, that he must go unto Jerusalem, and suffer many things of the elders and chief priests and scribes, and be killed, and the third day be raised up." It was on one of these occasions when He was speaking in this vein that Peter took Him—I take it that that means he even took Him by the arm—took Him aside to speak to Him, and—the audacity of this disciple!—he began to rebuke the Lord, saying: "Be it far from thee, Lord: this shall never be unto thee!" It was then our Lord turned upon Peter, and in words of excoriation which hardly find their equal anywhere in Scripture, He said to Peter: "Get thee behind me, Satan: thou art a stumbling-block unto me: for thou mindest not the things of God, but the things of men." "This shall never be unto Thee! Lord, be it far from Thee! To die, to go to Jerusalem, to be crucified. Be it far from Thee." How we can thank God that Peter's request and statement was never answered in the way he asked for it to be answered. For if our Lord had not gone to the cross, where should we be?

Now basically, I suppose, there are only two philosophies of life. Oh, there are many more, but they are variants of the two in one form or another. And these are clearly presented in this passage. One of them is in the words of Peter—and I would like to give you a more literal translation of what Peter actually said: "Pity Thyself, Lord! This shall never be unto Thee!" And multitudes in the world are living with that as the philosophy of their lives. Anything that would cause hardship, anything that would cause heartache, anything that would cause difficulty, anything that would cause them the least inconvenience—away with it! Circumvent it! Live for the things of time and sense, and find ease, find comfort, discover that which is pleasing to the flesh. That is one philosophy of life. But for the Christian, the source of that philosophy is forever settled and made absolutely clear by none other than the voice of the Son of God. He said that is out of the picture. He says that has the smell of the sulphurous flames of hell. That is Satan's philosophy. "Thou savorest not of the things that be of God, but the things that be of men."

The other philosophy is in the language of our Lord Jesus. He said, "Deny thyself." There you have the two possibilities. Pity thyself; deny thyself. And only the second is Christian. Now it was out of this circumstance, it was when Peter voiced the philosophy of men, when he gave voice to what Satan would have men do, to pity themselves, it was *then* that our Lord Jesus came forth to announce this principle so clearly. "If any man would come after me, it is not a matter of 'Pity thyself,' but a matter of 'Deny thyself,' and take up thy cross, and follow me."

My friends, it is high time we faced the fact that the Christian life is no picnic. It is no joy ride to heaven. The Lord Jesus never deceived His followers into thinking that Christianity was a picnic. Invariably He pointed out the hardships, the difficulties that they would encounter if they would follow Him. Deny thyself. Take up thy cross. And, may I say a word about the cross that we take up? I may have told you a story about Dr. P. W. Philpott. He was a Canadian, but ministered in the States, and went to be with the Lord not so long ago, rich in years. When I was a young pastor in the city of Philadelphia, Pennsylvania, Dr. Philpott responded to an invitation to come and visit us at my church. And he would take me aside on occasion and give me some pastoral advice; and I was very glad for it.

I remember on one occasion, in the dead of winter, we had had snow and sleet and ice and everything that made it hard for people to get around; and one night we were waiting for the congregation to get together. I was in the study, and he came in, and I rose to greet him. He did not let me sit down again, but stood right in front of me. Unfortunately there was a radiator behind me, and he kept backing me right into that hot radiator! He kept shaking his bony finger in front of my nose as he talked to me. And he said: "Let me tell you something that happened to me, when I was a pastor up in Canada. I noticed that there was a family absent from church for a couple of Sundays, so I went to call on them. Now," he said, "I don't advise you to do this, but I went early on Monday morning to call on this family." Well, I took my hat off to Dr. Philpott; if he was going early on Monday morning, here was one preacher that was not going early on Monday morning—that's washday in the States! But he could get away with it. And he said: "I rang the bell, and nobody came; so I rang again, and finally the good lady of the house came, her hair all disheveled, you know, and she was trying to straighten an apron. And she said, 'Oh, pastor, I'm so sorry you came today. I'm not prepared for you!' " That is exactly the way we like to get people, not prepared for us!

"And she said, 'Well, do come in, pastor!' " So he went in, and asked her why they had not been to church, and got all that straightened out. Then, because he was a family man, he took some things in that some of us might not have observed. He looked out of the window, and saw a storm was gathering. So he said, "I knew you were washing; I saw the clothes out in . . ."—well, you know, we call it "the backyard"—excuse me—" . . . the garden; don't you think maybe we had better go out and get some of those clothes down? There is a storm coming, and if it rains, you know what's going to happen." Well, my hat was off to him again. Any preacher who knows how to take down clothes . . .!

"Oh, no, pastor, it's just so wonderful to have you here, and to have you talk about the things of God. Now I just want you to read, and to pray."

And so he read; and then he looked out of the window again, and said, "That storm is just about to break. Before I pray, don't you think we ought to get those clothes in?"

"Oh, no, pastor, you just go ahead and pray."

And the heavens opened when he prayed. I mean literally! Oh, how it rained! But the little lady seemed unperturbed; and as the pastor was leaving he looked back—and I guess the little lady saw the look on his face, for she put her head out of the door and looked back, and she blanched. "Oh," she said. "Look! I was up at five o'clock this morning; I washed all those clothes so beautifully, and the line has broken, and look! Look at them in the mud! There they are!" Then she sobered, and said, "Pastor, I guess that's my cross!"

Then Dr. Philpott began to do it to me—it wasn't my clothes, but he began to do it to me! He said, "I shook my finger under the nose of that little lady, and I said to her, 'Don't you ever . . .' "—and he was coming closer to me, and I was moving farther back—" ' . . . don't you ever say that's your cross. Anything that can happen to your neighbor who isn't even a believer, can't be a cross to you if it happens to you. Your cross is what you suffer because you are a Christian.' "

I have never forgotten that, for he was right. "Deny yourself. Take up your cross. Follow me!" Deny yourself, yes. Say no to yourself. Yield yourself to the will of God. Say yes to God, so that even though it means saying no to the fondest ambition that you have, and the choicest desire that you have, and even the legitimate desires that you have, you are God's disciple: you deny yourself. You say yes to Christ, and follow Him.

I like the sweet reasonableness of the Lord. He did not just say that, but He added some reasons why. Would you think briefly with me of the reasons why? Why should we, who are children of God, do this that the Lord Jesus asks? Well, of course, because of His mercies. That is Romans 12:1–2. We would be ingrates if we did not respond: He gave us His all; how can we do less than give Him our all? Surely that is a good reason. But the Lord Jesus does not talk about that reason. He talks about three other things. Look at them.

First, "For whosoever would save his life shall lose it: and whosoever shall lose his life for my sake shall find it." What a paradox. What strange language is this. You have your life by losing it; and you lose your life by keeping it. And, look, my friend, that is so true that even some worldlings understand it; even some who do not know God understand it. That actually it is not our continual grasping and getting things for ourselves, finding ease and comfort, pitying ourself, that is going to enable us really to live. It is the giving of ourselves. And particularly—and this the worldling does not understand—particularly the giving of ourselves to the Lord Jesus, the handing over of our life to Him, the losing of our life to Him; the loosing, if you will, of our hand on our life, and handing it over to Him. Losing our life that way, we find it.

The only way truly to live is to be yielded to the Lord Jesus

Christ as God's servant. I want to testify very gladly, and very humbly: I did not know what life was until I yielded my all to the Lord Jesus Christ. Oh, how the devil has us baffled. Oh, how the world has us cooped up in a corner, not understanding that what God wants to give us is the best. "Thou wilt show me the path of life: in thy presence is fullness of joy: and in thy right hand are pleasures for evermore."

Oh, my friends, if you only knew what the Lord wants to give you! I have never found a saint of God all out for the Lord who has been sorry that he has gone all out for God. The only way truly to live is to deny yourself; to take up your cross, and follow Him.

Now the world looks at us, and when we do that they say, "Well, isn't he a somber individual! Isn't he a joyless soul!" And, you know, our newspaper cartoonists have their favorite picture of the Christian: he has a long, stovepipe black hat, a long coat that reaches almost down to his ankles, and a face as long as he is! Oh, yes! You know! The devil has them deceived. Listen, listen! Oh, my friend: "I am come that they might have *life*, and that they might have it more abundantly." The Lord Jesus gives you to know life—real, throbbing, pulsating life; without any morning-after-the-night-before: you know what I mean? Oh, it's great to be a Christian. It is great to be on the Lord's side. It is great to yield yourself to Him.

Says the Lord Jesus: "Deny yourself: take up your cross and follow me; because if you lose your life, if you lose your life in My will, if you lose control of your life and let it shift its moorings, and let Me become the Captain of your soul, then you will live; then life will be real and wonderful."

Look at the second reason. You will see it in verse 26: "What shall a man be profited, if he shall gain the whole world, and forfeit his life? Or what shall a man give in exchange for his life?" This business of living for God, this business of denying yourself and taking up your cross and following the Lord Jesus Christ, not only means that in that way you will fully live; it also means that you are making the most profitable use of the life span that God has given you. This change in translation is a good change; for the Lord puts a great value upon your life span here on earth. It is the most valuable possession that you have. I do not care how wealthy you are; I do not care how many stocks and bonds you have (the government will take care of that for you anyway!); I do not care what your name is. My friend, your most valuable possessions are those precious seconds, and minutes, and hours, and days, and weeks, months and years, that God gives you to live down here. Oh, that is a precious commodity. I do not wonder that my predecessor, Dr. Will H. Houghton, when he wrote that beautiful hymn, after the martyrdom of John and Betty Stam, put the prayer in it, "Lord, teach me the value of these hours."

Oh, what a precious commodity! They fly so fast. Says the apostle Paul, "Be not unwise, but wise—don't be foolish—*redeeming the time*"—buying up the opportunities. I suppose there is not one of us but that looks back upon his life and wishes he could live part of it over again, if not all of it, because we have wasted time, and have prostituted the use of that time; instead of using it for good, we have used it for evil. Time. Do you want to know how to make the best use of the life span that God has given you? Deny yourself: "Take up your cross, and follow Me. For what is a man profited if he shall gain the whole world, and forfeit his life? What shall a man give in exchange for his life?" Nothing, nothing.

So I find that discipleship means, first, truly living. It does not mean a joy ride to heaven; it does not mean that there are no trials and no burdens. But it does mean peace in your soul and joy in your heart, and a sense, a supreme sense, of the smile of the Lord upon you. It is *living*. And discipleship means that you are using your time on earth to the best possible advantage. The Lord Jesus says so.

But there is a third thing, in verse 27, "For the Son of man shall come in the glory of His Father. . . ." Deny yourself, take up your cross, follow Me—"for the Son of man shall come in the glory of the Father with his angels; and then shall he render unto every man according to his deeds." We are going to give an answer some day as to how we use this precious time. And the way to be best prepared for giving that answer is to be a disciple, is to deny yourself and take up the cross, and follow the Lord Jesus. Oh, yes, dear Christian, we know about the judgment seat of Christ theoretically. I suppose there are some of us that can enumerate all the judgments in the Bible, and give the various points under them; but wait a minute. Have you let it saturate your soul? Have you let it sink down into your heart, what it is going to mean to stand at the judgment seat of Christ?

Then shall every man "be made manifest before the judgment-seat of Christ," says II Corinthians 5:10. You will not just appear; you will be *manifest*. Everything will be stripped, everything absolutely open; there you stand to give an account for the deeds done in the body. You are going to stand there some day, and oh, how cheap, how miserably insufficient will seem some of the excuses we are making now, for not living out-and-out for God. We are going to give an answer. I do not know where—in a pillared hall, or under the great expanse of the dome of heaven—there is going to be a dais, and on that dais is going to be a throne, and on that throne the Son of God is going to sit. And you and I, individually, personally, one by one, are going to face the One whom we love, who gave Himself for us, and we are going to give an answer of the deeds done in the body.

Says the Lord Jesus, "If you want to be ready for that day, deny yourself, take up your cross, and follow Me." The three reasons: discipleship means that I really live—not just eke out existence, not just saunter along, but live, with all the throbbing, pulsating quality of real life. It means that I shall make the best possible use of the life span that God has given me. It means that when I stand at the judgment seat of Christ, I shall not have to be ashamed.

I remember reading a story—let me tell it to you in the first person, although the experience was not mine. I saw in a dream that I was in the celestial city, though when I traveled there I could not tell. I was one of a great multitude which no man could number, from all countries and people, from all times and ages. Somehow I found that the saint who stood next to me had been in heaven almost nineteen hundred years. "Who are you?" I said to him.

"I," said he, "was a Roman Christian. I lived in the days of the apostle Paul. I was one of those who died in Nero's persecution. I was covered with pitch, and fastened to a stake, and set on fire to light up Nero's gardens."

"How awful!" I exclaimed.

"No, no!" he said, "I was glad to do something for the Lord Jesus. He died on the cross for me."

The man on the other side then spoke. "I have been in heaven only a few hundred years. I came from an island in the South Seas. John Williams the missionary came and told me about the Lord Jesus, and I learned to love Him. My fellow countrymen killed the missionary, and they caught and bound me. I was beaten until I fainted, and they thought I was dead, but I revived. The next day they killed me, and cooked me, and ate me!"

"Oh, how terrible!" I said.

"No, no," he answered. "I was glad to die as a Christian. You see, the missionaries had told me that the Lord Jesus was scourged and crowned with thorns for me."

Then they both turned to me and said, "What did you suffer for Him? Or did you sell what you had and give it so that men like John Williams could tell the heathen about the Lord Jesus?" And I was speechless. And while they were both looking at me with sorrowful eyes I awoke, and it was a dream. But I lay on my soft bed awake for hours, thinking of the money I had wasted on my own pleasure, my extra clothing, and the many luxuries. And I realized that I did not know what the words of the Lord Jesus meant: "If any man would come after me, let him deny himself, and take up his cross, and follow me."

Bibliography

Culbertson, William. *The Faith Once Delivered: Keynote Messages from Moody Founder's Week.* Chicago: Moody, 1972.

______. *For Times like These.* Chicago: Moody, 1972.

______. *God's Provision for Holy Living.* Chicago: Moody, 1957.

Stevenson, Herbert F., ed. *Keswick's Triumphant Voice: Forty-eight Outstanding Addresses Delivered at the Keswick Convention, 1882–1962.* Grand Rapids: Zondervan, 1963.

Wiersbe, Warren W. *William Culbertson: A Man of God.* Chicago: Moody, 1974.

Part 2

Classic Books for the Preacher

14

Preaching on the Miracles

Many of the people we preach to week by week are secretly looking for the answer to the same questions that perplexed Gideon: "Oh my Lord, if the Lord be with us, why then is all this befallen us? and where be all his miracles which our fathers told us of. . . .?" (Judg. 6:13). In short, "If God is a God of miracles, why doesn't He do something?" Does He still heal the sick immediately, without means? Does He raise the dead? Do believers today have the right to expect Him to do for them in the twentieth century what He did for believers in the first?

Of course there are solutions to this problem that are less than Christian. You can deny the existence of God or of miracles. But these "solutions" create problems far worse than the original one, and they certainly do not square with the revelation in God's Word. As biblical preachers, we must go to the Bible and let God teach us His mind about the miraculous.

I suggest that you plan a course of messages on the miracles of the Bible. But before announcing the series, invest plenty of time in study, starting with C. S. Lewis's little masterpiece *Miracles*.

Lewis was greatly influenced in this area by George Macdonald and his book *The Miracles of Our Lord.* If you can locate a copy, read it carefully and note the seeds that later bore fruit in Lewis's work.

If it has been a long time since you considered miracles from an apologetical point of view, then study the relevant material in *Christian Apologetics* by Norman Geisler, *An Introduction to Christian Apologetics* by Edward Carnell, and *Studies in Theology* by Loraine Boettner. The article on miracles in *The Zondervan Pictorial Encyclopedia of the Bible* is an excellent introduction to the subject. A more popular treatment will be found in *Dear Agnos* by Arlie J. Hoover.[1]

Our purpose is not to turn sermons into addresses on theology. Our messages must always be theological, but they must first of all minister in a personal way to the hearts and lives of our listeners. The defense of the faith is but a preliminary step to the encouragement of the faithful. People live on promises, not explanations; and the human heart responds to the revelation of Jesus Christ as He is proclaimed in power.

Having surveyed the subject doctrinally and apologetically, you are now ready to outline a course of messages. You may want to begin with a message based on Judges 6:13—"What Ever Happened to Miracles?" Should believers today "put out the fleece" as Gideon did? Can we expect God to intervene in a miraculous way every time His people are in trouble? Is God willing to act but unable because of our unbelief ? Is it just as miraculous for God to work through means? People are asking these questions; perhaps we cannot answer them all in one message, but we can make a beginning.

The most comprehensive book on Bible miracles is *All the Miracles of the Bible* by Herbert Lockyer. After scanning this volume, you can decide what areas of revelation you want to tackle for your series: Old Testament miracles, miracles of Christ, apostolic miracles, forgotten miracles, misunderstood miracles, "sign miracles"

---

1. Norman Geisler, *Christian Apologetics* (Grand Rapids: Baker, 1976); Edward Carnell, *An Introduction to Christian Apologetics: A Philosophic Defense of the Trinitarian-Theistic Faith* (Grand Rapids: Eerdmans, 1948); Loraine Boettner, *Studies in Theology* (Grand Rapids: Eerdmans, 1947; reprinted—Philadelphia: Presbyterian and Reformed, n.d.); Gordon H. Clark, "Miracles," in Merrill C. Tenney, ed., *The Zondervan Pictorial Encyclopedia of the Bible*, 5 vols. (Grand Rapids: Zondervan, 1975), 4:241–50; Arlie J. Hoover, *Dear Agnos: A Defense of Christianity* (Grand Rapids: Baker, 1976).

in John's Gospel, healing miracles recorded by Dr. Luke, miracles in the life of Peter (a most interesting study), counterfeit miracles. The possibilities are many. Lockyer did not organize his book under those topics; but as you read it, you will readily see the variety of approaches you can take.

If you focus on the miracles of Christ, be sure to study that section in W. Graham Scroggie's indispensable *Guide to the Gospels.* He listed thirty-five different miracles, twenty-three of which relate to healing. Scanning this list, I discovered several miracles that our Lord performed on the Sabbath, which could be presented in a helpful series. While reading Scroggie, be sure to study the charts that show how the miracles are distributed throughout the four Gospels. You could preach a series on the miracles found only in John (there are six) or in Luke (again six). Mark has only two miracles not found in other Gospels.

The seven miracles recorded in John's Gospel have a special purpose and are worthy of pulpit treatment. Along with the standard commentaries on the fourth Gospel (I thoroughly enjoy those by Leon Morris, William Hendriksen, and Arthur W. Pink—although Pink at times goes overboard on typology),[2] you will want to study Merrill C. Tenney's excellent survey, *John, the Gospel of Belief. Expository Studies in St. John's Miracles* by Thomas Torrance is a fine study with helpful homiletical ideas. J. C. Ryle's classic *Expository Thoughts on the Gospels* is a gold mine of sane exegesis and warm-hearted exposition and application.[3]

Some standard works on the Gospel miracles should be at hand as you prepare to preach. *The Miraculous Element in the Gospels* by Alexander B. Bruce is a work of the highest standard, a companion volume to Bruce's *Parabolic Teaching of Christ.*[4] The former is

---

2. Leon Morris, *The Gospel According to John: The English Text with Introduction and Notes,* New International Commentary on the New Testament (Grand Rapids: Eerdmans, 1971); William Hendriksen, *Exposition of the Gospel According to John,* 2 vols., New Testament Commentary (Grand Rapids: Baker, 1953–1954); Arthur W. Pink, *Exposition of the Gospel of John* (Grand Rapids: Zondervan, 1975).

3. Merrill C. Tenney, *John, the Gospel of Belief: An Analytic Study of the Text* (Grand Rapids: Eerdmans, 1948); Thomas Torrance, *Expository Studies in St. John's Miracles* (London: Clarke, 1938); J. C. Ryle, *Expository Thoughts on the Gospels for Family and Private Use,* 7 vols. (New York: Carter, 1858–1870; reprinted—4 vols., Grand Rapids: Baker, 1977).

4. *The Parabolic Teaching of Christ: A Systematic and Critical Study of the Parables of Our Lord* (New York: Armstrong, 1883).

both a defense of the miraculous and an exposition of the Gospel narratives describing miracles.

The Miracles of Our Lord by John Laidlaw is not much help apologetically but makes a tremendous contribution homiletically. Next to Richard Trench's monumental *Notes on the Miracles of Our Lord,* Laidlaw's book has been the most helpful one in my library. For examples of solid preaching, read *The Miracles of Our Saviour Expounded and Illustrated* by the great Scottish preacher William M. Taylor. Another helpful volume is *Sermons on the Miracles* by Charles H. Spurgeon. Spurgeon had a gift for seeing practical truths in familiar Scripture passages, and this series is no exception.

Each miracle has unique characteristics and must be studied from that point of view. Why is the miracle of the coin in the fish's mouth (Matt. 17:24–27) the only Gospel miracle using money? Why is it recorded only in Matthew? Of the several accounts of the healing of blind men, how do they differ? Why do they differ?

I strongly recommend that you study the three resurrection miracles in the Gospels: that of the widow's son, the daughter of Jairus, and Lazarus. Here we have a twelve-year-old girl, a young man, and an older man. And in each case the Lord worked differently. Note that each person gave evidence of life in a different way. Surely we can relate these miracles to the great miracle of salvation (Eph. 2:1–10).

Our Lord's "water miracles" prove an interesting study, as do His miracles involving demonic forces. I have enjoyed preaching about the "minor miracles": healing Peter's mother-in-law, cursing the fig tree, healing a man's withered hand. His two "Gentile miracles" are interesting: healing the centurion's servant and the daughter of the Canaanite woman. The fact that He healed both at a distance is worth noting.

The apostolic miracles in the Book of Acts fit into the category of apologetics, according to Hebrews 2:1–4. You will find that the miracles of Peter and Paul parallel each other. For some reason preachers have neglected the miracles in the Book of Acts, and this is unfortunate.

No matter what text we preach, we must find, as Phillips Brooks said, "where truth touches life." To discuss a miracle of history without bringing its truths to bear upon present reality is to miss a great pastoral opportunity. The miracles reveal a God who cares, who knows the needs of His people and seeks to meet them. God worked, for the most part, in response to faith; and He did everything possible to strengthen the faith of His people. Certainly the miracles reveal God to us, God as seen both in Jesus Christ in the Gospels and in the Holy Spirit in Acts.

To be sure, there are deeper spiritual lessons in the miracles. While we may not agree with every detail of Pink's interpretations, his *Exposition of the Gospel of John* leads the field in explaining spiritual truths taught by the miracles. By the way, you will want to read the article on "miracle" in *The New International Dictionary of New Testament Theology*, as well as related articles in the *Theological Dictionary of the New Testament*.[5] These in-depth word studies indicate that God had more in mind in the miracles than meeting human need. Each miracle was a "sermon in action," and it is for us to discover the deeper truths in each miracle that apply to human life today.

Take the miracle of Jesus cursing the fig tree (Mark 11:12–26; Matt. 21:18–21). Surely it had its application to the fruitless nation of Israel, but its meaning is much broader. (Our Lord's parable of the fig tree in Luke 13:6–9 helps explain the Jewish context of the miracle.) Here are some practical lessons for today: Christ is seeking fruit; fruitlessness is sin; fruitlessness begins with the roots; fruitlessness is judged; fruitlessness can be corrected. The same Christ who judged the tree could have healed it. The tree could not decide to change, but we Christians can.

The raising of the widow's son (Luke 7:11–17) teaches us that Christ has power over death. I like to point out the three *meetings* at the city gate: (1) *two crowds met*—a sad crowd going to the cemetery and a joyful crowd following Jesus; (2) *two sufferers met*—a mother who had lost her only son and an only Son who had left His Father to come as the Man of sorrows; (3) *two enemies met*—the Prince of life and the last enemy, death. I do not think we are stretching a point or overspiritualizing Scripture when we see in our Lord's action a picture of the resurrection of the church and its reunion with Him when He returns.

The physical resurrection of Lazarus in John 11 is a perfect parallel to the spiritual resurrection of the believing sinner as described in Ephesians 2. Lazarus was dead; he could not help him-

5. Colin Brown, ed., *The New International Dictionary of New Testament Theology*, 3 vols. (Grand Rapids: Zondervan, 1975–1978); Gerhard Kittel and Gerhard Friedrich, eds., *Theological Dictionary of the New Testament*, trans. and ed. Geoffrey W. Bromiley, 9 vols. (Grand Rapids: Eerdmans, 1964–1974).

self; he was raised from the dead; he was loosed from the grave-clothes (the old life, Col. 3); he was seated with Christ (John 12:2); and by his life he helped win others to the Lord (John 12:9–11).

Why not preach a message that deals with Jesus' two miracles in Mark 5:21–43—healing the woman with the hemorrhage and raising Jairus's daughter? The contrast between the wealthy man and the poor woman, who meet at the feet of Jesus, is worthy of study. Because the woman was healed, the little girl died! How did Jairus feel toward the woman because she delayed the Lord? How did Jesus encourage Jairus's faith? Why did our Lord force the woman to confess her faith openly? There is scope for great preaching here! And how many people there are who have hidden needs they are ashamed to confess. How many there are who wonder at the delays of the Lord!

I do not suggest that you try to deal with all the miracles in one series. Put them into smaller packages so your people will have time to digest the truths you preach. "Blessed are the balanced!" applies to preaching as well as practicing the truth.

You may want to add a message on "The Man Who Did No Miracles"—John the Baptist (John 10:40–42). You would have expected John to do miracles: he had been born miraculously; he heralded a miraculous Savior; he was filled with the Spirit from before birth! John was not even delivered miraculously from prison the way Peter was. I sometimes contrast Lazarus and John the Baptist, for both led people to Christ. We have no recorded words of Lazarus, yet he was a walking miracle; we have a record of John's words, yet he did no miracles.

You might deal with the Book of Esther: it records no miracles, yet God providentially delivered His people. Or how about the three Hebrew children in Daniel 3 who were willing to obey God even if He did not miraculously deliver them! Our Lord's comment in Luke 16:27–31 shows that the Word of God has more power to convict and convert than miraculous events; II Peter 1:12–21 substantiates this.

Give yourself time to assimilate the meaning of the miraculous in the Word of God. Seek God's guidance as you assemble material and develop your series. Pray that God will help you reveal Christ's glory (John 2:11) and exalt His grace as you magnify His power to meet the needs of His people. For the greatest miracle is that of saving a person and building Christlike character into the person's life. Paul prayed for a miracle of healing but experienced a miracle of patience and power (II Cor. 12:1–10). The miracles of

God's grace are far greater than the miracles of God's government and power, and we can experience those miracles today.

Bibliography

Bruce, Alexander B. *The Miraculous Element in the Gospels: A Course of Lectures on the "Ely Foundation," Delivered in Union Theological Seminary.* New York: Armstrong, 1886.

Laidlaw, John. *The Miracles of Our Lord: Expository and Homiletic.* London: Hodder and Stoughton, 1890.

Lewis, C. S. *Miracles: A Preliminary Study.* New York: Macmillan, 1947.

Lockyer, Herbert. *All the Miracles of the Bible: The Supernatural in Scripture, Its Scope and Significance.* Grand Rapids: Zondervan, 1961.

Macdonald, George. *The Miracles of Our Lord.* New York: Routledge, 1870.

Pink, Arthur W. *Exposition of the Gospel of John.* 4 vols. Swengel, Pa.: Bible Truth Depot, 1923-?. Reprinted—1 vol. Grand Rapids: Zondervan, 1975.

Scroggie, W. Graham. *A Guide to the Gospels.* Know Your Bible. London: Pickering and Inglis, 1948.

Spurgeon, Charles H. *Sermons on the Miracles.* Library of Spurgeon's Sermons, edited by Charles T. Cook, vol. 3. Grand Rapids: Zondervan, 1958.

Taylor, William M. *The Miracles of Our Saviour Expounded and Illustrated.* New York: Armstrong, 1890.

Trench, Richard. *Notes on the Miracles of Our Lord.* London, 1846. Reprinted—Popular edition. Grand Rapids: Baker, 1949.

15

Preaching on the Parables

If you have not given at least one series on the parables of Jesus, then confess your sin, apologize to your congregation, and get to work! The parables are inexhaustible. You can preach them again and again and find new truths about man and God.

But beware! If you think you can outline a parable for a sermon and then paraphrase it, you are heading for disaster. Retelling the story is not the same as interpreting the truth of it or applying its message. It takes as much devoted study to unlock the parables as it does the doctrines taught by Paul in Romans or Ephesians. Each parable is like a many-faceted jewel. As the light shines through and you gaze from various angles, you discover new truths and new applications of old truths.

Before getting too far into your studies, read *Poet and Peasant* by Kenneth E. Bailey. This is the most exciting book on the parables since *The Waiting Father* by Helmut Thielicke. You do not need to agree with all of Bailey's ideas to profit greatly from his work. After reading *Poet and Peasant,* I revised several of my sermons in a series on the prodigal son. If you preach on the prodigal without consulting Bailey's book, you will be robbing yourself and your people. Bailey dealt only with Luke 11, 15, and 16; but his studies will help you understand all the parables.

The classic text on the parables is *Notes on the Parables of Our Lord* by Richard Trench. Be sure to purchase the edition with the footnotes in English if you do not remember your high-school Latin. Trench is always helpful, although he rarely dared to introduce a novel interpretation or application. For that you must turn to *The Parables and Metaphors of Our Lord* by G. Campbell Morgan. Morgan had that gift of penetrating a passage and coming up with such obvious truths that we wonder how we failed to see them first. He gave this series to the famous Westminster Chapel "Friday Night Bible School," and we are happy they were recorded for us to enjoy today. *The Parables and Metaphors of Our Lord* also deals with the symbols Jesus used in His teaching: for examples, the church as the light of the world and the salt of the earth. His studies of Peter as a rock and of "the temple of his body" are stimulating. You may want to do a series on "Pictures Jesus Painted" and use these familiar but little-understood metaphors.

Benjamin Keach's *Gospel Mysteries Unveil'd* and *Tropologia* have been reprinted (with different titles). Keach was the second pastor of the Baptist church that eventually became Charles H. Spurgeon's tabernacle. Keach began there in 1668 and remained for thirty-six years. Spurgeon commented on Keach's books: "Although our honored predecessor makes metaphors run on as many legs as a centipede, he has been useful to thousands. His work is old-fashioned, but it is not to be sneered at."[1]

The experienced preacher will have on his shelf the standard works on the parables: *The Study of the Parables* by Ada R. Habershon, *The Parables of Our Lord* by Marcus Dods, *The Parables of Our Lord* by William Arnot, and *The Parabolic Teaching of Christ* by Alexander B. Bruce. The more modern studies of the parables by George Henry Lang and Joachim Jeremias must not be ignored. Eta Linnemann's *Jesus of the Parables* leans heavily on form criticism, as does Jeremias's work; but the book is helpful.

What about sermons on the parables? I have already suggested that *The Waiting Father* by Thielicke is the finest modern production. Anything by Thielicke is certain to stimulate your mind or warm your heart. *Christ and the Meaning of Life* contains additional sermons on the parables. The well-known preacher and

1. *Commenting and Commentaries* (London: Passmore and Alabaster, 1876; reprinted—London: Banner of Truth, 1969), p. 155.

teacher of preachers George A. Buttrick has given us *The Parables of Jesus*. We do not agree with some of Buttrick's interpretations, but we admire his approach to the parables and his skill at interpreting them for the homiletician. Buttrick did his homework before writing this book! Other examples of how the parables can be preached are available in *The Parables* by Gerald H. Kennedy. This book overemphasizes the social gospel. Many of the parables have a social application, but Kennedy "reached" a bit here and there in applying these passages to social problems of the day. Both Kennedy and Buttrick suggested imaginative ways of dealing with the parables, and imagination (not fancy) is certainly needed in this kind of preaching.

For a meaty but traditional approach to the parables, read *The Parables of Our Saviour* by the great Scottish preacher William M. Taylor. Taylor pastored the Broadway Tabernacle, New York City, from 1872 to 1893 and gave the Yale Lectures on preaching in 1876 and 1886. He preached in the traditional Scottish style with solid exposition and personal application.

By the way, Spurgeon did some of his greatest preaching on the parables. The Kelvedon edition of his sermons has a volume on the parables, but that edition was severely edited and does not represent "pure Spurgeon." Check the *Metropolitan Tabernacle Pulpit* or the *Treasury of the New Testament*. Be warned, however, that it is easy to preach Spurgeon—so save him until after you have completed your personal study.

I have enjoyed preaching a series on Luke 15, "God's Lost-and-Found Department." The parable of the prodigal son and his neglected elder brother fascinates me, and I enjoy preaching the truths in it. *The Waiting Father* includes two sermons on the prodigal son. Spurgeon's *Twelve Sermons on the Prodigal Son* contains a wealth of material. You will also want to read *The Parable of the Father's Heart* by Morgan, and *The Prodigal* by Frank W. Boreham.[2] One of my favorite "prodigal books" is *Horns and Halos in Human Nature* by J. Wallace Hamilton.[3] I enjoy all of Hamilton's books, but *Horns and Halos* is my favorite. Hamilton was a unique pastor and preacher. I fear he did not have a strong gospel

---

2. Charles H. Spurgeon, *Twelve Sermons on the Prodigal Son and Other Texts in Luke 15, Delivered at the Metropolitan Tabernacle* (New York: Revell, n.d.; reprinted—Grand Rapids: Baker, 1976); G. Campbell Morgan, *The Parable of the Father's Heart* (New York: Revell, 1949); Frank W. Boreham, *The Prodigal* (London: Epworth, 1941).

3. Westwood, N.J.: Revell, 1954.

emphasis, but his insights into spiritual truth and human nature are most refreshing. This book contains fourteen sermons on the prodigal son. Another helpful little volume is one in the Short Course Series: *The Joy of Finding* by Alfred E. Garvie.[4] This volume deals only with the parable of the prodigal son and contains many helpful suggestions for the preacher. The appendix contains many helpful quotes on the parable from Alexander B. Bruce, Alfred Plummer and Walter F. Adeney.

Another specialized field is Matthew 13—the parables of the kingdom. Your treatment of these parables will depend on your definition of "the kingdom of heaven" and your interpretation of the Gospel of Matthew. The dispensational approach, as found in the *Scofield Reference Bible*, was presented ably by Arthur W. Pink in the little book *The Prophetic Parables of Matthew Thirteen*. Pink's interpretation reflects the dispensational position of J. N. Darby and William Kelly, as well as F. W. Grant. Morgan's *The Parables of the Kingdom* takes a different approach. For a modern sermonic treatment read *Behind History* by Ray C. Stedman. Most of us know Stedman as the gifted author of *Body Life*. Word Books is printing a number of his sermon series. I once heard Vance Havner say, "Too many of you preachers are more concerned with your dispensations than your dispositions." Do not make that mistake when expounding Matthew 13. Jesus used parables to impart life-changing truth. To relegate them to charts and outlines is to bury truth and starve souls. I think Stedman did a good job of blending interpretation and personal application.[5]

It is best to serve the parables in short courses. Depending on how you define the word *parable*, there are between fifty and sixty examples in the Gospels. I do not recommend that you cover all of them in one year. That would be too much of a good thing. You may want to preach a series of twelve messages on the more familiar parables. You could then use Matthew 13 or Luke 15 for a later series. I enjoyed doing Matthew 13 in the midweek service and Luke 15 in the evening service. After an interval, prepare a series on the lesser-known parables of our Lord, or perhaps on some of

---

4. *The Joy of Finding; or, God's Humanity and Man's Inhumanity to Man: An Exposition of Luke 15:11–32* (New York: Scribner, 1914).

5. Arthur W. Pink, *The Prophetic Parables of Matthew Thirteen* (Covington, Ky.: Calvary Book Room, n.d.); G. Campbell Morgan, *The Parables of the Kingdom* (New York: Revell, 1907); Ray C. Stedman, *Behind History* (Waco, Tex.: Word, 1976).

His metaphorical statements. The "judgment parables" in Matthew 21–25 make a good Lenten series.

The important thing is to obey Phillips Brooks and discover "where truth touches life." It is your job to *preach* the parables, not to tell a story and give a few tame exhortations. Live with the parables (and the best commentaries on them) until they get into your system and excite you. Once they excite you, they will excite your congregation.

One final caution: you cannot preach everything in a parable in one message. At a Bible conference I once spoke for over an hour on the parable of the sower. A friend said, "Would you come to my church and give that series?" The average congregation cannot digest that much truth at one time. Either hit the highlights of the parable or break the message down into a short series.

Those of you who want to venture into the Old Testament parables will get a great deal of help from *Expository Outlines on the Miracles and Parables of the Old Testament* by Trench and others. These forty-two studies should provide you with sufficient ideas for a series. The editor, however, has used the word *parable* in a broad sense, so be careful what passages you choose.

I have yet to find a congregation that does not benefit from a sermon on a parable.

Bibliography

Arnot, William. *The Parables of Our Lord.* London: Nelson, 1864.

Bailey, Kenneth E. *Poet and Peasant: A Literary-Cultural Approach to the Parables in Luke.* Grand Rapids: Eerdmans, 1976.

Bruce, Alexander B. *The Parabolic Teaching of Christ: A Systematic and Critical Study of the Parables of Our Lord.* New York: Armstrong, 1883.

Buttrick, George A. *The Parables of Jesus.* New York: Harper, 1928. Reprinted—Grand Rapids: Baker, 1973.

Dods, Marcus. *The Parables of Our Lord.* First series, *The Parables Recorded by St. Matthew;* second series, *The Parables Recorded by St. Luke.* London: Hodder and Stoughton, 1883–1886.

Habershon, Ada R. *The Study of the Parables.* New York: Cook, n.d. Reprinted—Grand Rapids: Kregel, 1957.

Jeremias, Joachim. *The Parables of Jesus.* Translated by S. H. Hooke. New York: Scribner, 1955.

Keach, Benjamin. *Gospel Mysteries Unveil'd; or, An Exposition of All the Parables and Many Express Similitudes Contained in the Four Evangelists, Spoken by Jesus Christ.* 4 vols. London, 1701.

Reprinted—*Exposition of the Parables in the Bible*. Grand Rapids: Kregel, 1974.

———. *Tropologia: A Key to Open Scripture Metaphors*. London, 1681. Reprinted—*Preaching from the Types and Metaphors of the Bible*. Grand Rapids: Kregel, 1972.

Kennedy, Gerald H. *The Parables: Sermons on the Stories Jesus Told*. New York: Harper, 1960.

Lang, George Henry. *The Parabolic Teaching of Scripture*. Grand Rapids: Eerdmans, 1955.

Linnemann, Eta. *Jesus of the Parables: Introduction and Exposition*. Translated by John Sturdy. New York: Harper and Row, 1967.

Morgan, G. Campbell. *The Parables and Metaphors of Our Lord*. New York: Revell, 1943.

Taylor, William M. *The Parables of Our Saviour Expounded and Illustrated*. New York: Armstrong, 1886.

Thielicke, Helmut. *Christ and the Meaning of Life: A Book of Sermons and Meditations*. Edited and translated by John W. Doberstein. New York: Harper, 1962.

———. *The Waiting Father: Sermons on the Parables of Jesus*. Translated by John W. Doberstein. New York: Harper, 1959.

Trench, Richard. *Notes on the Parables of Our Lord*. London, 1841. Reprinted—Popular edition. Grand Rapids: Baker, 1948.

Trench, Richard, et al. *Expository Outlines on the Miracles and Parables of the Old Testament*. London: Dickinson, 1890. Reprinted—Grand Rapids: Baker, 1974.

16

Sermon Series

Not every preacher thinks in terms of sermons in series. Some prefer to preach the Word week by week as the Spirit of God directs them. Charles H. Spurgeon was not a "series" preacher; neither was George W. Truett. Therefore a man must not think himself odd or backslidden if he prefers not to serve the spiritual food in courses.

But many others feel that the sermon series has distinct advantages for both the pastor and the church. To begin with, when a man (led by the Spirit) arranges a series of messages, he knows where he is going and can make better use of his preparation time. I cringe with embarrassment when I think of the hours and days I wasted in my first pastorate trying to determine a text for next Sunday's sermon. By the time I decided on one, I no longer had sufficient time left to study for and prepare the message.

This does not mean the preacher is locked into so rigid a program that the Spirit cannot give him a special message for that hour. On more than one occasion I have broken into a series with a special message, and the message had a greater impact because it was an interruption. But I believe, and I have learned by experience, that the Holy Spirit can prepare the preacher and the message weeks in advance as well as hours in advance. On many Sundays the message that had been scheduled months before turned out to be just the Word the congregation and pastor needed.

Most congregations thrive on series preaching. For one thing, a series arouses interest; and excitement and anticipation are good preparation for hearing God's Word. Series preaching exposes the people to various aspects of God's truth and, I might add, helps keep the preacher from riding his favorite homiletical hobbies. The inner man, just like the outer man, needs a balanced diet.

The pastor must take care, however, that church services not fall into a comfortable coffin due to sameness of diet. If I am expounding a different book of the Bible at each of the Sunday services, I should prepare something else for the midweek service. In fact I have tried to do the solid exposition on Sunday mornings (always with an evangelistic note, because that is when the unsaved attend church), and then do a more popular series in the evening service. At times I have reversed the schedule. The important thing is variety with balance. Sameness leads to tameness.

Some series are obvious: the Ten Commandments (and do not forget that eleventh commandment in John 13:34); the Beatitudes; the fruit of the Spirit in Galatians 5; the Lord's "I am" statements in the Gospel of John; His seven words from the cross; the seven churches of Asia Minor. But there are other series that are not as obvious, and I want to suggest some of them to you.

I borrowed an idea from one of George H. Morrison's sermons and did a series on "the refusals of Christ." You will find the original sermon in Morrison's book *Flood-tide.*[1] I called my series "When Jesus Said No" and dealt with: the miracle He refused to perform (Luke 4:1–4); the crown He refused to wear (John 6:14–29); the cup He refused to drink (Matt. 27:33–34); the prayer He refused to pray (John 17:15); the home He refused to visit (John 4:43–54); the disciple He refused to enlist (Mark 5:1–20); the visitors He refused to receive (John 12:20–36); the argument He refused to settle (Luke 12:13–34); and several others. As you read the Gospels, you will undoubtedly find many more examples.

The "fear not" statements of the Bible also make a helpful series, but please do not use all of them! Select a balanced list from both

---

1. London: Hodder and Stoughton, 1901. Reprinted—Grand Rapids: Baker, 1971.

testaments and be sure the circumstances involved touch on the varied problems and fears of life.

If you want to help your church family increase their ministries to each other, preach a series on the "one another" statements of the New Testament: love one another, edify one another, pray one for another. I counted about fourteen different passages that say "love one another"; and I have a list of twenty-two additional "one another" admonitions.

Another helpful series for the local church treats the biblical "pictures of the church": the family (and you could do an entire series on that theme), the army, the flock, the kingdom of priests, the temple, and others. In each message you can point out the privileges and responsibilities of the believer in the local church, and also the relationship of the pastor to the church. Guy King's delightful book *Brought In* will give you several helpful ideas, as will Robert Lee's *Similes of Our Lord and "His Own."*[2]

I had a delightful time with a Sunday evening series on Bible vocations. I called it "Help Wanted!" and dealt with such people as potters, goldsmiths, shepherds, fishermen, and carpenters. A few hours with your Bible dictionary and encyclopedia will supply all the vocations you need. *The Workmen of the Bible* by Donald Davidson contains homiletical studies of sixteen vocations and ends with a chapter on the unemployed; it is worth buying.

By all means preach on the great prayers of the Bible. Paul's prayers are worthy of study, and be sure to secure *Gleanings from Paul* by Arthur W. Pink and *The Prayers of St. Paul* by W. H. Griffith Thomas. Herbert Lockyer's encylopedic *All the Prayers of the Bible* is indispensable for a series like this. I once preached a series on "Famous Unanswered Prayers," which resulted in a different approach to teaching truths about prayer. What were the "unanswered prayers" in my series? Paul's prayer for healing in II Corinthians 12 was one. Two others were Salome's request for thrones for her two sons and Martha's prayer that Jesus rebuke Mary and put her to work. What about the prayer of the man of Gadara who was delivered from the legion of demons (Mark 5:18)? Note that three prayers were offered on that occasion: the demons prayed that Jesus would send them into the swine, the villagers that Jesus would leave, and the man that he might go with Jesus

---

2. *Brought In: Talks on the Positive Side of Christian Experience* (London: Marshall, Morgan, and Scott, 1949); *Similes of Our Lord and "His Own,"* Mildmay Devotional Series, no. 1 (London: Pickering and Inglis, 1930).

and serve Him. Our Lord answered the first two prayers affirmatively, but not the third!

Night scenes of the Bible have always been a good series. I need not list the events for you because you know them well. Have you ever preached a series on the "sleepers of the Bible"? Start with Adam in Genesis 2 (imagine waking up and discovering you are married!), and be sure to note the three times Peter went to sleep. I once did a series on "Bible fires" that proved helpful: the burning bush, the burning of God's Word (Jer. 36), the three Hebrew children in the furnace, the "strange fire" of Leviticus 10, the bonfire at Ephesus (Acts 19:11–20), and the lake of fire.

Mentioning "strange fire" reminds me of several "strange things" in the Bible that could comprise series: strange fire, strange incense (Exod. 30:9), strange land (Ps. 137:4), strange work (Isa. 28:21). Please do not treat these texts as novelties. The fact that you are giving a popular setting to the messages does not justify shallow preparation and barren content. I have discovered that the Spirit of God teaches people new truths when we put them in new settings, and that often He catches a believer unawares who might resist the truth given in a verse-by-verse exposition.

In a single sermon Spurgeon once preached on all the "I have sinned" texts of the Bible, but he was one of the few who could get away with it. These texts make a splendid series because they teach the difference between true repentance (illustrated by David and the prodigal son) and false (Pharaoh, Balaam, Judas, and Saul), and they highlight the miracle of God's grace in forgiving and restoring the erring sinner. Check your concordance for other examples. You might balance these confessions of sin with a series on "great confessions of faith": those of Joseph (Gen. 50:24–26); Joshua (Josh. 24:15); Elijah (I Kings 18); Job (Job 13:15); Peter (Matt. 16:16); Paul (Acts 27:21–26); and I am sure you can think of others.

By all means preach a series on the "great words of the gospel." I think my title for such a series was "The Vocabulary of Victory," and I preached on justification, sanctification, adoption, propitiation, and other great doctrines. H. A. Ironside's *Great Words of the Gospel* is an example of this kind of preaching. Never be afraid to preach Bible doctrine, but be sure you make it meaningful to believers today.

We must occasionally preach about the great personalities of the Bible, and here the possibilities are many. Clarence Macartney and Clovis Chappell were both masters of this kind of preaching, and their books are available today in reprint editions. Here are some ideas: people who said no; forgotten people; failures who made good; men who wanted to die; great women; people who received new names; saints in strange places (examples: Abraham in Egypt, Lot in Sodom, Peter by the enemy fire). You could do a course on the life of a personality such as David, Abraham, Elijah, Peter, and Paul. Excellent biographical studies by F. B. Meyer will help point the way;[3] also consult *The Representative Men of the Bible* and *The Representative Women of the Bible* by George Matheson. Alexander Whyte's *Bible Characters* series is rich with spiritual insight. I have also been helped by J. Sidlow Baxter's *Mark These Men* and William S. LaSor's *Great Personalities of the Bible*.

What more shall I say? Time would fail me to write about series dealing with: Bible doors, invitations, paradoxes, benedictions, promises; great Bible chapters, titles and names of Christ, titles and names of the Holy Spirit, names of God in the Old Testament, and many more. As you live in your Bible and keep your homiletical senses alert, you will discover new ways to package old truths of the Word of God.

A few closing words of counsel.

If you find that a series is not really generating interest and accomplishing something, end it early. I once bravely started a series on Moses, beginning with his birth, and after a few weeks found myself struggling to stay above water. As young as I was, I was smart enough to quit. The people thanked me.

Never announce a sensational series or message unless you can produce the goods. Andrew W. Blackwood once announced a series on heaven, only to discover that each week he had less and less to say. When he got to his message on "The Geography of Heaven," he was sorry he had ever started. A topic or sermon title that looks exciting in your notebook may prove to be a dud when you begin preparing the actual message. The late R. G. Lee used to warn against "laying a foundation for a skyscraper and then building a chicken coop on it." Good advice!

Unless your people can take more, limit your series to six to ten messages, or at the most twelve. If you try to exhaust the subject, you may also exhaust the congregation. W. Graham Scroggie once started a long series from Romans, and week by week his crowd evaporated. A not-too-gentle note from a church member forced Scroggie to realize he was not made for long, detailed series. So he

3. See chap. 6, note 5.

shifted to the shorter "overview" series that made his ministry so effective. Never fight in Saul's armor; you may kill yourself and your church.

Finally, advertise your series in advance and distribute nicely printed cards or folders that describe it. I have had the joy of leading people to Christ who came to church to hear a series of messages I was preaching. But be sure your advertising does not promise more than you can deliver.

A sermon series in the hands of a dedicated preacher can be an effective way to teach the Word and build the church. Certain seasons of the year (Advent and Lent in particular), lend themselves to special series, but our people are always hungry for new pastures where there is nourishment for their souls. Keep your preaching biblical and balanced (a "breather" between series is helpful), and God will bless the people through your preaching.

Bibliography

Baxter, J. Sidlow. *Mark These Men: Practical Studies in Striking Aspects of Certain Bible Characters.* Grand Rapids: Zondervan, 1960.

Davidson, Donald. *The Workmen of the Bible.* London: Clarke, 1937

Ironside, H. A. *Great Words of the Gospel.* Chicago: Moody, 1944.

LaSor, William S. *Great Personalities of the Bible.* Westwood, N.J.: Revell, 1965

Lockyer, Herbert. *All the Prayers of the Bible.* Grand Rapids: Zondervan, 1959.

Matheson, George. *The Representative Men of the Bible.* 2 vols. London: Hodder and Stoughton, 1902–1903.

———. *The Representative Women of the Bible.* Edited by William Smith. London: Hodder and Stoughton, 1907.

Pink, Arthur W. *Gleanings from Paul: Studies in the Prayers of the Apostle.* Chicago: Moody, 1967.

Thomas, W. H. Griffith. *The Prayers of St. Paul.* The Short Course Series, edited by John Adams. Edinburgh: Clark, 1914.

Whyte, Alexander. *Bible Characters.* 6 vols. Edinburgh: Oliphant, Anderson, and Ferrier, 1898–1902. Reprinted—1 vol. Grand Rapids: Zondervan, 1968.

17

Books of Quotations

One of my favorite pastimes is paging through books of quotations. This is more than an opportunity for relaxation because I usually discover a statement that opens the door to an aspect of truth I have never considered. For example, the statement "Liberty is not an end; it is a means" is excellent for a series of sermons on Galatians. The fact that the statement is a quotation from Benito Mussolini only emphasizes the point more—he abused that liberty and it killed him.

Books of quotations are a marvelous literary and spiritual adventure. We preachers know (and our people suspect) that nothing we say is really original. All we do is package it in a new way. Even the great Charles H. Spurgeon confessed: "Thoughts belong to everybody, brethren. I must not wonder if other people steal my thoughts, since I have stolen so many of other people's. For my part, I beg, borrow, and steal from every conceivable quarter; *but* when I steal a man's coat, I tear it all to pieces and make a waistcoat out of it."[1] Or to change the image, Spurgeon milked many cows, but he made his own butter. You and I should do the same, and good books of quotations will help.

Most people use quotation books for two valid purposes: to locate and document an elusive quotation, and to find material to buttress an argument or illustrate a thought. This does not mean that we carelessly borrow other men's ideas and sprinkle them throughout our message the way a cook drops mushrooms on a pizza. It means that we read what others have said, try to understand it, and then practically apply it in our own ministries.

I read quotation books to learn. A good quotation is worth a dozen paragraphs of explanation. Good quotations, especially contradictory ones, help me understand a topic better and give me a broader glimpse of the truth. Most of us read what we agree with and avoid everything else. But we are apt to learn as much from our enemies as our friends. The French essayist Montaigne wrote, "Nothing is so firmly believed as that which a man knoweth least." While this statement is not always true, it points up the fact that we tend to avoid the contrary view lest it undermine our confidence in what we believe. You can learn even more, if the material is documented, by going to the original sources. I have encountered many new and exciting writers while browsing through quotation books and at the same time have confronted some new and exciting thoughts.

Dictionary of Quotations, edited by Bergen Evans, is my favorite. For many years Evans was chairman of the English department at Northwestern University (located in Evanston, Illinois). When I was a seminary student in Chicago, my fiancée and I sometimes attended Evans's "Down You Go" program at the WGN-TV studio. I still marvel at this man's learning; he could serve as a living card catalog at the Library of Congress.

Dictionary of Quotations is over two thousand pages long and contains complete indexes. The book is arranged topically, and the material is documented. Notes explain the context of the quotations, archaic language, or some sidelight that helps make the material interesting and useful. Evans is especially good at tracing the original sources of familiar quotations. President Franklin D. Roosevelt is popularly credited with originating this statement: "The only thing we have to fear is fear itself." But Evans discovered that Henry David Thoreau wrote something similar in his journal;

1. In William Williams, *Personal Reminiscences of Charles Haddon Spurgeon* (London: Religious Tract Society, 1895), pp. 141–42.

and Montaigne included it in an essay. Roosevelt apparently liked to borrow and adapt, which is a good thing to do if you remember your debts. I urge you to add the *Dictionary of Quotations* to your library. Take time to read the preface, in which the editor summarized what quotations are all about and how we should treat them. His humor is apparent throughout the volume—a delight to read and use and a bargain at any price.

The two classic books of quotations are of course *The Oxford Dictionary of Quotations* edited by Alice Mary Smyth and *Familiar Quotations* edited by John Bartlett. Both volumes are arranged by author, so their main use is for locating and documenting quotations. You cannot look up *duty* or *faith* and find a number of appropriate quotations, as with Evans's volume. You can look up key words in the extensive index, but this is not as convenient. You will not need both books in your library, so browse through each and decide which better meets your needs. I feel the Oxford volume leans more heavily on English literature. I should mention *Bartlett's Unfamiliar Quotations* edited by Leonard Louis Levinson. This volume is not related to Bartlett's *Familiar Quotations.* It is a collection of unfamiliar material that the editor felt was worth preserving. The quotations are not documented, so you have no idea when the statement appeared or in what context. It is dangerous to use a quotation out of context, so I would counsel you to document them.

One of the better contemporary books is *Magill's Quotations in Context* edited by Frank N. Magill. The editor documented his sources, and he gave enough of the context to make the material meaningful. There are about two thousand entries, and many are from contemporary personalities known to today's congregations.

For those who like "great thoughts" in the classic mold, *The New Dictionary of Thoughts* will fill the bill. This work began in 1852 with *Jewels for the Household.* In the 1891 edition the editor, Tyron Edwards, wisely changed the title to *Dictionary of Thoughts.* Later editors revised and enlarged the book and changed the title again. The material is arranged topically, and an "author's reference index" will help you identify writers. (*Webster's Biographical Dictionary* is your best tool for identifying people quoted in these books. And while you are at it, check on name pronunciations.)[2] The cross-referenced "subject finder" will help you locate material on many topics. I was surprised to find twelve different listings under *change* and sixteen under *thought.*

2. Springfield, Mass.: Merriam, 1976.

Granted, some of these quotations are museum pieces; but many are still good currency and can be wisely invested today. I was happy to see Jean Ingelow's statement, "I have lived to thank God that all my prayers have not been answered"; and Richard Trench's, "Prayer is not overcoming God's reluctance; it is laying hold of His highest willingness."

This leads me to a word of caution: a quotation is helpful in a sermon only if the source or the context are meaningful to the listeners. Most people know who William Shakespeare was, but beware of hitting your congregation with an unfamiliar quotation from an equally unfamiliar writer. True, a good quotation can carry itself and does not need to be strengthened by the source. But if your quotation has a great thought, meaningful context, and familiar source, then you have some powerful ammunition to fire. "The goal of all life is death," said Sigmund Freud. What a statement to use in introducing a sermon on Philippians 1:21. Or how about using this statement to introduce a message on Matthew 2: "Christ cannot possibly have been a Jew. I don't have to prove that scientifically. It is a fact." This was said in 1935 by Joseph Goebbels, propaganda minister for Adolf Hitler. Younger members may not know Goebbels, but they do know Hitler.

I often use quotations to get attention at the beginning of a sermon. A quotation can also serve as an illustration—to illumine a truth or vividly nail down a point. The more striking it is, the better. Suppose you are preaching on Psalm 106:15—"And he gave them their request; but sent leanness into their soul." Your theme is the tragedy of answered prayer. (When prayer is selfish, the answer is a tragedy.) Why not open with the statement from Oscar Wilde, "When the gods wish to punish us, they answer our prayers"? Or suppose you are preaching from Genesis 1 about the creation of man. Friedrich Wilhelm Nietzsche's statement "Woman was God's second mistake" would certainly get the attention of the congregation. Is man a mistake? This could be the springboard for an exposition of the passage that man is made in God's image and is *not* a mistake.

Let me suggest a book that may "turn you off" at first because it is filled with quotations from theological and political rebels: *The Great Quotation* edited by George Seldes. The introductory essays are entertaining and helpful, so be sure to read them—particularly "Uses and Misuses of Quotations." The topics covered are usually overlooked by other quotation books: "means of production," "individual," "skepticism," and other topics relating to politics and government. Both author and subject indexes are helpful, although the latter is not necessary since the book is arranged by subjects.

Expect to get angry as you read—and do not agree with everything you read. This book is worth having and reading, if only to let you know how the other half thinks. The brief section on "The Jews" is, by itself, worth the price of the book.

At the other extreme is *The Encyclopedia of Religious Quotations* edited by Frank S. Mead. This beautifully produced volume covers the usual topics from "adversity" to "zeal," with a generous blending of Scripture quotations, hymns, poems, and miscellaneous items. There are subject and author indexes. The emphasis is on classic authors, but there are enough contemporary quotes to prevent this book from becoming just another collection. Another useful volume of the same genre is a *Handbook of Preaching Resources from English Literature* edited by James D. Robertson. While limited in size, this collection contains some excellent material: just enough context is supplied for each quotation.

A final suggestion is *Contemporary Quotations* compiled by James B. Simpson. The material comes from speeches and writings since 1950. It abounds in quotations from well-known politicians, actors and actresses, and famous people whose names are still familiar. There are four main divisions: (1) the nation, (2) the world, (3) man, and (4) communications and the arts. The documentation is excellent, and so is the subject index. But the author index is not adequate for identifying those quoted. Often the editor identifies the person when he is first mentioned. It includes the famous statement made by the Duke of Windsor and quoted by *Look* magazine: "The thing that impresses me most about America is the way parents obey their children." Here too is the statement by Charles Lawrence, the forgotten man who developed the engine for Charles Lindbergh's plane: "Who ever heard of Paul Revere's horse?" (Did you ever preach about the blessing of helping other people succeed?)

To stimulate your thinking or arouse your interest in a subject, there is no better friend than a good book of quotations. These books contain errors as well as truths, and the people quoted did not always live up to their words (nor do we, for that matter). But I find quotation books to be enjoyable friends, helpful workers, and stimulating teachers. I trust you will too.

Bibliography

Bartlett, John, ed. *A Collection of Familiar Quotations.* Cambridge, Mass.: Bartlett, 1855. Reprinted—*Familiar Quotations: A Collection of Passages, Phrases, and Proverbs Traced to Their Sources in An-*

cient and Modern Literature. 9th ed. Boston: Little and Brown, 1900.

Edwards, Tyron, ed. *The New Dictionary of Thoughts: A Cyclopedia of Quotations from the Best Authors of the World, Both Ancient and Modern, Alphabetically Arranged by Subjects*. Revised by C. N. Catrevas, Jonathan Edwards, and Ralph Emerson Browns. New York: Standard, 1957.

Evans, Bergen. *Dictionary of Quotations*. New York: Delacorte, 1968.

Levinson, Leonard Louis, ed. *Bartlett's Unfamiliar Quotations*. Chicago: Cowles, 1971.

Magill, Frank N., ed. *Magill's Quotations in Context*. 2 series. New York: Harper and Row, 1965–1969.

Mead, Frank S., ed. *The Encyclopedia of Religious Quotations*. Westwood, N.J.: Revell, 1965.

Robertson, James D., ed. *Handbook of Preaching Resources from English Literature*. New York: Macmillan, 1962. Reprinted—Grand Rapids: Baker, 1972.

Seldes, George, ed. *The Great Quotations*. New York: Stuart, 1960. Reprinted—New York: Pocket, 1972.

Simpson, James B., ed. *Contemporary Quotations*. New York: Crowell, 1964. Reprinted—New York: Galahad, 1974.

Smyth, Alice Mary, ed. *The Oxford Dictionary of Quotations*. 2d ed. New York: Oxford University, 1953.

Peter M. Roget

18

The Thesaurus

I cannot reach for my copy of Peter M. Roget's *Thesaurus of English Words and Phrases* without thinking of two famous Scotsmen: Sir James Barrie and Alexander Whyte. Barrie is one of Scotland's best-known authors and perhaps is most famous for *Peter Pan*, a story that still captivates children and adults. While a young man at Edinburgh University, Barrie attended Whyte's Bible classes. In fact he and Whyte both came from Kirriemuir, a part of Scotland that Barrie made famous in some of his books. When the young writer left Edinburgh in 1882, he took with him a letter of introduction from Whyte, which probably helped him land his first journalistic position. The two were good friends, and each admired the other's wizardry with words.

What do these two Scotsmen have to do with Roget's *Thesaurus*? Simply this: both were confirmed users of it. Whyte's biographer, G. F. Barbour, said of him: "He always kept a copy of Roget's *Thesaurus* on his desk."[1] And Barrie gave us a hint of his

1. *The Life of Alexander Whyte* (London: Hodder and Stoughton, 1923), p. 293.

interest when he said of Captain Hook in *Peter Pan:* "The man is not wholly evil—he has a *Thesaurus* in his cabin." Those of us who love words may have to revise our dark opinions of the captain.

Peter Mark Roget was born in 1779 in London, where his father was pastor of the French Protestant Church in Soho. Shortly after Peter's birth his father died, leaving young Peter to be raised by his mother Catherine, a frustrated woman whose hypochondria grew worse every year. His Uncle Samuel understood the boy best and generously provided for the family's needs. Catherine was constantly writing to her brother that young Peter was "thin and pale as usual," and she was sure the boy would die of tuberculosis like his father. Peter showed an interest in science and mathematics, so medicine seemed the ideal vocation. In 1793 he enrolled at the university in Edinburgh. Catherine did her utmost to make a third-floor apartment into home for herself and the two children. She had two great concerns: Peter's health and her budget. In letters to her brother, she repeatedly hinted for extra money and expressed concern about her son's health. She worried about his late hours of study (she wanted him in bed before eleven) and complained about inadequate libraries in Edinburgh. No matter what ailment the children had—or she assumed they had—she fed them generous doses of Godbald's Syrup.

It was not easy to be a medical student at the university in those days. Out of a class of four hundred, perhaps twenty would earn degrees. In May 1797 Catherine was sure Peter would never make it after he came down with tuberculosis and missed weeks of school. Catherine sent detailed reports to her brother and poured patent medicines into her son. "I entreated him the day before yesterday," she wrote on 10 June, "to try Godbald's Vegetable Balsam, which has, God be thanked, caused so great a change in his complaints that yesterday he ate heartily some rice pudding and a little beef." After a summer's rest and a short holiday, Peter's health improved and he resumed his studies. He was one of only twelve awarded the M.D.

Peter had a passion for organization. Identification and classification were the systole and diastole of his academic heart. As a doctor he majored in anatomy and physiology, seeking to identify and classify the parts and organs of the body. Medical science was in sad shape in those days, and Roget was a pioneer in exact scientific study. He helped organize several scientific societies in London, and in most of them Roget became librarian or secretary in charge of gathering and publishing bulletins of scientific interest.

Following his graduation, Roget spent five years in what his biographer called "postgraduate wanderings" in Bristol, London, and Geneva. In April 1804 he settled in Manchester to build his medical practice and continue private scientific studies. He helped found a medical society there and lectured on human physiology. But perhaps the most important thing he did in those years was to purchase a notebook and start compiling and classifying lists of English words. This notebook, begun in 1805, was the nucleus for his *Thesaurus*. No man with any drive to succeed could long remain away from London, so in January 1809 Roget moved back, locating just two blocks from Uncle Samuel and a short distance from the British Museum.

In the years that followed, Roget joined almost every important medical and scientific organization in London. True, his uncle's name (and purse) paved his way, but once in, Roget held his own. He always managed to meet the right people, be seen in the right places, and hold the right offices. He was lionized by some and despised by others. Once he became an organization officer, he stayed in office and made sure the rule book was followed—and the library correctly classified. On several occasions he was challenged by younger members who wanted to get fresh air into the organizations, but he managed to hold on. Roget was fated to live at a time when science in general and medicine in particular were going through a convulsive transition, and he was not given to sudden change.

Roget carried on his practice, lectured at medical schools and societies, and continued his science experiments. He found time to marry in 1824; two weeks later he read a paper at the Royal Society: "Explanation of an Optical Deception in the Appearance of the Spokes of a Wheel Seen Through Vertical Apertures." That sounds confusing, but this paper led to the invention of the motion picture. Conclusions from Roget's investigation of the London water supply during some epidemics came close to what Louis Pasteur discovered years later. A power struggle in the Royal Society forced Roget to leave office as senior secretary on 30 November 1847. What seemed a defeat for science was a victory for literature, for he now had time to work on his beloved notebooks with their endless lists of words.

In 1849 he actually began to write *Thesaurus of English Words and Phrases*, the book that has perpetuated his name more than anything he wrote in the scientific field. (He was sure that *Animal and Vegetable Physiology Considered with Reference to Natural Theology*, two volumes published in 1834, would keep his name alive for centuries. Even articles he wrote for the *Encyclopaedia Britannica* have been forgotten.) More than twenty million copies of various editions of the *Thesaurus* have been distributed since it was first published in May 1852.

Roget was not a linguist or a philologist; he was an organizer. He wrote his *Thesaurus* because he realized that the classification of words according to the ideas they represent makes a wonderful tool for effective communication. Many people use the *Thesaurus* as a dictionary of synonyms. To do so is to ask for trouble. I can still hear my professor of homiletics saying: "Beware, gentlemen! The *Thesaurus* will sell you short every single time!" Roget's book contains no definitions or etymologies. It simply arranges words and phrases into six useful categories, which are subdivided into hundreds of different sections.

I will never forget how stunned I was when, as a junior-high-school student, I bought my first *Thesaurus* and tried to decipher Roget's system. I was certain I would need to know philosophy to understand such categories as "Intrinsicality" and "Extrinsicality," "Adjunct" and "Remainder," and "Obstinacy" and "Tergiversation." Like most users of *Thesaurus*, I turned to the extensive index, but I have since learned that the best way to use the book is the way Roget arranged it: by category and class.

The preacher who is addicted to alliteration searches his *Thesaurus* to find a word that means "opposition" and starts with *C*. (Alliteration, if it comes naturally, can strengthen a sermon; but if it is forced, it does more harm than good.) He turns to *Opposition* and discovers such possibilities as "contravention, counteraction, collision, conflict, competition." If he uses one of these words without finding out what it means and how it differs from the other, he may find himself excommunicating his congregation. *Conflict* and *competition* are not synonymous. Mark Twain said that "the difference between the right word and the almost right word is the difference between lightning and the lightning bug." The *Thesaurus* can start you on the right trail, but use a dictionary to get to your destination. I enjoy using *Webster's New Dictionary of Synonyms* and the *Funk and Wagnalls Standard Handbook of Synonyms, Antonyms, and Prepositions*.

I suggest you get acquainted with the "categories" and "classes" that Roget and his editorial successors have worked out. They will help you see words as tools and as expressions of concrete ideas. As you become acquainted with these arrangements, you will realize the complexity and richness of the English language. Roget planned it this way. His greatest concern was truth, and he believed that order is the first step toward truth. If Roget knew that millions of people use his book to do crossword puzzles, he would probably be deeply offended. And if he knew that an edition "in dictionary form" had been published, he would be highly scandalized. (I have used that edition, but it is not half as good as a regular dictionary of synonyms.) Roget continued to enlarge and improve his book until he died, and then members of his family took over. There are numerous "popular" editions available today, but the true student of words will want the best.

About the time Roget was buried, a young Presbyterian preacher was completing his ministry as an assistant in Glasgow. The following year he moved to Edinburgh and began a ministry that would bless the evangelical world for years. I wonder if Whyte ever visited Roget's grave at West Malvern and silently paid tribute to the man who gave him the book that he always kept on his desk.

Bibliography

Fernald, James C. *Funk and Wagnalls Standard Handbook of Synonyms, Antonyms, and Prepositions.* Rev. ed. New York: Funk and Wagnalls, 1947.

Roget, Peter M. *Thesaurus of English Words and Phrases, Classified and Arranged so as to Facilitate the Expression of Ideas and Assist in Literary Composition.* London: Longman, Brown, Green, and Longmans, 1852. Reprinted—*Roget's International Thesaurus.* 3d ed. New York: Crowell, 1962.

Webster's New Dictionary of Synonyms: A Dictionary of Discriminated Synonyms with Antonyms and Analogous and Contrasted Words. Springfield, Mass.: Merriam, 1973.

19

Anthologies

A wit has described an anthologist as "a man who sits home and raids a good book." Certainly no serious student would limit his reading to anthologies, but this genre does have a ministry to the reader who knows how to use it. Anthologies are not substitutes for the original works that provided the excerpts. Apart from their entertainment and educational value, anthologies help introduce us to different authors and viewpoints we might miss in regular reading. Some of my most rewarding literary experiences have started with an excerpt in an anthology. Even a brief introduction can lead to a lasting friendship.

At the top of my list is *A Diary of Readings* edited by John Baillie, the well-known professor of divinity at the University of Edinburgh from 1934 to 1956 and principal of New College until his death in 1960. This is a collection of extracts from many writers and many times that ought to be read and pondered today. Baillie described the book as "an anthology of pages suited to engage serious thought." And he warned in the foreword: "Some pages may be thought difficult, but it does us no hurt to have our minds stretched a little, even when we do not fully comprehend."

The editor has not limited himself to any one school theologically or ecclesiastically. In these pages I find the Puritan John Owen, the Anglican Phillips Brooks, psychologist William James, apologist C. S. Lewis, and even Albert Schweitzer. I do not always agree with what I read, but this does not hinder me from reading and learning and, I trust, growing. This book especially helps me on those "dry days" when mind and heart need a bit of extra priming. This kind of book—or any book—is no substitute for my Bible; but it often so illuminates the Word that God brings new truths to my heart or makes old truths shine with new light. Since there is one selection for each day of the year, you may use this volume as a "thinking man's daily devotional"; but you may also keep it near your desk or easy chair simply for occasional reading. Caution: do not open the book until your mind is in gear. If A. W. Tozer was right in saying that one test of a good book is that you have to put it down and start thinking for yourself, then *A Diary of Readings* is a good book. It makes you think—and it makes you *want* to think. After all, are we not to love the Lord with the mind as well as the heart?

The Practical Cogitator makes no pretense to any religious commitment, but its content has often led me into theological by-paths never planned by the editors. Subtitled *The Thinker's Anthology*, this amazing book was edited by Charles P. Curtis, Jr., and Ferris Greenslet. It was published in 1945 and has enjoyed wide popularity in spite of the fact that the selections are not what you would call popular or familiar. One guideline for the selections was: "Nothing that is not worth re-reading. Some things that can be chewed over almost indefinitely." The thirteen sections (nearly 700 pages) cover "man in search of himself," history, nature, community, liberty, justice, and a host of other important topics and subtopics. The first excerpt is from Oliver Wendell Holmes, Jr.: "Any two philosophers can tell each other all they know in two hours." The final quotation is from Leonardo da Vinci: "In rivers the water that you touch is the last of what has passed and the first of that which comes: so with time present."

This is the kind of book you can drop into your briefcase and carry along on a trip. I suggest you keep several sheets of note paper in the book so you can jot down ideas that are sure to come as you read, and then transfer these thoughts to your permanent file when you get home. (We should never read without having note paper on hand. Unrecorded thoughts become lost thoughts.) But this is *not* a book to speed-read or swallow in great gulps. Read, think, apply; then read again, always bringing the light of Scripture to bear on the matter. You cannot help but grow.

George Macdonald: An Anthology edited by Lewis is a priceless collection of 365 excerpts from the writings of this Scottish poet-mystic-novelist, who influenced Lewis in his Christian commitment. Many consider Macdonald's books imaginative but dull, and according to Lewis's preface to this collection, he seemed to agree: "Some of his best things are thus hidden in his dullest books. My task here has been almost one of exhumation." Macdonald had to resign from his pastorate in Arundel, Sussex, because of his generous views about the salvation of the heathen, but otherwise his beliefs could hardly be termed "liberal." His Christianity was an enjoyable experience; he saw God as the loving Father at the heart of all that is in the world and the Bible, sin excepted. There is a penetrating quality to his writing. He never stays on the surface of an idea, but digs into the very center, and then tries to get it into the center of our being. This brief collection (128 pages) may be your best introduction to Macdonald.

Most "religious anthologies" are useless to the busy pastor, because they say either too much or too little. But two on my shelf I value: *Anthology of Jesus* edited by Sir James Marchant, and *The Fellowship of the Saints* edited by Thomas S. Kepler. The Marchant collection has 383 pages of excerpts arranged in forty-two sections, covering every aspect of our Lord's life and ministry. The material is selected from the very finest in Christian prose and poetry, including sermons, hymns, lectures, theological treatises, church creeds, Christian classics, and books that most of us would perhaps overlook in our Christological studies. The index to authors includes Charles H. Spurgeon and Samuel Rutherford, along with John Henry Newman and G. K. Chesterton! The contributors are a varied group, but that is exactly what I want in an anthology. The twelve selections on the ascension would enrich any sermon on that topic; and the material on faith in Christ is equally stirring. As with all good anthologies, this one includes an index to sources, allowing you to read the originals and benefit even more. As a devotional aid, *Anthology of Jesus* is one of the best.

Kepler was for many years a student of the mystics and their writings, and I consider *The Fellowship of the Saints* the best single volume of this kind. Beginning with the church fathers and going up to the twentieth century, Kepler included the best writings of the greatest spiritual leaders of the church, always with a view to helping the reader grow in his own spiritual life. The editor's preface answers the question "What is a saint?" and you may or may not agree with him. (He is not talking about salvation, but daily living.) The selections from 137 spiritual writers cover many aspects of the Christian life: worship, prayer, service, humility, suffering, death (John Donne, naturally), and even Christian social action. "A New Set of Devotional Exercises" by Douglas V. Steere is one of my favorites, as is John Wesley's counsel on "Christian Behavior." The apostle Paul did not need to read John Flavel's "In Prosperity and Adversity," but I need to read it often. Here too is Robert Leighton's "Rules and Instructions for a Holy Life," with that matchless statement, "Thou must keep thy memory clean and pure, as it were a wedlock-chamber. . . ." Of course we must have an excerpt from that Scottish mystic Henry Scougal, whose *Life of God in the Soul of Man* ought to be required reading for every Christian.[1]

Devotional writing has a tendency to go to extremes. Either it is so theological that it fails to touch the heart, or it is so experience-centered that it elevates the writer without glorifying the Lord. The selections in *The Fellowship of the Saints* do not fall into these extremes. For the most part they are based on Scripture, and yet they are personal and practical without being academic. These old saints—especially the Puritans—had a way of expressing profound truths in unforgettable sentences, without becoming sentimental. If you buy only one anthology of the writings of the "great saints," buy this one.

At this point I should meet an objection that often arises. Certain of these writers belonged to branches of Christendom some of whose doctrines evangelicals cannot endorse. Are we making a mistake by reading their works, endangering rather than nourishing our spiritual lives? Paul's admonition in I Thessalonians 5:21 certainly applies: "Prove all things; hold fast that which is good." One must do this even when reading a book or article by a recognized evangelical. Only the Bible is inspired, and all other writing must be tested by that standard. But the fact that some of these writers belonged to religious communities whose doctrines we cannot wholly accept does not mean the writers *themselves* have nothing to say to us. I have never felt I must agree entirely with a writer or speaker in order to learn from him. (In fact I sometimes learn more from those with whom I disagree.) Bernard of Clairvaux, St. John of the Cross, and Thomas Aquinas, to name but a few, belonged to religious orders outside our evangelical Protestant tradition; yet they can say something to us about God from their experience. It is our responsibility, led by the Holy Spirit, to separate essentials from accidentals and receive what the Lord pro-

1. Originally published in 1677. Edited by Winthrop S. Hudson and republished in 1948 (Philadelphia: Westminster).

vides. When I recommend a book written by someone not an evangelical, I am not issuing a blanket endorsement of all the book says or the author believes. Surely when Paul quoted Epimenides and Aratus in Acts 17:28, not even the people at Mars Hill concluded that the apostle endorsed *all* that these heathen poets had written.

Four more anthologies, none of which has any direct relationship to theology, help us understand different aspects of life, and this understanding cannot but help us in our ministries. *Letters to Mother*, edited by Charles Lincoln Van Doren, is just that: a collection of letters written by famous people to their mothers. Here you find letters from scientists and churchmen, explorers and writers, statesmen and poets—and each letter is alive with homiletical possibilities. Here is Harry S. Truman's famous letter to "Mama and Mary" in which he said: "I had hurried to the White House to see the President, and when I arrived, I found I *was* the President." What a way to introduce a sermon on the call of Moses or Isaiah! And here is Nathaniel Hawthorne writing to his mother: "I have not yet concluded what profession I shall have. Being a minister is of course out of question. I should not think that even you could desire me to choose so dull a way of life." Quite a contrast to John Wesley's letter to his mother, dated 28 May 1725, in which he said: "I can't think that when God sent us into the world He had irreversibly decreed that we should be perpetually miserable in it." *Letters to Mother* is delightful reading and is filled with material that can nicely illustrate truths from the Word of God.

A Treasure of the World's Great Diaries, edited by Philip Dunaway and Mel Evans, ought to be on your shelf. It opens with excerpts from one of the most famous diaries of all time, Anne Frank's; and it closes with a dramatic section from *Hiroshima Diary* by Dr. Michihiko Hachiya. Between these two war-time excerpts are pages from diaries written by people as far apart in time and space as Davy Crockett and Samuel Pepys (one of the most famous diarists of English literature). The Quaker John Woolman is here, as are Queen Victoria, Henry David Thoreau, Thomas A. Edison, George Washington, and a host of "unknown greats" whom I enjoyed getting to know.

I close with two books on special themes. *The Book of Friendship* edited by Elizabeth S. Selden seeks to be "an international anthology" on friendship. Despite some sticky sentimentalism, there are valuable insights on human relationships. The closing section contains quotations from Scripture that touch on friendship—including David and Jonathan and the parable of the good Samaritan.

The Blessings of Old Age edited by Marjorie Eleanor Maxwell is good to have on hand. The population is getting older, and more and more "senior saints" attend our services. I appreciate the editor's wise selections from the Bible, as well as from the poets, ancient and modern. The first section on "Youth and Age" provides new material on the "generation gap." The second section presents "portraits" of old age, and here is Donne saying:

> No Spring, nor Summer Beauty hath such grace
> As I have seen in one Autumnal face.

The third section, "Memories," is captivating. It opens with Cicero saying, "Now the harvest of old age is, as I have often said, the memory and rich store of blessings laid up in earlier life." The sections on death and on life after death are rich and should help supplement God's truth in funeral messages.

I have found these nine anthologies enriching and enjoyable. Some are still in print; others you will have to hunt out in used-book stores. They are worth the search.

Bibliography

Baillie, John, ed. *A Diary of Readings: Being an Anthology of Pages Suited to Engage Serious Thought, One for Every Day of the Year, Gathered from the Wisdom of Many Centuries.* New York: Scribner, 1955.

Curtis, Charles P., Jr., and Greenslet, Ferris, eds. *The Practical Cogitator; or, The Thinker's Anthology.* Rev. ed. Boston: Houghton Mifflin, 1953.

Dunaway, Philip, and Evans, Mel, eds. *A Treasure of the World's Great Diaries.* Garden City, N.Y.: Doubleday, 1957.

Kepler, Thomas S., ed. *The Fellowship of the Saints: An Anthology of Christian Devotional Literature.* New York: Abingdon-Cokesbury, 1948. Reprinted—*An Anthology of Devotional Literature.* Grand Rapids: Baker, 1977.

Macdonald, George. *George Macdonald: An Anthology.* Edited by C. S. Lewis. New York: Macmillan, 1947.

Marchant, James, ed. *Anthology of Jesus.* New York: Harper, 1926.

Maxwell, Marjorie Eleanor, ed. *The Blessings of Old Age: An Anthology.* London: Faber and Faber, 1954.

Selden, Elizabeth S., ed. *The Book of Friendship: An International Anthology.* Boston: Houghton Mifflin, 1947.

Van Doren, Charles Lincoln, ed. *Letters to Mother: An Anthology.* Great Neck, N.Y.: Channel, 1959.

20

A Basic Library

My books are tools, and I use them. I cannot afford to be a book collector; neither the budget nor the diminishing shelf space (and house space!) permits such a luxury. If I discover that a book is no longer useful to me, I give it to someone who can use it. I am not sentimental about my tools: if they are not working *for* me, they are working *against* me. (I do confess to owning some "collector's items" that I discovered in used-book sales, including some presentation copies containing valuable autographs. But that is another story.)

Over the years I have been asked to make a list of books that have helped me in preaching; what follows is an attempt to fulfill that request. As you scan these pages, please keep in mind that this is not a "definitive bibliography" (if such a thing is possible) nor was it prepared with the scholar in mind. This book list is for pastors and preachers, men who must use their study time wisely.

My including a book does not mean I endorse everything in it or all that the author believes. My excluding your favorite book does not mean I condemn it.

In the chapter that follows I sometimes give author and title, sometimes just the author. More-complete information about each book is available in the bibliography at the end of the chapter.[1]

Please do not rush out and purchase every book that I or any other writer recommends. In the early years of my ministry, I did that; it filled my shelves, emptied my wallet, and did not greatly enrich my ministry. While you do not want to reject too quickly a book that has proved itself, neither do you want to buy something that will never prove profitable.

Be sure to grow in your appreciation of books. Titles that do not interest you today may become very exciting in a few years. In the early years of my ministry, I scorned Joseph Parker; today I revel in him.

Do not gather books so quickly that they remain strangers to you. Get to know each one, even if you cannot read it immediately. An educated person is not one who knows all the answers, but one who knows where to find them. Beware of "short-cut" books that hand you predigested pabulum. A. W. Tozer said that the best books are those that make us think for ourselves. Books are tools, not crutches.

I enjoy my library. Each book is a friend that converses with and teaches me. It is not necessary for a library to be large to be effective. Better to have fewer of the best books than to clutter your shelves with volumes that cannot serve you well. Above all, love your books, use them, and dedicate all you learn to the service of Jesus Christ.

Books About Books

The Minister's Library by Cyril J. Barber is indispensable if you are serious about building a good library. The author issues *Periodic Supplements* to update the original volume. Some of the technical books Barber lists may not be needed by the average pastor, but he should be acquainted with them. Every young pastor should be given a copy of this book along with his ordination certificate!

---

1. The only exceptions are commentaries in series for which abbreviations are given on pp. 289–90. The author's name in these cases is given in the text, and the series abbreviation follows in parentheses. By referring to the list of abbreviations, you can discover the publisher of the series and the date(s) of publication.

Commenting and Commentaries by Charles H. Spurgeon was first published in 1876, so you will not find in it many recent titles! Spurgeon glorified the Calvinists, gored the Arminians, and disparaged J. N. Darby and the dispensationalists. But in spite of this, we love him and thank him for his wise and witty words about books. Fortunately some of the titles he recommended are now back in print. Be sure to read the opening lecture!

The Best Books by W. J. Grier reads like the catalog of a Puritan bookstore. Grier emphasized Reformed theology and Puritan commentators, so this book is a perfect companion to Spurgeon's. The author knows books and has certainly listed some of the finest. You cannot go too far wrong following his suggestions, even if you do not agree with his theology.

Wilbur M. Smith's *Treasury of Books for Bible Study* is a modern classic that should be in your library. Smith was probably the greatest evangelical bibliographer of his generation. Smith's *Chats from a Minister's Library* were originally aired over WMBI, the radio station of the Moody Bible Institute. I recall hearing some of these talks and sensing—even from a radio broadcast—Smith's enthusiasm for books.

A Reader's Guide to Religious Literature by Beatrice Batson deals with classical religious literature, beginning with the early Middle Ages. If you are tired of "the books of the hour" and want to be enriched by "the books of the ages," you should consult this volume. Alexander Whyte fed his soul on Dante, yet most preachers today dismiss *The Divine Comedy* as a piece of medieval, Roman Catholic fantasy. How I wish the church would start drinking at these wells again!

The Lifetime Reading Plan by Clifton Fadiman is like a key to buried treasure. The author listed more than one hundred classics and, in a series of brief essays, tells why they are important today. I have followed Fadiman's suggestions for many years and have benefited greatly. The author's "Preliminary Talk" is worth reading often!

Christianity Today publishes annual issues that deal with books published during the previous twelve months. Scholars in various fields compile book lists and make comments. These issues are valuable and worth keeping.

Some of your most helpful sources of bibliography are scholarly books and encyclopedias. The volumes of the *New International Commentary* are especially helpful. Articles in both the *Wycliffe Bible Encyclopedia* and *The Zondervan Pictorial Encyclopedia of the Bible* conclude with good bibliographies.

Finally, some colleges and seminaries publish book lists compiled by their faculties. A letter to the librarian or dean of education would get the information you need.

The Bible

Each preacher must have an overall picture of divine revelation if he is to handle God's Word honestly and meaningfully. When he takes a text from Isaiah 40, he must know where the prophet Isaiah fits into the picture and how chapter 40 relates to the rest of that book—and for that matter, to the rest of the Bible. Congregations desperately need to understand the Bible *as a whole*, and not just isolated books and passages.

Explore the Book by J. Sidlow Baxter is a favorite of mine. The author is certainly one of our greatest Bible teachers and expositors. He called these studies "a basic and broadly interpretive course," and they are that. No matter what your degree or training, you would do well to read straight through these studies over the course of a year and take them to heart.

W. Graham Scroggie's *Unfolding Drama of Redemption* is a three-volume set covering the entire Bible, including the intertestamental period. Scroggie was Baxter's predecessor at famed Charlotte Baptist Chapel in Edinburgh, and both men possess the gift of analysis and synthesis. Again, do not put these books on your shelf; *read and study them.* And add to them *Know Your Bible*, another Scroggie work that will increase your understanding of the Word of God.

Living Messages of the Books of the Bible by G. Campbell Morgan has been available since 1912, and yet it continues to minister. Morgan had the unique ability to seize the heart of a book or a passage and to make the Scriptures live. His *Analyzed Bible* is a companion volume. In *The Unfolding Message of the Bible* Morgan rehearsed the "whole sweep" of divine revelation, showing how the books of the Bible relate to each other. It is the most pastoral of his analytical books, being very warm and personal.

Let it be said from the very first that the best commentaries on the entire Bible are those in which each Bible book is treated by a man who has devoted himself to mastering that book. No one set of commentaries is complete or final; no one-volume commentary can meet all your needs.

The Pulpit Commentary was first published between 1880 and

1919. There are many editions, both in the United States and Britain. If you find a used set at a comfortable price, and if you have room on your shelves for twenty-three volumes (or more, depending on the edition), then buy it. However, you must know that: (1) the introductions are limited and outdated; (2) the exegesis, while usually sound and helpful, is not abreast of modern studies; and (3) the homiletical helps are, for the most part, useless. Some enterprising publisher should bring out *The New Pulpit Commentary*.

What about John Peter Lange's commentary? Charles H. Spurgeon praised it, and several generations of Bible students have used it. You must wade through a great deal of material to dig out the nuggets, and the exegesis is not in tune with more up-to-date commentaries. I have especially enjoyed the comments on Genesis, Psalms, Proverbs, Mark, and Luke.

As for the famous commentary by Robert Jamieson, A. R. Fausset, and David Brown, Spurgeon said: "Of this I have a very high opinion." Who am I to argue with the master? The material by Brown stands out above the rest. Again, the material is old but sturdy. A learned friend of mine complained that "everytime you face a hard passage in the Bible and look into JFB, they have nothing to say on it!" This may be an exaggeration. I think the set is useful but not indispensable.

If you can locate the six-volume edition of the *Expositor's Bible*, buy it immediately! It takes up less space than the original fifty-volume set, and not everything in the original set is worth owning. Samuel H. Kellogg on Leviticus is a classic; so is Alexander Maclaren on the Psalms and on Colossians.

The Expositor's Bible Commentary edited by Frank E. Gaebelein promises to be a very useful tool. It employs the New International Version for its text—certainly a happy choice. I recommend it.

Expositions of Holy Scripture by Alexander Maclaren is a homiletical well that never runs dry. I have often warned young preachers not to read Maclaren too early in their sermon preparation, for they will be tempted to preach him! You should own this set, read it, and learn from it.

James Hastings's *Speaker's Bible* is eighteen volumes rich with sermonic material. True, you will find paragraphs that are theologically wrong and that have been proved wrong by history (some sermons were written when social evolution and world peace were favorite themes). But if you will mine these pages, you will be enriched. Hastings's *Great Texts of the Bible*, a twenty-volume set, is worth the space you assign to it. It suffers from some of the weaknesses of *The Speaker's Bible,* but it has so many strengths that you dare not ignore it.

Most one-volume Bible commentaries are a disappointment, but *The New Bible Commentary* edited by Francis Davidson is one of the better ones.

The Old Testament

Gleason L. Archer's *Survey of Old Testament Introduction* leads the field, in my opinion. Running a close second is *The Old Testament Speaks* by Samuel J. Schultz. Merrill F. Unger's *Introductory Guide to the Old Testament* and Edward J. Young's *Introduction to the Old Testament* are both older works but still very useful.

Two helpful books on Old Testament themes are *New Perspectives on the Old Testament* edited by J. Barton Payne and *Classical Evangelical Essays in Old Testament Interpretation* edited by Walter C. Kaiser, Jr.

Basic books on Old Testament theology are those by J. Barton Payne and Walter C. Kaiser, Jr. Two classic works are those of Gustav Oehler and A. B. Davidson. Davidson's book is infected with a bit of liberal theology but is still worth reading. Use Payne's book as your compass, and you cannot stray.

These books have been most helpful to me in Old Testament research: *Old Testament History* by Charles F. Pfeiffer; *A Scientific Investigation of the Old Testament* by Robert Dick Wilson (a classic work by a great scholar); *The Biblical World* edited by Charles F. Pfeiffer (a beautifully illustrated handbook to the geography and peoples of the Old Testament); *A Survey of Israel's History* by Leon J. Wood; *Historical Geography of the Holy Land* by George A. Turner; *The Wycliffe Historical Geography of Bible Lands* by Charles F. Pfeiffer and Howard F. Vos (the book to buy if you buy only one in this field); *The Pentateuch in Its Cultural Environment* by G. Herbert Livingston (a well-written introduction, with an excellent treatment of ancient literature, including the Dead Sea Scrolls, and its relationship to Moses' writings). *The Macmillan Bible Atlas* by Yohanan Aharoni and Michael Avi-Yonah contains 264 maps, plus numerous other drawings and charts, illustrating every major event in Bible history. The text is concise. This book is valuable.

Genesis. In spite of his tendency to spiritualize and go to extremes in typology, Arthur W. Pink is very helpful. While in that frame of mind, secure *Genesis to Deuteronomy* by Charles Henry Mackintosh; Dwight L. Moody told everyone to read CHM, but Charles H. Spurgeon criticized him. F. B. Meyer's *Five Books of Moses* is a helpful devotional commentary, as is W. H. Griffith Thomas's *Genesis* (DC).[2] More critical commentaries are those of H. C. Leupold (my favorite) and Derek Kidner (TOTC). In his *Genesis Record* Henry M. Morris gleaned helpful truths from many sources, added his own insights, and presented it all from a "scientific" point of view. His many works on the Bible and science lead us to respect what he has written on Genesis.

Hebrew Ideals by James Strahan is not a critical commentary or even an explanatory one. It is a treatment of the "ideals" evident in the Book of Genesis: e.g., separation, blessedness, integrity, judgment, love, home. For rich spiritual insight and practical application, this book is superior.

While some aspects of his theology disturb me, Helmut Thielicke is still in my opinion a great writer and preacher. His series of sermons on Genesis 1–11 is called *How the World Began* and is worth reading. Thielicke can make ancient history meaningful to contemporary man. Would that people with a more conservative theology could follow his example!

Edward J. Young's studies of Genesis 1 and Genesis 3 are valuable. *The Gospel in Genesis* by Henry Law and *Types in Genesis* by Andrew J. Jukes are helpful studies of typology. M. R. DeHaan's *Portraits of Christ in Genesis* is useful. *The Study of the Types* by Ada R. Habershon is a classic treatment; though not limited to Genesis, I mention it here.

Exodus. The best commentaries are those by Arthur W. Pink, F. B. Meyer (DC), and John J. Davis. For typology in this book, I suggest: *These Are the Garments* and *Made According to Pattern* by Charles W. Slemming; *From Egypt to Canaan* and *The Tabernacle in the Wilderness* by John Ritchie; *Christ in the Old Testament* by T. W. Callaway; *The Gospel in Exodus* by Henry Law; *Teaching from the Tabernacle* by C. Sumner Wemp; *Christ in the Passover* by Ceil and Moishe Rosen; and two excellent volumes by Henry W. Soltau—*The Tabernacle, the Priesthood, and the Offerings* and *The Holy Vessels and Furniture of the Tabernacle.* Books on the Ten Commandments are legion. I prefer those by Lehman Strauss, William Barclay, Alan Redpath, G. Campbell Morgan, Thomas Watson, Joy Davidman, Elton Trueblood (*Foundations for Reconstruction*) and R. W. Dale.

---

2. Reprinted—Grand Rapids: Eerdmans, 1946.

Leviticus-Deuteronomy. Apart from commentary sets on the entire Bible, Leviticus does not receive lavish treatment. I enjoy Andrew Bonar and Samuel H. Kellogg (EB). On the typology of the offerings, I use the works of Andrew J. Jukes and H. A. Ironside. Numbers also suffers from neglect. Irving L. Jensen's commentary (EBC) is brief but helpful. Deuteronomy has been given slightly better treatment. P. C. Craigie's commentary (NICOT) is choice, and Samuel J. Schultz, an acknowledged scholar, wrote a warm-hearted though brief exposition of the book (EBC).

Joshua-Ruth. Good studies of Joshua are those of Arthur W. Pink, H. A. Ironside, W. Graham Scroggie, Alan Redpath, and F. B. Meyer. The finest commentary on Judges to appear in recent years is that of Leon J. Wood. Arthur E. Cundall's exposition of Judges (TOTC) and Leon Morris's of Ruth (TOTC), bound in one volume, are also excellent. Other good analyses of Ruth are those of Philip Mauro, Henry Moorhouse, J. Vernon McGee, George E. Gardiner, and Samuel Cox.

The Historical Books. By all means secure *A Harmony of the Books of Samuel, Kings, and Chronicles* by William D. Crockett and *The Mysterious Numbers of the Hebrew Kings* by Edwin R. Thiele. As for "preaching helps" in this area, standard commentaries are a bit lacking. The volumes in the *Expositor's Bible* contain good material, and the old *Cambridge Bible* has some excellent volumes. In both sets you will find some traces of higher criticism, but the wise student knows how to handle it. H. A. Ironside's expositions of Ezra-Esther are helpful for spiritual insights and applications. Alan Redpath on Nehemiah is satisfying, J. Vernon McGee on Esther helpful. Often secondhand copies of the old *Devotional Commentary* are available; they have helpful sermonic material on these books. The *Christ in the Bible* series by A. B. Simpson is good for typology and spiritual lessons from history.

Job. In *Commenting and Commentaries* Charles H. Spurgeon listed over forty titles on Job, about the same number as for Romans! Spurgeon himself preached at least eighty-eight sermons on Job. I doubt that most preachers need that many commentaries, or that they will preach that many sermons from this book. The volume in John Peter Lange's commentary is especially good. The two volumes on Job in Albert Barnes's *Notes on the Old Testament* are exceptionally good. Joseph Caryl's work (originally twelve volumes published between 1644 and 1666, now abridged) "can scarcely be superceded or surpassed," wrote Spurgeon.

John Edgar McFadyen's survey of the book contains much helpful material; it is not a verse-by-verse commentary. James Strahan included both commentary and practical exposition. G. Campbell

Morgan's study is so good you will be tempted to preach it. H. L. Ellison wrote one of the best surveys of the book. Theodore H. Robinson's survey is also helpful. For devotional studies see Jessie Penn-Lewis, J. Allen Blair, and Andrew W. Blackwood, Jr. If you have a flair for psychology, you will enjoy William E. Hulme, C. G. Jung, and Ralph E. Hone.

Psalms. My favorite commentary is that of A. F. Kirkpatrick (CB).[3] The two volumes by Derek Kidner (TOTC) are a delight to use; I would not part with them. Commentaries by Joseph Addison Alexander and J. J. Stewart Perowne are also valuable. The three volumes by Alexander Maclaren (EB) beautifully blend careful exegesis and sensitive exposition. Compare these studies of the Psalms with Maclaren's treatment of them in his *Expositions*. For survey and introduction, no one compares with W. Graham Scroggie (in *Know Your Bible*). A. C. Gaebelein combined devotional truth with prophetic interpretations. The lover of alliterative outlines will revel in those of Arthur G. Clarke.

I must confess to having mixed emotions about Charles H. Spurgeon's monumental *Treasury of David.* Spurgeon's own expositions and comments are worth reading, but the antiquarian nuggets dug up by his secretary, John L. Keys, are musty and at times a bit comical; and the "hints to the village preacher" contain little that is preachable today. It is worth owning, but waste no time reading the miscellaneous material. Concentrate on Spurgeon, and the set will enrich you.

The Titles of the Psalms by James W. Thirtle is fascinating and seems to make sense. Thirtle's *Old Testament Problems* is also worth owning. Both are out of print. If you enjoy the Covenanters, then the commentary by David Dickson will rejoice your soul. Alexander Maclaren's *Life of David as Reflected in His Psalms* is required reading, as is John Ker's *Psalms in History and Biography*.

Books on individual Psalms are limited. The two best on Psalm 119 are by Charles Bridges and S. Franklin Logsdon (*The Song of a Soul Set Free*). Andrew Murray wrote a beautiful exposition of Psalm 51, D. Martyn Lloyd-Jones of Psalm 73 (*Faith on Trial*), and John Stevenson of Psalm 22. My favorite studies of Psalm 23 are those of John Stevenson, William Allen Knight (*The Song of Our Syrian Guest*), and W. Phillip Keller.

Proverbs. Charles Bridges's commentary is the classic. Derek Kidner's work on this book (TOTC) is as delightful as that on Genesis and the Psalms; his essays on subjects in Proverbs are most

3. Reprinted—Fincastle, Va.: Scripture Truth.

helpful. While not as detailed or profound, H. A. Ironside demonstrated his sanctified common sense and spiritual wisdom. For a modern series of messages on topics in Proverbs, see that of James T. Draper, Jr. The old study by William Arnot is a gold mine of spiritual truth.

Ecclesiastes. H. C. Leupold's commentary is probably the best. Samuel Cox (EB) is helpful. F. C. Jennings has written a popular devotional treatment. C. H. Welch's fine little study opens up new areas of truth, even if one does not follow the author's ultradispensational interpretation of Scripture. The series of messages by David Allan Hubbard is excellent; I highly recommend it.

Song of Solomon. Charles H. Spurgeon preached fifty-nine sermons from this book (an amazing feat in Victorian England!), fifty-two of which have been reprinted in *The Most Holy Place*. Watchman Nee produced a practical study, as did J. Hudson Taylor (*Union and Communion*). The commentary by Wendell P. Loveless is still useful, the one by H. A. Ironside sane, the one by Clarence E. Mason (*Love Song*) the best recent one. Mason followed the "Ironside plot" of the book and explained who is speaking in each "song" and what they are saying.

The Prophets. Kyle M. Yates supplied helpful background material for, and major themes of, each prophet, but he gave us two Isaiahs and no Daniel. Samuel J. Schultz and Edward J. Young wrote excellent studies of the prophetic message and ministry. Andrew W. Blackwood showed how to preach from the prophetic books.

Isaiah. Edward J. Young's three-volume commentary certainly needs no recommendation from me. He took the amillennial approach, but his work is still valuable for all serious students. Young's separate study of Isaiah 53 is one of the best on that chapter. F. C. Jennings's commentary has passed the test of time. It is both devotional and explanatory, taking the Plymouth Brethren viewpoint. W. E. Vine, also Brethren, wrote a brief study that is full of nuggets of truth. Albert Barnes's two volumes are also excellent. For the basic material you need on Isaiah's "servant section" and his proclamation of the Messiah, see F. B. Meyer, Alan A. MacRae, David Baron (a classic), and Robert D. Culver (*The Sufferings and the Glory of the Lord's Righteous Servant*). For an analysis of Isaiah, read G. Campbell Morgan's *Analyzed Bible*.

Jeremiah-Lamentations. R. K. Harrison (TOTC) is most satisfying on these books. G. Campbell Morgan showed how the careful preacher can expound them in a contemporary way. Two excellent studies of the prophet Jeremiah's personality are by F. B. Meyer and David M. Howard. H. A. Ironside's commentary is not detailed, but it gives you the broad spiritual messages of these books and their application. Ironside wrote with evangelical warmth.

Ezekiel-Daniel. Charles Lee Feinberg's commentary on Ezekiel is the best from the premillennial point of view, H. L. Ellison's from the amillennial. On Daniel, Lehman Strauss and John F. Walvoord are the basic premillennial interpreters, and H. C. Leupold is the main amillennial one. Leon J. Wood wrote one of the best recent studies of Daniel. Geoffrey R. King took a different tack in some areas, but he wrote with a refreshing style and remained evangelical. Two excellent studies on Daniel 9 and the seventy weeks are those by Sir Robert Anderson and Alva J. McClain.

Minor Prophets. H. A. Ironside's exposition of the minor prophets is one of his best. I have already mentioned *Preaching from the Prophets* by Kyle M. Yates. The commentary by George L. Robinson, a great scholar, is a classic. G. Campbell Morgan gave the full text of each book, an explanatory analysis (not just an outline), and the "permanent message" of each prophet. Morgan was at his best here. Homer Hailey supplied commentary and paraphrase of each book, mixing in spiritual insights and practical applications along the way. He furnished an introduction and outline to each book. Two works that are old but useful, even though infected a bit with liberal interpretations, are those by E. B. Pusey and George Adam Smith (EB). Charles Lee Feinberg's study of the minor prophets is also excellent.

On Hosea specifically I recommend G. Campbell Morgan; on Amos, Roy Lee Honeycutt and John Edgar McFadyen; on Jonah, Patrick Fairbairn, J. Allen Blair, and Hugh Martin; on Habakkuk, D. Martyn Lloyd-Jones (*From Fear to Faith*); on Haggai, Thomas V. Moore; on Zechariah, David Baron (a recognized Hebrew-Christian scholar whose commentary is *the* commentary on this book), Charles Lee Feinberg, Merrill F. Unger, and F. B. Meyer; and on Malachi, G. Campbell Morgan and Thomas V. Moore.

The New Testament

New Testament Introduction by Donald Guthrie is essential. The author, abreast of the latest problems and trends in New Testament studies, ably defended a conservative position. He included a helpful bibliography. *The New Testament: An Historical and Analytic Survey* by Merrill C. Tenney has been a standard college and seminary textbook since 1953. The companion volume, *New Testament Times*, puts New Testament people and events into their historical setting.

My favorite Greek lexicon is that of George Abbott-Smith. It is a handy volume for the desk, and it usually answers the question quickly. When it does not, I refer to the ponderous volume by Walter Bauer.

The Synonyms of the New Testament by Richard Trench is a standard, although occasionally it needs to be updated by the *Theological Dictionary of the New Testament*, edited by Gerhard Kittel and Gerhard Friedrich. These ten volumes (including the helpful index volume) contain more information than any one preacher could begin to digest in his lifetime. You need not be an expert in either Greek or Hebrew to appreciate and use this set. To be sure, the articles are uneven in theological emphasis and scholarship; but a careful use of them will enrich you and your sermons. Another valuable work translated from German is the three-volume *New International Dictionary of New Testament Theology* edited by Colin Brown. The Greek and Hebrew words are transliterated.

Most students prefer A. T. Robertson's *Word Pictures in the New Testament* to Marvin R. Vincent's older *Word Studies in the New Testament* (though I wish Robertson had not anglicized the Greek words). J. A. Bengel's *Gnomon of the New Testament* has been reprinted and is worth owning. (The Greek word *gnomon* means "a pointer, as on a sun-dial; an interpreter." Bengel wanted his books to point the way, not to explain Scripture exhaustively. He gave "hints" instead of long comments.)

My favorite "cheater" is *A Parsing Guide to the Greek New Testament* compiled by Nathan E. Han. I also confess to using Alfred Marshall's handy *Interlinear Greek-English New Testament* and W. E. Vine's *Expository Dictionary of New Testament Words*. I am not embarrassed to consult *The Englishman's Greek Concordance* compiled by G. V. Wigram, who also gave us *The Englishman's Hebrew and Chaldee Concordance*.

William Barclay was certainly one of the most productive writers of religious books of his generation. His *Daily Study Bible* is excellent for word studies and historical information but is very weak theologically. His *New Testament Wordbook* and *More New Testament Words* are valuable studies of Greek words. While you are at it, buy also his *Flesh and Spirit: An Examination of Galatians 5:19–23*.

Light from the Ancient East by Adolf Deissmann is an old standard you must not ignore. The many Greek word studies and New Testament commentaries by Kenneth S. Wuest have been brought together in *Word Studies from the Greek New Testament.* Wuest was a beloved instructor for many years at the Moody Bible Institute. At times he squeezed Greek words until they were about to bleed; but his simple studies reveal a love for Christ and devotion to the Word.

Bishop Henry Alford wrote his famous four-volume *Greek Testament* especially for people who know little or no Greek; his *New Testament for English Readers* is an abridgment of this work.

My favorite New Testament commentary is that of R. C. H. Lenski. I smile whenever this scholar stabbed the "chiliasts" or those who reject infant baptism; yet I profit greatly from his sane and spiritually sensitive exposition. You do not have to be a Greek scholar to benefit from Lenski. Another good commentary on the New Testament is that of William Hendriksen. This able teacher-preacher has not yet completed the entire New Testament; we pray God will spare and sustain him for his task. The author gets right to the point, and you invariably know where he stands. He always sees the practical side of God's truth. You have here a scholar's mind and a pastor's heart! No one can afford to be without the *New International Commentary on the New Testament;* all the volumes are good, and some are masterpieces, such as Leon Morris on John and John Murray on Romans. One of the better one-volume commentaries is *A New Testament Commentary* edited by G. C. D. Howley.

James Hastings's *Dictionary of Christ and the Gospels* and *Dictionary of the Apostolic Church* are still valuable to the serious student and ought to be in every preacher's library.

The Gospels. W. Graham Scroggie's *Guide to the Gospels* is indispensable. The author examined each Gospel individually, then their relationship to each other. Digesting the information in these pages is the equivalent of taking a postgraduate seminar. *The Genius of the Gospels* by Merrill C. Tenney examines the Gospels as historical documents, biographical sketches, homiletic treatises, and spiritual guides. *Four Views of Christ* by Andrew J. Jukes examines the characteristics of each Gospel. As far as expositions are concerned, those of G. Campbell Morgan and J. C. Ryle are basic.

As for books on the life of Christ, Alfred Edersheim's stands at the head of the line. Do not purchase an abridged edition; get the original two volumes and read them. John Peter Lange's study is a classic, as are those of David Smith, James Stalker (*Christ, Our Example* and *The Life of Jesus Christ*), Alexander B. Bruce (*The Training of the Twelve*), Frederic W. Farrar, and Alexander Whyte. Newer works include those of William Barclay, John F. Walvoord, Robert D. Culver, J. W. Shepard, and H. Brash Bonsall. I believe that G. Campbell Morgan's book *The Crises of the Christ* was his finest. In it Morgan dealt with the seven "crisis experiences" of our Lord, from His birth to the ascension. Morgan also wrote *The Teaching of Christ*, a study of what Jesus taught about God, man, and other subjects. Two other helpful volumes are *To Understand the Bible—Look for Jesus* by Norman Geisler and *Christ in All the Scriptures* by A. M. Hodgkin.

To study the virgin birth of Christ, secure the classic by J. Gresham Machen, then add the works of Howard A. Hanke and Robert G. Gromacki. Two classics on the deity of Christ are volumes by Wilbur M. Smith and Benjamin B. Warfield. I have already suggested books on the miracles and parables of our Lord in chapters 14 and 15.

Studies of the passion and death of Christ are legion, so concentrate on basic ones. The three volumes by Klaas Schilder are not easy reading, nor are you likely to react positively to all the ideas in them, but they are valuable. James Stalker's *Trial and Death of Jesus Christ* is a classic. I always get help and spiritual blessing from *The Suffering Saviour* by F. W. Krummacher and from *The Day of the Cross* by W. M. Clow. *The Passion and Death of Christ* by Charles H. Spurgeon is a collection of twelve sermons that trace the events in order. Marcus L. Loane is a careful scholar and gifted writer, and his *Place Called Calvary* dealt primarily with the seven words of Christ from the cross. *The Seven Sayings of the Saviour on the Cross* by Arthur W. Pink is a gold mine of spiritual nuggets, and so is *Gold from Golgotha* by Russell Bradley Jones. An older book, *Testament of Love* by Hubert Simpson, deals with the seven words in a tender and profound way.

You ought to preach a series on John 17 and the high-priestly prayer of Christ. Obtain for this the works of Henry Barclay Swete, Thomas Manton, Charles Ross, Handley C. G. Moule, Marcus Rainsford, Peter Green, and John R. W. Stott (in *Christ the Liberator*). As for the resurrection of Christ, go to books by Merrill C. Tenney, W. J. Sparrow Simpson, Marcus L. Loane, B. F. Westcott, and Donald Grey Barnhouse (*The Cross Through the Open Tomb*). Tenney's *Vital Heart of Christianity* is small but very practical. The standard works on Christ's ascension are those of William Milligan and Henry Barclay Swete.

Homiletic Studies in the Gospels, compiled and edited by Harald F. J. Ellingsen, is a treasure-trove for preachers! Ellingsen knows books *and* good preaching.

I will now list a few helpful volumes on the individual Gospels. Please keep in mind that the standard commentaries I have already recommended (Lenski, Hendriksen, NICNT, Lange) will not usually be repeated.

Matthew. John A. Broadus's commentary has survived the test of time, while other volumes in the American Commentary on the New Testament have been forgotten. Broadus was a careful scholar and a great teacher of preachers. Donald Grey Barnhouse ("*His Own Received Him Not, But . . .*") gave a dispensational survey of the book in true Barnhouse style; this is a very helpful study. W. H. Griffith Thomas showed in his commentary his scholarship, devotion to Christ, and ability to analyze and outline Scripture. You may also want to secure A. C. Gaebelein's commentary.

Books on the Sermon on the Mount abound, but I enjoy those by D. Martyn Lloyd-Jones (the best single work from the conservative point of view), Guy King (a devotional study containing good material you will want to share), Arthur W. Pink (a detailed and helpful work, but it tends toward legalism in places), F. B. Meyer (Meyer needs no recommendation from me!), Helmut Thielicke (fifteen sermons that display the author's usual insights and surprises), C. F. Hogg and J. B. Watson (not a detailed study but to the point; sections on the sermon's application to today and its parallels in the Epistles are very helpful), and Robert Govett (an old work that is a bit too literalistic for me but is filled with choice thoughts; Charles H. Spurgeon said Govett was a hundred years ahead of his time).

Before I wrote my book on the beatitudes, I read dozens of others. Almost all of them said the same thing or said nothing! But in addition to the standard commentaries and those already listed on the Sermon on the Mount, I can recommend those by William Barclay, Spiros Zodhiates, J. D. Jones (*The Way into the Kingdom*), Frank W. Boreham, and Ralph W. Sockman (*The Higher Happiness*)—although I do not agree with all of Sockman's theology.

Along with William Barclay's book on the Lord's Prayer, others worth owning are those by Helmut Thielicke, J. D. Jones, and James W. Thirtle.

The Pharisees and Jesus by A. T. Robertson is the best on this subject that I have seen. Robertson originally gave these chapters as lectures at Princeton Theological Seminary. A. C. Gaebelein wrote a useful study of the difficult Olivet Discourse.

Mark. The best "preaching commentary" is that of J. D. Jones (DC);[4] you should get it. A. T. Robertson wrote a beautiful "sketch" of John Mark that is based on the author's exhaustive knowledge of the Greek New Testament. E. Schuyler English's commentary explains the text, maintains the theme of the book, and helps the student; what more could you want? The two scholarly commentaries you should buy are those of Henry Barclay Swete and Vincent Taylor.

Luke. I recommend the commentary by Frédéric Godet.

John. The best introduction and survey is the one by Merrill C. Tenney. The best *general* commentary is that of Arthur W. Pink. For Greek exegesis and in-depth studies, read both William Hendriksen and Leon Morris (NICNT). A. T. Robertson's *Divinity of Christ in the Gospel of John* is a classic study of this important theme. For more modern discussions see Morris's *Studies in the Fourth Gospel*. W. H. Griffith Thomas's studies in the life and writings of John have all the merits for which the author is noted.

Acts. *A Harmony of the Life of St. Paul* by Frank J. Goodwin does for Paul's life what a Gospel harmony does for Christ's. *The Odyssey of Paul* by George Ogg deals with chronology. As for introductions to Paul's life and letters, that of W. J. Conybeare and J. S. Howson has long been the standard. I use it in connection with the work of David Smith. By all means purchase F. F. Bruce's *Paul: Apostle of the Heart Set Free*. Anything by Bruce is worth reading, but this book is particularly valuable since it "distills" Bruce's lifetime of Pauline studies. *The Apostles* by Donald Guthrie is also excellent.

James S. Stewart's *Man in Christ* is a theological interpretation of Paul, his experiences and doctrines, and it ought to be read by every serious student. For a more detailed study see that of Herman Ridderbos. For sermonic studies see the works of F. B. Meyer and of William M. Taylor (in *Bible Biographies*).

The Environment of Early Christianity by Samuel Angus and *The Defense of the Gospel in the New Testament* by F. F. Bruce explain the intellectual and cultural milieu of the early church.

The Cities of St. Paul and *Pictures of the Apostolic Church*, both by the great Pauline scholar Sir William Ramsay, are still important. To update them, secure *Cities of the New Testament* by E. M.

4. Reprinted—Fincastle, Va.: Scripture Truth.

Blaiklock and *An Archaeologist Follows the Apostle Paul* by James L. Kelso. *St. Paul the Traveller and the Roman Citizen*, also by Ramsay, is a standard work of such stature that it needs no recommendation from me.

Three little books that I rarely see are: *St. Paul in Damascus and Arabia* by George Rawlinson, *St. Paul at Rome* by Charles Merivale, and *St. Paul in Asia Minor* by E. H. Plumptre, all part of "The Heathen World and St. Paul" series.

Baker Book House has reprinted the valuable *Voyage and Shipwreck of St. Paul* by James Smith. Baker has also reprinted A. T. Robertson's *Paul the Interpreter of Christ* and *Epochs in the Life of Paul*, both useful tools.

Along with the standard commentaries (and F. F. Bruce's in the NICNT is superb), add those by Thomas Walker (written by a missionary to India, this older work is worth many of the newer books combined), G. Campbell Morgan (shows how a long narrative book can become exciting exposition), Alexander Maclaren (rich and practical material in his *Bible Class Expositions*, which also has volumes on the four Gospels), and Irving L. Jensen (the best *analysis* of the book). Also secure Morgan's *Birth of the Church*, an exposition of Acts 2.

A good survey of the Holy Spirit in Acts can be obtained from studies by J. H. E. Hull and H. E. Dana. *The Metaphors of St. Paul* by J. S. Howson is a small but priceless book on Paul's use of illustrations from army life, architecture, agriculture, and athletics.

Romans. Before you purchase any others, buy the basic commentaries by William Sanday and Arthur C. Headlam (ICC), Charles Hodge, Handley C. G. Moule (EB), Robert Haldane, D. Martyn Lloyd-Jones (six volumes cover 3:20–8:39 and ought to be studied by every preacher), William R. Newell, and Donald Grey Barnhouse (ten volumes originally, containing excellent preaching, great illustrations, and solid food). Then if you want more, add those of Handley C. G. Moule (CB), James Madison Stifler, and W. H. Griffith Thomas.

Chapter 8 is ably handled by Marcus L. Loane, A. Skevington Wood (*Life by the Spirit*), John R. W. Stott, and Watchman Nee (*The Normal Christian Life*). Chapters 9–11 are a battleground! For the premillennial interpretation read A. C. Gaebelein (*The Jewish Question*) and Alva J. McClain (*The Jewish Problem and Its Divine Solution*); for the amillennial, H. L. Ellison.

I Corinthians. Excellent commentaries have been written by Thomas Charles Edwards (based on the Greek text but useful to any careful student), G. Campbell Morgan (excellent, written in

Morgan's typical expository fashion), Leon Morris (so outstanding that I must mention it; not all the volumes in the TNTC are as good, however), and W. E. Vine (a careful study based on a thorough knowledge of the Greek text, but for the English reader). Two recent studies geared to the layman but also helpful to the pastor are those of Robert G. Gromacki and James L. Boyer. *Pastoral Problems in I Corinthians* by John Stanley Glen has some helpful insights. Two classic commentaries are those by Frédéric Godet and Charles Hodge. Alan Redpath's series of messages on this book is pastoral and practical.

It is too bad that many books treat I Corinthians 13 in a shallow manner. To avoid sentimentality, read the works of Jonathan Edwards (*Charity and Its Fruits*), E. M. Blaiklock, J. D. Jones, and Charles G. Finney (*Attributes of Love*).

II Corinthians. Basic works that complement each other are those by Charles Hodge and Handley C. G. Moule. Also valuable are those of G. Campbell Morgan, Geoffrey B. Wilson (brief but helpful), John Heading (Plymouth Brethren), and Alan Redpath (a series of sermons that shows intense personal suffering on the preacher's part).

Galatians. The essential commentaries are those of J. B. Lightfoot, John Brown, and C. F. Hogg and W. E. Vine. Also helpful are those by John R. W. Stott, Lehman Strauss, William Ramsay, Handley C. G. Moule, and Merrill C. Tenney.

Ephesians. Standard commentaries are those by John Eadie, Charles Hodge, and Handley C. G. Moule (CB).[5] Also good are those of Ruth Paxson (*The Wealth, Walk, and Warfare of the Christian,* a delightful devotional study with excellent analysis and outlines) and F. F. Bruce (brief but most helpful). Five volumes of D. Martyn Lloyd-Jones's exposition of this book are now available. For a very detailed exposition of the Christian armor passage, see William Gurnall. For examples of pastoral preaching through Ephesians, see Harold J. Ockenga.

Philippians. The standard works are by John Eadie, J. B. Lightfoot, Alfred Plummer, and Marvin R. Vincent (ICC). Also helpful are studies by J. A. Motyer, A. T. Robertson, Handley C. G. Moule, Guy King, John Henry Jowett, Paul S. Rees, and F. B. Meyer.[6]

Colossians-Philemon. The standard commentaries on Colossians are by John Eadie and J. B. Lightfoot. Other valuable works are

5. Reprinted—Grand Rapids: Kregel, 1977.

6. Reprinted—Grand Rapids: Baker, 1952.

those by Handley C. G. Moule (a deeply devotional commentary based on a profound knowledge of the Greek text), Alexander Maclaren in the *Expositor's Bible* (a masterpiece of scholarship and exposition), W. H. Griffith Thomas (deeply spiritual and very practical), Guy King (maintains his delightful series of expositions at a high level), and William Barclay (an excellent commentary that is not part of the *Daily Study Bible*). Moule, Maclaren (EB), and Thomas also cover Philemon.

Thessalonians. The two volumes by Leon Morris (NICNT and TNTC) are tremendous. D. Edmond Hiebert's work is useful, but I wish the author had not taken so much space surveying the opinions of other commentators. C. F. Hogg and W. E. Vine crammed their commentary with useful information and good exposition. If you can handle the Greek text, the most scholarly of the old works is that of Charles J. Ellicott. For sermonic exposition, see Harold J. Ockenga.

Pastoral Epistles. The two volumes on I and II Timothy by D. Edmond Hiebert (EBC) are excellent, as is the volume on all the pastoral epistles by Homer A. Kent, Jr. Other good commentaries on the pastorals are by Donald Guthrie (a superior work in the TNTC), W. E. Vine (follows Vine's usual capable approach to exegesis and application), and Alfred Plummer (EB). For simple devotional studies see those of Guy King on the two epistles to Timothy. Eugene Stock's "plain talks" on the themes in these letters are valuable; every pastor ought to study these fifty chapters carefully.

Hebrews. The most exhaustive treatment is that of John Owen. Philip Edgcumbe Hughes's volume is essential for your library; I cannot recommend it too much! F. F. Bruce's commentary (NICNT) is great. John Brown's work is a faithful standard that is most satisfying. The work of Arthur W. Pink is useful, as is William R. Newell's classic. For a devotional approach, read Andrew Murray; for a general survey, G. Campbell Morgan. Among the newer studies I have enjoyed that of Homer A. Kent, Jr. The two volumes by Adolph Saphir are excellent. Joseph A. Seiss's work is a classic, as is B. F. Westcott's. W. H. Griffith Thomas's commentary consists of a series of excellent homiletical studies.

Three helpful volumes on Hebrews 11 are by G. Campbell Morgan (*The Triumphs of Faith*), R. E. O. White, and E. W. Bullinger. An excellent study of the "warning passages" and the problem of apostasy is that of R. E. Glaze, Jr. But the best treatment I have seen is found in the study by James T. Draper, Jr. Draper, while furnishing an example of how one pastor preached through Hebrews, interpreted the warning passages in the same way as had M. R. DeHaan. I happen to agree with this interpretation!

James. Thomas Manton's commentary is a classic, but please do not imitate his detailed exposition! Puritan congregations had more time on their hands than do believers today. I have enjoyed using Robert Johnstone's work. Spiros Zodhiates' collection of studies, originally given over the radio, are based on the Greek text but popular in presentation. Also useful are commentaries by Guy King (another of his delightful devotional expositions), J. A. Motyer (*The Tests of Faith*, a fine example of careful exegesis and pastoral concern), and Lehman Strauss (another example of clear exposition).

Peter's Epistles. Everybody recommends the commentary of the saintly Robert Leighton, archbishop of Glasgow. I have used it with profit, but I have received even more help from that of Edward Gordon Selwyn. The latter work is based on the Greek text but is not highly technical. W. H. Griffith Thomas furnished a good survey of Peter's life that relates events to his letters. For devotional studies consult the works of John Henry Jowett, F. B. Meyer, and Paul S. Rees.

John's Epistles. Three classics stand out: those of Robert S. Candlish, B. F. Westcott, and Robert Law. John R. W. Stott's commentary (TNTC) is also superior. F. F. Bruce's is not as full as some of his commentaries, but it is still excellent. Another smaller work is that of W. E. Vine. For a devotional exposition, read Guy King.

Jude. S. Maxwell Coder's commentary (EBC) is brief but very satisfying; Richard Wolff's, helpful; Thomas Manton's a classic (376 pages on twenty-five verses!).

Revelation. When I study this difficult book, I keep nearby the commentaries by Lehman Strauss, John F. Walvoord, Robert H. Mounce (NICNT), Walter Scott, and William R. Newell. Strauss showed his familiarity with the works in the field but did not hesitate to state and defend his own views; Wilbur M. Smith thought very highly of Strauss's commentary. Walvoord's expertise in the field of prophecy is well known; his book is a perfect complement to Strauss's. Mounce's work is scholarly and tries to avoid extremes. Scott's is a classic treatment of the English text. Newell's is another classic work from the premillennial perspective. Other helpful commentaries are those by W. A. Criswell, Joseph A. Seiss, Merrill C. Tenney, and Gary G. Cohen. The best amillennial treatment I have found is that of William Hendriksen. Also amillennial and good is that of Albertus Pieters. I have profited greatly from both Hendriksen and Pieters.

On the letters to the seven churches, read G. Campbell Morgan, William Barclay, William Ramsay, and Richard Trench.

Bible Personalities

The standard is *The Greater Men and Women of the Bible* edited by James Hastings, six volumes containing a wealth of material on key persons of biblical history. Some enterprising editor should update this set. Alexander Whyte's *Bible Characters* is a collection of the great preacher's messages which focus on one key aspect of the subject's personality and use that to illumine his life. In *The Representative Men of the Bible* and *The Representative Women of the Bible* George Matheson, the blind scholar-preacher, saw more than most of us see! Like Whyte, Matheson centered on one important area of the person's life, but Matheson's treatment is much broader than Whyte's. Herbert Lockyer's *All the Men of the Bible* and *All the Kings and Queens of the Bible* are not detailed but are still helpful. In *Meet Yourself in the Bible* Roy L. Laurin selected twenty-eight persons and showed how God gave them victory in a particular area of life. William S. LaSor's *Great Personalities of the Bible* provide excellent background material and good practical applications. In *Bible Biographies* William M. Taylor studied Joseph, Moses, David, Ruth, Esther, Elijah, Daniel, Peter, and Paul. Here is excellent, solid Bible exposition, given in the traditional Scottish way. I also use Harold J. Ockenga's *Women Who Made Bible History*.

Good studies of David have been written by Arthur W. Pink and Alan Redpath. Some excellent volumes on Elijah are those of Arthur W. Pink, Leon J. Wood, W. W. Fereday, and Elijah P. Brown. On Elisha see books by J. T. Mawson and F. W. Krummacher (a classic).

Books on preaching are referred to throughout *Listening to the Giants*, as well as the companion volume, *Walking with the Giants*. Biographies and autobiographies of famous preachers are also mentioned often. For books on doctrine, church history, and other related fields, consult the larger bibliographies.

Happy hunting!

Abbreviations

CB—*Cambridge Bible for Schools and Colleges*. Cambridge: Cambridge University, 1884–1899.

DC—*Devotional Commentary.* London: Religious Tract Society, 1905-1931.

EB—*Expositor's Bible.* 1888-1905. Reprinted—Grand Rapids: Eerdmans, 1943.

EBC—*Everyman's Bible Commentary.* Chicago: Moody, 1970-.

ICC—*International Critical Commentary.* New York: Scribner, 1895-1937.

NICNT—*New International Commentary on the New Testament.* Grand Rapids: Eerdmans, 1951-.

NICOT—*New International Commentary on the Old Testament.* Grand Rapids: Eerdmans, 1976-.

TNTC—*Tyndale New Testament Commentary.* Grand Rapids: Eerdmans, 1957-1974.

TOTC—*Tyndale Old Testament Commentary.* Downers Grove, Ill.: InterVarsity, 1974-.

Bibliography

Abbott-Smith, George. *A Manual Greek Lexicon of the New Testament.* New York: Scribner, 1922.

Aharoni, Yohanan, and Avi-Yonah, Michael. *The Macmillan Bible Atlas.* Rev. ed. New York: Macmillan, 1977.

Alexander, Joseph Addison. *The Psalms, Translated and Explained.* 1850. Reprinted—Grand Rapids: Baker, 1975.

Alford, Henry. *The Greek Testament.* 5th ed. 4 vols. 1871-1877. Reprinted—Grand Rapids: Baker, 1976.

———. *The New Testament for English Readers.* 2 vols. 1863-1866. Reprinted—Chicago: Moody.

Anderson, Robert. *The Coming Prince; or, The Seventy Weeks of Daniel with an Answer to the Higher Criticism.* 10th ed. 1915. Reprinted—Grand Rapids: Kregel.

Angus, Samuel. *The Environment of Early Christianity.* New York: Scribner, 1914.

Archer, Gleason L. *A Survey of Old Testament Introduction.* Rev. ed. Chicago: Moody, 1974.

Arnot, William. *Laws from Heaven for Life on Earth: Illustrations of the Book of Proverbs.* New York: Nelson, 1857. Reprinted—Grand Rapids: Kregel.

Barber, Cyril J. *The Minister's Library.* Grand Rapids: Baker, 1974.

Barclay, William. *The All-Sufficient Christ: Studies in Paul's Letter to the Colossians.* Philadelphia: Westminster, 1963.

———. *The Beatitudes and the Lord's Prayer for Everyman.* New York: Harper and Row, 1968.

———. *Daily Study Bible.* Rev. ed. 17 vols. Philadelphia: Westminster, 1975-1976.

———. *Flesh and Spirit: An Examination of Galatians 5:19-23.* 1962. Reprinted—Grand Rapids: Baker, 1976.

——— *Jesus as They Saw Him: New Testament Interpretations of Jesus.* New York: Harper and Row, 1962.

______. *Letters to the Seven Churches*. New York: Abingdon, 1958.
______. *A New Testament Wordbook*. New York: Harper, 1956.
______. *More New Testament Words*. New York: Harper, 1958.
______. *The Ten Commandments for Today*. New York: Harper and Row, 1973.
Barnes, Albert. *Notes on the Old Testament, Explanatory and Practical*. 9 vols. 1840–1868. Reprinted—Grand Rapids: Baker, 1949–1950.
Barnhouse, Donald Grey. *The Cross Through the Open Tomb*. Grand Rapids: Eerdmans, 1961.
______. *Exposition of Bible Doctrines, Taking the Epistle to the Romans as a Point of Departure*. 10 vols. Grand Rapids: Eerdmans, 1958–1964.
______. *"His Own Received Him Not, But . . .": The Turning Point in the Ministry of Christ*. New York: Revell, 1933.
Baron, David. *The Servant of Jehovah: The Sufferings of the Messiah and the Glory That Should Follow: An Exposition of Isaiah 53*. New York: Doran, 1922.
______. *The Visions and Prophecies of Zechariah: "The Prophet of Hope and of Glory."* 1918. Reprinted—Fincastle, Va.: Scripture Truth.
Batson, Beatrice. *A Reader's Guide to Religious Literature*. Chicago: Moody, 1968.
Bauer, Walter; Arndt, William F.; Gingrich, F. Wilbur; and Danker, Frederick W. *A Greek-English Lexicon of the New Testament and Other Early Christian Literature*. 2d ed. Chicago: University of Chicago, 1979.
Baxter, J. Sidlow. *Explore the Book: A Basic and Broadly Interpretive Course of Bible Study from Genesis to Revelation*. 6 vols. Grand Rapids: Zondervan, 1960.
Bengel, J. A. *Gnomon of the New Testament*. Translated by Charlton T. Lewis and Marvin R. Vincent. 2 vols. 1860–1862. Reprinted—*New Testament Word Studies*. Grand Rapids: Kregel, 1971.
Blackwood, Andrew W. *Preaching from Prophetic Books*. New York: Abingdon-Cokesbury, 1951.
Blackwood, Andrew W., Jr. *Devotional Introduction to Job*. Grand Rapids: Baker, 1959.
Blaiklock, E. M. *Cities of the New Testament*. Westwood, N.J.: Revell, 1965.
______. *The Way of Excellence: A New Translation and Study of I Corinthians 13 and Romans 12*. Grand Rapids: Zondervan, 1968.
Blair, J. Allen. *Living Obediently: A Devotional Study of the Book of Jonah*. Neptune, N.J.: Loizeaux, 1963.
______. *Living Patiently: A Devotional Study of the Book of Job*. Neptune, N.J.: Loizeaux, 1966.
Bonar, Andrew. *A Commentary on the Book of Leviticus*. 3d ed. 1852. Reprinted—Grand Rapids: Baker, 1978.
Bonsall, H. Brash. *The Person of Christ*. London: Christian Literature Crusade, 1967.
Boreham, Frank W. *The Heavenly Octave: A Study of the Beatitudes*. 1935. Reprinted—Grand Rapids: Baker, 1968.
Boyer, James L. *For a World like Ours: Studies in I Corinthians*. Grand Rapids: Baker, 1971.
Bridges, Charles. *Exposition of Psalm 119, as Illustrative of the Character and Exercises of Christian Experience*. London: Seeley and Burnside, 1830.
______. *An Exposition of the Book of Proverbs*. 1847. Reprinted—Grand Rapids: Zondervan, 1959.

Broadus, John A. *Commentary on the Gospel of Matthew*. American Commentary on the New Testament. Philadelphia: American Baptist Publication Society, 1886.

Brown, Colin, ed. *The New International Dictionary of New Testament Theology*. 3 vols. Grand Rapids: Zondervan, 1975–1978.

Brown, Elijah P. *The Raven and the Chariot: New Thoughts on Elijah the Tishbite*. New York: Eaton and Mains, 1907.

Brown, John. *An Exposition of the Epistle of Paul the Apostle to the Galatians*. Edinburgh: Oliphant, 1853.

______. *An Exposition of the Epistle of the Apostle Paul to the Hebrews*. Edited by David Smith. 2 vols. 1862. Reprinted—London: Banner of Truth, 1964.

Bruce, Alexander B. *The Training of the Twelve*. 1871. Reprinted—Grand Rapids: Kregel, 1971.

Bruce, F. F. *The Defense of the Gospel in the New Testament*. Rev. ed. Grand Rapids: Eerdmans, 1977.

______. *The Epistles of John: Introduction, Exposition, and Notes*. Old Tappan, N.J.: Revell, 1970.

______. *The Epistle to the Ephesians: A Verse-by-Verse Exposition*. Westwood, N.J.: Revell, 1961.

______. *Paul: Apostle of the Heart Set Free*. Grand Rapids: Eerdmans, 1977.

Bullinger, E. W. *The Great "Cloud of Witnesses": Being a Series of Papers on Hebrews 11*. London: Eyre and Spottiswoode, 1911.

Callaway, T. W. *Christ in the Old Testament*. New York: Loizeaux, 1950.

Candlish, Robert S. *The First Epistle of John*. 1866. Reprinted—Grand Rapids: Zondervan, 1952.

Caryl, Joseph. *An Exposition with Practical Observations on the Book of Job*. 12 vols. 1644–1666. Reprinted—1 vol. Grand Rapids: Kregel.

Clarke, Arthur G. *Analytical Studies in the Psalms*. 1949. Reprinted—Grand Rapids: Kregel.

Clow, W. M. *The Day of the Cross: A Course of Sermons on the Men and Women and Some of the Notable Things of the Day of the Crucifixion of Jesus*. 1909. Reprinted—Grand Rapids: Baker, 1955.

Cohen, Gary G. *Understanding Revelation: An Investigation of the Key Interpretational and Chronological Questions Which Surround the Book of Revelation*. Chicago: Moody 1978.

Conybeare, W. J., and Howson, J. S. *The Life and Epistles of St. Paul*. 2 vols. 1854. Reprinted—Grand Rapids: Eerdmans, 1953.

Cox, Samuel. *The Book of Ruth: A Popular Exposition*. London: Religious Tract Society, 1876.

Criswell, W. A. *Expository Sermons on Revelation*. 5 vols. Grand Rapids: Zondervan, 1961–1966.

Crockett, William D. *A Harmony of the Books of Samuel, Kings, and Chronicles: The Books of the Kings of Judah and Israel*. 1897. Reprinted—Grand Rapids: Baker, 1951.

Culver, Robert D. *The Life of Christ*. Grand Rapids: Baker, 1976.

______. *The Sufferings and the Glory of the Lord's Righteous Servant*. Moline, Ill.: Christian Service Foundation, 1958.

Dale, R. W. *The Ten Commandments*. New York: Hodder and Stoughton, n.d.

Dana, H. E. *The Holy Spirit in Acts*. 2d ed. Kansas City: Central Seminary, 1943.

Davidman, Joy. *Smoke on the Mountain: The Ten Commandments in Terms of Today*. Philadelphia: Westminster, 1970.

Davidson, A. B. *The Theology of the Old Testament.* Edited by S. D. F. Salmond. New York: Scribner, 1904.

Davidson, Francis, ed. *The New Bible Commentary.* Grand Rapids: Eerdmans, 1954.

Davis, John J. *Moses and the Gods of Egypt: Studies in the Book of Exodus.* Grand Rapids: Baker, 1971.

DeHaan, M. R. *Hebrews: Twenty-Six Simple Studies in God's Plan for Victorious Living.* Grand Rapids: Zondervan, 1959.

______. *Portraits of Christ in Genesis.* Grand Rapids: Zondervan, 1966.

Deissmann, Adolf. *Light from the Ancient East: The New Testament Illustrated by Recently Discovered Texts of the Graeco-Roman World.* New rev. ed. Translated by Lionel R. M. Strachan. 1927. Reprinted—Grand Rapids: Baker, 1978.

Dickson, David. *A Brief Explication of the Psalms.* 3 vols. 1653–1654. Reprinted—*A Commentary on the Psalms.* 2 vols. London: Banner of Truth, 1959.

Draper, James T., Jr. *Hebrews: The Life That Pleases God.* Wheaton, Ill.: Tyndale, 1976.

______. *Proverbs: The Secret of Beautiful Living.* Wheaton, Ill.: Tyndale, 1977.

Eadie, John. *A Commentary on the Greek Text of the Epistle of Paul to the Colossians.* 1856. Reprinted—Grand Rapids: Baker, 1979.

______. *A Commentary on the Greek Text of the Epistle of Paul to the Ephesians.* 1854. Reprinted—Grand Rapids: Baker, 1979.

______. *A Commentary on the Greek Text of the Epistle of Paul to the Philippians.* 1859. Reprinted—Grand Rapids: Baker, 1979.

Edersheim, Alfred. *The Life and Times of Jesus the Messiah.* 1883. Reprinted—Grand Rapids: Eerdmans.

Edwards, Jonathan. *Charity and Its Fruits: Christian Love as Manifested in the Heart and Life.* Edited by Tyron Edwards. 1852. Reprinted—London: Banner of Truth, 1969.

Edwards, Thomas Charles. *A Commentary on the First Epistle to the Corinthians.* 2d ed. London: Hodder and Stoughton, 1885.

Ellicott, Charles J. *A Critical and Grammatical Commentary on St. Paul's Epistles to the Thessalonians.* 1858. Reprinted—Grand Rapids: Zondervan.

Ellingsen, Harald F. J. *Homiletic Thesaurus on the Gospels.* 3 vols. 1949–1950. Reprinted—*Homiletic Studies in the Gospels.* Grand Rapids: Baker, 1972.

Ellison, H. L. *Ezekiel: The Man and His Message.* Grand Rapids: Eerdmans, 1956.

______. *From Tragedy to Triumph: The Message of the Book of Job.* Grand Rapids: Eerdmans, 1958.

______. *The Mystery of Israel: An Exposition of Romans 9–11.* Grand Rapids: Eerdmans, 1966.

English, E. Schuyler. *Studies in the Gospel According to Mark: A Comprehensive Exposition of the Gospel of the Servant-Son of God.* New York: Our Hope, 1943.

Fadiman, Clifton. *The Lifetime Reading Plan.* Rev. ed. New York: Crowell, 1978.

Fairbairn, Patrick. *Jonah: His Life, Character, and Mission, Viewed in Connexion with the Prophet's Own Times, and Future Manifestations of God's Mind and Will in Prophecy.* 1849. Reprinted—Grand Rapids: Kregel.

Farrar, Frederic W. *The Life of Christ.* 2d ed. 2 vols. 1874. Reprinted—Portland: Fountain, 1976.

Feinberg, Charles Lee. *God Remembers: A Study of the Book of Zechariah*. 1951. Portland: Multnomah, 1977.
———. *The Minor Prophets*. Chicago: Moody, 1976.
———. *The Prophecy of Ezekiel: The Glory of the Lord*. Chicago: Moody, 1969.
Fereday, W. W. *Elijah the Tishbite*. Kilmarnock: Ritchie, 1966.
Finney, Charles G. *Attributes of Love: A Section from "Lectures on Systematic Theology."* Minneapolis: Bethany Fellowship, 1963.
Gaebelein, A. C. *The Book of Psalms*. New York: Our Hope, 1939.
———. *The Gospel of Matthew: A Complete Analysis of Matthew with Annotations*. 1914. Reprinted—Neptune, N.J.: Loizeaux.
———. *The Jewish Question*. New York: Our Hope, 1912.
———. *The Olivet Discourse, Matthew 24-25: An Exposition*. 1906. Reprinted—Grand Rapids: Baker, 1969.
Gaebelein, Frank E., ed. *The Expositor's Bible Commentary*. Grand Rapids: Zondervan, 1976-.
Gardiner, George E. *The Romance of Ruth*. Grand Rapids: Kregel, 1977.
Geisler, Norman. *Christ: The Theme of the Bible*. 1968. Reprinted—*To Understand the Bible—Look for Jesus*. Grand Rapids: Baker, 1979.
Glaze, R. E., Jr. *No Easy Salvation: A Careful Examination of the Question of Apostasy in Hebrews*. 1966. Reprinted—New Orleans: Insight, 1974.
Glen, John Stanley. *Pastoral Problems in I Corinthians*. Philadelphia: Westminster, 1964.
Godet, Frédéric. *Commentary on St. Paul's First Epistle to the Corinthians*. Translated by A. Cusin. 2 vols. 1886-1887. Reprinted—Grand Rapids: Zondervan.
———. *A Commentary on the Gospel of St. Luke*. Translated by E. W. Shalders and M. D. Cusin. 2 vols. 1875. Reprinted—Grand Rapids: Zondervan.
Goodwin, Frank J. *A Harmony of the Life of St. Paul*. 1895. Reprinted—Grand Rapids: Baker, 1951.
Govett, Robert. *The Sermon on the Mount Expounded*. 3d ed. 1885. Reprinted—London: Thynne, 1932.
Green, Peter. *Our Great High Priest: Thoughts on the Seventeenth Chapter of St. John's Gospel*. New York: Longmans and Green, 1939.
Grier, W. J. *The Best Books: A Guide to Christian Literature*. London: Banner of Truth, 1968.
Gromacki, Robert G. *Called to Be Saints: An Exposition of I Corinthians*. Grand Rapids: Baker, 1977.
———. *The Virgin Birth: Doctrine of Deity*. Nashville: Nelson, 1974.
Gurnall, William. *The Christian in Complete Armour; or, A Treatise on the Saints' War Against the Devil*. 3 vols. 1655-1662. Reprinted—London: Banner of Truth, 1964.
Guthrie, Donald. *The Apostles*. Grand Rapids: Zondervan, 1975.
———. *New Testament Introduction*. 3d ed. Downers Grove, Ill.: Inter-Varsity, 1971.
Habershon, Ada R. *The Study of the Types*. 1911. Reprinted—Grand Rapids: Kregel, 1973.
Hailey, Homer. *A Commentary on the Minor Prophets*. Grand Rapids: Baker, 1972.
Haldane, Robert. *Exposition of the Epistle to the Romans*. 1835ff. Reprinted—London: Banner of Truth, 1966.
Han, Nathan E., comp. *A Parsing Guide to the Greek New Testament*. Scottdale, Pa.: Herald, 1971.

Hanke, Howard A. *The Validity of the Virgin Birth.* Grand Rapids: Zondervan, 1964.
Hastings, James, ed. *Dictionary of Christ and the Gospels.* 2 vols. 1906-1908. Reprinted—Grand Rapids: Baker, 1973.
______, ed. *Dictionary of the Apostolic Church.* 2 vols. 1916-1922. Reprinted—Grand Rapids: Baker, 1973.
______, ed. *The Greater Men and Women of the Bible.* 6 vols. Edinburgh: Clark, 1913-1916.
______, ed. *The Great Texts of the Bible.* 20 vols. 1910-1915. Reprinted—Grand Rapids: Baker, 1977.
Hastings, James, and Hastings, Edward, eds. *The Speaker's Bible.* 18 vols. 1923-1932. Reprinted—Grand Rapids: Baker, 1978.
Heading, John. *Second Epistle to the Corinthians.* Kilmarnock: Ritchie.
Hendriksen, William. *More Than Conquerors: An Interpretation of the Book of Revelation.* Grand Rapids: Baker, 1939.
______. *New Testament Commentary.* Grand Rapids: Baker, 1953-.
Hiebert, D. Edmond. *The Thessalonian Epistles: A Call to Readiness: A Commentary.* Chicago: Moody, 1971.
Hodge, Charles. *A Commentary on the Epistle to the Ephesians.* 1856. Reprinted—Grand Rapids: Baker, 1980.
______. *A Commentary on the Epistle to the Romans.* 1835. Reprinted—Grand Rapids: Eerdmans.
______. *An Exposition of the First Epistle to the Corinthians.* 1857. Reprinted—Grand Rapids: Eerdmans, 1956.
______. *An Exposition of the Second Epistle to the Corinthians.* 1857. Reprinted—Grand Rapids: Eerdmans, 1953.
Hodgkin, A. M. *Christ in All the Scriptures.* 1908. Reprinted—London: Inter-Varsity, 1936.
Hogg, C. F. and Vine, W. E. *The Epistle of Paul the Apostle to the Galatians.* London: Pickering, 1922.
Hogg, C. F., and Vine, W. E. *The Epistles of Paul the Apostle to the Thessalonians.* Glasgow: Pickering and Inglis, 1914.
Hogg, C. F., and Watson, J. B. *The Sermon on the Mount.* London: Pickering, 1934.
Hone, Ralph E., ed. *The Voice out of the Whirlwind: The Book of Job.* San Francisco: Chandler, 1960.
Honeycutt, Roy Lee. *Amos and His Message: An Expository Commentary.* Nashville: Broadman, 1963.
Howard, David M. *Words of Fire, Rivers of Tears: The Man Jeremiah.* Wheaton, Ill.: Tyndale, 1976.
Howley, G. C. D., ed. *A New Testament Commentary: Based on the Revised Standard Version.* Grand Rapids: Eerdmans, 1969.
Howson, J. S. *The Metaphors of St. Paul.* London: Strahan, 1868.
Hubbard, David Allan. *Beyond Futility: Messages of Hope from the Book of Ecclesiastes.* Grand Rapids: Eerdmans, 1976.
Hughes, Philip Edgcumbe. *A Commentary on the Epistle to the Hebrews.* Grand Rapids: Eerdmans, 1977.
Hull, J. H. E. *The Holy Spirit in the Acts of the Apostles.* Cleveland: World, 1968.
Hulme, William E. *Dialogue in Despair: Pastoral Commentary on the Book of Job.* Nashville: Abingdon, 1968.
Ironside, H. A. *Addresses on the Book of Joshua.* New York: Loizeaux, 1950.
______. *Addresses on the Song of Solomon.* New York: Loizeaux, 1933.

———. *Lectures on the Levitical Offerings.* New York: Loizeaux, 1951.

———. *Notes on the Book of Proverbs.* New York: Loizeaux, 1907.

———. *Notes on the Books of Ezra, Nehemiah, and Esther.* New York: Loizeaux, 1951.

———. *Notes on the Minor Prophets.* New York: Loizeaux, 1942.

———. *Notes on the Prophecy and Lamentations of Jeremiah, the "Weeping Prophet."* New York: Loizeaux, 1906.

Jamieson, Robert; Fausset, A. R.; and Brown, David. *A Commentary, Critical, Experimental, and Practical on the Old and New Testaments.* 1901. Reprinted—Grand Rapids: Eerdmans, 1935.

Jennings, F. C. *Old Groans and New Songs: Being Meditations on Ecclesiastes.* New York: Loizeaux, 1920.

———. *Studies in Isaiah.* New York: Loizeaux, 1935.

Jensen, Irving L. *Acts: An Inductive Study: A Manual of Bible-Study-in-Depth.* Chicago: Moody, 1968.

Johnstone, Robert. *Lectures, Exegetical and Practical, on the Epistle of James.* 1871. Reprinted—Grand Rapids: Baker, 1954.

Jones, J. D. *The Greatest of These: Addresses on I Corinthians 13.* London: Hodder and Stoughton, 1925.

———. *The Model Prayer.* London: Clarke, n.d.

———. *The Way into the Kingdom.* London: Religious Tract Society, 1900.

Jones, Russell Bradley. *Gold from Golgotha.* Chicago: Moody, 1945.

Jowett, John Henry. *The Epistles of St. Peter.* The Practical Commentary on the New Testament. 1906. Reprinted—Grand Rapids: Kregel, 1970.

———. *The High Calling: Meditations on St. Paul's Letter to the Philippians.* New York: Revell, 1909.

Jukes, Andrew J. *The Characteristic Differences of the Four Gospels, Considered as Revealing Various Relations of the Lord Jesus Christ.* 1853. Reprinted—*Four Views of Christ.* Edited by James Shiffer Kiefer. Grand Rapids: Kregel, 1966.

———. *The Law of the Offerings, Considered as the Appointed Figure of the Various Aspects of the Offering of the Body of Jesus Christ.* 1848. Reprinted—Grand Rapids: Kregel, 1976.

———. *The Types of Genesis Briefly Considered as Revealing the Development of Human Nature in the World Within, and Without, and in the Dispensations.* 4th ed. 1857. Reprinted—*Types in Genesis.* Grand Rapids: Kregel, 1976.

Jung, C. G. *Answer to Job.* Translated by R. F. C. Hull. 1954. Reprinted—Princeton, N.J.: Princeton University, 1972.

Kaiser, Walter C., Jr., ed. *Classical Evangelical Essays in Old Testament Interpretation.* Grand Rapids: Baker, 1972.

———. *Toward an Old Testament Theology.* Grand Rapids: Zondervan, 1978.

Keller, W. Phillip. *A Shepherd Looks at Psalm 23.* Grand Rapids: Zondervan, 1970.

Kelso, James L. *An Archaeologist Follows the Apostle Paul.* Waco, Tex.: Word, 1970.

Kent, Homer A., Jr. *The Epistle to the Hebrews: A Commentary.* Grand Rapids: Baker, 1972.

———. *The Pastoral Epistles: Studies in I and II Timothy and Titus.* Chicago: Moody, 1958.

Ker, John. *The Psalms in History and Biography.* Edinburgh: Elliott, 1886.

King, Geoffrey R. *Daniel: A Detailed Explanation of the Book.* Rev. ed. Grand Rapids: Eerdmans, 1966.

King, Guy. *A Belief That Behaves: An Expositional Study of the Epistle of James.* London: Marshall, Morgan, and Scott, 1941.

______. *Crossing the Border: An Expositional Study of Colossians.* London: Marshall, Morgan, and Scott, 1957.

______. *The Fellowship: An Expositional and Devotional Study of I John.* London: Marshall, Morgan, and Scott, 1963.

______. *Joy Way: An Expositional Application of the Epistle to the Philippians.* London: Marshall, Morgan, and Scott, 1952.

______. *A Leader Led: A Devotional Study of I Timothy.* London: Marshall, Morgan, and Scott, 1951.

______. *New Order: An Expositional Study of the Sermon on the Mount.* London: Marshall, Morgan, and Scott, 1943.

______. *To My Son: An Expositional Study of II Timothy.* London: Marshall, Morgan, and Scott, 1944.

Kittel, Gerhard, and Friedrich, Gerhard, eds. *Theological Dictionary of the New Testament.* Translated and edited by Geoffrey W. Bromiley. 9 vols. Grand Rapids: Eerdmans, 1964–1974.

Knight, William Allen. *The Song of Our Syrian Guest.* Boston: Pilgrim, 1904.

Krummacher, F. W. *Elijah the Tishbite.* 1837. Reprinted—Grand Rapids: Baker, 1977.

______. *The Suffering Saviour: Meditations on the Last Days of Christ.* Translated by Samuel Jackson. 1850. Reprinted—Chicago: Moody, 1948.

Lange, John Peter, ed. *A Commentary on the Holy Scriptures: Critical, Doctrinal, and Homiletical, with Special Reference to Ministers and Students.* Edited and translated by Philip Schaff. 24 vols. 1865–1879. Reprinted—12 vols. Grand Rapids: Zondervan, 1960.

______. *The Life of the Lord Jesus Christ: A Complete Critical Examination of the Origin, Contents, and Connection of the Gospels.* Edited by Marcus Dods. Translated by Sophia Taylor and J. E. Ryland. 1872. Reprinted—Grand Rapids: Zondervan, 1958.

LaSor, William S. *Great Personalities of the Bible.* Westwood, N.J.: Revell, 1965.

Laurin, Roy L. *Meet Yourself in the Bible.* Findlay, Ohio: Dunham, 1946.

Law, Henry. *Christ Is All: The Gospel of the Pentateuch.* 4 vols. 1867. Vols. 1 (*The Gospel in Genesis*) and 2 (*The Gospel in Exodus*) reprinted—London. Banner of Truth.

Law, Robert. *The Tests of Life: A Study of the First Epistle of St. John.* 3d ed. 1914. Reprinted—Grand Rapids: Baker, 1978.

Leighton, Robert. *A Practical Commentary upon the First Epistle General of St. Peter.* 2 vols. 1693–1694. Reprinted—1 vol. Grand Rapids: Kregel, 1972.

Lenski, R. C. H. *Interpretation of the New Testament.* 12 vols. Minneapolis: Augsburg, 1933–1946.

Leupold, H. C. *Exposition of Daniel.* 1949. Reprinted—Grand Rapids: Baker, 1969.

______. *Exposition of Ecclesiastes.* 1952. Reprinted—Grand Rapids: Baker, 1966.

______. *Exposition of Genesis.* 2 vols. 1942. Reprinted—Grand Rapids: Baker, 1949.

Lightfoot, J. B. *The Epistles of St. Paul.* 3 vols. 1865–1875. Reprinted—Grand Rapids: Zondervan, 1957.

Livingston, G. Herbert. *The Pentateuch in Its Cultural Environment.* Grand Rapids: Baker, 1974.

Lloyd-Jones, D. Martyn. *The Christian Soldier: An Exposition of Ephesians 6:10–20.* Grand Rapids: Baker, 1978.

———. *The Christian Warfare: An Exposition of Ephesians 6:10–13.* Grand Rapids: Baker, 1977.
———. *Faith on Trial.* Grand Rapids: Eerdmans, 1965.
———. *God's Ultimate Purpose: An Exposition of Ephesians 1:1–23.* Grand Rapids: Baker, 1979.
———. *God's Way of Reconciliation: Studies in Ephesians 2.* Grand Rapids: Baker, 1972.
———. *From Fear to Faith.* Downers Grove, Ill.: InterVarsity, 1953.
———. *Life in the Spirit, in Marriage, Home, and Work: An Exposition of Ephesians 5:18–6:9.* Grand Rapids: Baker, 1975.
———. *Romans: An Exposition.* Grand Rapids: Zondervan, 1971–.
———. *Studies in the Sermon on the Mount.* 2 vols. Grand Rapids: Eerdmans, 1959–1960.
Loane, Marcus L. *The Hope of Glory: An Exposition of the Eighth Chapter in the Epistle to the Romans.* Waco, Tex.: Word, 1969.
———. *Our Risen Lord.* Grand Rapids: Zondervan, 1968.
———. *The Place Called Calvary.* Grand Rapids: Zondervan.
Lockyer, Herbert. *All the Kings and Queens of the Bible: Tragedies and Triumphs of Royalty in Past Ages.* Grand Rapids: Zondervan, 1961.
———. *All the Men of the Bible: A Portrait Gallery and Reference Library of More Than 3,000 Biblical Characters.* Grand Rapids: Zondervan, 1958.
Logsdon, S. Franklin. *The Song of a Soul Set Free.* Kalamazoo, Mich.: Masters, 1976.
Loveless, Wendell P. *Christ and the Believer in the Song of Songs.* Chicago: Moody, 1945.
McClain, Alva J. *Daniel's Prophecy of the Seventy Weeks.* Grand Rapids: Zondervan, 1940.
———. *The Jewish Problem and Its Divine Solution.* Winona Lake, Ind.: BMH, 1972.
McFadyen, John Edgar. *A Cry for Justice: A Study in Amos.* New York: Scribner, 1912.
———. *The Problem of Pain: A Study in the Book of Job.* London: Clarke, n.d.
McGee, J. Vernon. *Exposition on the Book of Esther.* Wheaton, Ill.: Van Kampen, 1951.
———. *Ruth: The Romance of Redemption.* 1943. Reprinted—*In a Barley Field.* Glendale, Calif.: Regal, 1968.
Machen, J. Gresham. *The Virgin Birth of Christ.* 1930. Reprinted—Grand Rapids: Baker, 1965.
Mackintosh, Charles Henry. *Genesis to Deuteronomy: Notes on the Pentateuch.* 6 vols. 1880–1882. Reprinted—1 vol. Neptune, N.J.: Loizeaux, 1972.
Maclaren, Alexander. *Bible Class Expositions.* 6 vols. London: Hodder and Stoughton, 1892–1894.
———. *Expositions of Holy Scripture.* 32 vols. 1904–1910. Reprinted—17 vols. Grand Rapids: Baker, 1974.
———. *The Life of David as Reflected in His Psalms.* New York: Macmillan, 1885.
MacRae, Alan A. *The Gospel of Isaiah.* Chicago: Moody, 1977.
Manton, Thomas. *An Exposition of John 17.* London: Banner of Truth, 1959.
———. *A Practical Commentary or an Exposition with Notes on the Epistle of Jude.* 1658. Reprinted—London: Banner of Truth, 1958.
———. *A Practical Commentary or Exposition on the General Epistle of James.* 1651. Reprinted—London: Banner of Truth, 1962.

Marshall, Alfred. *The Interlinear Greek-English New Testament: The Nestle Text with a Literal English Translation*. Grand Rapids: Zondervan, 1958.

Martin, Hugh. *The Prophet Jonah: His Character and Mission to Nineveh*. 1866. Reprinted—London: Banner of Truth, 1958.

Mason, Clarence E. *Love Song*. Chicago: Moody, 1976.

Matheson, George. *The Representative Men of the Bible*. 2 vols. London: Hodder and Stoughton, 1902–1903.

———. *The Representative Women of the Bible*. Edited by William Smith. London: Hodder and Stoughton, 1907.

Mauro, Philip. *Ruth: The Satisfied Stranger*. New York: Revell, 1920.

Mawson, J. T. *Delivering Grace, as Illustrated in the Words and Ways of the Prophet Elisha*. London: Pickering and Inglis, 1932.

Merivale, Charles. *St. Paul at Rome*. New York: Young, 1877.

Meyer, F. B. *Christ in Isaiah*. 1895. Reprinted—Fort Washington, Pa.: Christian Literature Crusade, 1970.

———. *The Directory of the Devout Life: Meditations on the Sermon on the Mount*. 1904. Reprinted—*The Sermon on the Mount*. Grand Rapids: Baker, 1959.

———. *The Five Books of Moses: A Devotional Commentary on Each Chapter from Genesis, Leviticus, Exodus, Numbers, Deuteronomy*. London: Marshall, Morgan, and Scott, 1955.

———. *Jeremiah: Priest and Prophet*. London: Morgan and Scott. 1847.

———. *Joshua and the Land of Promise*. New York: Revell, 1893.

———. *Paul: A Servant of Jesus Christ*. New York: Revell, 1897.

———. *The Prophet of Hope: Studies in Zechariah*. 1900. Reprinted—Fort Washington, Pa.: Christian Literature Crusade.

———. *Tried by Fire: Expositions of the First Epistle of Peter*. 1895. Reprinted—Fort Washington, Pa.: Christian Literature Crusade, 1970.

Milligan, William. *The Ascension and Heavenly Priesthood of Our Lord*. New York: Macmillan, 1892.

Moore, Thomas V. *The Prophets of the Restoration; or, Haggai, Zechariah, and Malachi*. 1856. Reprinted—*A Commentary on Haggai and Malachi*. London: Banner of Truth, 1960.

Moorhouse, Henry. *"Ruth the Moabitess" and Other Bible Readings*. London: Morgan and Scott, 1913.

Morgan, G. Campbell. *The Acts of the Apostles*. New York: Revell, 1924.

———. *The Analyzed Bible*. 10 vols. New York: Revell, 1907–1911.

———. *The Answers of Jesus to Job*. 1935. Reprinted—Grand Rapids: Baker, 1973.

———. *The Birth of the Church*. Edited by Jill Morgan. Old Tappan, N.J.: Revell, 1968.

———. *The Corinthian Letters of Paul: An Exposition of I and II Corinthians*. New York: Revell, 1946.

———. *The Crises of the Christ*. New York: Revell, 1903.

———. *The Four Gospels*. London: Oliphants, 1956. Reprinted—*An Exposition of the Four Gospel Narratives*.

———. *God's Last Word to Man: Studies in Hebrews*. 1936. Reprinted—Grand Rapids: Baker, 1974.

———. *Hosea: The Heart and Holiness of God*. 1934. Reprinted—Grand Rapids: Baker, 1974.

———. *The Letters of Our Lord: A First-Century Message to Twentieth-Century*

Christians: Addresses Based upon the Letters to the Seven Churches of Asia. London: Pickering and Inglis, 1945.

———. *Living Messages of the Books of the Bible.* 2 vols. New York: Revell, 1912.

———. *The Minor Prophets: The Men and Their Messages.* Westwood, N.J.: Revell, 1960.

———. *Studies in the Prophecy of Jeremiah.* New York: Revell, 1931.

———. *The Teaching of Christ.* New York: Revell, 1913.

———. *The Ten Commandments.* 1901. Reprinted—Grand Rapids: Baker, 1974.

———. *The Triumphs of Faith.* 1944. Reprinted—Grand Rapids: Baker, 1973.

———. *The Unfolding Message of the Bible: The Harmony and Unity of the Scriptures.* Westwood, N.J.: Revell, 1961.

———. *"Wherein?" Malachi's Message to the Men of Today.* 1898. Reprinted—*Malachi's Message for Today.* Grand Rapids: Baker, 1972.

Morris, Henry M. *The Genesis Record: A Scientific and Devotional Commentary on the Book of Beginnings.* Grand Rapids: Baker, 1976.

Morris, Leon. *Studies in the Fourth Gospel.* Grand Rapids: Eerdmans, 1969.

Motyer, J. A. *Philippian Studies: The Richness of Christ.* Chicago: Inter-Varsity, 1966.

———. *The Tests of Faith.* London: Inter-Varsity, 1970.

Moule, Handley C. G. *Colossian Studies: Lessons in Faith and Holiness from St. Paul's Epistles to the Colossians and Philemon.* 1898. Reprinted—*Colossian and Philemon Studies: Lessons in Faith and Holiness.* Grand Rapids: Zondervan.

———. *The Cross and the Spirit: Studies in the Epistle to the Galatians.* London: Seeley, 1898.

———. *The High Priestly Prayer: A Devotional Commentary on the Seventeenth Chapter of St. John.* London: Religious Tract Society, 1908.

———. *Philippian Studies: Lessons in Faith and Love from St. Paul's Epistle to the Philippians.* 1897. Reprinted—Grand Rapids: Zondervan, 1962.

———. *The Second Epistle to the Corinthians: A Translation, Paraphrase, and Exposition.* Edited by A. W. Handley Moule. London: Pickering and Inglis, 1962.

Murray, Andrew. *Have Mercy upon Me: The Prayer of the Penitent in the Fifty-first Psalm, Explained and Applied.* New York: Randolph, 1895.

———. *The Holiest of All: An Exposition of the Epistle to the Hebrews.* New York: Revell, 1894.

Nee, Watchman. *The Normal Christian Life.* London: Witness and Testimony, 1958.

———. *Song of Songs.* Fort Washington, Pa.: Christian Literature Crusade, 1965.

Newell, William R. *The Book of the Revelation.* Chicago: Scripture Press, 1935.

———. *Hebrews, Verse by Verse.* Chicago: Moody, 1947.

———. *Romans, Verse by Verse.* Chicago: Moody, 1938.

Ockenga, Harold J. *The Church in God: Expository Values in Thessalonians.* Westwood, N.J.: Revell, 1956.

———. *Faithful in Christ Jesus: Preaching in Ephesians.* New York: Revell, 1948.

———. *Women Who Made Bible History: Messages and Character Sketches Dealing with Familiar Bible Women.* Grand Rapids: Zondervan, 1962.

Oehler, Gustav. *Theology of the Old Testament.* Edited by George E. Day. Translated by Ellen D. Smith and Sophia Taylor. 1883. Reprinted—Grand Rapids: Zondervan.

Ogg, George. *The Odyssey of Paul.* Old Tappan, N.J.: Revell, 1968.

Owen, John. *An Exposition of the Epistle to the Hebrews.* 2d ed. 7 vols. 1812–1814. Reprinted—4 vols. Evansville, Ind.: Sovereign Grace, 1960.

Paxson, Ruth. *The Wealth, Walk, and Warfare of the Christian.* New York: Revell, 1939.

Payne, J. Barton, ed. *New Perspectives on the Old Testament.* Waco, Tex.: Word, 1970.

———. *The Theology of the Older Testament.* Grand Rapids: Zondervan, 1962.

Penn-Lewis, Jessie. *The Story of Job: A Glimpse into the Mystery of Suffering.* 3d ed. Bournemouth: Overcomer Book Room, n.d.

Perowne, J. J. Stewart. *The Book of Psalms: A New Translation, with Introductions and Notes, Explanatory and Critical.* 2 vols. 1864–1868. Grand Rapids: Zondervan, 1976.

Pfeiffer, Charles F., ed. *The Biblical World: A Dictionary of Biblical Archaeology.* Grand Rapids: Baker, 1966.

———. *Old Testament History.* Grand Rapids: Baker, 1973.

Pfeiffer, Charles F., and Vos, Howard F. *The Wycliffe Historical Geography of Bible Lands.* Chicago: Moody, 1967.

Pfeiffer, Charles F.; Vos, Howard F.; and Rea, John. *Wycliffe Bible Encylopedia.* 2 vols. Chicago: Moody, 1975.

Pieters, Albertus. *Studies in the Revelation of St. John.* Grand Rapids: Eerdmans, 1943.

Pink, Arthur W. *An Exposition of Hebrews.* 3 vols. Grand Rapids: Baker, 1954. Reprinted—1 vol.

———. *Exposition of the Gospel of John.* 4 vols. 1923ff. Reprinted—1 vol. Grand Rapids: Zondervan, 1975.

———. *An Exposition of the Sermon on the Mount.* Grand Rapids: Baker, 1950.

———. *Gleanings in Exodus.* Chicago: Moody, 1962.

———. *Gleanings in Genesis.* 1922. Reprinted—Chicago: Moody, 1966.

———. *Gleanings in Joshua.* Chicago: Moody, 1964.

———. *The Life of David.* 2 vols. Grand Rapids: Zondervan, 1958.

———. *The Life of Elijah.* Rev. ed. London: Banner of Truth, 1963.

———. *The Seven Sayings of the Saviour on the Cross.* Grand Rapids: Baker, 1958.

Plummer, Alfred. *A Commentary on St. Paul's Epistle to the Philippians.* London: Scott, 1919.

Plumptre, E. H. *St. Paul in Asia Minor and at the Syrian Antioch.* New York: Pott and Young, 1877.

Pusey, E. B. *The Minor Prophets: A Commentary, Explanatory and Practical.* 2 vols. 1892–1895. Reprinted—Grand Rapids: Baker, 1950.

Rainsford, Marcus. *Lectures on John 17.* 2d ed. 1876. Reprinted—*Our Lord Prays for His Own: Thoughts on John 17.* Chicago: Moody, 1950.

Ramsay, William. *The Cities of St. Paul: Their Influence on His Life and Thought: The Cities of Eastern Asia Minor.* 1907. Reprinted—Grand Rapids: Baker, 1979.

———. *A Historical Commentary on St. Paul's Epistle to the Galatians.* 1899. Reprinted—Grand Rapids: Baker, 1979.

———. *The Letters to the Seven Churches of Asia and Their Place in the Plan of the Apocalypse.* 1904. Reprinted—Grand Rapids: Baker, 1979.

———. *Pictures of the Apostolic Church, Its Life and Teaching.* Philadelphia: *Sunday School Times, 1910.*

———. *St. Paul the Traveller and the Roman Citizen*. 3d ed. 1897. Reprinted—Grand Rapids: Baker, 1979.

Rawlinson, George. *St. Paul in Damascus and Arabia*. London: SPCK, 1877.

Redpath, Alan. *Blessings out of Buffetings: Studies in II Corinthians*. Westwood, N.J.: Revell, 1965.

———. *Law and Liberty: A New Look at the Ten Commandments in the Light of Contemporary Society*. Old Tappan, N.J.: Revell, 1978.

———. *The Making of a Man of God: Studies in the Life of David*. Westwood, N.J.: Revell, 1962.

———. *The Royal Route to Heaven: Studies in I Corinthians*. Westwood, N.J.: Revell, 1960.

———. *Victorious Christian Living: Studies in the Book of Joshua*. Westwood, N.J.: Revell, 1955.

———. *Victorious Christian Service: Studies in the Book of Nehemiah*. Westwood, N.J.: Revell, 1958.

Rees, Paul S. *The Adequate Man: Paul in Philippians*. Westwood, N.J.: Revell, 1959.

———. *Triumphant in Trouble: Studies in I Peter*. Westwood, N.J.: Revell, 1962.

Ridderbos, Herman. *Paul: An Outline of His Theology*. Translated by John Richard de Witt. Grand Rapids: Eerdmans, 1975.

Ritchie, John. *From Egypt to Canaan; or, The Exodus and Pilgrimage of Israel, Illustrative of the Believer's Redemption, Salvation, Walk, and Warfare*. Kilmarnock: Ritchie, n.d.

———. *The Tabernacle in the Wilderness*. N.d. Reprinted—Grand Rapids: Kregel.

Robertson, A. T. *The Divinity of Christ in the Gospel of John*. 1916. Reprinted—Grand Rapids: Baker, 1976.

———. *Epochs in the Life of Paul: A Study of Development in Paul's Career*. 1909. Reprinted—Grand Rapids: Baker, 1974.

———. *Making Good in the Ministry: A Sketch of John Mark*. 1918. Reprinted—Grand Rapids: Baker, 1976.

———. *Paul's Joy in Christ: Studies in Philippians*. 1917. Reprinted—Grand Rapids: Baker, 1979.

———. *Paul the Interpreter of Christ*. 1921. Reprinted—Grand Rapids: Baker, 1976.

———. *The Pharisees and Jesus*. New York: Scribner, 1920.

———. *Word Pictures in the New Testament*. 6 vols. 1930-1933. Reprinted—Nashville: Broadman, 1943.

Robinson, George L. *The Twelve Minor Prophets*. 1926. Reprinted—Grand Rapids: Baker, 1978.

Robinson, Theodore H. *Job and His Friends*. London: SCM, 1954.

Rosen, Ceil, and Rosen, Moishe. *Christ in the Passover: Why Is This Night Different?* Chicago: Moody, 1978.

Ross, Charles. *The Inner Sanctuary: An Exposition of John 13-17*. London: Banner of Truth, 1967.

Ryle, J. C. *Expository Thoughts on the Gospels for Family and Private Use*. 7 vols. 1858-1870. Reprinted—4 vols. Grand Rapids: Baker, 1977.

Saphir, Adolph. *The Epistle to the Hebrews: An Exposition*. 2d ed. 2 vols. 1902. Reprinted—Grand Rapids: Zondervan.

Schilder, Klaas. *Christ Crucified*. Translated by Henry Zylstra. 1940. Reprinted—Grand Rapids: Baker, 1979.

______. *Christ in His Suffering.* Translated by Henry Zylstra. 1938. Reprinted—Grand Rapids: Baker, 1979.

______. *Christ on Trial.* Translated by Henry Zylstra. 1939. Reprinted—Grand Rapids: Baker, 1979.

Schultz, Samuel J. *The Old Testament Speaks.* New York: Harper, 1960.

______. *The Prophets Speak: Law of Love, the Essence of Israel's Religion.* New York: Harper and Row, 1968.

Scott, Walter. *Exposition of the Revelation and Prophetic Outlines.* 2d ed. New York: Our Hope, n.d.

Scroggie, W. Graham. *A Guide to the Gospels.* London: Pickering and Inglis, 1948.

______. *Know Your Bible: A Brief Introduction to the Scriptures.* Rev. ed. 2 vols. London: Pickering and Inglis, 1965. Reprinted—1 vol.

______. *The Land and Life of Rest: The Book of Joshua in the Light of the New Testament.* London: Pickering and Inglis, 1950.

______. *The Unfolding Drama of Redemption: The Bible as a Whole.* 3 vols. London: Pickering and Inglis, 1953–1971.

Seiss, Joseph A. *The Apocalypse: A Series of Special Lectures on the Revelation of Jesus Christ.* 1865. Reprinted—Grand Rapids: Zondervan.

______. *Popular Lectures on the Epistle of Paul the Apostle to the Hebrews.* 1846. Reprinted—*Lectures on Hebrews.* Grand Rapids: Baker, 1954.

Selwyn, Edward Gordon. *The First Epistle of St. Peter: The Greek Text, with Introduction, Notes, and Essays.* London: Macmillan, 1946.

Shepard, J. W. *The Christ of the Gospels: An Exegetical Study.* Grand Rapids: Eerdmans, 1946.

Simpson, A. B. *Christ in the Bible.* 20 vols. Harrisburg, Pa.: Christian Publications, 1886.

Simpson, Hubert. *Testament of Love.* New York: Abingdon, 1935.

Simpson, W. J. Sparrow. *Our Lord's Resurrection.* 1905. Reprinted—Grand Rapids: Zondervan.

Slemming, Charles W. *Made According to Pattern: A Study of the Tabernacle in the Wilderness.* Rev. ed. 1956. Reprinted—Fort Washington, Pa.: Christian Literature Crusade, 1964.

______. *These Are the Garments: A Study of the Garments of the High Priest of Israel.* Rev. ed. 1955. Reprinted—Fort Washington, Pa.: Christian Literature Crusade, 1963.

Smith, David. *The Days of His Flesh: The Earthly Life of Our Lord and Saviour Jesus Christ.* 8th ed. 1910. Reprinted—Grand Rapids: Baker, 1976.

______. *The Life and Letters of St. Paul.* New York: Doran, 1920.

Smith, James. *The Voyage and Shipwreck of St. Paul: With Dissertations on the Life and Writings of St. Luke, and the Ships and Navigation of the Ancients.* 4th ed. Edited by Walter E. Smith. 1880. Reprinted—Grand Rapids: Baker, 1978.

Smith, Wilbur M. *Chats from a Minister's Library.* Grand Rapids: Baker, 1951.

______. *The Supernaturalness of Christ: Can We Still Believe in It?* 1940. Reprinted—Grand Rapids: Baker, 1974.

______. *A Treasury of Books for Bible Study.* Grand Rapids: Baker, 1960.

Sockman, Ralph W. *The Higher Happiness.* New York: Abingdon-Cokesbury, 1950.

Soltau, Henry W. *The Holy Vessels and Furniture of the Tabernacle.* 1851. Reprinted—Grand Rapids: Kregel, 1969.

———. *The Tabernacle, the Priesthood, and the Offerings.* 1884. Reprinted—Grand Rapids: Kregel, 1974.

Spence, H. D. M., and Exell, Joseph S., eds. *The Pulpit Commentary.* 52 vols. 1880–1919. Reprinted—23 vols. Grand Rapids: Eerdmans, 1963.

Spurgeon, Charles H. *Commenting and Commentaries.* 1876. Reprinted—London: Banner of Truth, 1969.

———. *The Most Holy Place: Sermons on the Song of Solomon Delivered at the Metropolitan Tabernacle and New Park Street Chapel.* 1896. Reprinted—Pasadena, Tex.: Pilgrim.

———. *The Passion and Death of Christ.* Grand Rapids: Eerdmans, 1965.

———. *The Treasury of David: Containing an Original Exposition of the Book of Psalms . . .* 7 vols. 1882–1887. Reprinted—Grand Rapids: Baker, 1977.

Stalker, James. *Imago Christi: The Example of Jesus Christ.* 1889. Reprinted—*Christ, Our Example.* Grand Rapids: Zondervan, 1960.

———. *The Life of Jesus Christ.* Rev. ed. New York: Revell, 1891.

———. *The Trial and Death of Jesus Christ: A Devotional History of Our Lord's Passion.* 1894. Reprinted—Grand Rapids: Zondervan.

Stevenson, John. *Christ on the Cross: An Exposition of the Twenty-Second Psalm.* London: Jackson, 1844.

———. *The Lord Our Shepherd: An Exposition of the Twenty-Third Psalm.* New York: Carter, 1845.

Stewart, James S. *A Man in Christ: The Vital Elements of St. Paul's Religion.* 1935. Reprinted—Grand Rapids: Baker, 1975.

Stifler, James Madison. *The Epistle to the Romans: A Commentary, Logical and Historical.* Chicago: Moody, 1960.

Stock, Eugene. *Plain Talks on the Pastoral Epistles.* London: Scott, 1914.

Stott, John R. W. *Men Made New: An Exposition of Romans 5–8.* London: Inter-Varsity, 1966.

———. *The Message of Galatians.* London: Inter-Varsity, 1968.

Stott, John R. W., et al. *Christ the Liberator: Urbana 70.* Downers Grove, Ill.: InterVarsity, 1971.

Strahan, James. *The Book of Job Interpreted.* Edinburgh: Clark, 1913.

———. *Hebrew Ideals: A Study of Genesis 11–50.* 3d ed. Edinburgh: Clark, 1915.

Strauss, Lehman. *The Book of the Revelation: Outlined Studies.* Neptune, N.J.: Loizeaux, 1972.

———. *Devotional Studies in Galatians and Ephesians.* New York: Loizeaux, 1957.

———. *The Eleven Commandments.* 2d ed. Neptune, N.J.: Loizeaux, 1975.

———. *James, Your Brother: Studies in the Epistle of James.* Neptune, N.J.: Loizeaux, 1972.

———. *The Prophecies of Daniel.* Neptune, N.J.: Loizeaux, 1969.

Swete, Henry Barclay. *The Ascended Christ: A Study in the Earliest Christian Teaching.* London: Macmillan, 1910.

———. *The Gospel According to St. Mark: The Greek Text with Introduction, Notes, and Indices.* 1892. Reprinted—Grand Rapids: Eerdmans.

———. *The Last Discourse and Prayer of Our Lord: A Study of St. John 14–17.* London: Macmillan, 1913.

Taylor, J. Hudson. *Union and Communion.* 1894. Reprinted—Minneapolis: Bethany Fellowship, 1971.

Taylor, Vincent. *The Gospel According to St. Mark: The Greek Text with Introduction, Notes, and Indexes.* London: Macmillan, 1952.

Taylor, William M. *Bible Biographies*. 8 vols. 1874-1891. Reprinted—5 vols. Grand Rapids: Baker, 1961-1962.
Tenney, Merrill C. *Galatians: The Charter of Christian Liberty*. Rev. ed. Grand Rapids: Eerdmans, 1971.
______. *The Genius of the Gospels*. Grand Rapids: Eerdmans, 1951.
______. *Interpreting Revelation*. Grand Rapids: Eerdmans, 1957.
______. *John, the Gospel of Belief: An Analytic Study of the Text*. Grand Rapids: Eerdmans, 1948.
______. *The New Testament: An Historical and Analytic Survey*. Grand Rapids: Eerdmans, 1953.
______. *New Testament Times*. Grand Rapids: Eerdmans, 1965.
______. *The Reality of the Resurrection*. New York: Harper and Row, 1963.
______. *Resurrection Realities: "Now Is Christ Risen."* 1945. Reprinted—*The Vital Heart of Christianity*. Grand Rapids: Zondervan, 1964.
______, ed. *The Zondervan Pictorial Encyclopedia of the Bible*. 5 vols. Grand Rapids: Zondervan, 1975.
Thiele, Edwin R. *The Mysterious Numbers of the Hebrew Kings: A Reconstruction of the Chronology of the Kingdoms of Israel and Judah*. 1951. Reprinted—Grand Rapids: Eerdmans, 1965.
Thielicke, Helmut. *How the World Began: Man in the First Chapters of the Bible*. Translated by John W. Doberstein. Philadelphia: Muhlenberg, 1961.
______. *Life Can Begin Again: Sermons on the Sermon on the Mount*. Translated by John W. Doberstein. Philadelphia: Fortress, 1963.
______. *Our Heavenly Father: Sermons on the Lord's Prayer*. Translated by John W. Doberstein. 1960. Reprinted—Grand Rapids: Baker, 1974.
Thirtle, James W. *The Lord's Prayer: An Interpretation, Critical and Expository*. London: Morgan and Scott, 1915.
______. *Old Testament Problems: Critical Studies in the Psalms and Isaiah*. New York: Frowde, 1907.
______. *The Titles of the Psalms: Their Nature and Meaning Explained*. New York: Frowde, 1905.
Thomas, W. H. Griffith. *The Apostle John: Studies in His Life and Writings*. 1923. Reprinted—Grand Rapids: Eerdmans, 1953.
______. *The Apostle Peter: Outline Studies in His Life, Character, and Writings*. 1904. Reprinted—Grand Rapids: Eerdmans, 1946.
______. *Hebrews: A Devotional Commentary*. N.d. Reprinted—Grand Rapids: Eerdmans, 1962.
______. *Outline Studies in the Gospel of Matthew*. Edited by Winifred G. T. Gillespie. Grand Rapids: Eerdmans, 1961.
______. *St. Paul's Epistle to the Romans: A Devotional Commentary*. Grand Rapids: Eerdmans, 1946.
______. *Studies in Colossians and Philemon*. Edited by Winifred G. T. Gillespie. Grand Rapids: Baker, 1973.
Trench, Richard. *Commentary on the Epistles to the Seven Churches in Asia, Revelation 2-3*. 5th ed. London: Paul, Trench, and Trübner, 1890.
______. *The Synonyms of the New Testament*. 1854. Reprinted—Grand Rapids: Eerdmans, 1950.
Trueblood, Elton. *Foundations for Reconstruction*. 1946. Reprinted—Waco, Tex.: Word, 1972.
Turner, George A. *Historical Geography of the Holy Land*. Grand Rapids: Baker, 1973.

Unger, Merrill F. *Introductory Guide to the Old Testament.* Grand Rapids: Zondervan, 1951.

———. *Zechariah.* Grand Rapids: Zondervan, 1963.

Vincent, Marvin R. *Word Studies in the New Testament.* 4 vols. 1887–1900. Reprinted—Grand Rapids: Eerdmans.

Vine, W. E. *A Comprehensive Dictionary of the Original Greek Words with Their Precise Meanings for English Readers.* 4 vols. 1939–1941. Reprinted—*Expository Dictionary of New Testament Words.* Westwood, N.J.: Revell, 1956.

———. *The Epistles of John: Light, Love, Life.* Grand Rapids: Zondervan, 1965.

———. *The Epistles to Timothy and Titus: Faith and Conduct.* Grand Rapids: Zondervan, 1965.

———. *I Corinthians.* Grand Rapids: Zondervan, 1961.

———. *Isaiah: Prophecies, Promises, Warnings.* London: Oliphants, 1946.

Walker, Thomas. *The Acts of the Apostles.* Indian Church Commentaries. 1906. Reprinted—Chicago: Moody, 1965.

Walvoord, John F. *Daniel, the Key to Prophetic Revelation: A Commentary.* Chicago: Moody, 1971.

———. *Jesus Christ Our Lord.* Chicago: Moody, 1969.

———. *The Revelation of Jesus Christ: A Commentary.* Chicago: Moody, 1966.

Warfield, Benjamin B. *The Lord of Glory: A Study of the Designations of Our Lord in the New Testament with Especial Reference to His Deity.* 1907. Reprinted—Grand Rapids: Baker, 1974.

Watson, Thomas. *The Ten Commandments.* London: Banner of Truth, 1959.

Welch, C. H. *Ecclesiastes: An Exposition.* Banstead: Berean, 1952.

Wemp, C. Sumner. *Teaching from the Tabernacle.* Chicago: Moody, 1976.

Westcott, B. F. *The Epistles of St. John: The Greek Text, with Notes and Essays.* 3d ed. 1892. Reprinted—Grand Rapids: Eerdmans, 1955.

———. *The Epistle to the Hebrews: The Greek Text, with Notes and Essays.* 3d ed. 1903. Reprinted—Grand Rapids: Eerdmans, 1955.

———. *The Revelation of the Risen Lord.* London: Macmillan, 1881.

White, R. E. O. *The Exploration of Faith: Triumphs of Hebrews 11.* Chicago: Moody, 1969.

Whyte, Alexander. *Bible Characters.* 6 vols. 1898–1902. Reprinted—1 vol. Grand Rapids: Zondervan, 1968.

———. *The Walk, Conversation, and Character of Jesus Christ Our Lord.* 1905. Reprinted—Grand Rapids: Baker, 1975.

Wiersbe, Warren W. *Live like a King: Making the Beatitudes Work in Daily Life.* Chicago: Moody, 1976.

———. *Walking with the Giants: A Minister's Guide to Good Reading and Great Preaching.* Grand Rapids: Baker, 1976.

Wigram, G. V. *The Englishman's Greek Concordance of the New Testament.* 9th ed. 1903. Reprinted—Grand Rapids: Zondervan, 1970.

———. *The Englishman's Hebrew and Chaldee Concordance of the Old Testament.* 1843. Grand Rapids: Zondervan, 1970.

Wilson, Geoffrey B. *II Corinthians: A Digest of Reformed Comment.* Edinburgh: Banner of Truth, 1973.

Wilson, Robert Dick. *A Scientific Investigation of the Old Testament.* 1926. Reprinted—Chicago: Moody.

Wolff, Richard. *A Commentary on the Epistle of Jude.* Grand Rapids: Zondervan, 1960.

Wood, A. Skevington. *Life by the Spirit.* Grand Rapids: Zondervan, 1963.

Wood, Leon J. *Commentary on Daniel.* Grand Rapids: Zondervan, 1973.

———. *Distressing Days of the Judges.* Grand Rapids: Zondervan, 1975.

———. *Elijah: Prophet of God.* Des Plaines, Ill.: Regular Baptist, 1968.

———. *A Survey of Israel's History.* Grand Rapids: Zondervan, 1970.

Wuest, Kenneth S. *Word Studies from the Greek New Testament for the English Reader.* 4 vols. Grand Rapids: Eerdmans, 1966.

Yates, Kyle M. *Preaching from the Prophets.* New York: Harper, 1942.

Young, Edward J. *The Book of Isaiah: The English Text, with Introduction, Exposition, and Notes.* 3 vols. Grand Rapids: Eerdmans, 1965.

———. *Genesis 3: A Devotional and Expository Study.* London: Banner of Truth, 1966.

———. *An Introduction to the Old Testament.* Grand Rapids: Eerdmans, 1958.

———. *Isaiah 53: A Devotional and Expository Study.* Grand Rapids: Eerdmans, 1952.

———. *My Servants, the Prophets.* Grand Rapids: Eerdmans, 1952.

———. *Studies in Genesis 1.* Grand Rapids: Baker, 1973.

Zodhiates, Spiros. *The Behavior of Belief: An Exposition of James Based upon the Original Greek Text.* Grand Rapids: Eerdmans, 1966.

———. *The Pursuit of Happiness: An Exposition of the Beatitudes of Christ in Matthew 5:1–11 and Luke 6:20–26, Based upon the Original Greek Text.* Grand Rapids: Eerdmans, 1966.

Part 3

Miscellania

21

The Theology of Dwight L. Moody

"I don't like your theology!" a woman told Dwight L. Moody after hearing him preach.

"Theology!" the evangelist replied. "I didn't know I *had* any theology!"

Although he had not received seminary training, Moody knew his Bible, knew what he believed, and preached what he believed. He was against dead creedalism and often said: "A creed is the road or street. It is very good as far as it goes, but if it doesn't take us to Christ, it is worthless." He abhorred preaching that emphasizes doctrines divorced from the living Christ. "Feeding on doctrines is like trying to live on dry husks," he said. "I pity a person who has to be fed religion with a theological spoon." But he had a theology, whether or not he recognized it.

I once heard a popular preacher tell a large congregation of students that they had to choose between being "deep Bible students" or winners of souls. Charles H. Spurgeon and R. A. Torrey would have laughed at that, for both were great scholars and even greater soul-winners.

Dwight L. Moody was neither scholar nor theologian, but a definite system of belief governed both his life and his ministry. How he developed this system, where it came from, and what it meant to him are all discussed in the book *Love Them In: The Proclamation Theology of D. L. Moody*, written by Stanley N. Gundry.[1] I consider this the most important book on Moody since Wilbur M. Smith's monumental *Annotated Bibliography of D. L. Moody.*[2] In fact Gundry's research supplements Smith's and even corrects it in a few minor instances. I doubt that any serious student of American evangelism will avoid Gundry's book, with its important information and interpretations. It is a valuable contribution to the study not only of Moody but also of American historical theology.

Thanks to Gundry's careful scholarship, the real Moody can now stand up and be recognized. Would Moody approve modern methods of evangelism? Was he really as "liberal" in his theology as his son Paul claimed? Where would he stand on the modern charismatic movement? Did he adjust his theology to his successful evangelistic methods, or did the methods grow out of his beliefs? Gundry faced and solved these questions and more, making his study a practical analysis of evangelism.

The author has done his homework, as a survey of the bibliography indicates. He analyzed all of Moody's sermons beginning with 1873. He had access to the wealth of materials in the Moody Bible Institute "Moodyana Collection," including valuable newspaper reports of Moody's campaigns and sermons. He read all the biographies, pro and con, and his evaluation of them is one of the great assets of the book. I especially appreciate the way he answered James F. Findlay, Jr., author of *Dwight L. Moody.*[3] Findlay did not understand Moody's convictions about the atonement and the return of Christ. I am happy that Gundry has set the record straight.

The book opens with a survey of Moody's life and work. This chapter is one of the best summaries of Moody's life and ministry *in historical context* that I have read. The author carefully explained the denominational situation in Moody's day so that we will not read today's situation into Moody's life. While this first chapter is not a substitute for a longer biography, it does contain some facts I had not seen elsewhere.

---

1. Chicago: Moody, 1976.

2. Chicago: Moody, 1948.

3. *Dwight L. Moody, American Evangelist, 1837–1899* (Chicago: University of Chicago, 1969; reprinted—Grand Rapids: Baker, 1973).

In chapter 2 the author came to grips with his theme: theology's role in Moody's message. That Moody was first of all a soul-winner is obvious to anyone who has read his sermons. "I have not come to preach this or that doctrine," he would affirm. "I preach the 'whosoever.' " To those who asked why he did not preach election or sanctification, he said, "Why don't you preach them yourself?" When asked where his creed could be found, he replied simply, "In Isaiah 53."

These statements (and many others like them) do not imply that Moody was against theology, but that he was against theology that leaves no room for evangelism. Moody was constantly learning from others; in fact this is why he went to Britain in 1867 and again in 1872. He loved nothing better than an informal discussion about the Word of God among men of like faith. "What did God give you out of the Bible today?" he would often ask a friend. And he was constantly adding new ideas to his collection of envelopes that served as a sermon file.

Some have accused Moody of wedding the theology of Charles G. Finney to his own "big-business methods" from shoe-salesman days. Gundry answered this wrong interpretation with a scholarly discussion of Moody's relationship to Finney, settling the matter once for all. You will also find in this chapter what Moody believed about premillennialism, the use of the inquiry room, and the value of advertising and its relationship to the work of the Spirit. In this day of reports and statistics, Moody's views on "counting converts" might be helpful. "Mr. Moody never counted converts, or traded on the spiritual successes he gained," wrote his son-in-law, A. P. Fitt. "He deprecated the boastful use of statistics. People used to ask him what were the most notable conversions he had achieved, and the greatest meetings he ever conducted. They could not draw him out on such matters."

In the next three chapters Gundry dealt with the three pillars of Moody's preaching: ruined by the fall, redeemed by the blood, regenerated by the Spirit. These same points are found on the Henry Varley memorial in Bristol, England, but it is doubtful that Moody borrowed them from Varley. Like the familiar "He saves, He keeps, He satisfies" of a generation ago, these "three R's" were familiar in Moody's day. When you recall how popular evolution was then, you can appreciate Moody's courage in preaching the fall of man and salvation as a crisis experience, not a process. He did not major on judgment; he emphasized God's love. He did preach a sermon on hell in most of his campaigns, but he did so lovingly. R. W. Dale said that Moody was the only man he ever heard who had a right to preach on hell, because Moody could not preach on it without shedding tears. Henry Moorhouse taught Moody the meaning of God's love, a lesson Moody never forgot. In fact he had "God Is Love" spelled out in gas lights at the front of his church auditorium in Chicago. How Moorhouse changed Moody's view of God's love is told in chapter 4. I have often used the story in sermons.

Chapter 6 focuses on "Taking the Remedy" and deals with the historic problem of election and free will. Moody emphasized man's will in his sermons. (He once claimed that "the elect are the whosoever wills, and the non-elect are the whosoever won'ts." I cannot document it, but I read somewhere that he once prayed, "Lord, save the elect—and then elect some more!") It is well known that Moody greatly admired Spurgeon and that Spurgeon defended Moody and Ira Sankey when they were ministering in England. Spurgeon thought Moody's emphasis was not as Calvinistic as his own, but this did not keep him from having fellowship with the evangelist. Moody did not deny the doctrine of election; he simply felt it is a "family matter for the saints" and should not be preached to sinners.

In chapter 7 the author examined Moody's beliefs about living the Christian life. Moody did not keep his converts in "deep freeze" until they matured. "Now, if you want to be a useful, happy Christian," he said, "just get to work and do not go to sleep. Find some church where you can find something to do. If you want to be a healthy Christian you have got to work."

Moody's concern about social problems such as poverty and drunkenness is discussed here. Gundry pointed out that the great evangelist "failed to appreciate the complexity of the problems arising from industrialization, urbanization, and immigration." He felt that individual salvation would cure society's ills. But Moody was never calloused toward those in need. The words at the front door of his first church buildings are still at the front doors of the Moody Church in Chicago: "Ever welcome to this house of God are strangers and the poor."

One of the book's most valuable discussions is in the chapter titled "The Holy Spirit and the Believer." Unfortunately certain groups have tried to use Moody's personal experience to back up their own teachings about the Holy Spirit. Gundry has effectively answered them. Moody did not speak in tongues, nor did he encourage it in his meetings. He did not believe in sinless perfection, and he used the phrase "baptism of the Spirit" only in reference to power for witnessing and Christian service.

Moody's views of the local church are examined in chapter 8. "If

I know my own heart," he told a Northfield meeting in 1887, "I love the Church more than anything else on this earth." But he hated "this miserable sectarian spirit." He did not openly criticize ministers as George Whitefield had and Billy Sunday would. (Sunday once called a group of New York City preachers "white-livered, black-hearted mugs"—and the great John Henry Jowett was sitting in the group!) Moody encouraged new converts to unite with a church and support the pastor. Some have accused Moody of being "ecumenical" in the modern sense. Gundry has shown the error of this thinking. Moody wanted the churches and denominations to unite in soul-winning efforts, but he did not encourage a super-church or even the erasing of denominational distinctives. I was amazed to discover that Moody had preached at the Mormon Tabernacle and that during his first visit to Salt Lake City, he had openly denounced the teachings of Joseph Smith. Moody did not take a hard line against the Roman Catholics, although he clearly explained how he differed from them in doctrine.

The final two chapters deal with Moody's view of prophecy and the Bible. In chapter 9 Gundry, in one of the best discussions of dispensationalism I have ever seen, showed how Moody was strongly influenced by the Plymouth Brethren. (They did not influence his ecclesiology; he agreed with Spurgeon.) Not even the Brethren agreed on their prophetic views, particularly the idea of a secret rapture before the tribulation. Moody did not draw a chart of future events, but he did preach that Jesus Christ can return at any moment and that no signs must precede His coming.

The strongest contribution of chapter 10 is the discussion of Moody's relationship to "higher criticism" and to men like George Adam Smith and Henry Drummond, liberal thinkers in their day. Moody's son Paul, who was sympathetic with the liberal movement of the 1920s, tried to convince others that his father's sympathies would also have been with men like Harry Emerson Fosdick who were "preaching the love of God." Torrey effectively refuted this statement in a strong article in the October 1923 issue of the *Moody Bible Institute Monthly;* he followed it with another article in the December issue. Gundry clearly proved that Moody was not a liberal, even though some of his friends were. Gundry cited many statements from Moody's sermons showing that the great evangelist warned against these liberal attacks on the Bible. He told a Northfield gathering in 1898, "If a minister begins to pick the Bible to pieces, get up and get out!"

Moody never preached a sermon or wrote a book on the relationship of theology to evangelism, but his whole life and ministry developed that theme. Gundry has now systematized this with warmth of spirit and depth of scholarship. I am grateful for his insights into Moody's life and work, because they have helped me examine my own soul winning. Moody was balanced: he did not so emphasize doctrine that he neglected evangelism, and yet his evangelism was not so pragmatic that it lacked doctrinal foundation. The end did not justify the means in Moody's thinking. We need to strike this balance today and to realize that quantity and quality join hands in the doctrines of the Word of God.

If you ask for one book in your stocking next Christmas, ask for *Love Them In: The Proclamation Theology of D. L. Moody*. And really read it. You will experience the dual blessing of getting to know a great man better and of sharpening your theological focus. What more could one ask?

Betsey Holton Moody

22

The Women in Moody's Ministry

If ever a preacher was a man's man, it was Dwight L. Moody. Men flocked to hear him, and they soon found themselves caught up in the cause of Christ. Moody's circle of friends and acquaintances included men of every rank and calling, many of whom were famous in their own right but who found their greatest satisfaction in serving Christ under Moody's direction. Whether he preached to them, gave them jobs to do, or asked them for money, Moody was an evangelist whom men could trust.

But several women were also influential in the evangelist's life and ministry. The first was his mother, Betsey Holton Moody. The Holtons came to the United States from England in 1634, one year after the Moody family had arrived. Both families eventually settled in Northfield, Massachusetts.

Betsey Holton married Edwin Moody on 3 January 1828, and they settled on a small farm. Dwight Lyman, born on 5 February 1837, was their sixth child. John Pollock said in his biography of Moody: "Edwin Moody . . . was a genial, shiftless, lazy fellow, adored by his wife Betsey and their numerous offspring, popular with the neighbors, but addicted to more whiskey than was good for his heart."[1] On 28 May 1841 Edwin died, leaving seven children and a pregnant wife. The next month Betsey gave birth to twins, Sam and Lizzie. This stretched the family's meager resources to the breaking point.

Friends—and some relatives—urged Betsey to break up the home and scatter the children into families where they would get better care. She refused. She sacrificed to bring up her seven boys and two girls as a united family. Betsey probably often cried herself to sleep at night, but to her children she was always the wall of strength. She sent them to the First Congregational Church, pastored by the Rev. Oliver C. Everett, a moderate Unitarian. (Young Dwight often rounded up friends and took them to Sunday school.) Betsey taught her children to work hard, be honest, never give up, and always show compassion to the needy. Though her table had no luxuries (or necessities) to spare, she always shared.

When Dwight left for Boston in 1854, his mother gave him five dollars and encouraged him to work hard at her brother's shoe store. On 21 April 1855 a Sunday school teacher, Edward Kimball, led young Moody to Christ. On 18 September 1856 Moody went to Chicago, began working in a Sunday school and the YMCA, and eventually became the most successful evangelist of his day. He faithfully wrote to his mother, who was skeptical of her son's "radical" activities. Betsey Holton Moody did not yet possess and enjoy the same Christian faith that her son did.

In 1875, after great success in England, Moody returned to Northfield, bought property, and made it his home. In spite of opposition from local pastors, Moody held a meeting in one of the churches, hoping to reach for Christ some of his friends and relatives—particularly his mother. "I will be a Unitarian till I die," she had said; but on 17 October she stood at the invitation. Moody was so overcome that he wept for joy. Betsey was seventy years old when she received Christ. She died in February 1896, giving a clear witness of her confidence in Christ.

There is no question that Moody's mother had given him the kind of training that helped make him the man he was. Today's generation would call it "puritanical," but it made for rock-like character, no matter how rough the exterior might have been.

It fell to another woman to polish that character—Emma Revell Moody, the evangelist's wife. In his delightful book *My Father: An*

---

1. *Moody: A Biographical Portrait of the Pacesetter in Modern Mass Evangelism* (New York: Macmillan, 1963), p. 4.

Intimate Portrait of Dwight Moody, Paul Moody wrote: "If in retrospect our home seemed so ideal, the secret was my mother. My father's admiration for her was as boundless as his love. To the day of his death, I believe, he never ceased to wonder at two things—the use God had made of him despite what he considered his handicaps, and the miracle of having won the love of a woman he considered so completely his superior, with such a different temperament and background."[2]

Emma Revell was born in London on 5 July 1843. Her father was a shipbuilder who retired because of poor health and in 1849 moved to Chicago. The Revells had strong Baptist convictions, and Moody first saw Emma when she was teaching a Sunday school class at First Baptist Church. Two years later her family moved across from John V. Farwell, one of Moody's businessmen-volunteers. Farwell recruited Emma for Moody's Sunday school. Moody began to cultivate her friendship, and in 1860 they were officially engaged. On 28 August 1862 they were married. They set up their first home on Chicago's north side, where most of Moody's Sunday school work would be done.

You could not find a husband and wife more opposite than Dwight and Emma Moody. She was fragile and sickly; he was bursting with energy and rarely knew what it was to be ill. She suffered with asthma and headaches most of her life. Dwight was an extrovert; Emma preferred to remain in the background. She was well-educated, while her husband functioned with perhaps a fifth-grade education. And she was "polished" in the best British fashion; he had yet to be polished. But she was exactly what he needed—the perfect balance wheel and at times the perfect brake. She bore him three children: Emma (1864), William (1869), and Paul (1879). Sometimes Emma's parents cared for the children so she could travel with her husband. More frequently she stayed home with the children, praying for and encouraging her husband.

In 1875 Dwight, Emma, and the family moved to Northfield. The reserved British girl became an American farm girl. She raised a garden, canned fruits and vegetables, enjoyed the outdoors with the children, and occasionally took long drives into the woods alone with her husband. She handled his finances, wrote many of his letters, and saw to it, when he was away from home, that the children received their Bible training. Among Moody's last words were: "Mamma, you have been a good wife to me!" Emma survived her famous husband by only a few years, dying in 1903.

2. (Boston: Little and Brown, 1938), p. 52.

Two other women who made a lasting contribution to Moody's life and ministry were Sarah Cooke and her friend, Mrs. Hawxhurst. "Auntie Sarah" had come to Chicago from England. She and her husband, who was in the meat business, were Free Methodists. Mrs. Hawxhurst had lost her husband and moved to Chicago to live with her daughter. In 1871, while attending a camp meeting, "Auntie Sarah" became burdened that the Lord would give Moody "the baptism of the Holy Ghost and of fire." She and Mrs. Hawxhurst told Moody they were praying for him, but he told them to pray for the lost. But Moody soon was concerned enough to ask them to pray with him every Friday afternoon. Sarah reported that on 6 October 1871 Moody was so burdened for power that he actually "rolled on the floor and in the midst of many tears and groans, cried to God to be baptized with the Holy Ghost and fire."[3] One month later, while walking down Wall Street in New York City, Moody experienced such a filling of God's Spirit that he had to "ask Him to stay His hand."

The last woman I want to introduce is Miss Emma Dryer, who could well be called the "mother of Moody Bible Institute." Dryer, born in Massachusetts, came to Chicago in 1870 to work in a home for wayward girls. An excellent teacher and administrator, she served on the faculty of the State Normal School. When Moody dedicated the new tabernacle in 1871, Dryer was assisting in the Bible classes for women; and in 1873 Moody asked her to join the church staff and direct all the women's work. This included teaching Bible classes, directing sewing classes and other meetings, and visiting women.

Moody had attended the Mildmay Institutes in England and been impressed with this approach to Bible teaching. He later told Dryer that he wanted to build an institution in Chicago along the lines of Mildmay and that he would "make it the *first work* of his life." Dryer was skeptical. "Before the YMCA?" she asked.

"Yes," Moody replied. "Nothing will come between me and this work."

The establishing of a Christian school in Chicago had long been a concern of Dryer, and she was determined that the evangelist not change his mind. Originally Moody wanted to limit the student body to girls only. What about the young men? "Let the theological seminaries take 'em," he answered. "We'd find ourselves in hot water quick if we undertook to educate young men."

---

3. In Wilbur M. Smith, ed., *An Annotated Bibliography of D. L. Moody* (Chicago: Moody, 1948), p. 153.

Moody then left for Britain, not returning to the States until August 1875. Northfield was his first love, so he did not spend much time in Chicago, but at every opportunity Dryer reminded him of his promise to start a school. In 1879 Moody sent her to study Bible schools in Britain. Her experiences only deepened the burden for a school in Chicago. In 1883 she founded the successful "May Institutes" at the Chicago Avenue Church, the successor to Moody's North Side Tabernacle. These annual Bible lectures were presented by a well-known preacher or teacher. The lectures were held in the YMCA building, but Dryer kept praying for a definite educational ministry apart from both the YMCA and the church. During 1883 and 1884 she encouraged a special weekly prayer meeting for the establishing of a "Bible-work in Chicago." Finally in 1885 Moody agreed to start a school provided that the finances came in. He also agreed to give three months a year to the work once it was organized. It is interesting that Moody first wanted to establish the school in New York City because he felt "Chicago was not prepared for it."

The money came in, and Moody kept his promise. On 22 January 1886 he gave his famous "Farwell Hall" address, in which he called for the training of "gap-men" to serve the Lord in the churches. On 5 February 1887 the Chicago Evangelization Society was founded. The new ministry had problems, and in July 1887 Moody resigned from the work. Finally Moody agreed to stay with it, but Dryer left it. Mrs. Cyrus McCormick, who had been involved in the situation, gave Dryer $25,000 to carry on her own Bible ministry, and thus the infant school was saved.

Moody Bible Institute has remained true to the Word and has played a significant role in world evangelism. And Moody's name and ministry are better known because of the Institute than any other work he founded.

Moody was a man's man, but he was wise enough to know that he could not do the job alone. So God gave him several women to labor with him in the gospel. And you and I are that much richer because he and they faithfully fulfilled God's will.

Bibliography

Powell, Emma Moody. *Heavenly Destiny: The Life Story of Mrs. D. L. Moody*. Chicago: Moody, 1943.

23

Henry Varley

(1835–1912)

Henry Varley would have been a famous man had he never met Dwight L. Moody. But for some reason people remember Varley most for his telling the evangelist: "The world has yet to see what God can do with and for and through and in a man who is fully and wholly consecrated to Him." He made that statement in 1872 after a prayer meeting with several guests at Henry Bewley's estate in Dublin, but oddly enough Varley later did not recall having said it. A year later, when Moody returned to England, he told Varley: "Those were the words sent to my soul, through you, from the living God. As I crossed the wide Atlantic the boards of the deck . . . were engraved with them, and when I reached Chicago the very paving stones seemed marked with them. Under the power of those words I have come back to England, and I felt that I must not let any more time pass until I let you know how God used your words to my inmost soul."

The words of Henry Varley consistently pierced the human heart, for he was one of the most effective evangelists and revivalists of his time. "Varley," said Charles H. Spurgeon one day, "you are the only man in London I envy. You can go where you please and hold great missions throughout the country, and many souls are won for Christ. Now I admit my pond is a pretty big one; but I can't keep on catching the same fish. . . ." Varley often preached at the Metropolitan Tabernacle, a privilege Spurgeon did not give to many, and as the result of one Sunday's ministry there, over fifty people joined the church.

Henry Varley was born in 1835 in the little town of Tattershall, Lincolnshire. His father, not a particularly religious man, operated a small brewery and malt-house. But Varley's mother was a devoted evangelical who saw to it that her seven children learned to honor the Lord. Henry was eleven when his mother died. His father, unable to make ends meet, broke up the family. So young Varley was thrust into life, penniless, friendless, and with no promise of success.

He went to London and tried one job after another, finally finding what seemed to be a good position with a small butcher shop. However, the owner expected him to cheat the customers, and young Henry, though still unconverted, refused. In 1851 he found a new position with Thomas Pickworth, a successful butcher and devoted Christian. Varley was converted to Christ in August of that year. At about the same time he fell in love with Sarah Pickworth, the owner's daughter, whom he married six years later. The young Christian became active in the YMCA and Sunday school, and he soon discovered a gift for public speaking and began giving occasional "Sunday school addresses." (Spurgeon started his ministry the same way.)

But 1854 brought the cholera plague to London, and Varley, now in his own little butcher shop, suffered a financial setback from which he could not recover. Part of the problem was a partner who preferred drinking to selling, but it was obvious to Varley that his opportunities in London were limited. With Joshua 1:7 as his encouragement, he sailed for Australia. There Varley preached Christ, and though he found no wealth for himself, he did lead some men to Christ. He moved to Melbourne, where he turned down a job that would have required him to work on Sunday. But he finally joined the Langton brothers and quickly made himself almost indispensable. Within six months he saved enough money to purchase a business of his own. When he left Australia in June 1857 and sold the business, he never received the promised money. No matter: he was on his way home to Britain and his wife, and he had enough capital to begin again in London.

He was twenty-three when he established his own meat business, and he let it be known that he was in partnership with God. The business prospered, and so did his ministry. He and his wife were associated with a Baptist church at Westbourne Grove, but their real concern was for a slum known as Notting Dale. (Charles Dickens said that Notting Dale "contained one thousand inhabitants and three thousand pigs.") A Congregational church had established a mission school there, and the pastor, John Stoughton, asked Varley to supervise it. This was the kind of challenge Varley lived for: evangelism in the hard places, with nothing to trust but the promises of God. About a dozen adults attended his first service, but the congregations soon increased and many were won to Christ. Varley encouraged new converts to unite with area churches, but they refused. (Moody faced this same problem with his converts in Chicago.) So Varley started the Free Tabernacle at the corner of St. James Square, Notting Dale. This new church with no denominational connections offended the pastor and people at the Westbourne Grove church. Varley was censured for his ecclesiastical sins and urged to repent. Instead he resigned from the church.

The ecclesiastical convictions of Spurgeon and Varley are a study in contrast. Varley had Plymouth Brethren leanings and was not too excited over denominations. Spurgeon was a staunch Baptist. Varley refused ordination and repudiated the title "Reverend." "Plain Henry Varley is all I mean to be to the end of my days," he said.

Spurgeon playfully called Varley "a bad Baptist and a half-bred Plymouth Brother," to which Varley replied, "Show me some scriptural authority for calling myself a Baptist, and I will fall in at once."

"But we must be called by some name," Spurgeon argued.

"That is so," said Varley, "but how will this do—'a good minister of Jesus Christ'?"

On the Henry Varley memorial tablet in Brighton are the words: "His creed was simple—Ruin by the fall, Redemption by the blood of Christ, Regeneration by the Holy Ghost." These "three R's" were characteristic of Moody and often appeared in his sermons.

"Varley's Tabernacle," which had a seating capacity of one thousand, opened in 1860. Unlike Spurgeon's tabernacle, Varley's had room for a large choir and a harmonium. Spurgeon, no great lover of choir music, would not permit instruments in his services. It is worth noting that Varley influenced the father and two uncles of Gipsy Smith, and it was Varley who later baptized them. Along with the preaching ministry, Varley organized a soup kitchen, tea meetings for the poor, the distribution of Christmas gifts to neglected children, and a "Workman's Hall" club to keep men out of taverns. Not forgetting his own background, he instituted "The Butcher's Festival," which annually drew hundreds of butchers. All of this had one purpose: the winning of lost souls to Jesus Christ.

These words, spoken to Varley by Rev. John Offord, profoundly altered Varley's life: "My dear young brother, I have a deep conviction that the Lord is going to use you in a yet more wonderful manner. Be sure and go where He leads." The result was not immediate, but the seed had been planted. In 1869 Varley sold his business to his brother-in-law, a great step of faith since he had a wife and five children to support, the tabernacle to direct, and very little savings (he had given most of it away). "The pastor as a soul-winner is in the *retail* business," he told Spurgeon, "but the evangelist is in the wholesale." "My husband was born with his hat on," said Mrs. Varley, and she was right. No sooner did Varley return home from one evangelistic campaign than he was off to another. At first he concentrated on the cities of Great Britain and tried, as much as possible, to return to the tabernacle for Sunday services. But it soon became clear that the Lord had bigger plans for him.

In September 1874 he made the first of seven trips to North America, and God gave such a tremendous awakening in Brantford, Ontario, that over a thousand people received Christ. The bars and poolrooms were almost emptied. Seven years later it was reported that the Brantford police had nothing to do. When Varley returned in 1898, he found only two places licensed to sell alcohol. During that same tour Varley got enthusiastic permission from P. T. Barnum to preach in the Hippodrome in New York City. For three Sundays the evangelist addressed twenty thousand people, with hundreds standing outside.

If my count is correct, Varley made thirty-five trips during this later ministry: ten to Australia; seven to North America; five to South Africa, India, the Holy Land, and parts of Europe; and thirteen back to his native Britain. It was obvious that he could not maintain his ministry at the tabernacle and still obey the call to world evangelism, so in 1882 he resigned. Six years later he moved to Australia. He would have been better off to purchase a boat, because he returned to Australia only six times in the next twenty-four years.

In 1893 he assisted Moody in his great World's Fair ministry in

Chicago. Knowing Varley's effectiveness with the down-and-outer, Moody assigned him to a section of the city known for vice and crime. "More crimes and murders are committed there than in any other portion of the city," Varley wrote home. But God again gave him great crowds—eighty percent men—and great harvests. From 1897 to 1900, Varley conducted the "Great Tour," preaching in key cities in North America and Great Britain. In January 1897 he visited San Francisco for a second time, and one of the young men who assisted in the meetings was H. A. Ironside. Young Ironside often conducted seven street meetings a day and then took interested people to the evening service, where he ushered and managed the book table. Varley made a lasting impression on Ironside, convincing him that the winning of souls and the teaching of believers are complementary ministries, not competitive.

God's "gospel wholesaler" traveled almost constantly between Australia, Great Britain, and North America, winning lost souls and bringing spiritual quickening to the churches. His name shows up in connection with Northfield and Winona Lake, and we see him teamed up in conferences with John McNeill, G. Campbell Morgan, and A. C. Dixon. Varley and his wife settled once again in England, and on 30 March 1912, sitting quietly by the fire, he died. Thomas Spurgeon officiated at his funeral.

If there are any "secrets" to Henry Varley's ministry, they are concentration, courage, and prayer. He never hesitated to name sins and fight them openly. He wrote: "I am more and more persuaded that we, as Christian workers, lose a great deal of power by not openly challenging the evils that are ruining our brothers and sisters." During his years in Australia, Varley openly attacked the opium trade in cities, gambling, vice, and the sins of "slumlords." But prayer was the great source of Varley's power, as Moody learned when he visited him in London in 1867. "I visited that man to find the secret of his success," said Moody. "At home he prayed for the meeting. After supper, as we were rattling along through stone streets of London, he said, 'Now, brother, let us have prayer for that meeting.' " Moody confessed that "rattling through the streets wasn't exactly a comfortable place to pray"—but God answered and people were converted.

"Amongst the great evangelists of the Victorian era," said F. B. Meyer, "few will shine with greater brilliance than my beloved friend, Henry Varley." He was the man who challenged Moody, the man whom Spurgeon envied, the man God used because he dared to trust Him and obey His call.

Bibliography

Varley, Henry. *"The Christian Ambassador" and Other Addresses*. New York: Willard, 1875.

———. *Christ's Coming Kingdom; or, The Lord's Reign on Earth*. 3d ed. London: Holness, 1893.

———. *Terse Talk on Timely Topics*. London: Nisbet, 1884.

Varley, Henry, Jr. *Henry Varley's Life Story*. London: Holness, 1916

24

Samuel Johnson

(1709–1784)

Although I have often written about biographies of great men, I have never before written about the biography that is justly called the greatest in the English language—James Boswell's *The Life of Samuel Johnson*.

Samuel Johnson was a genius—a man with a computer-like memory and a mind that could assemble, analyze, organize, and present ideas so uniquely that the greatest people of his day clamored to sit and listen to him. He possessed such a store of knowledge that he could discuss anything with intelligence and profit. Johnson also had (as Boswell put it) "a certain continual power of seizing the useful substance of all that he knew, and exhibiting it in a clear and forcible manner. . . ." When he read, he "devoured the heart out of it" and was never distracted. His *Dictionary of the English Language*, a labor of nine years, won him little money, but immortal fame and the unquestioned position as "the great Cham of Literature." "Cham" is the title of the sovereign of Tartary. (In his first edition Boswell spelled it "Chum," and nobody knew what he was talking about.)

Why is Boswell's *Life of Samuel Johnson* a classic, and why has it brought pleasure to readers for nearly two hundred years? Why would anyone read a book about an eccentric writer who loved to sit at the table with friends, eat big meals, and converse on any subject? And not only converse, but argue so vehemently that his opponents were often overpowered, if not by logic at least by noise? "There is no arguing with Johnson," said playwright Oliver Goldsmith. "If his pistol misses fire, he knocks you down with the butt-end of it!"

The main attraction of *The Life of Samuel Johnson* is the man himself—gigantic in body and mind, and expansive with pen and tongue. He was eccentric and sometimes brutal. His sarcasm could cut down the most formidable opponent, yet his wit and wisdom were so rich that even his enemies read what he wrote and envied him. When a friend of Johnson advised Boswell to tone down some of Johnson's faults, Boswell replied: "No, madam, I will not cut his claws or make my tiger a cat to please anyone!" Much of the pleasure of reading Boswell's book is knowing that we are seeing Johnson (as Cromwell put it) "warts and all." We do not always agree with his words or his actions, but we are glad to have an unretouched photograph instead of a glamorous portrait.

The only word you can apply to Samuel Johnson is *massive.* He never graduated from a university, yet Oxford University granted him a master's degree, and later a doctorate, on the strength of his learning and literary productivity. He claimed that he never read a book through, yet he always knew what a book said. (And Johnson was blind in one eye.)

Johnson confessed that he "always felt an inclination to do nothing." There was a "natural indolence" about him that delighted his friends and despaired his publishers. He promised to have the dictionary completed in three years; it took him nine. "It was strange to think," wrote Boswell, "that the most indolent man in Britain had written the most laborious work, the *Dictionary of the English Language.*" While he was writing the dictionary, Johnson was also publishing the *Rambler,* a paper that came out twice each week and contained essays written by Johnson on "moral and religious" themes. On the strength of these essays, Johnson received his M.A. from Oxford.

James Boswell was a great observer and recorder of the men and events of his day. This Scottish lawyer, who longed to be identified with the great people of that era, was a born keeper of journals. Boswell was only twenty-two when he dared to invite himself into Johnson's life, but Johnson adored him for it. There was enough vanity in Johnson to enjoy Boswell's attention, yet enough sanity to keep the hero-worshiping lawyer from going too far.

Boswell antedated the modern psychologist in the way he questioned Johnson and encouraged him in his conversation. Instead of asking, "What are your views of educating children?" Boswell would introduce a quotation, give a hypothetical situation, or even deliberately pick an argument. Using a literary giant as the focal point, Boswell enabled readers to look at life through the mind and heart of Samuel Johnson. Johnson knew what it was to be poor and rejected, and he knew what it was to mobilize his God-given forces to work his way from hack journalist to the *pontifex maximus* of the literary world.

Johnson was a religious man, something Boswell was not. In his dictionary Johnson was careful to quote no writer whose books would undermine religion or morals. He defended the Christian faith, including miracles, and held to the deity of Christ and the efficacy of His atonement. At age 72 Johnson dictated a short "sermon" to Boswell in which he magnified the work of Christ on the cross: "The great sacrifice for the sins of mankind was offered at the death of the Messiah, who is called in Scripture 'the Lamb of God that taketh away the sins of the world.' " Johnson's lifestyle was not like that of such Christian contemporaries as John Wesley and George Whitefield. His expressions of faith were limited to the liturgies of the Anglican church. But his prayers indicate he was a converted man.

Johnson was melancholy, and his Christianity lacked joy. Boswell repeatedly mentioned Johnson's fits of melancholy and obsession with death. No doubt Boswell's sense of humor and "devil may care" attitude helped lift Johnson out of gloom and despair. Johnson constantly suffered physically, and he had a growing fear that he would one day go mad. For all his practical piety, he was not sure of salvation, and he claimed that no man could be sure. Boswell said that Johnson "saw God in clouds," but he needed the sunshine of God's grace and love.

Johnson's spiritual life was quickened when, as a student at Oxford, he read William Law's *Serious Call to a Devout and Holy Life*. It was not the dull book he had expected, and from that time religious faith was a prominent part of his thinking and living. Years later he called Law's book "the finest piece of hortatory theology in any language."

Johnson's convictions about preaching are worth considering. One day Boswell brought up the Methodists and praised them for their success in reaching the masses. "Sir," replied Johnson, "it is owing to their expressing themselves in a plain and familiar manner, which is the only way to do good to the common people, and which clergymen of genius and learning ought to do from a principle of duty. . . ." He believed that a minister ought to serve God and not look for a comfortable living, as did many of the clergy in his day. "The life of a parson, of a conscientious clergyman, is not easy," he said. "I would rather have Chancery suits upon my hands than the cure [care] of souls."

When asked about Wesley, Johnson said, "He can talk well on any subject." Johnson's only criticism of Wesley was that he never sat long enough to engage in serious conversation. He was not as generous to Whitefield, whose popularity he attributed to "the peculiarity of his manner. He would be followed by crowds were he to wear a nightcap in the pulpit, or were he to preach from a tree." Both Whitefield and Johnson attended Pembroke College, Oxford. Johnson was not sympathetic with the evangelist's methods, although he admired his eloquence and Christian character. "He did not draw attention by doing better than others, but by doing what was strange," said Johnson, alluding no doubt to Whitefield's open-air preaching.

Read Boswell and discover what Johnson thought about John Bunyan, Richard Baxter, Isaac Watts, William Cowper, John Donne, and hundreds of other preachers and famous people. Find out how he detested the actions of the American colonies, and how he opposed their "insurrection" against Great Britain. His thinking about women preachers is worth quoting, whether you agree with it or not: "Sir, a woman's preaching is like a dog's walking on his hind legs. It is not done well; but you are surprised to find it done at all." Read his views on capital punishment, education, marriage, travel, and a host of other topics.

The Life of Samuel Johnson is a long book and should be read in segments. My favorite edition is the two-volume one in Everyman Library. Be sure to read the quoted letters and the footnotes. In the footnotes Boswell scored some of his best hits against other biographers of Johnson. Scholars have calculated that Johnson and Boswell were together for less than three hundred days during their twenty-one–year friendship. Yet out of these days Boswell put together the most complete picture we have of this great man of letters. For information on the first fifty-four years of Johnson's life, Boswell depended on existing documents, interviews with friends, and Johnson himself. The book begins to scintillate from 1763 when Boswell took notes, stored conversations in his memory, and filled pages in his journal.

After Boswell's masterpiece you may want to read John Wain's *Samuel Johnson: A Biography.* Wain is professor of poetry at Oxford. This modern biography interprets Johnson's emotional afflictions and his Christian faith. It also emphasizes Johnson's kindness to those in need. At his own expense he fed, clothed, and housed as motley a group of people as you would ever find. His Christian faith may have been gloomy, but it was practical. Another classic biography of Johnson, published in 1977, is one by the noted Harvard scholar W. Jackson Bate. This book analyzes Johnson's psychology with great skill, including his religious fears and battles. *The Religion of Dr. Johnson and Other Essays* by William Thomas Cairns is a sympathetic study that should be supplemented by Bate's biography.

Scattered throughout *The Life of Samuel Johnson* are many of the doctor's prayers. He often wrote a special prayer when beginning a new venture, such as writing the dictionary or taking a trip. Johnson's *Prayers and Meditations* was edited and published by George Strahan after Johnson's death. Elton Trueblood also edited a collection of his prayers.

Boswell wrote at the end of his biography of Johnson that "the more his character is considered, the more he will be regarded by the present age, and by posterity, with admiration and reverence." Throughout his life Boswell was wrong about many things, but about this he was right.

Bibliography

Bate, W. Jackson. *Samuel Johnson.* New York: Harcourt Brace Jovanovich, 1977.

Boswell, James. *The Life of Samuel Johnson, LL.D.: Comprehending an Account of His Studies and Numerous Works, in Chronological Order; a Series of His Epistolary Correspondence and Conversations with Many Eminent Persons; and Various Original Pieces of His Composition, Never Before Published.* 2 vols. London: Dilly, 1791. Reprinted—Everyman Library. New York: Dutton, 1949.

Cairns, William Thomas. *"The Religion of Dr. Johnson" and Other Essays.* New York: Oxford University, 1946. Reprinted—Freeport, N.Y.: Books for Libraries, 1969.

Johnson, Samuel. *Prayers and Meditations.* Edited by George Strahan. London: Cadell, 1785.

———. *Doctor Johnson's Prayers.* Edited by Elton Trueblood. London: SCM, 1947. Reprinted—Folcroft, Pa.: Folcroft Library Editions, 1976.

Wain, John. *Samuel Johnson.* New York: Viking, 1975.

John Bunyan

25

Bunhill Fields

If you ever want to visit John Bunyan, Isaac Watts, John Owen, Susanna Wesley, and a host of other great Christians, then make your way to Bunhill Fields. This quaint cemetery is located on City Road in London, across the street from Wesley's Chapel. Be sure to visit the chapel first, especially the grave of John Wesley in the garden behind the chapel. Then cross City Road into Bunhill Fields and enter a different world.

Bunhill Fields, an old burial ground, probably was first called Bone-Hill Fields. Some 120,000 bodies are buried here, with the last burial recorded on 5 January 1854. The people whose remains mingle in this dust were Dissenters. Because they refused to follow the teaching of the established church, they could not be buried in consecrated ground. So they were interred at Bunhill Fields. This place is sacred to Christians who believe in liberty of conscience, the preaching of the Word, and the winning of lost souls. Many are buried here who "loved not their lives unto the death" and who willingly died in defense of God's truth.

Walk through the east gate and take the main path toward the center to find the tomb of John Bunyan, author of *Pilgrim's Progress* and many other works. This great monument would have been lost to us were it not for the Earl of Shaftesbury, who directed a generous public subscription that restored it in 1862. The tomb itself excites any lover of *Pilgrim's Progress.* On one side is a pilgrim carrying his heavy burden; on the other, the burden rolling away from the pilgrim! The inscription is simple: "John Bunyan, Author of the 'Pilgrim's Progress.' Obt. 31st August, 1688. AEt. 60." The year 1978 was the 300th anniversary of the publication of *Pilgrim's Progress.* Charles H. Spurgeon claimed he had read *Pilgrim's Progress* at least one hundred times, and he referred to it in many sermons. John Henry Jowett attributed his pure English style to his familiarity with Bunyan's masterpiece.

When my wife and I, with Dr. and Mrs. Howard Sugden, visited Bedford, England, the famous Bunyan Meeting House was locked. We watched hundreds drive past the large Bunyan statue on St. Peter's Street and wondered how many passers-by knew much about the man. In Elstow, near Bedford, we visited the famous Moot Hall, which dates back to 1500. This museum depicts English life in Bunyan's day (1628–1688). The jail list is there with Bunyan's name, as is a heavy door from the very jail in which Bunyan was confined.

The definitive Bunyan biography is *John Bunyan: His Life, Times, and Work*, by John Brown. Be sure to purchase the tercentenary edition, revised by another great Bunyan scholar, Frank Mott Harrison. Brown had devoted his life to Bunyan research, and Harrison continued his work. By the way, Harrison's book *John Bunyan: A Story of His Life* is an excellent study. But let no book replace *Pilgrim's Progress.* Every gospel-preaching pastor ought to master it. It may not make Spurgeons out of us, but it certainly will help us better understand the Christian conflict and the way of victory.[1]

Take the path east of Bunyan's tomb, and you cannot miss the tomb inscribed "John Owen, D.D.," a great English scholar and preacher who died in 1683. While a student at Oxford he allowed himself only four hours' sleep each night to spend more time in study. When he started his ministry, Owen was probably not converted. One Sunday in London, he went to hear a great Presbyte-

---

1. John Brown, *John Bunyan: His Life, Times, and Work*, rev. Frank Mott Harrison (London: Hulbert, 1928); Frank Mott Harrison, *John Bunyan: A Story of His Life* (London: Hulbert, 1928; reprinted—London: Banner of Truth, 1964).

rian preacher, only to discover that a substitute was preaching. But the unknown preacher's message reached Owen's heart, and he received assurance of peace with God. His tongue and pen were mighty weapons for the Lord. The 1850 edition of his complete works contains twenty-four large volumes. Some of his works are available today in reprint editions. They are wordy but meaty, a treasure-house for the serious student.

Owen and Bunyan are buried near each other, which is providential because their lives and ministries intersected. Owen interceded with Bishop Barlow of Lincoln to have Bunyan released from jail. And Owen encouraged Bunyan to publish *Pilgrim's Progress* and even recommended him to his own publisher. When King Charles II chided the learned Dr. Owen for going to hear Bunyan preach, the scholar replied: "I would willingly exchange all my learning for that tinker's power of touching men's hearts."

In the section across from Owen, near the entrance path, is the marker for Thomas Goodwin's grave. Some years ago lightning struck the tomb and split the top; all you can read now is "Thomas Goodwin, D.D." He died in 1679 at age eighty, leaving behind a rich legacy of books. Goodwin was converted in his student days while attending a funeral service. The sermon text was Luke 19:41–42, and the simple message profoundly affected him. Refusing to bow to the established church, Goodwin cast his lot with the nonconformists and became one of their greatest scholars and saints. He was a member of the Westminster Assembly in 1643. During the London fire of 1666, Goodwin lost a large part of his library. He served as chaplain to Oliver Cromwell. His writings were published in five large volumes, reprint editions of which are available today. The great Alexander Whyte fed his soul on the works of Thomas Goodwin.

Retracing our steps and walking west, we pass Bunyan, then the graves of the Cromwells (not Oliver or Richard), and to the right discover the grave of Susanna Wesley, mother of John and Charles—and seventeen other children! In spite of her busy life, she spent at least one hour each morning and evening in prayer and meditation. She personally taught and prayed with her children. For a fascinating study of the Wesley family, read *Family Circle* by Maldwyn Edwards.[2] You will meet not only Susanna the mother, but also Sammy, John, Charles, Hetty, Martha, Anne, and others of the circle.

---

2. *Family Circle: A Study of the Epworth Household in Relation to John and Charles Wesley* (London: Epworth, 1949).

As we continue west and cross an intersecting path, we turn to the right (past the "sunken tomb") and come to the large tomb of John Gill, successor of Benjamin Keach and illustrious predecessor of Spurgeon. Gill was actually the fourth pastor of the church that came to be known as "Spurgeon's Tabernacle." He came in 1720 and remained until his death in 1771. Statements like "As sure as John Gill is in the bookseller's shop" and "As sure as Dr. Gill is in his study" were current in his day and aptly described his interests. Gill's *Body of Divinity* is perhaps his best-known work. For 122 Sunday mornings Gill preached from the Song of Solomon. The sermons were published, and Spurgeon wrote in his personal copy, "This priceless work of my learned predecessor has always been helpful to me." If a pastor today preached 122 sermons on the Song of Solomon, he would probably be asked to resign! Gill did not compromise. He was an ambassador, not a diplomat. When a member of his congregation warned him that a certain book he had written would cause him to lose friends and income, he replied: "I can afford to be poor, but I cannot afford to injure my conscience." Spurgeon in his own courage patterned himself after both Bunyan and Gill.

If we cross the path into the north section, we can walk along several winding paths and visit more interesting graves. A number of hymn writers are here, some of whom are practically forgotten: David Denham, John Rippon, Samuel Stennett, William Shrubsole (who wrote the tune "Miles' Lane"), Joseph Hart ("Come, Ye Sinners, Poor and Needy"), Joseph Swain, and, of course, Isaac Watts. Also buried here, but about as far away from Watts as he can be and still be in the cemetery, is Thomas Bradbury. He and Watts broke fellowship over the doctrine of the Trinity. "Let's have none of Mr. Watts's *whims!*" Bradbury once shouted in a church service.

We could walk around Bunhill Fields for hours and profit from looking into the histories of the men and women whose dust rests here. We could visit the grave of Abraham Hume, whose tomb was damaged by a huge crowd that visited Bunhill expecting to see a resurrection. A rumor circulated in 1708 that a certain Dr. Emms, buried there, would be raised on 25 May. The crowd was so great that day that several markers and tombs were damaged. Needless to say, the good doctor never got above the ground.

Literature buffs should note that Daniel Defoe, author of *Robinson Crusoe,* is buried here. One of Defoe's schoolmates was Samuel Wesley, father of John and Charles. Defoe was forever getting into trouble with the government or going into debt. He spent time in Newgate Prison, was sued for libel, and stood in the stocks.

Baptists might want to visit the grave of Dan Taylor (1738–1816). He was converted by the Methodists when about twenty years old but soon disagreed with their doctrines. He was willing to walk 120 miles in the winter to be baptized in a river by a Baptist minister!

Some of the epitaphs are outright humorous, like the one for Dame Mary Page:

> In 67 months she was tap'd 66 times,
> Had taken away 240 gallons of water,
> Without ever repining at her case,
> Or ever fearing the operation.

Not far from Gill's resting-place is the grave of Thomas Hutchings (1768–1827), whose death is interesting. He was in his pulpit on 25 February 1827 when he suffered a stroke. He was praying: "Lord, we are dying creatures; prepare us for life, prepare us for death, and for eternal glory, for Christ's sake. Amen." Then the stroke hit him; he lingered a few days and then died.

One final fact: when you visit Bunhill Fields, notice the great number of pastors who served their churches for twenty-five years or more. Some of them served one congregation for as long as fifty years. Pastors did not move quickly in those days. Gill pastored his church for more than fifty years. His successor, Rippon, ministered there for sixty-three years. And Spurgeon preached there for nearly forty years.

I have visited Bunhill Fields twice, and each time I have felt a sense of awe and devotion. Even in the midst of a noisy city, Bunhill Fields still has a holy hush of God over it. I cannot help but give thanks to God for the sacrificial ministries of the people buried there. How much poorer we would be without Bunyan and Watts and Owen and Wesley! And there are hundreds of unknown saints whose bodies rest beneath that city sod. Someday we shall meet them. Meanwhile we give thanks for their devotion to Christ, a devotion that, for many of them, meant suffering and death.

26

Marks of Maturity in the Ministry

The work that the pastor does cannot be separated from the life that he lives. A man may be a successful surgeon and, at the same time, a compulsive gambler; or he may teach algebra with great success and get drunk every weekend. But the man in the ministry reproduces after his kind. This is why Paul warned Timothy, "Take heed unto thyself, and unto the doctrine. . . ." (I Tim. 4:16). Bad character can never live with good doctrine. Unless the truth is written on the pastor's heart and revealed in his life, he can never write it on the hearts of others.

It is for this reason that maturity is essential in the work of the ministry. As the pastor matures, his people mature; for the work we do flows out of the life we live. Paul was concerned that young Timothy's "profiting" be seen by all men (I Tim. 4:15), and that word *profiting* was an apt choice. It means "pioneer advance into new territory." Paul wanted to see Timothy mature—move into new areas of spiritual understanding and growth—because then his church would also mature to the glory of God.

There is a great difference between age and maturity. Age is a quantity of time; maturity is a quality of experience. Unfortunately not everyone who grows old, grows up! The man who says, "I've been pastoring for twenty years!" has no guarantee that he is ministering in a mature manner, because age and experience are no guarantees of maturity. They are only opportunities for maturity.

There are several ways to measure maturity. I want to focus on one: the ability to make distinctions. In his prayer for the Philippians, Paul desired that they "may approve things that are excellent" (Phil. 1:10), or that they "may distinguish the things that differ." A little child thinks all four-footed animals are dogs until he discovers the existence of cats, mice, hamsters, and a multitude of other creatures. The ability to make distinctions that are important is one mark of the mature man. With this in mind I would like to suggest several distinctions that, to me, mark the man who is maturing in the ministry.

Activity or ministry. To begin with, the maturing pastor knows the difference between activity and ministry. He knows that not all activity is ministry—in fact, it might be a detour around real ministry!—and that some ministry requires very little activity but a great deal of intensity. A Sunday bulletin that looks like an airlines timetable does not always indicate that God's people are serving the Lord. It could mean they are living on substitutes. The mature pastor is not against activity, because he knows that Spirit-filled people will be busy serving others; but he does not make activity the sole test of the spiritual level of the church.

Activity can simply mean doing a job and getting it over with; ministry means sharing a life. In I Thessalonians 2:7–8 Paul compared the faithful pastor to a nursing mother who imparts her very life to the children! It may be pressing the illustration too far, but ministry means nursing the children, while activity means mixing a formula and turning the family over to a babysitter! The man who truly ministers is fulfilling a calling to the glory of God, not serving a calendar for the praise of men.

Multiplying activities is not always the way to God's blessing. I know a church that prided itself in its busy schedule; there was something every night of the week. Some of the people asked that the church board make Monday a "family night" so that members could stay home and enjoy their families. The board agreed. Unbelievable as it sounds, a few weeks later the members were asking to have the regular Monday-evening program restored. They explained: "We just sit home and look at each other and don't know what to do!" What a tragedy that a "busy church" had incapacitated them for the job of building beautiful human relationships at home! After living for years on substitutes, the people did not know the real thing when it came their way.

Every pastor owes it to himself and his church to examine carefully the church program as well as his own schedule. Each committee, organization, activity, and office should be tested. Has some of the temporary scaffolding become part of the permanent structure? Or to change the figure, is a growing body being forced to wear baby clothes? We do not perform surgery on the baby to make him fit the garments; we get new garments! A breath of fresh air would blow through the local church that has the courage to separate activity from ministry.

We must face the fact that some pastors actually enjoy endless activity and full schedules. Perhaps it gives them a feeling of accomplishment. Or perhaps (and this may be closer to the truth) it gives them an excuse not to get so close to the people that they have to pay a price to serve the Lord. When a man is "on the run," people with broken hearts do not seek him out. Keeping active on the organizational and denominational treadmill can ease a pastor's conscience as he neglects prayer and meditation and a close confrontation with the needs that his people face. Every man knows the plague of his own heart, so I must not judge; but I cannot help feeling that heaven has a special reward for that pastor who has had the courage to say with Jeremiah, "Take away her battlements; for they are not the Lord's" (Jer. 5:10).

Principles or methods. The maturing pastor also knows the difference between principles and methods. The old couplet puts it perfectly:

> Methods are many, principles are few;
> Methods always change, principles never do.

For example, it is a basic principle of the ministry that no man can be saved apart from the Word of God. How you get God's Word to him is quite something else. You may preach to him, hand him a tract, or invite him to your home for a cookout and converse with him in a casual way. Or it is a principle that the local church must pray if God is going to bless. The methods you use to get your people to pray will vary, and what works in rural Iowa may not work in metropolitan Chicago. Some churches thrive on early-morning prayer breakfasts; others use prayer cells in the homes. No one method is more inspired than another, and the pastor who marries a method may have to divorce it when he moves to his next pastorate.

The beginning pastor and the immature pastor become intoxicated with methods. Consciously or unconsciously they "imitate the big men" and fall in love with every new idea that is generated. It matters not that Saul's armor does not fit; the immature man will stumble around in it anyway because "this is what everybody is doing these days." Try to convince him that there is really nothing new under the sun, and he will look at you with alarm. Try to convince him that the methods must fit the man, and he will become suspicious of you and your orthodoxy. After all, there is today an orthodoxy of method as well as of doctrine, and sometimes it appears that the former is more important than the latter.

Right methods, and methods that are effective and biblical, are certainly important. A man said to Dwight L. Moody, "Mr. Moody, I don't like your methods."

"Well, I'm always looking for better methods," the evangelist replied. "What methods do *you* use?"

"I have no methods," the man replied sheepishly.

"Then I'll stick to my own," said Moody.

But we need to remember that methods deal with the *how* and *what* of the ministry; principles deal with the *why*. It is valuable to know *what* works; but it is also valuable to know *why* it works. Psalm 103:7 illustrates this truth: "He made known his ways unto Moses, his acts unto the children of Israel." Israel knew *what* God was doing; but Moses knew *why* God was doing it.

A man builds his principles out of his own personal experience with the Word of God. He is careful to test his methods by his principles. When a man ministers according to principle, there is stability to his work; there are roots that will not be shaken by every wind of doctrine. The man who follows God-given principles is not attracted by all the latest fads, nor does he seek the approval of men. "He that doeth the will of God abideth for ever"; he that adopts all the latest methods is forgotten as soon as are the methods.

Popularity or success. This leads to a third mark of maturity: knowing the difference between popularity and success. Barabbas was popular but hardly a success. Popularity is a passing thing; success is permanent. (Of course sin can transform a successful pastor into a failure; but the work of an obedient man continues to help others.) The man who courts popularity with men may find himself a stranger to God and His blessing.

"If I take care of my character," said Moody, "my reputation will take care of itself." The mature man knows that the most important part of his life is the part that only God sees. What he is in the closet is much more important than what he is in the pulpit. The man who fails in the secret place will ultimately fail in the public place. The mature man majors on building Christian character: he saturates himself with the Word; he spends time in prayer; he battles sin. He lets patience have her perfect work so that he can become still more mature in Christ (James 1:4). He is not quick to jump into the spotlight; like Joseph he knows that God has His purposes and His times.

The immature man covets praise and success in the eyes of men. He revels in statistics and in comparing his work with the work of others. He forgets the warning of Paul about those who, "measuring themselves by themselves, and comparing themselves among themselves, are not wise" (II Cor. 10:12). He belongs to a "mutual admiration society" and is very unhappy if someone is not praising him and his work. He is unmindful of the counsel in II Corinthians: "Not he that commendeth himself is approved, but whom the Lord commendeth" (10:18).

When God wants to build a ministry, He first builds a man, a man of character and faithfulness. He tests him with a few things; if he proves faithful, He promotes him to many things (Matt. 25:21). But if He sees that popularity is the governing force of a man's life, God abandons him just as He abandoned King Saul and Demas. The mature pastor majors on being a success in the eyes of God, no matter what others say.

Opinion or conviction. The maturing pastor can also distinguish between opinion and conviction. Actually there are three concepts that must not be confused: prejudice, opinion, and conviction. Prejudice is an unthinking thing, buried in a man's upbringing; it is blind and dangerous. The man who says "I feel" is probably operating on the basis of prejudice. Opinion is better educated; it is usually based on experience and reveals itself when a man says "I think." But for a man to say "I know!" demands conviction. If I refuse to fly to Denver because "I just don't like airplanes," then that is prejudice. If I say, "The last three times I was up, I became very ill," then that is opinion. But if I say, "My doctor examined me and discovered I have inner-ear trouble and must stay off planes," then I am speaking from conviction. The tragedy is that many pastors think they are showing conviction when others see only stubbornness based on prejudice and opinions!

The Pharisees in Jesus' day claimed to have convictions, and because of their convictions they crucified the Son of God. Nobody, not even Jesus, could convince them that their so-called convictions were merely traditional opinions that they had never examined critically and honestly. Perhaps the orthodox today need to take this to heart. A man's maturity is tested by the way he acts toward those who disagree with him. A mature man can disagree without becoming disagreeable; he can love the truth without hating his critic. The man who refuses to examine the other side of the question is announcing his immaturity and writing his own ticket to failure. The mature man is open to truth, because he knows that all truth comes from God. He is kind to pastors of different beliefs because he realizes that "we know in part" (I Cor. 13:9) and that seeking truth is a lifelong challenge.

The immature man thinks he always has to be right. He forgets that we have our treasure in earthen vessels and that even Joshua and Peter occasionally made mistakes. As the winds of change blow across the world, the immature man runs into his private storm shelter and curses the wind; or worse yet, he mounts his trusty steed and becomes an evangelical Don Quixote who tilts windmills and prides himself at being a "fool for Christ's sake." A fool, perhaps; for Christ's sake—that remains to be seen. The mature man is not afraid of change because he has built on the Rock and belongs to a kingdom that cannot be shaken (Heb. 12:25–29). If God's winds blow away some of the rigging, he does not scuttle the ship, knowing that God will never destroy anything that His people need. The mature man will abandon his prejudices, examine his opinions, test his convictions. He wants to be sure he is basing his ministry on true convictions, not secondhand opinions. He may discover he is actually hiding behind his opinions because deep inside he fears they may be wrong! If so, he will face this honestly and ask God for guidance.

In short, the mature man will remember the counsel of Augustine: "In essentials, unity; in doubtful questions, liberty; in all things, charity."

Acting or reacting. In connection with this, consider a fifth mark of maturity: knowing the difference between acting and reacting. Men act; children and animals react. This difference is subtle; but as Mark Twain said, so is the difference between *lightning* and *lightning bug*.

Some reactions are good for us: jumping back when we touch something hot, or turning away when we confront something dirty.

But life is more than a series of conditioned reflexes; problems must be faced, decisions must be made, people must be helped. The pastor whose life and ministry are controlled by specific purposes does not have to react; he can simply act because he knows what must be done. The man who constantly reacts is always the victim of circumstances, the puppet of people who know how to pull strings. He lives in constant fear; he "explodes" when his ideas are rejected. He is not in control of the situation because he is not in control of himself!

The man who acts is the man who walks with God and is sure of his calling. He know himself—weaknesses as well as strengths—and he knows the work God wants him to finish. He knows how to listen without arguing and interrupting. "He that answereth a matter before he heareth it, it is folly and shame unto him," says Proverbs 18:13, and good advice this is. The mature man thinks with his mind, not with his glands. He is governed by a divine purpose, so he never complains about the circumstances. After all, God is bigger than circumstances! The immature man can never accomplish much because the situation is never right. As the old Roman proverb puts it, "When the pilot does not know which port he is heading for, no wind is the right wind." Immaturity thrives on excuses, maturity on challenges.

The maturing pastor knows where he is going, and his church knows that he does. "But none of these things move me," he says with Paul, "neither count I my life dear unto myself, so that I might finish my course with joy, and the ministry, which I have received of the Lord Jesus, to testify of the gospel of the grace of God" (Acts 20:24). He has in his private notebook a list of goals—some long-range, some immediate. He has a set of priorities; he knows what must be done first. He permits nothing to turn him from the task; he does not neglect his own vineyard while trying to help everyone else with their work. "My life—my course—my ministry!"

Dictatorship or leadership. A sixth mark of maturity is this: distinguishing between dictatorship and leadership. Churches rise or fall on leadership. Certainly it is true that all believers are one in Christ; but it is also true that God has set some believers over the local church as spiritual leaders. The church is an organism; but if an organism is not organized, it will die. When I accepted my first church, a saintly pastor counseled me: "Remember, there can be only one leader in a church; and if that leader is not the pastor, it will be somebody else—and you'll have trouble!"

How can we tell a leader from a dictator? Sometimes it is not easy, but perhaps a few suggestions will help. A leader *shows* the church what to do by example; the dictator *tells* the church what to do. A leader depends on humility, prayer, and love; a dictator depends on pressure, force, and fear. The true leader goes before and encourages; the dictator stands behind and drives. The leader leads by serving; the dictator expects others to serve him. The leader rejoices when God gets the glory and others get the credit; the dictator takes both the credit and the glory for himself. The leader builds people; the dictator uses people and then drops them when he is through exploiting them.

One test of leadership is this: What kind of people does one's ministry attract? Usually the dictator attracts "small people" who desperately need the security and popularity of a great man, and who must lose their own identities as they inflate the ego of their hero. A true leader attracts people who believe in his cause and who are willing to work with him to extend it. They do not lose their identities in the leader; rather they grow under his leadership. A dictator manufactures cookie-cutter followers who imitate him; a leader grows other leaders who themselves mature under his guidance. Unfortunately even a dedicated leader attracts some weak people who need to bask in the light of his greatness. Where the light shines the brightest, the bugs fly in. But a true leader will not be deceived by this shallow idol worship.

A leader is always harder on himself than he is on others. "The chief is servant of them all." A dictator may take risks, but he will not pay the price he asks his followers to pay. There is always a convenient scapegoat around who will gladly pay the price and think himself fortunate to have the privilege of dying. The Pharisees were spiritual dictators; they laid burdens on the backs of the people, yet did nothing to help the people carry them. This is why Jesus warned His disciples, "Call no man on earth your father!" The mature man is no man's disciple, nor does he want any other man to be his disciple. He is happy to be a disciple of Jesus Christ.

Sermons or messages. There are certainly other marks of the mature pastor, but I will close with this one: he knows the difference between a sermon and a message. From the chef's point of view, it is the difference between the recipe and the meal. Or from the builder's point of view, it is the difference between the blueprints and the final structure.

A young pastor just out of seminary said to me: "I feel my main job is to preach the Word. I don't go for this business of calling on my people." When I asked him whether he planned to preach sermons or messages, he was not quite sure what I meant. I tried to explain that we preach to real people, not to nameless crowds, and that the Word of God must be made meaningful to our people in a practical way. Unless the preacher is a pastor, unless he knows his people, he cannot bring them messages. He can only prepare outlines and preach sermons—and then wonder why the people do not grow.

A faithful shepherd will lead the flock into the pastures it needs. There are seasons to the soul, and there are seasons to the ministry of a church. The pastor is a spiritual steward; his task is to feed the household "their portion of meat in due season" (Luke 12:42). He had better know the appetites and needs of the family, or his diet may make them sick instead of strong! The ivory-tower preacher who descends twice a week with a divine oracle may attract a host of people who prefer to be anonymous and left alone; but he will probably not bind up the brokenhearted or dry many tears. People with honest spiritual needs can tell when the pastor really cares.

A sermon need not cost us very much: a bit of reading, some main points (preferably alliterated), a few stories . . . and that's it! But a message is costly. "Preaching that costs nothing accomplishes nothing," said John Henry Jowett, and he is right. But David said it first:"Neither will I offer . . . unto the Lord my God of that which doth cost me nothing" (II Sam. 24:24). Unless the Word of God smashes through our own lives, burning and cutting, tearing down and building up, we have no right to give it to others. The man who can "whip out" a sermon in a few hours on Saturday evening, after wasting a whole week of opportunity for meditation, may see what men call "results," but he will never see what God calls lasting fruit. A real message flows out of a broken heart, a heart open to God and to God's people. The man with a message steps into the pulpit saying: "My heart is inditing a good matter: I speak of the things which I have made touching the king: my tongue is the pen of a ready writer" (Ps. 45:1).

A sermon is "put together" like a tossed salad; a message is "beaten oil for the sanctuary." The man with a sermon speaks from authorities; the man with a message speaks from authority. He has felt the fire in his bones, and nothing can silence his lips. He has walked with Christ in the way, and therefore the Word is burning in his heart. In him the Word becomes flesh.

The writing of a sermon comes from learning; the preparing of a message comes from living. The ideal is a combination of both. The man of God must meet the Lord on the mountain top, hearing His voice and seeing His glory. But he must also come into the valley to share the battles and burdens of God's people. The mature man is not elated when he hears, "Wasn't that a great sermon!" But he quietly thanks God when he hears someone say, "Pastor, your message spoke to my heart today. I needed it."

In this day when the key word seems to be *bigger*—and we thank God for every increase in His vineyard—it might be wise for us to add another word: *better*. God wants numerical increase; but He also wants spiritual maturity. The one is not the enemy of the other. If maturity were the enemy of evangelism, God would never have used Paul. His great desire was to "present every man perfect [mature] in Christ Jesus" (Col. 1:28). But an immature pastor will never develop mature people.

How does God mature us? Through the Word of God and prayer. Through problems and suffering and misunderstanding. Through sacrifice and service. In fact the very problems that discourage us today may be the tools God is using to make us grow in grace. Maturity does not come overnight unless you are a mushroom. Maturity demands time, deep roots, weathering storms. "And he shall be like a tree planted by the rivers of water. . . ." The process of maturing is a lifetime challenge because the standard of achievement is not our favorite preacher but "the measure of the stature of the fulness of Christ."

Our world is a gigantic playpen in which grown-up children fight over their expensive toys. The need of the hour is maturity, and the man of the hour is the preacher of the Word. We pastors dare not be little children at a time when God is looking for mature men to build His church.

Index of Persons

Abbott, Lyman, 98
Abbott-Smith, George, 280
Adeney, Walter F., 240
Aharoni, Yohanan, 274
Aitken, William Hay M. H., 181
Alexander, Charles M., 182
Alexander Joseph Addison, 277
Alford, Henry, 281
Anderson, Robert, 182, 279
Andrewes, Lancelot, 77
Angus, Samuel, 284
Aquinas, Thomas, 266
Aratus of Soli, 267
Archer, Gleason L., 274
Aristotle, 98
Armerding, Carl, 201
Arnot, William, 238, 278
Augustine, 38, 105, 350
Avi-Yonah, Michael, 274

Bailey, Kenneth E., 237–38
Baillie, John, 263–64
Ball, Alwyn, 79
Barber, Cyril J., 270
Barbour, A. H., 111
Barbour, C. F., 111, 257
Barbour, George F(reeland), 109
Barbour, Jane Elizabeth, 111
Barbour, Robert W., 109, 111
Barclay, Robert, 168
Barclay, William, 275, 280, 282, 283, 287, 289
Barlow, ———, 141
Barlow, Thomas, 341
Barnes, Albert, 276, 278
Barnhouse, Donald Grey, 282, 283, 285
Barnum, P. T., 328
Baron, David, 278, 279
Barrie, James, 257–58
Bartlett, John, 251
Bate, W. Jackson, 337
Batson, Beatrice, 271
Bauer, Walter, 280

Baur, F. C., 51
Baxter, J. Sidlow, 178, 247, 272
Baxter, Richard, 336
Bell M'Kenzie, 61
Bengel, J. A., 280
Bernard of Clairvaux, 266
Bewley, Henry, 325
Birrell, Charles M., 91, 95, 97
Blackwood, Andrew W., Sr., 247, 278
Blackwood, Andrew W., Jr., 277
Blaiklock, E. M., 284–85, 286
Blair, J. Allen, 277, 279
Boettner, Loraine, 230
Bonar, Andrew, 276
Bonar, Horatius, 176
Bonsall, H. Brash, 282
Booth, William, 182
Boreham, Frank W., 239, 283
Boswell, James, 333–37
Bounds, E. M., 178
Boyer, James L., 286
Bradbury, Thomas, 342
Bridges, Charles, 277
Broadus, John A., 283
Brock, William, 90
Bromley, John, 36 n
Brookes, James H., 79
Brooks, Phillips, 232, 241, 264
Brown, Archibald G., 181
Brown, Charles R., 188
Brown, Colin, 280
Brown, David, 273
Brown, Elijah P., 289
Brown, John (b. 1784), 286, 287
Brown, John (b. 1830), 340
Bruce, Alexander B., 231, 238, 240, 282
Bruce, F. F., 284, 285, 286, 287, 288
Buchman, Frank, 16
Buckland, William, 39
Buckley, J. M., 113
Bullinger, E. W., 287
Bunyan, John, 160, 336, 339, 340, 341, 342, 343
Buttrick, George A., 239

Cairns, William Thomas, 337
Callaway, T. W., 275
Candlish, Robert S., 288
Carnell, Edward, 230
Caryl, Joseph, 276
Chadwick, Owen, 48
Chafer, Lewis Sperry, 142
Champness, Thomas, 181
Chapman, J. Wilbur, 97, 182, 202–4
Chappell, Clovis, 246
Charles II, 341
Chesterton, G. K., 265
Christopher, ———, 141
Church, R. W., 17, 19, 48
Cicero, 268
Clarke, Arthur G., 277
Clow, W. M., 282
Coder, S. Maxwell, 213, 288
Cohen, Gary G., 288
Conant, Judson E., 190
Connolly, Francis X., 21
Conybeare, W. J., 284
Cooke, Sarah (Anne), 322
Cowper, William, 336
Cox, Samuel, 276, 278
Craigie, P. C., 276
Criswell, W. A., 288
Crockett, Davy, 267
Crockett, William D., 276
Cromwell, Oliver, 334, 341
Cromwell, Richard, 341
Cuff, William, 181
Culbertson, William, 201, 211–16
Culver, Robert D., 278, 282
Cumming, Elder, 181
Cummins, G. D., 212
Cundall, Arthur E., 276
Curtis, Charles P., Jr., 264

Dale, R. W., 49, 51, 154, 181, 188, 275, 313
Dana, H. E., 285
Dante, 271
Darby, J. N., 240, 271
Darwin, Charles, 110
Davidman, Joy, 275
Davidson, A. B., 274
Davidson, Donald, 245
Davidson, Francis, 274
Davidson, Randall, 157
Davis, John J., 275
Dawson, W. J., 183
Defoe, Daniel, 342
DeHaan, M. R., 275, 288
Deissmann, Adolf, 281
DeLaura, David J., 21
Denham, David, 342
Denney, James, 185

Dewhirst, J. W. T., 153–54
Dickens, Charles, 327
Dickson, David, 277
Dixon, A. C., 126–27, 177, 182, 184, 329
Dods, Marcus, 110, 111, 238
Donne, John, 266, 268, 336
Draper, James T., Jr., 278, 287–88
Drummond, Henry, 107–13, 154, 171, 181, 185, 191, 315
Dryer, Emma, 322–23
Duff, ——, 184
Dunaway, Philip, 267

Eadie, John, 286
Eden, George R., 49, 51
Edersheim, Alfred, 281–82
Edison, Thomas A., 267
Edward VIII (Duke of Windsor), 253
Edwards, Jonathan, 50, 191, 193, 286
Edwards, Maldwyn, 341
Edwards, Thomas Charles, 285
Edwards, Tyron, 251
Eliot, George. *See* Evans, Mary Ann
Ellicott, Charles J., 287
Ellingsen, Harald F. J., 283
Ellison, H. L., 277, 279, 285
Emms, ——, 342
English, E. Schuyler, 197, 199, 201, 284
Epimenides, 267
Evans, Bergen, 250–51
Evans, Mary Ann (George Eliot), 187
Evans, Mel, 267
Everett, Oliver C., 320

Fadiman, Clifton, 271
Fairbairn, A. M., 154
Fairbairn, Patrick, 279
Farrar, Frederic W., 282
Farwell, John V., 321
Fausset, A. R., 273
Feinberg, Charles Lee, 279
Feltham, F. J., 127
Fereday, W. W., 289
Findlay, James F., Jr., 312
Finney, Charles G., 50, 178–79, 193, 286, 313
Fitt, A. P., 313
Flavel, John, 266
Fletcher, John, 166
Fosdick, Harry Emerson, 315
Frank, Anne, 267
Freud, Sigmund, 252
Friedrich, Gerhard, 38, 280
Froude, Richard Hurrell, 16, 37
Fullerton, W. Y., 92, 95, 125, 186

Gaebelein, A. C., 277, 283, 284, 285
Gaebelein, Frank E., 273
Gardiner, George E., 276
Garrett, Charles, 181
Garvie, Alfred E., 240
Geisler, Norman, 230, 282
Gill, John, 342, 343
Gillespie, Winifred G. T., 143
Gladstone, William, 47
Glaze, R. E., Jr., 287
Glen, John Stanley, 286
Godet, Frédéric, 284, 286
Goebbels, Joseph, 252
Goldsmith, Oliver, 334
Goodell, ——, 194
Goodwin, Frank J., 284
Goodwin, Thomas, 341
Gordon, A. J., 182
Gordon, Charles William (Ralph Connor), 109
Govett, Robert, 283
Graham, Billy, 197
Grant, F. W., 240
Grant, Ulysses S., 78
Gray, James M., 139, 212
Green, Peter, 282
Greenslet, Ferris, 264
Grier, W. J., 271
Griffith, William, 140
Gromacki, Robert G., 282, 286
Guinness, H. Grattan, 182
Guinness, Harry, 182
Gundry, Stanley N., 312–16
Gurnall, William, 286
Guthrie, Donald, 279, 284, 287

Habershon, Ada R., 238, 275
Hachiya, Michihiko, 267
Hadley, Sam, 202–4
Hailey, Homer, 279
Haldane, Robert, 285
Hall, Newman, 181
Hallam, Arthur, 36
Hamilton, J. Wallace, 239–40
Hammontree, Homer, 201
Han, Nathan E., 280

Hanke, Howard A., 282
Hardie, (James) Keir, 171
Harrison, Frank Mott, 340
Harrison, R. K., 278
Hart, Joseph, 342
Haslam, William, 181
Hastings, James, 273–74, 281, 289
Havner, Vance, 240
Hawthorne, Nathaniel, 267
Hawxhurst, ______, 322
Heading, John, 286
Headlam, Arthur C., 285
Hendriksen, William, 231, 281, 283, 284, 288
Henry, Matthew, 184, 191
Hermansen, Howard A., 201
Hiebert, D. Edmond, 287
Hitler, Adolf, 252
Hodder, H. M., 110–11
Hodge, Charles, 285, 286
Hodgkin, A. M., 282
Hogg, C. F., 283, 286, 287
Holledge, Tom, 124
Holledge, William, 124
Holmes, Oliver Wendell, Jr., 264
Hone, Ralph E., 277
Honeycutt, Roy Lee, 279
Hoover, Arlie J., 230
Hort, F. J. A., 48, 51
Houghton, Will(iam) H., 212–13, 215, 216, 223
Howard, David M., 279
Howley, G. C. D., 281
Howson, J. S., 284, 285
Hubbard, David Allan, 278
Hughes, Hugh Price, 181
Hughes, Philip Edgcumbe, 287
Hull, J. H. E., 285
Hulme, William E., 277
Hume, Abraham, 342
Hutchings, Thomas, 343
Huxley, Thomas Henry, 186

Ingelow, Jean, 252
Ironside, H(enry) A(llan) (Harry), 197–201, 246, 276, 278, 279, 329
Ironside, Sophia (Stafford), 198

James I, 77, 81
James, William, 264
Jamieson, Robert, 273
Jay, William, 184
Jeffries, James, 89
Jennings, F. C., 278
Jensen, Irving L., 276, 285
Jeremias, Joachim, 238
John of the Cross, 266
Johnson, Jack, 89
Johnson, Samuel, 333–37
Johnstone, Robert, 288
Jones, J. D., 156, 157, 283, 284, 286
Jones, Russell Bradley, 282
Jowett, John Henry, 40, 126, 153–58, 177, 181, 193, 286, 288, 315, 340, 353
Jukes, Andrew J., 275, 276, 281
Jung, C. G., 277

Kaiser, Walter C., Jr., 274
Keach, Benjamin, 238, 342
Keble, John, 16, 37
Keller, W. Phillip, 277
Kelly, William, 240
Kellogg, Samuel H., 273, 276
Kelso, James L., 285
Kemp, Joseph W., 175–79
Kennedy, Gerald H., 239
Kennedy, James W., 112
Kent, Homer A., Jr., 287
Kepler, Thomas S., 265, 265–66
Ker, John, 277
Keys, John L., 277
Kidner, Derek, 275, 277
Kilpatrick, ______, 180
Kimball, Edward, 320
King, Geoffrey R., 279
King, Guy, 245, 283, 286, 287, 288
Kingsley, Charles, 21
Kirkpatrick, A. F., 277
Kittel, Gerhard, 38, 280
Knight, William Allen, 277
Krummacher, F. W., 282, 289

Laidlaw, John, 232
Lang, George Henry, 238
Lange, John Peter, 273, 276, 282, 283
LaSor, William S., 247, 289
Laurin, Roy L., 289
Law, Henry, 275
Law, Robert, 288
Law, William, 335

Lawrence, Charles, 253
Lawrence, T. E., 142
Lee, James Prince, 48
Lee, R. G., 247
Lee, Robert, 245
Leighton, Robert, 266, 288
Lenski, R. C. H., 281, 283
Leupold, H. C., 275, 278, 279
Levinson, Leonard Louis, 251
Lewis, C. S., 229–30, 264, 265
Liddon, Henry, 48, 50
Lightfoot, J(oseph) B(arber), 40, 47–52, 286
Lincoln, Abraham, 89
Lindbergh, Charles, 253
Linnemann, Eta, 238
Livingston, G. Herbert, 274
Lloyd-Jones, D. Martyn, 157, 277, 279, 283, 285, 286
Loane, Marcus L., 282, 285
Lockhart, William, 17
Lockyer, Herbert, 230–31, 245, 289
Lodge, Oliver J., 187
Logsdon, S. Franklin, 200, 201, 277
Loveless, Wendell P., 278
Lowth, Robert, 208
Luther, Martin, 187, 193

Macartney, Clarence, 246
McCheyne, Robert Murray, 214
McClain, Alva J., 279, 285
McCormick, Nettie (Fowler), 323
Macdonald, F. C., 51
Macdonald, George, 211, 230, 265
MacDuff, John Ross, 62
McFadyen, John Edgar, 276, 279
McGee, J. Vernon, 276
Macgregor, George H. C., 181
Machen, J. Gresham, 282
Mackay, W. P., 176
Mackenzie, Peter, 181
Mackintosh, Charles Henry, 275
Maclaren, Alexander, 181, 273, 277, 285, 287
Maclaren, Ian. *See* Watson, John
Macmillan, Donald, 62 n
McNeill, John, 329
McPheeters, Thomas S., 78
MacRae, Alan A., 278
Magill, Frank N., 251
Mantle, Gregory, 181
Manton, Thomas, 282, 288
Marchant, James, 265
Marshall, Alfred, 280
Martin, Hugh, 279
Martin, Samuel, 157
Mason, Clarence E., 278
Matheson, George, 61–65, 154, 247, 289
Maurice, F. D., 36
Mauro, Philip, 276
Mawson, J. T., 289
Maxwell, Marjorie Eleanor, 267–68
Mead, Frank S., 253
Melanchthon, Philipp, 193
Mellor, Enoch, 153
Merivale, Charles, 285
Meyer, F(rederick) B(rotherton), 89–97, 126, 181, 247, 275, 276, 278, 279, 283, 284, 286, 288, 329
Miall, Edward, 186
Miller, Harry, 182
Milligan, William, 283
Montaigne, 250, 251
Moody, Betsey (Holton), 319–20
Moody, Dwight L(yman), 78, 79, 91–93, 107–8, 108–9, 111–12, 113, 125, 126, 182, 193, 198, 275, 311–16, 319–23, 325, 327, 328–29, 329, 348, 349
Moody, Edwin, 319–20
Moody, Emma, 321
Moody, Emma (Revell), 320–21
Moody, Lizzie, 320
Moody, Paul (D.), 113, 315, 321
Moody, Samuel, 320
Moody, William (R.), 321
Moore, Thomas V., 279
Moorhouse, Henry, 276, 314
Morgan, G. Campbell, 40, 80, 97, 156, 184, 186, 192, 238, 239, 272, 275, 276–77, 278, 279, 281, 282, 285, 285–86, 286, 287, 289, 329
Morris, Henry M., 275
Morris, Leon, 231, 276, 281, 284, 286, 287
Morrison, George H., 36, 64, 244
Morrison, Robert, 191
Motyer, J. A., 286, 288
Moule, Handley C. G., 52, 141, 181, 282, 285, 286, 287

Mounce, Robert H., 288
Muller, George, 182
Murray, Andrew, 176, 182, 277, 287
Murray, James, 36
Murray, John, 281
Mussolini, Benito, 249

Nee, Watchman, 278, 285
Nero, 224
Newell, William R., 285, 287, 288
Newman, John Henry, 15–21, 37, 265
Newton, ______, 104
Nicoll, W. Robertson, 15, 48, 96, 107, 110, 112, 156
Nietzsche, Friedrich Wilhelm, 252

Ockenga, Harold J., 286, 287, 289
O'Connell, Marvin R., 17
Oehler, Gustav, 274
Offord, John, 328
Ogg, George, 284
Olford, Stephen, 91, 214
Orr, James, 181
Owen, John, 264, 287, 339, 340–41, 343

Page, Mary, 343
Parker, Joseph, 97, 157, 181, 192, 270
Pasteur, Louis, 259
Paxson, C. E., 79
Paxson, Ruth, 286
Payne, J. Barton, 274
Penn-Lewis, Jessie, 277
Pentecost, George F., 182
Pepys, Samuel, 267
Perowne, J. J. Stewart, 277
Pfeiffer, Charles F., 274
Phelps, William Lyon, 112
Philpott, P. W., 199, 219–21
Pickworth, Thomas, 326
Pierson, A. T., 125, 154, 182
Pieters, Albertus, 288
Pink, Arthur W., 231, 233, 240, 245, 274, 275, 276, 282, 283, 284, 287, 289
Plato, 98
Plummer, Alfred, 240, 286, 287
Plumptre, E. H., 285
Pollock, John, 319
Polycarp, 191
Porritt, Arthur, 157
Pusey, E. B., 16, 279

Rainsford, Marcus, 282
Ramsay, William, 284, 285, 286, 289
Rawlinson, George, 285
Redpath, Alan, 91, 275, 276, 286, 289
Rees, Paul S., 286, 288
Revere, Paul, 253
Ridderbos, Herman, 284
Rippon, John, 342, 343
Ritchie, John, 275
Roberts, Evan J., 193
Roberts, Richard, 181, 193
Robertson, A. T., 280, 283–84, 284, 285, 286
Robertson, F. W., 17
Robertson, James D., 253
Robinson, George L., 279
Robinson, Theodore H., 277
Roget, Catherine, 258
Roget, Peter M(ark), 257–61
Roosevelt, Franklin D., 250–51
Rose, Hugh James, 37
Rosen, Ceil, 275
Rosen, Moishe, 275
Ross, Charles, 282
Russell, J. H., 175
Rust, Arthur, 92
Rutherford, Samuel, 265
Ryle, J. C., 231, 281
Ryrie, Charles C., 80–81

Sanday, William, 285
Sandburg, Carl, 89
Sankey, Ira (D.), 91, 108, 111, 126, 182, 314
Saphir, Adolph, 287
Scarborough, Lee R., 189
Schilder, Klaas, 282
Schultz, Samuel J., 274, 276, 278
Schweitzer, Albert, 264
Scofield, C(yrus) I(ngerson), 77–81
Scott, Walter, 288
Scougal, Henry, 266
Scroggie, J. M., 176
Scroggie, W. Graham, 139, 176, 178, 231, 247–48, 272, 276, 277, 281
Seiss, Joseph A., 287, 288
Selden, Elizabeth S., 267
Seldes, George, 252

Selwyn, Edward Gordon, 288
Shaftesbury, Earl of (Anthony Ashley Cooper), 340
Shakespeare, William, 252
Sharp, B. Oswald, 140
Shepard, J. W., 282
Shrubsole, William, 342
Simpson, A. B., 276
Simpson, A. R., 111
Simpson, Hubert, 185, 282
Simpson, James B., 253
Simpson, W. J. Sparrow, 282
Slemming, Charles W., 275
Smith, David, 282, 284
Smith, George Adam, 108, 109, 112, 279, 315
Smith, Gipsy, 327
Smith, James, 285
Smith, Joseph, 315
Smith, W. Robertson, 110
Smith, Wilbur M., 212, 271, 282, 288, 312
Smyth, Alice Mary, 251
Sockman, Ralph W., 283
Socrates, 98
Soltau, Henry W., 275
Sophocles, 98
Spurgeon, Charles, 123–24, 125
Spurgeon, Charles H(addon), 38, 39, 47, 50, 92, 97, 123–27, 178, 181, 191, 232, 238, 239, 243, 246, 249–50, 265, 271, 273, 275, 276, 277, 278, 282, 283, 311, 314, 315, 325–26, 326, 328, 329, 340, 342, 343
Spurgeon, James (A.), 125
Spurgeon, Lila (Rutherford), 125, 127
Spurgeon, Susannah (Thompson), 123, 124–25
Spurgeon, Thomas, 123–27, 178, 329
Stalker, James, 107, 109, 181, 282
Stam, Betty, 223
Stam, John, 223
Stanley, Arthur P., 186
Stedman, Ray C., 240
Steere, Douglas V., 266
Stennett, Samuel, 342
Stevenson, John, 277
Stewart, Alex H., 201
Stewart, James S., 63, 284
Stifler, James Madison, 285
Stock, Eugene, 287
Stott, John R. W., 282, 285, 286, 288
Stoughton, John, 327
Strahan, George, 337
Strahan, James, 275, 276
Strauss, Lehman, 275, 279, 286, 288
Sugden, Howard, 340
Sunday, Billy, 315
Swain, Joseph, 342
Swete, Henry Barclay, 282, 283, 284

Taylor, Dan, 343
Taylor, J. Hudson, 278
Taylor, Vincent, 284
Taylor, William M., 232, 239, 284, 289
Temple, Frederick, 140
Temple, William, 19
Tenney, Merrill C., 231, 279–80, 281, 282, 282–83, 284, 286, 288
Tennyson, Alfred, 36
Thiele, Edwin R., 276
Thielicke, Helmut, 237, 238, 275, 283
Thirtle, James W., 277, 283
Thomas a Kempis, 101
Thomas, W(illiam) H(enry) Griffith, 139–43, 245, 275, 283, 284, 285, 287, 288
Thoreau, Henry David, 250, 267
Thucydides, 98
Torrance, Thomas, 231
Torrey, R. A., 50, 113, 139, 182, 311, 315
Tozer, A. W., 264, 270
Trench, Richard (Chenevix), 35–40, 232, 238, 241, 252, 280, 289
Trevor, Meriol, 21
Trueblood, Elton, 275, 337
Truett, George W., 243
Truman, Harry S., 267
Turner, George A., 274
Twain, Mark, 260, 350

Unger, Merrill F., 274, 279
Urquhart, Andrew, 177

Van Doren, Charles Lincoln, 267
Varley, Henry, 182, 313, 325–29
Varley, Sarah (Pickworth), 326, 328, 329
Victoria, Alexandrina, 38, 267
Vincent, Marvin R., 280, 286

Vinci, Leonardo da, 264
Vine, W. E., 278, 280, 286, 287, 288
Vos, Howard F., 274

Wain, John, 337
Walker, Miles, 93
Walker, Thomas, 285
Walvoord, John F., 279, 282, 288
Wanamaker, John, 191
Warfield, Benjamin B., 282
Washington, George, 267
Watkinson, William L., 181
Watson, J. B., 283
Watson, John (Ian Maclaren), 109, 112
Watson, Thomas, 275
Watts, Isaac, 191, 336, 339, 342, 343
Weaver, Richard, 182
Webb-Peploe, H. W., 181
Welch, C. H., 278
Wells, Bombardier, 89
Wemp, C. Sumner, 275
Wesley, Anne, 341
Wesley, Charles, 341, 342
Wesley, Hetty, 341
Wesley, John, 51, 193, 266, 267, 335, 336, 339, 341, 342, 343
Wesley, Martha, 341
Wesley, Samuel, Sr., 341, 342
Wesley, Samuel, Jr., 341
Wesley, Susanna, 339, 341
Westcott, B. F., 48, 49, 51, 166, 282, 287, 288
Whately, Richard, 15, 39
White, Frank, 182
White, R. E. O., 287
White, W. D., 21
Whitefield, George, 178, 193, 315, 335, 336
Whittle, Daniel W., 182
Whyte, Alexander, 15, 16, 17–18, 19, 21, 110, 111, 154, 181, 247, 257, 261, 271, 282, 289, 341
Wiersbe, Warren W., 213, 283
Wigram, G. V., 280
Wilberforce, Samuel, 38, 39, 40
Wilberforce, William, 38
Wilde, Oscar, 252
Williams, John, 224
Wilson, Geoffrey B., 286
Wilson, Robert Dick, 274
Winchester, Alex B., 142
Windsor, Duke of. *See* Edward VIII
Wolff, Richard, 288
Wood, A. Skevington, 285
Wood, G. R. Harding, 143
Wood, Leon J., 274, 276, 279, 289
Woolman, John, 267
Wuest, Kenneth S., 281

Yates, Kyle M., 278, 279
Young, Dinsdale, 127
Young, Edward J., 274, 275, 278

Zodhiates, Spiros, 283, 288